Sadlier **PHONICS** Reading

Sadlier **Little Books BIG Books** Reading

Teaching Phonics in a Balanced Literacy Program

- Literature-Driven Thematic Units
- Structured Skills Instruction
- Phonics in Context
- Real Reading Experiences

An Essential Component of a Balanced Literacy Program for Today's Teaching Strategies

Recent studies show that a comprehensive and balanced approach to phonics instruction is the key to helping children become better readers. Although some children learn to read and understand what they read with little or no direct skills instruction, most students need and benefit from structured and systematic phonics instruction that includes phonemic awareness, an important early predictor of future success in reading.

Sadlier Phonics presents a balanced and integrated approach to teaching phonics that will reinforce, enrich, and support your total reading program.

Little Books and Big Books for shared, guided, and independent reading—40 leveled readers in each format—provide emergent, early, and fluent readers with opportunities for the transfer of newly acquired skills to real reading experiences.

Engaging Literature

Word Building Strategies

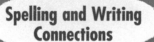

Spelling and Writing Connections

Student Manipulatives

Punchout Letter and Picture Cards

> *"**Sadlier Reading** will help to integrate phonics, spelling and writing into our present language arts curriculum."*
>
> Sr. Dawn Gear, G.N.S.H.
> Atlanta, GA

Curriculum Integration

Real Reading Experiences

Home-Involvement Activities

Sadlier Reading *supports* and *extends* your basal reader... Call for **Correlations!**

TEACHER'S EDITION

Flexible Organization

Literature-Driven Thematic Units

	Skill Focus	Unit Theme	Literature Selection
LEVEL K			
Unit 1	Listening Skills, Motor Skills, Visual Discrimination	Ready, Set, Go!	Rides by Ilo Orleans
Unit 2	Letter Recognition Aa-Zz	Animals from A to Z	Zoo by John Travers Moore
Unit 3	Initial Consonants (f, m, s, t, h, b)	We Are Special!	Happy Birthday to Me! by Carmen Muñoz
Unit 4	Initial Consonants (l, d, c, n, g, w)	Off to Work!	Work by Babs Bell Hajdusiewicz
Unit 5	Initial Consonants (p, r, k, J, q, v, y, z)	Food, Fabulous Food!	Yellow Butter by Mary Ann Hoberman
Unit 6	Short Vowels (a, i, o, u, e)	Moving Along	Jump or Jiggle by Evelyn Beyer
LEVEL A			
Unit 1	Auditory Discrimination	Book Buddies	Good Books, Good Times by Lee Bennett Hopkins
Unit 2	Letter Recognition and Consonant Sounds	Celebrations	Parades by Karama Fufuka
Unit 3	Short Vowels	Creepy, Crawly Bugs	Bugs by Margaret Wise Brown
Unit 4	Long Vowels	Save Our Earth	Yesterday's Paper by Mabel Watts
Unit 5	Consonant Blends	Sensational Senses	Ears Hear by Lucia & James L. Hymes, Jr.
Unit 6	Consonant Digraphs	Rain or Shine	Clouds by Christina G. Rossetti
Unit 7	Word Structure (Inflectional Endings, Compound Words, Contractions)	All About Growing	Tommy by Gwendolyn Brooks

	Skill Focus	Unit Theme	Literature Selection
LEVEL B			
Unit 1	Initial, Medial, and Final Consonants	*Friends Around the World*	*A Friend* by Betsy Jones Michael
Unit 2	Short Vowels	*Splish! Splash!*	*Sampan* by Tao Lang Pee
Unit 3	Long Vowels	*Earth, Trees, and Me*	*Trees* by Harry Behn
Unit 4	Variant Consonant Sounds and Consonant Blends	*In the City*	*City Street* by Lois Lenski
Unit 5	Compound Words, y as a Vowel, Consonant Digraphs, r-controlled Vowels	*Going Places*	*The Museum Door* by Lee Bennett Hopkins
Unit 6	Vowel Pairs, Vowel Digraphs, Diphthongs	*A Rainbow of Colors*	*What Is Brown?* by Mary O'Neill
Unit 7	Contractions and Word Endings	*Numbers Count!*	*Numbers, Numbers* by Lee Blair
Unit 8	Suffixes, Prefixes, Synonyms, Antonyms, Homonyms	*Outdoor Fun*	*Swinging* by Irene Thompson
LEVEL C			
Unit 1	Consonants and Consonant Variants	*Fall into Autumn*	*Autumn Leaves* by Aileen Fisher
Unit 2	Short and Long Vowels	*Sounds of Music*	*Song* by Ashley Bryan
Unit 3	Syllables, Consonant Blends, Compound Words, y as a Vowel, Consonant Digraphs	*What If . . . ?*	*Sunflakes* by Frank Asch
Unit 4	r-controlled Vowels, Vowel Digraphs, Diphthongs	*Super Sports*	*The Sidewalk Racer* by Lillian Morrison
Unit 5	Contractions and Word Endings	*Genius at Work*	*I Made a Mechanical Dragon* by Jack Prelutsky
Unit 6	Suffixes, Prefixes, Multisyllabic Words	*Space Fantasy*	*Space Campers' Song* by Anastasia Suen
Unit 7	Synonyms, Antonyms, Homonyms, Dictionary Skills	*Wacky Words, Riddles and Rhymes*	*Have You Ever Seen?* (Anonymous)

Scope and Sequence

Level K

Level A

	Level K
Literature Selections	5, 27, 69, 101, 133, 165
Phonics Alive at Home	6, 28, 70, 102, 134, 166
Listening Skills	7-10
Motor Skills	11-12
Visual Discrimination	13-20
Auditory Discrimination	21-26
Letter Recognition	29-68
Initial Consonants	71-100, 103-132, 135-160, 163-164
Final Consonants	161-162
Medial Consonants	
Short Vowels	167-178
Long Vowels	
Final **y** as a Vowel	
Consonant Blends	
Consonant Digraphs	
Inflectional Endings	
Compound Words	
Contractions	
Soft and Hard **c** and **g**	
Syllabication	
r-controlled Vowels	
Vowel Pairs and Digraphs	
Diphthongs	
Plurals	
Words Ending in **le**	
Suffixes	
Prefixes	
Synonyms, Antonyms, Homonyms	
Sounds of **s**	
Schwa	
Singular and Plural Possessives	
Dictionary Skills	
Take-Home Books	181-192
Student Skills Assessment Checklist	179-180
Punchout Letter and Picture Cards	193-200

Page numbers refer to the Student Edition.

Level A	Level B	Level C
5, 13, 83, 147, 225, 249, 269	5, 17, 47, 67, 89, 121, 149, 179	5, 19, 49, 81, 113, 147, 179
6, 14, 84, 148, 226, 250, 270	6, 18, 48, 68, 90, 122, 150, 180	6, 20, 50, 82, 114, 148, 180
7-12		
15-16, 35-36, 55-56, 73-74		
17-22, 24-30, 32-34, 37-42, 44-50, 52-54, 57-62, 64-72, 76-78, 81-82	7-8, 13-16	7, 10, 15-18
23-24, 31, 43, 51-52, 63-64, 71, 75, 78, 81-82	9-10, 13-16	8, 10, 15-18
79-82	11-16	9-10, 15-18
85-146, 221-222, 224	19-46	21-32, 45-48
149-212, 217-220, 223-224	49-66	33-48
213-219	95-98, 119	67-70, 79
227-248	75-88	53-64, 79
251-268	99-108, 119	71-80
271-274, 283-284	163-170, 173-178	135-146, 171, 174
275-278, 283, 285	91-92, 97-98, 119	65-66, 69-70, 79, 169, 174
279-283, 286	151-158, 177	123-126, 145
	69-74, 87	11-12, 14-18
	93-94	51-52, 60, 66, 68, 75, 87-88, 97-98, 106, 115-118, 120, 122, 140, 155-158, 164, 167-178
	109-120	83-92, 111
	123-140, 147	93-102, 111
	141-148	103-112
	159-162	127-130, 133-134, 145
	171-172	119-120, 145, 170, 174
	181-188, 205	149-160, 172, 174, 175-177
	189-194, 205	161-166, 173-177
	195-206	181-190, 201
		13-18
		121-122
		131-134, 145
		191-202
289-304	209-224	205-208
287-288	207-208	203-204
305-312		

Level B

Level C

Sadlier PHONICS Reading

LEVEL K

Letter recognition lessons, which continue the theme of the unit, include picture cues, engaging art, and practice in recognizing, naming, and printing letters.

Lesson organization allows for flexible introduction of letters and sounds.

Name_____

Time to Talk

RRR

Rr

R

Directions: Wagon and **dragon** rhyme. Look at the picture.
...ee whose names rhyme.

LESSON 10:

Time to Talk **lessons encourage oral language development, phonemic awareness, vocabulary building, and auditory discrimination.**

Name_____

Time to Talk

Directions: The **gardener** is taking care of his garden. **Gardener** begins with the sound of g. Look at the picture. Talk about all of the things that begin with the sound of g.

LESSON 72: Introducing the Sound of Initial Consonant g

121

Strategically placed *Remember* **lessons provide cumulative review and practice.**

Name _____

Mm   hN   Tt
Oc   Ss
gQ   pP   Rn

Tt   Take toys to the tub.

Directions: Trace the partner letters **Tt** with your finger. Then cut out the pictures at the bottom of the page. If the picture name begins with the same sound as **toy**, glue it on the tub.

86   LESSON 54: Recognizing Initial Consonant t

Games, mazes, and cut-and-paste activities provide meaningful letter-sound recognition practice.

Dance!   Dance!   Dance!

Dd

6

Directions: Print the partner letters ... Then say the name of each picture. Circle the picture in ... h the sound of **d**.

110   LESSON 66: Recognizing and Writing In...

Letter-sound correspondence is developed through motivating illustrations, theme-related text, model letters, and generous write-on lines.

Time to Write

See my favorites.

This is my favorite color.   This is my favorite food.

This is my favorite thing to do.

Directions: Share some of your favorite things.

84   LESSON 53: Applying Phonics to Writing

Time to Write **lessons encourage children to transfer phonics skills to writing experiences.**

Sadlier Little Books BIG BOOKS Reading

NEW!

LEVEL K

for Emergent Readers (PreK–1)

Twenty exciting LITTLE BOOKS for guided and independent reading and BIG BOOKS for shared and modeled reading written especially for emergent readers by a diverse group of authors and illustrators. This delightful series printed in a variety of formats and shapes captures children's interest, introduces high-frequency words, and helps develop comprehension skills. Familiar experiences, natural language, repetition, and rhyme make reading come alive.

Decodable and consistently placed text helps ensure reading success. Each story builds phonemic awareness with a focus on a specific initial consonant sound. Numerous reading and writing experiences encourage beginning literacy and language development.

The "Dear Family" feature involves the entire family in early literacy activities. Discussion questions foster oral language and vocabulary development.

Audiocassettes bring each story to life!

Some seagulls

Some sailboats

He makes a mess with milk.

He makes a mess with mud.

Create a literacy environment in your classroom!

Set 4
Level K, Emergent Readers (PreK–1)
Initial Consonants j, q, v, y, z; Final Consonant x

Title	Phonemic Awareness Strategy	Beginning Print Concepts	Applied Phonics Skill	Comprehension Skill	Story Summary
J My Name Is Jess Fiction	Distinguishing rhyming words	• Understanding that both print	Initial	Identifying	With just a little help from a friend,
When Mr. Quinn Snored Fiction	Segm word sound				
Valentine's Checkup Fiction	Blend to m				
The Yellow Yarn Mystery Fiction	Addin spoke				
Colors at the Zoo Nonfiction	Produ rhym				

Set 3
Level K, Emergent Readers (PreK–1)
Initial Consonants g, w, p, r, k

Title	Phonemic Awareness Strategy	Beginning Print Concepts	Applied Phonics Skill	Comprehension Skill	Story Summary
Goldilocks and the Three Bears Fiction	Substituting the beginning sound in a spoken word	• Recognizing familiar sight words • Predicting text	Initial Consonant g	Dramatizing a Story	Goldilocks causes quite a bit of pandemonium as she makes herself right
Wait for Me Fiction	Distin spoke				
Patty and Pop's Picnic Fiction	Segm word sound				
Here Comes the Rain! Fiction	Blend to m				
Keeping Baby Animals Safe Nonfiction	Isolat in a s				

Set 2
Level K, Emergent Readers (PreK–1)
Initial Consonants b, l, d, c, n

Title	Phonemic Awareness Strategy	Beginning Print Concepts	Applied Phonics Skill	Comprehension Skill	Story Summary
A Basket Full of Surprises Fiction	Producing a rhyming word.	• Understanding the concepts of *letter and word*	Initial Consonant b	Classifying Objects	Billy finds a basket full of surprises in the basement. But the biggest
What Does Lucy Like? Fiction	Distin in spo sente				
The Dinosaur Dance Fiction	Addin spoke				
Count with Me Nonfiction	Remo a spo				
Nora Plays All Day Fiction	Blend to m				

Set 1
Level K, Emergent Readers (PreK–1)
Initial Consonants f, m, s, t, h

Title	Phonemic Awareness Strategy	Beginning Print Concepts	Applied Phonics Skill	Comprehension Skill	Story Summary
Felix, the Very Hungry Fish Fiction	Isolating the initial sound in a spoken word	• Holding a book right side up • Understanding parts of a book and their functions	Initial Consonant f	Making Predictions	Felix is very hungry. He gulps down some yummy bugs; but when he sees a fat, juicy worm, he's too clever to take the bait.
Messy Moose Fiction	Blending sounds together to make a word	• Understanding the terms *author* and *illustrator* • Recognizing that both print and pictures convey meaning	Initial Consonant m	Sequencing	Messy Moose doesn't mean to— but somehow he always manages to make a mess! But not to worry, Messy Moose always cleans up too!
What Do You See by the Sea? Nonfiction	Distinguishing syllables in spoken words and sentences	• Knowing when to turn the page • Finding/Matching a word in text	Initial Consonant s	Distinguishing Fantasy/Reality	Come visit the seashore and see all kinds of wonderful things by the sea!
Show and Tell Fiction	Segmenting a spoken word into individual sounds	• Understanding that text is read from left to right • Recognizing the concepts of *letter and word*	Initial Consonant t	Retelling a Story	Find out what some kindergartners take to school for show and tell. Then decide what you'd take!
Harry's Hat Fiction	Substituting the beginning sound in a spoken word to make a new word	• Recognizing uppercase and lowercase letters • Identifying a sentence	Initial Consonant h	Recognizing Main Idea and Details	Harry's hat is even better than his grandpa's fishing hat and his mom's hard hat. Just wait until you see Harry's hat!

Sadlier PHONICS Reading

*"In **Sadlier Phonics** students develop decoding skills through the integration of literature and effective phonics instruction."*

Stephanie Brazell
Thousand Oaks, CA

LEVEL A

Decoding strategies **are practiced in context. Reading for meaning is emphasized through comprehension activities.**

Convenient two-page pull-out lessons accommodate a flexible sequence of instruction.

Quality literature, **chosen for its special appeal to children, sets the theme and introduces the phonics skills for each unit.**

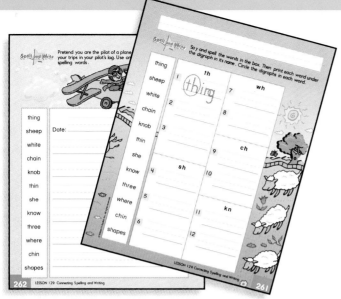

Look and Learn **lessons review phonics skills, using vivid photography and nonfiction stories that encourage cross-curricular connections.**

Look at the pictures. Then read and talk about them.

All living things grow.
Sunflowers grow.
So do animals like tigers.
You're growing, too. Aren't you?

Try matching the young plants
and animals to the older ones.
How are they the same?
How are they different?
How do they change as they grow?

Look at a baby picture of yourself.
How have you changed?

LESSON 140: Words with Endings, Compound Words, and Contractions in Context 283

Spell and Write **lessons focus attention on the transfer of phonics skills to writing. Each spelling list introduces and provides practice with high-frequency words.**

Check-Up **lessons offer multiple forms of assessment for continuous evaluation of student progress.**

Check-Up Fill in the circle next to the name of each picture.

1. ○ tip ○ tape ○ tap
2. ○ bit ○ bite ○ boat
4. ○ pain ○ pin ○ pine
5. ○ cane ○ cone ○ kite
7. ○ soap ○ side ○ sail
8. ○ slide ○ slid ○ slate
10. ○ cot ○ cat ○ coat
11. ○ goat ○ gate ○ get
12. ○ hide ○ hot ○ had
13. ○ ran ○ rain ○ rose
14. ○ robe ○ rob ○ ripe
15. ○ cub ○ cap ○ cut

184 LESSON 90: Assessing Long Vowels a, i, o

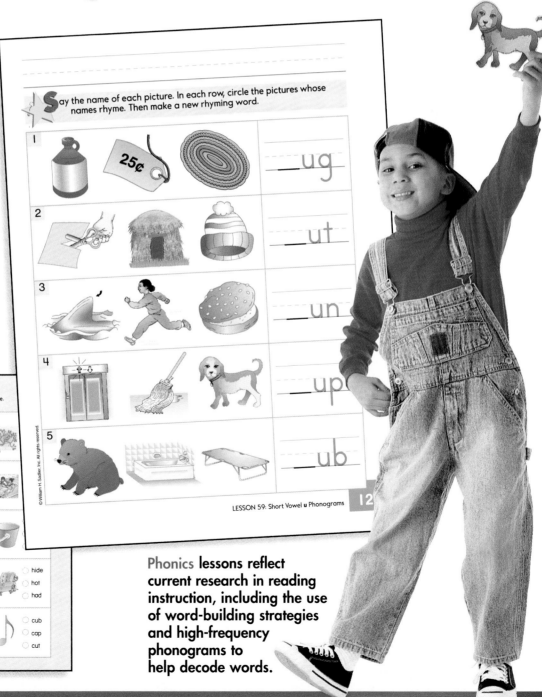

Say the name of each picture. In each row, circle the pictures whose names rhyme. Then make a new rhyming word.

1. ___ug
2. ___ut
3. ___un
4. ___up
5. ___ub

LESSON 59: Short Vowel **u** Phonograms

12

Phonics lessons reflect current research in reading instruction, including the use of word-building strategies and high-frequency phonograms to help decode words.

LEVEL A

for Early Readers (K–2)

Easy-to-read, colorful LITTLE BOOKS for guided and independent reading and BIG BOOKS for shared and modeled reading have been written by a diverse group of authors and illustrators. This exciting series provides beginning readers with the support of repeated language patterns, predictable events, and a strong picture-text match.

Original stories focusing on short vowels and long vowels encourage children to transfer phonics skills and apply decoding strategies to real reading and writing experiences! Each story uses high-frequency words and helps develop comprehension skills.

An engaging "Dear Family" page helps beginning readers develop literacy skills in and out of the classroom! Activities encourage children to read at home.

Classroom Library Level A includes:
- 10 Big Books (1 of each title)
- 100 Little Books (10 of each title)
- 2 Teacher's Resource Guides
- Classroom Storage/Display Unit

Code # 0939-X

June put ice cubes in the tub.
But it was no use.

June got down her big blue robe.
But it was no use.

reate a literacy environment
n your classroom!

Set 1	Level A, Early Readers (K–2) Short Vowels		
Title	Applied Phonics Skill	Comprehension Skill	Story Summary
...ander Ant Cools Off ...on	Short a	Dramatizing a Story	Alexander Ant gets very hot walking home one day. He makes a big splash when he finally cools off!
...ixed Up ...on	Short i	Comparing & Contrasting	Imagine what things would be like if they got all mixed up. You might discover that you prefer some things just as they are.
...to Make a Crocodile ...on	Short o	Identifying Steps in a Process	Making a picture of a crocodile is easy and lots of fun. Unless, that is, you do too good a job.
...Bear Cubs Like to Do ...iction	Short u	Recalling Details	Bear cubs like to sleep, play, eat nuts and honey, and, of course, give big bear hugs.
...Tell! ...on	Short e	Drawing Conclusions	A whispered secret changes every time one child repeats it to another ... until it gets back to the boy whose secret it was in the first place.

Set 2	Level A, Early Readers (K–2) Long Vowels		
Title	Applied Phonics Skill	Comprehension Skill	Story Summary
Wake Up, Sleepyheads! Fiction	Long a	Summarizing	Hibernating "sleepyheads" wake each other up to enjoy the dawn of spring.
Niles Likes to Smile Fiction	Long i	Making Inferences	Find out why Niles likes to smile. You may be surprised!
Joey's Rowboat Fiction	Long o	Sequencing	Joey and his dad find an abandoned rowboat. They fix it up together. Now they're ready to see if it will float.
A Hippo in June's Tub Fiction	Long u	Retelling a Story	June tries everything she can think of to get a rude hippo out of her bathtub, with no luck. In the end, though, the solution turns out to be quite easy.
Come Meet Some Seals Nonfiction	Long e	Recognizing Facts	Come along and find out some interesting facts about seals—including where they live, what they do, and what's a seal's favorite meal.

LEVEL B

*"**Sadlier Phonics** inspires children to build on what they have learned and apply skills within an integrated curriculum."*
Sr. Martina Anne Erdlen, I.H.M.
Immaculata, PA

High-interest *Look and Learn* nonfiction photo essays, focusing on the phonics skills used in context, conclude each thematic unit.

Lessons introduce more advanced phonics skills including *r*-controlled vowels, vowel digraphs and diphthongs, inflectional endings, suffixes and prefixes, synonyms, antonyms, and homonyms.

Consistent use of triple-lines for student writing throughout the entire Student Edition.

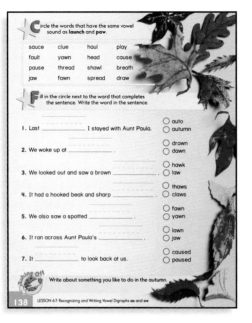

Taking Off suggests activities for individuals or cooperative learning groups to extend the phonics lesson.

Spell and Write lessons invite students to write for different purposes.

Helpful Hints help students understand and remember phonics generalizations.

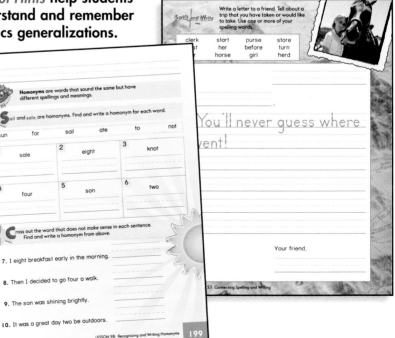

LEVEL C

Child-engaging poetry, by well-known authors, sets the theme and illustrates phonics and structural analysis skills in context.

Meaning is emphasized as phonics skills are taught and applied.

Cloze activities encourage students to apply syntactic, semantic, and graphophonic cues as they read longer passages for meaning.

Reading Strategies encourage children to transfer what they already know about some words to help them read new words.

Critical thinking is promoted through thought-provoking questions and discussion.

Written assessments are one of many tools provided to help monitor mastery of reading skills.

LEVEL B

for Fluent Readers (1–3)

A motivating series of LITTLE BOOKS for guided and independent reading and BIG BOOKS for shared and modeled reading—designed especially for more advanced readers by a diverse group of authors and illustrators. Longer stories have more fully developed plots and greater variation in both sentence structure and vocabulary. Illustrations enhance each story and contribute to the overall meaning.

This series focuses on more advanced phonics and comprehension skills. While reading, children learn to apply these skills in the context of a wide variety of genres.

A "Dear Family" page in each book features activities for the family to encourage reading at home. These activities reinforce comprehension, word-study, and writing skills.

Create a literacy environment in your classroom!

GETTING TO KNOW
SHARKS
By Jennifer Jacobson

Where do sharks live?

Basking shark in chilly water

Reef shark in warm water

Sharks live in the sea. Most sharks live where the water is warm. But others live where the water is chilly.

Some sharks swim in deep water far from shore. But not all of them do! Some swim in shallow water close to land.

Set 1 — Level B, Fluent Readers (1–3): Consonant Blends and Consonant Digraphs

Title	Applied Phonics Skill	Comprehension Skill	Story Summary
Why Coyote Howls at Night — Fiction	Initial l-blends (bl, cl, fl, gl, pl, sl)	Distinguishing Fantasy/Reality	In this folktale, Coyote rides on a star. After flying with Coyote, you'll know why he howls at night.
The Tongue Twister Prize — Fiction	Initial r-blends (br, cr, dr, fr, gr, pr, tr)	Identifying Problem/Solution	Greta wins a tongue twister contest. But the prize for winning is *not* what Greta expects!
Ah-choo! — Fiction	Initial s-blends (sl, sm, sn, sp, st, str, sw)	Identifying Steps in a Process	Something is making Stanley sneeze, but what can it be? Stanley has to find out!
Getting to Know Sharks — Nonfiction	Initial Consonant Digraphs (th, sh, wh, ch, kn, wr)	Recognizing Facts	You'll discover where sharks live, what they eat, and many other facts in this nonfiction book.
The Trash Can Band — Fiction	Final Consonant Digraphs (ck, th, sh, ch)	Making Judgments	The Trash Can Band makes quite a racket in quiet Beech Rock, but the townspeople don't mind.

Set 2 — Level B, Fluent Readers (1–3): Word Study and Structural Analysis

Title	Applied Skill	Comprehension Skill	Story Summary
Too Small Jill — Fiction	Contractions	Retelling a Story	It seems like Jill is too small to help when the family rabbit disappears, but Jill shows her family that she's bigger than they think.
Discovering Dinosaurs — Nonfiction	Plurals	Classifying Information	Travel back in time millions of years to "dig up" amazing dinosaur facts.
The Cheerful King — Fiction	Suffixes and Prefixes	Sequencing	The king's wish is to be able to cry like everyone else. By the end of this story, the king is in tears!
The Lion and the Mouse — Fiction	Synonyms and Antonyms	Drawing Conclusions	The lion learns an important lesson about friendship when his life is saved by a little mouse.
Buggy Riddles — Fiction	Homonyms	Making Inferences from Pictures	A very clever bug shares a lot of funny riddles about fellow insects.

Sadlier Phonics Reading

Teacher's Editions
Make Connections Th[...]

A PLANNING RESOURCE

- appears at the beginning of each unit
- gives an at-a-glance survey of the unit
- accommodates a flexible sequence of instruction.

Provides Additional Teaching Resources

- gives ideas for hands-on games and blackl[...] master activities
- illustrates activities for the Phonics Puncho[...]
- suggests language activities for the ESL stu[...]
- explains interactive computer, audio, and video activities
- provides a wealth of assessment strategies

A LITERATURE CONNECTION
Exciting poetry

- introduces each unit
- enhances the theme of the unit

A HOME CONNECTI[...]
Phonics Alive at Home
(English and Spanish)

- provides an overview of the [...]
- explains the phonics concepts
- presents easy-to-do activities and projects

Take-Home Books support beginning lit[...]

- provide reading enjoyment f[...] whole family
- put phonics skills in context
- increase students' vocabulary

evelop Literacy!

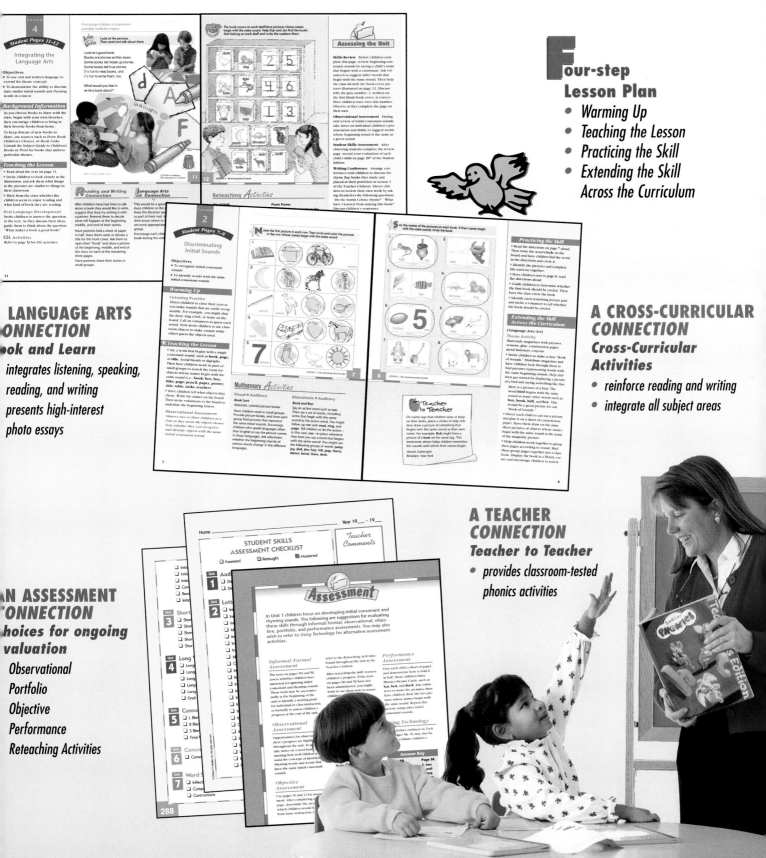

Four-step Lesson Plan

- **Warming Up**
- **Teaching the Lesson**
- **Practicing the Skill**
- **Extending the Skill Across the Curriculum**

LANGUAGE ARTS CONNECTION
ook and Learn

- integrates listening, speaking, reading, and writing
- presents high-interest photo essays

A CROSS-CURRICULAR CONNECTION
Cross-Curricular Activities

- reinforce reading and writing
- integrate all subject areas

A TEACHER CONNECTION
Teacher to Teacher

- provides classroom-tested phonics activities

AN ASSESSMENT CONNECTION
hoices for ongoing valuation

- Observational
- Portfolio
- Objective
- Performance
- Reteaching Activities

T-15B

Classroom Posters and Phonics Picture Cards

CLASSROOM POSTERS

- *Colorful classroom posters of unit literature selections build children's interest in the theme of the unit.*

- *Four sets of posters are available. Set K, Set A, Set B, and Set C.*

PHONICS PICTURE CARDS

A boxed set of durable full-color picture cards depict familiar objects and reinforce letter-sound correspondences.

ALPHABET POSTERS

26 unforgettable animal characters help develop letter recognition, phonemic awareness, and sound-symbol correspondence.

Sadlier PHONICS

LEVEL B

Jane M. Carr   Joanne M. McCarty

Patricia Scanlon   Anne F. Windle

Program Consultants

Grace R. Cavanagh, Ed.D.
Principal, P.S. 176
Board of Education
New York, New York

Patricia N. Grant
Director, Early Childhood Program
Sacred Heart School, Vailsburg
Newark, New Jersey

Eleanor M. Vargas
Resource Specialist Teacher
Los Angeles Unified School District
Los Angeles, California

Vilma M. Vega, Ed.D.
Elementary Curriculum Supervisor
Hillsborough County Public Schools
Tampa, Florida

Donna A. Shadle
Kindergarten Specialist
St. Paul Elementary School
North Canton, Ohio

Deborah A. Scigliano
First Grade Teacher
Assumption School
Pittsburgh, Pennsylvania

Sadlier-Oxford
A Division of William H. Sadlier, Inc.
New York, New York 10005–1002

Advisors

Stephanie Hart Brazell
Kindergarten/First Grade Teacher
Thousand Oaks, California

Sr. Paul Mary Janssens, O.P.
Principal
Aurora, Illinois

Sue Pecci
First Grade Teacher
Winter Springs, Florida

Debra L. Bates
Kindergarten/First Grade Teacher
Cleveland, Ohio

Damaris Hernandez Reda
Assistant Principal
New York, New York

Sr. Dawn Gear, G.N.S.H.
Principal
Lilburn, Georgia

Theresa A. Kenney–Martinez
First Grade Teacher
Pomona, California

Anita Shevette
Kindergarten Teacher
Pomona, California

Sr. Paulette Marie Gregoire, R.J.M.
Principal
Fall River, Massachusetts

Noelle Deinken
Kindergarten Teacher
Thousand Oaks, California

Mary Lee Gedwill
Second Grade Teacher
North Olmstead, Ohio

Angela L. Stankiewicz
Principal
New Bedford, Massachusetts

JoAnne Nardone, Ed.D.
Program Review Specialist
New York, New York

Sr. Francis Helen Murphy, I.H.M.
Editorial Advisor
Immaculata, Pennsylvania

Rosemarie Valente
Second Grade Teacher
Newark, New Jersey

Laura A. Holzheimer
Title 1 Reading Teacher
Grades 1–3
Cleveland, Ohio

Sophia Finger, Ed.D.
Assistant Principal
New York, New York

Kelly Johnston Hackett
Instructional Technology
    Consultant
Orlando, Florida

Mary L. Brown
Kindergarten/First Grade
Multi–Age Teacher
Chillicothe, Ohio

Karen Jalowiec Losh
Fort Wayne, Indiana

Acknowledgements

Every good faith effort has been made to locate the owners of copyrighted material to arrange permissions to reprint selections. In several cases this has proved impossible. The publisher will be pleased to consider necessary adjustments for future printings for any owner whose rights may have been unintentionally infringed.

Thanks to the following for permission to reprint the copyrighted materials reprinted below:

"A Friend" (text only) by Betsy Jones Michael, reprinted with permission of the author.

"Trees" A Poem (text only) by Harry Behn. A Bill Martin Book published by Henry Holt and Company. Copyright 1949 Harry Behn. © Renewed 1977 Alice L. Behn. Used by permission of Marian Reiner.

"City Street" (text only) by Lois Lenski © 1954 from WE LIVE IN THE CITY. Reprinted with permission of The Lois Lenski Covey Foundation.

"The Museum Door" (text only) by Lee Bennett Hopkins, reprinted by permission of Curtis Brown, Ltd. Copyright © 1987 by Lee Bennett Hopkins.

"What is Brown?" (text only), from HAILSTONES AND HALIBUT BONES by Mary O'Neill and Leonard Weisgard, Ill. Copyright © 1961 by Mary LeDuc O'Neill. Used by permission of Doubleday, a division of Bantam Doubleday Dell Publishing Group, Inc.

Letter models in this program were used with permission of the publisher, Zaner-Bloser, Inc., Columbus, OH. From HANDWRITING A WAY TO SELF EXPRESSION, copyright, 1993.

Product Development and Management: Leslie A. Baranowski

ISBN: 0–8215–0812–1 (Teacher's Edition); ISBN: 0–8215–0802–4 (Student's Edition)

3456789/9

Dear Teacher,

Reading ability develops in an encouraging environment where language learning is meaningful and functional. As children grow in literacy they become proficient at recognizing semantic, syntactic, and graphophonic cues and using them to extract meaning from printed text. We believe that phonics instruction is an integral part of the total reading process.

Sadlier Phonics reflects current approaches to literacy instruction and is built upon the following sound principles:

- Early and structured phonics instruction is fundamental to a complete and effective beginning reading program.
- Phonics skills are best learned through meaningful contextual lessons that feature quality literature.
- Students need ample opportunity to practice and apply letter-sound correspondences.
- The language arts (listening, speaking, reading, and writing) are interrelated and mutually supportive.

After giving much critical attention to the latest reading research and consulting with educators across the country, we are proud to present a balanced and integrated approach to phonics instruction. Children will delight in the literature-driven, theme-based lessons, which provide an exciting context for learning decoding skills.

We hope that you and your students enjoy *Sadlier Phonics* and that it helps you inspire a lifelong love of reading!

Sincerely,

The Authors

Contents

1 Initial, Medial, and Final Consonants
Theme: Friends Around the World

2 Short Vowels

Theme: The Wonders of the Water

Vowel Pairs, Vowel Digraphs, Vowel Diphthongs
Theme: A Rainbow of Colors

Contractions and Word Endings
Theme: Numbers Count!

Suffixes, Prefixes, Synonyms, Antonyms, and Homonyms

Theme: Outdoor Fun!

PHONICS WORKSHOP

WHAT IS PHONICS?

In *Beginning to Read: Thinking and Learning About Print*, Marilyn Adams defines *phonics* as "a system of teaching reading that builds on the alphabetic principle, a system in which a central component is the teaching of correspondences between letters or groups of letters and their pronunciations." Phonics helps children make the connection between words they hear and say and words they see in print.

WHY TEACH PHONICS?

Phonics is an essential ingredient of a balanced reading program. Without phonics instruction, many children would not have the necessary skills to decode words. Studies suggest that children who are taught phonics become not only more proficient readers, but also better spellers.

Research confirms that phonemic awareness correlates closely with reading achievement and subsequent school success. The ultimate goal of phonics instruction is not to teach children a set of isolated skills, but rather to teach them skills and strategies they can use each and every time they encounter print.

The teaching of phonics, however, does *not* mean that reading methodologies should be abandoned. There is no one "right" way to teach a child how to read. The key to teaching children how to read is to combine phonics instruction with other reading materials and methods to give students the best possible chance at achieving literacy.

BAT
CAT
HAT

Thematic instruction provides a framework and context for learning. Although the main focus of the theme centers on developing children's ability to read and write, the theme may also naturally integrate other areas of the curriculum such as science, social studies, music, math, art, and health.

Each *Sadlier Phonics* student book is organized around topical themes. An engaging piece of poetry introduces each theme and presents each unit's phonics skills in context. The theme concept continues throughout the lessons, which utilize original rhymes, stories, captivating artwork, and colorful photos. Each unit concludes with a theme-related photo essay.

The time you spend on any given theme will vary, based on the expected learner outcomes. Establish a comfortable pace for you and your students, allowing time to capitalize on children's particular interests and their enthusiasm for the topic.

At the beginning of each new theme, take inventory of children's prior knowledge. An effective way to do so is to make a K-W-L chart. Before starting the unit, record what children already **know** about the theme topic under the K heading. Ask what they **want** to learn about the topic, and write their questions under the W heading. As you progress through the unit, write what children have **learned** under the L column.

You may want to develop a chart of "theme words." Write the theme topic on a sheet of chart paper, and post it on a wall in your classroom. Have children add words to the chart throughout the unit. The chart can serve as a reference for spelling and writing activities.

The *Sadlier Phonics* Teacher's Edition is also chock-full of theme activities. Look under the *"Extending the Skills Across the Curriculum"* section of each lesson plan for hands-on learning activities linked to the unit theme.

K W L CHART

K	W	L
Some bugs help us.	How many legs do bugs have?	Most bugs have six legs.
Praying mantises are bugs.	What do praying mantises eat?	Praying mantises eat other bugs.

You can build excitement about reading by creating a classroom that is rich in print and language. In such an atmosphere children will start to understand beginning print concepts, explore and play with language, and begin to use writing to communicate their thoughts and ideas.

Take a look around your classroom. Are there opportunities for children to interact constantly with print? You may wish to add these print sources to the walls, ceiling, and floor of your classroom:
• Poetry posters • Calendars • Maps • Schedules • Word charts • Bulletin boards • Job lists • Alphabet strips • Signs and labels • Experience charts • Message boards • Recipes • Class roster.

An environment that fosters literacy would also include reading and writing corners. How you set up these areas will depend on your space limitations. When planning, remember that these areas should be easily accessible to children.

DESIGNING A READING CORNER

A reading corner will nurture independent reading. In setting up the space, be sure to include a wide variety of printed materials, such as:
• Books of various levels • Theme-related books • Magazines • Newspapers • Plays • Poetry • Student-made books • Class stories.

Books may be brought from home by children, borrowed from your school or local library, or donated by parent groups. You will want to add to and change the selection regularly.

DESIGNING A WRITING CORNER

A writing corner should encourage experimentation with the written word and provide opportunities for creative expression and personal communication. In setting up a writing corner, you'll want to include as many of the following items as possible:
• All kinds of paper (lined and unlined, note pads, index cards, self-stick notes, stationery, and construction paper) • Office supplies (paper clips, a stapler, scissors, and a hole punch) • Pencils, pens, crayons, and markers • Rubber letter stamps and ink pads • Dictionaries • A telephone book and a class directory • Writing journals • Computers and typewriters • Writing portfolios.

There should be an area where children can share and display their writing.

CURRICULUM INTEGRATION

Sadlier Phonics provides teachers with meaningful activities for total curriculum integration.

WHY SHOULD YOU INTEGRATE PHONICS WITH OTHER SUBJECT AREAS?

Curriculum integration represents a holistic approach to learning that • enables students to make relevant connections to life • promotes the transfer of learning • provides for multiple intelligences • reinforces skills through contextual experiences.

WHAT CURRICULUM CONNECTIONS CAN BE MADE WITH PHONICS?

Phonics is a part of a total language arts program. In support of that approach, the *Sadlier Phonics* lesson plans abound with activities that foster critical thinking and oral language development as they enhance listening, speaking, reading, writing, and spelling skills. Suggested science, social studies, math, health, music, and art related activities incorporate the relevant phonics skills and give children immediate opportunities to apply their newly learned skills.

HOW IS PHONICS INTEGRATED WITH OTHER CURRICULUM AREAS?

To see how practical and enjoyable *Sadlier Phonics* makes the process of integrating curricula, let's look at a typical second grade unit.

The "Numbers Count!" unit begins with a "fun" poem. The lesson plans are loaded with references to trade books, songs, and purposeful writing activities. And, of course, a unit on "numbers" ties right in with grade-level appropriate math concepts. While studying the inflectional endings **ed** and **ing**, children also learn about time by making paper-plate clocks and read books such as *The Cuckoo-Clock Cuckoo* and *Around the Clock with Harriet*. In addition, students pattern their writing after a well-known author.

These kinds of cross-curricular activities bridge learning and prevent skills from being taught in isolation.

PHONICS: AN ESSENTIAL PART OF THE INTEGRATED LANGUAGE ARTS PROGRAM

Sadlier Phonics recognizes that listening, speaking, reading, and writing are interrelated and are mutually supportive. The program provides structured phonics lessons within an integrated language arts approach to instruction so that students apply phonics skills and strategies to reading, spelling, and writing activities. These authentic experiences emphasize the importance of what children are learning and make the lessons relevant and sensible.

Integrating the Language Arts lessons can be found in the Teacher's Edition.

The use of common, concrete, and well-illustrated vocabulary, such as that which generally supports phonics, is particularly well-suited to the ESL student in your classroom. Effective phonics instruction adds exponentially to a student's oral, reading, and writing vocabularies because phonics integrates the four language processes— listening, speaking, reading, and writing. Phonics instruction enables ESL students to work on speaking and writing English before they develop strong oral vocabularies.

Applying knowledge of letters and sounds also improves ESL students' pronunciation. They no longer have to rely on rote mimicking of what they hear while they lack awareness of the written form. ESL students can sound out many words that they otherwise might not hear spoken. They pronounce words more clearly because they are aware of the letter-sound correspondences.

ESL scenarios will vary. One class might be made up entirely of Spanish-speaking children and a teacher who is fluent in Spanish; another might include eight children who speak languages other than English–each of which is different and none of which the teacher knows. Instructional framework will depend on the number of students, available space, and budget constraints.

The ESL activities in the *Sadlier Phonics* Teacher's Edition are designed to support the process, common to all class settings, of helping children develop their receptive (listening/reading) and expressive (speaking/writing) abilities.

ADDRESSING CHILDREN'S LEARNING STYLES

The three basic styles, or modalities, through which we learn are the visual, the auditory, and the kinesthetic.

The *Sadlier Phonics* program addresses the different learning styles of students through the multisensory activities provided in the Teacher's Edition. Choose the activities that make sense for your group of learners.

THE VISUAL LEARNER The visual learner best acquires knowledge by seeing the material being presented. Activities that include reading and writing provide the context to reach these students. For example, having the visual learner find words in literature that demonstrate the phonics skill being studied is a good way to capitalize on his or her visual strengths. Another way to appeal to a child's visual awareness is to write a class-composed poem or an experience story on the board or on chart paper where the child can see it.

By providing a print-rich environment, you constantly enable visual learners to find meaning in and learn from the print around them. Poems, posters, stories, and other written materials enrich and enliven their learning experiences.

THE AUDITORY LEARNER The auditory learner needs to hear the material to best assimilate it. Using a variety of spoken and sung activities to enhance learning plays to the auditory learner's strength. Listening to a poem or story is a joy for such children. Read aloud every day, both for enjoyment and for purposeful learning. As you read aloud, ask questions that require attention to auditory cues, such as questions that require children to identify rhyming words or words that contain a specific sound.

THE KINESTHETIC LEARNER
The kinesthetic learner learns best through movement and his or her sense of touch. Allow children to move as much as possible. Gross motor movements are beneficial, especially for the developing young child. Writing on the board, manipulating picture and letter cards, and working with a felt board are some strategies that actively involve kinesthetic learners.

Tracing tactile letters and drawing letters in sugar, salt, or even pudding are good ways to help kinesthetic learners learn letter formation. Sandpaper letters are great to use, too! Any manipulative activity that you choose is bound to captivate these "in-touch" learners.

PHONICS ALIVE AT HOME

Young children's literacy development depends largely on their language experiences at home. Parents and caretakers can not only help children develop sound reading skills but also help instill in children a love for reading.

Many parents and caretakers may want to help their children become successful readers, but may not know *how* to do so. Help parents over this stumbling block by spending time at your first school open house or teacher-parent conferences explaining the reading methods used in your classroom.

Share the suggestions below with parents and caretakers. If they frequently visit your classroom, post the suggestions on a special bulletin board as reminders. You might also include the ideas in your next parent newsletter.

STORY TIME Read to your child every day! Make it a relaxed time. Bedtime is often a good time to share a favorite story or a brand-new one.

TALK IT OVER As you read, pause frequently to discuss the illustrations and progress of the story. When you finish a book, ask your child to summarize it or tell about his or her favorite part.

TRY IT TOGETHER As your child's reading skills develop, make time to read aloud together. Track the words with your finger, pausing occasionally to allow your child to read to you.

LIBRARY TIME Help your child obtain a library card. Visit your local library often and allow your new cardholder to choose the books he or she wants to read.

A BOOK OF MY OWN Books make wonderful gifts! You might arrange times when your child can choose and purchase a book for a special occasion or as a special reward.

REVIEW SCHOOLWORK Reading over phonics worksheets with your child helps reinforce what he or she has learned and provides opportunities for the child to show off knowledge. Treat errors as opportunities to teach.

BE A ROLE MODEL Make sure your child sees you reading something every day.

BRING READING HOME! Help your child see how learning to read affects life outside of school. You might start by making your child aware of directions for playing a game or preparing a packaged food, signs on stores and roads, and names of items on your shopping list.

Sadlier Phonics provides a convenient take-home letter at the beginning of each unit in the Student Edition. The instructions — in English and Spanish — explain the unit skills and suggest some easy-to-do activities that will help phonics come alive at home.

USING TECHNOLOGY

Today, children can hear and see language come to life through multimedia technology. To create a rich, multisensory experience for your students, *Sadlier Phonics* has integrated technology lessons in its comprehensive approach to teaching phonics. Each unit contains a two-page "Tech Talk" section. Computer Connection activities that are interspersed throughout the lessons link the skills being taught with experiences related to the unit theme.

Utilizing readily available computer software, *Sadlier Phonics* leads you step-by-step through activities that focus on using and working with language in a variety of contexts. From producing audio and video files, to accessing information on the Internet, to sending letters to pen pals via E-mail, students actively practice phonics skills while developing computer literacy.

Recognizing that each classroom is configured differently, Sadlier gives you flexibility in using the material. So, if the number of machines is limited, all students can participate. Another option lets you use a large-screen monitor or an overhead LCD (liquid crystal display) panel, thus permitting you to work on a single machine while displaying the on-screen material to the entire class. Your knowledge of individual learning styles will come into play when you decide whether an activity should involve a small group, partners, or one child working alone.

Technology can connect school and home and so help families become more involved with their children's learning. You may photocopy the "Tech Talk" pages so children have the opportunity to work on them on their home computers. Technology can also increase your effectiveness as an educator, enabling you to monitor student progress continuously and make on-the-spot assessments.

But, to fully access the potential of this powerful learning tool, technology must be integrated into the curriculum. *Sadlier Phonics* does just that by providing experiences that help to guide your students onto the highway of technological opportunity!

ASSESSMENT

Assessment is a continuing process by which we monitor and evaluate children's progress. To help you successfully assess your students, each unit of *Sadlier Phonics* contains a Teacher's Edition section that offers multiple strategies for assessment, including blackline masters.

Suggestions for different methods of evaluation are discussed under these headings:
- Informal/Formal • Observational
- Objective • Portfolio • Performance
- Teacher • Technology.

INFORMAL/FORMAL TESTS are provided for each unit. They help you ascertain what children know or have learned about the skills being taught. Informal testing at the beginning of a unit might identify a starting point for individual or class instruction. A test given at the end of the unit assesses students' progress in mastering specific skills.

OBSERVATIONAL Student performance in the classroom should be observed and recorded frequently. Try to set aside five to fifteen minutes a day to observe two or three students so that you observe each child about every two to three weeks. Observe students in a variety of learning situations; specific instances for doing so are highlighted in the lesson plans.

OBJECTIVE Periodic unit reviews help you determine whether children have mastered the skills being taught. Reteaching activities in the Teacher's Edition can then be used with those students who need more instruction. The aforementioned unit tests could also be used at this point to assess progress objectively.

PORTFOLIO An icon in the lesson plans indicates portfolio opportunities. Have children keep a portfolio of drawings and writing that demonstrate their emergent reading and writing skills, how they have improved, and where they may still have difficulty. Schedule individual conferences periodically, and encourage self-evaluation.

PERFORMANCE Classroom-based projects allow you to evaluate listening skills, comprehension, and visual recognition and help you determine whether children have correctly assimilated specific phonics skills. Suggestions for classroom projects can be found in each unit. A discussion of how children complete the "Phonics Alive at Home" project is another way to assess whether unit skills have been mastered.

TECHNOLOGY "Tech Talk" activities provide yet another way to monitor student progress.

Theme:

*Friendship is the same,
no matter where you go.*

Overview

Unit 1 introduces children to consonant sounds as they learn that friendship links people around the world.

Objectives

- To enjoy a poem about friends
- To recognize consonant sounds in context
- To write consonants in words

Thematic Teaching

Have children form a circle and share their ideas about ways in which friends are important to them. Encourage children to discuss what friends do for each other and difficulties that might come up between them. Explain the importance of being sensitive to those who may feel as though they do not have friends. Tell children they can show their sensitivity by making these people feel included.

Display the Poetry Poster "A Friend," and refer to it throughout the unit.

Betsy Jones Michael

Betsy Jones Michael has been reading and writing poems since she was a child. A storyteller and teacher of young children, Jones Michael believes that things are most easily remembered when in rhyme or rhythmic poetry. In her poem "A Friend," the poet wants to convey the sentiment "just one good friend is all a person needs" and that "between good friends, words are not always necessary."

Individual Lessons

Lesson	Skill Focus
1	Introduction to Initial Consonants
2	Recognizing and Writing Initial Consonants
3	Recognizing and Writing Final Consonants
4	Recognizing and Writing Medial Consonants
5	Reviewing Consonants
6	Integrating the Language Arts

Take-Home Book: *Friends of Mine*

Curriculum Integration

Writing Children write letters to friends and express their ideas about friendship on pages 10, 12, 14, and 15.

Social Studies Making friends, getting along with others, and using globes and maps are topics that appear on pages 8, 14, and 15.

Art A creative activity that complements phonics learning appears on page 12.

Optional Learning Activities

Multisensory Activities Children enjoy visual, auditory, tactile, and kinesthetic learning activities throughout the unit.

Multicultural Connection Children learn about cultural diversity through activities about *futbol* and finding a penpal on pages 8 and 14.

Thematic Activities Assorted activities develop the unit theme in the *Extending the Skill Across the Curriculum* aspect of each lesson.

Assessment Strategies

Multiple strategies such as *Observational Assessment,* writing portfolios, written end-of-unit assessments, and the *Skills Checklist* at the back of the Student Edition will help you assess children's mastery of phonics skills throughout Unit 1.

Theme-Related Resources

Ikeda, Daisaku. *Over the Deep Blue Sea.* New York: Alfred A. Knopf, 1993.

The Magical Forest. Celebrity Home Entertainment, 1994.

Rolling Harvey Down the Hill. Listening Library, 1993.

Assessment

In Unit 2 children focus on recognizing and writing initial, medial, and final consonants. The following are suggestions for evaluating these skills through informal/formal, observational, objective, portfolio, and performance assessments. You may also wish to refer to *Using Technology* for alternative assessment activities.

Informal/Formal Assessment

The test on page 5D assesses whether children have mastered identifying initial, medial, and final consonants. This tool may be used informally at the beginning of the unit to identify a starting point for individual or class instruction, or formally at the end of the unit to assess children's progress.

Observational Assessment

Specific opportunities for observation are highlighted in the lesson plans. In addition, there are many opportunities throughout the unit to observe children identifying consonants, whether it is having them say a word such as **paint** and tell that it begins with the consonant **p** or watching as children perform a *Computer Connection*.

Objective Assessment

Use the assessment pages throughout the unit. After completing each assessment page, determine the area(s) in which children would benefit from more instruction; then refer to *Reteaching Activities* found throughout the unit in the Teacher's Edition. After reteaching the skill, reassess children's progress.

Portfolio Assessment

Reread the poem "A Friend." Tell children what a good deed is. Have them brainstorm a list of good deeds they might do for a friend. Write their responses on the board. Ask volunteers to name the initial, medial, and/or final consonant in each word.

Direct children to make a gift box for a friend. Tell children to write on paper one or two good deeds they would like to do for a friend. You might want the children to decorate or illustrate their good deeds.

Provide small gift boxes for children. Have them put their good deed papers in the box and then wrap it. Beforehand, direct children to copy their good deed papers and place the copy in their portfolios.

Performance Assessment

Set up three stations around the classroom—one station each for initial, medial, and final consonants. At each station have an appropriate list of words.

On the board write "Initial," "Medial," and "Final." Tell children to copy the titles on separate sheets of paper. Have children rotate among the stations and write the correct consonants on their answer sheets.

Using Technology

To evaluate children's progress, have them complete the *Tech Talk* activities on pages 5I–5J of the Teacher's Edition.

Answer Key	
Page 5D	
1. six	7. wagon
2. door	8. camel
3. hat	9. robot
4. top	10. kite
5. fan	11. ruler
6. cat	12. box

ay the name of each picture. Then write the letter that stands for the missing sound.

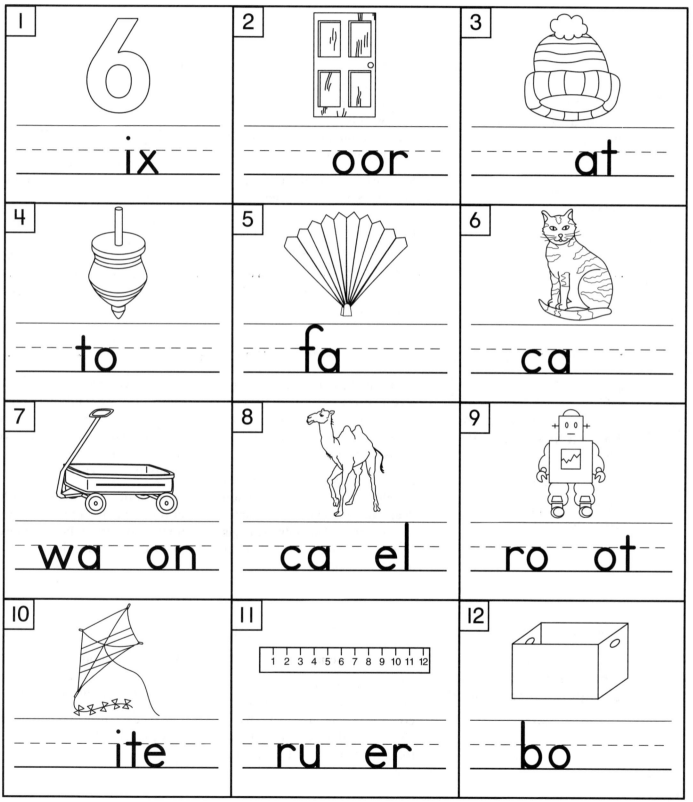

1	2	3
__ix	__oor	__at
4	5	6
to__	fa__	ca__
7	8	9
wa__ on	ca__ el	ro__ ot
10	11	12
__ite	ru__ er	bo__

Blackline Master 1: Assessing Initial, Medial and Final Consonants   **5D**

Game Time

▲▽▲▽▲▽▲▽▲▽▲▽ A Friend Is Calling ▲▽▲▽▲▽▲▽▲▽▲▽

Blackline Master 2 p.5F

Objective: To identify initial and final consonant sounds

Players: pairs

Materials: crayons, scissors

⚙ Duplicate Blackline Master 2 and give a copy to each child. Direct each partner to choose one color with which to color the phones at the bottom of his or her sheet and then cut them out.

⚙ Invite each pair to use the colored phones as markers as they move along the phone line on one of their game boards. Tell partners to take turns saying a picture name, identifying its beginning sound, and then laying in place

a phone marker until they reach the end.

⚙ Have pairs repeat the process with ending sounds. Then have them name other words that have the same beginning or ending sound before marking each picture.

⚙ Encourage children to play a version of the game at home, in which they name household words to match the pictures' beginning and ending sounds.

▲▽▲▽▲▽▲▽▲▽▲▽ A Friendly Match ▽▲▽▲▽▲▽▲▽▲▽▲

Blackline Master 3 p.5G

Objective: To match initial and final consonant sounds

Players: pairs

Materials: glue, construction paper

⚙ Duplicate Blackline Master 3 and give a copy to each pair. Have children glue their copies onto construction paper, cut out the cards, and color the pictures.

⚙ Have one player in each pair deal out all the cards. Direct each non-dealer to lay down a card, name the picture, and identify the beginning and ending sounds. Remaining players should respond by

laying down a picture whose name either begins or ends with one of the sounds identified. Tell children to position the cards in a neat vertical column and to pass if they do not have a card to play.

⚙ The first player with no cards left or the player holding the least number of cards when no more plays are possible wins.

▲▽▲▽▲▽▲▽▲ Just Between Buddies ▲▽▲▽▲▽▲▽▲

Objective: To generate words that begin with a specific consonant sound

Players: pairs

⚙ Assign a consonant to each pair.

⚙ Direct partners to use words that begin with that consonant to compose a sentence that tells about something friends can do together. For example: **B**ill and

Barb like to **b**ounce **b**alls in **B**oston; **S**ally and **S**am skate on the sidewalk in the summer.

⚙ Call on each pair to recite its sentence for the class.

A Friend Is Calling

A Friendly Match

ESL Activities

Best Friends *Page 5*

Invite each child to write a few sentences describing his or her best friend. Remind children that a best friend might be an adult, family member, or pet. Have each child attach a photo or illustration to the description sheet and present the picture-essay to the class. Use prompts such as the following to guide children:

● What is your friend's name?
● How old is your friend?
● Where does she or he live?
● What do you enjoy doing together?
● What do you like about your friend?
● How long have you known your friend?
● What does your friend look like?

Friends' Day *Page 5*

Plan a Friends' Day. Prepare a letter explaining the event to children's parents. For the day's festivities, have children invite a friend to class and introduce the friend by describing his or her interests, school, family, and so on. Encourage children to invite friends from other countries to share their native customs with the class. Have the class question the guests. Meanwhile, prepare a list of each guest's characteristics and interests. After all guests have been introduced, have children match the characteristics you have listed with the names of the guests.

Making New Friends *Page 5*

Ask children to interview a classmate they do not know well in order to "make a new friend." Suggest questions to help children through the interviews. For example:

● Where does your new friend live?
● Does he or she come from another country?
● What does she or he like to do for fun?
● What is his or her favorite subject in school?

Have children reverse roles and repeat the interviewing process. Then allow time for each child to tell the class about her or his new friend.

Long-Distance Pals *Page 15*

Arrange a pen-pal program between students in your class and students in different schools. Help children write simple letters to their pen pals. Provide sentence prompts such as the following:

● My name is _____ .
● I am _____ years old.
● I am in the second grade.
● I like to _____ .

Who's Your Friend? *Page 15*

Present to the class pictures of children dressed according to the custom of their native lands. Discuss the pictures, identify each country portrayed, and share some of the distinctive characteristics or traditions of its people. Then introduce the following sentence patterns to bring discussion back to children in the class:

● My friend is from....
● Where is your friend from?

Invite several children to stand before the class, and give a picture that shows at least one person to each. Direct one child to introduce his or her friend in the picture; pass the follow-up question pattern to the next child. Let the chain of responses continue until all children holding pictures have made an introduction.

Friendly Dialogue *Page 15*

Have children select partners. Direct each pair to develop a dialogue between two friends who meet to play together on the weekend. Use these questions to guide children:

● How will you greet your friend?
● What will you do with your friend?
● Where will you go?
● What will you say when you leave your friend?

5H

TECH TALK

Consonant Capers

Objectives

● To recognize initial, medial, and final consonant sounds

● To use a program such as Kid Works™ 2* to make a class consonant book

Preparation
Have children brainstorm words that characterize a friend or a friendship. Encourage children to name things that would describe a best friend. List the words on the board, and have children identify the initial, medial, and final consonants in each word.

One Step at a Time

1 Have children work independently or in small groups. Direct children on Kid Works™ 2 to select a background picture by clicking on the coloring book in Story Illustrator.

2 Have children use the stamps to add pictures about friendship to the background and save their work.

3 Tell children to switch to Story Writer and write a few sentences about friends or friendship to go with their picture. Tell them to retrieve their friendship scene from the Picture Box and place it at the beginning of their story.

4 Have children print their illustrated documents through Story Player.

5 Direct children to identify the consonants in all the words. Have them underline the beginning consonants in green, the medial consonants in yellow, and the final consonants in red.

Class Sharing

Have students or groups share their pages with the class. Tell them to ask the class to identify the consonants at the beginning, middle, or end of the words in the sentences about friendship. Then compile all the pages into a class consonant book, and display it in the Reading Corner.

My friends and I play and sing outside.

Friendly E-Mail

Objectives
- To practice recognition of initial, medial, and final consonant sounds
- To use E-mail to correspond with children around the United States

Preparation
Use the journal *Classroom Connect* or a similar resource to obtain names of teachers willing to maintain ongoing communications between their classes and yours.

Explain to children that electronic mail, E-mail, is a way to communicate with others who might be far away. Display a map of the United States, and ask children to name states they have been to or know about. Tell them they are going to communicate with other second graders across the United States. Explain to your class that these other children will be their E-mail friends.

One Step at a Time

1. Help children compose a descriptive introduction about themselves to send to another class.

2. Ask children to name things to include in the introduction. They might name the city or town where they live, and describe the weather and what kinds of work people do there. Have children tell about what they are studying in school, particularly in phonics Unit 1.

3. Write the above information and name of each child on chart paper. Have volunteers identify the beginning, medial, and final consonants of all the names.

4. Enter all the information, highlight the consonants identified, and send it to another second-grade class. Ask for the same kind of information in return.

Class Sharing

On a wall map, have a volunteer pinpoint where children in both classes live. Use a piece of yarn to connect the two points. Help children calculate the distance between the classes.

Display the information you receive from the other class around the map. Ask children to identify the consonants and consonant sounds.

Try to maintain communication with this class throughout the year.

Help a Friend

VIDEO

Show the video *The Magical Forest* (Celebrity Home Entertainment). Have the class describe the helpful things the animals did. Then direct children to tell about a time they helped a friend and how it felt to be helpful.

Together, make a list of helpful acts and circle the initial, medial, and final consonants.

Have children work in groups. Tell each group to select a helpful activity to role-play. You might videotape the helpful hints for parents' night.

All referenced software is listed under Computer Resources on page T46.

Literature Introduction to Initial Consonants

Objectives
- To enjoy a poem about friendship
- To identify all the consonants

Starting with Literature

- Read aloud "A Friend" on page 5. Focus attention on the illustration, and encourage students to discuss how the picture shows that the children are friends.
- Invite children to recite the poem with you. Then ask them to tell about the special places they like to go to with friends.

Developing Critical Thinking
Have a volunteer read aloud the questions at the bottom of the page. Engage children in a discussion about why it is nice to have a friend. Ask them to suggest ways of making new friends. List ideas on the board.

Introducing the Skill

- Call attention to the alphabet chart in your room. Elicit from the class that **a, e, i, o,** and **u** are vowels and that all the other letters are consonants.
- Write **friend** and **fun** on the board. Ask children to name all the consonants in each word.

Practicing the Skill

- Have each child choose a word from the poem, say the word, and name its consonants. Then invite students to find two words in the poem that begin with the same consonant.

ESL Activities
Refer to page 5H.

A Friend

It's fun to have a friend!
Someone to see and stay with
To walk and talk and play with
To laugh and shout HURRAY with
It's fun to have a friend!

We might not even talk!
We might just sit and giggle
Until we wiggle-wiggle
Or leap and jump and jiggle
We might not even talk!

It's fun to have a friend!
To hold a hand and go with
To ask and learn and know with
To sing and dance and grow with
It's fun to have a friend!

Betsy Jones Michael

Critical Thinking   Encourage children to see the need
Why is it fun to have a friend?   to be welcoming to new friendships.
How can you make new friends?

LESSON 1: Introduction to Initial, Medial, and Final Consonants   **5**

Theme Words

Friends Reread the poem "A Friend." Ask children to name some of their friends. Print these names on the word chart. Ask children what they like to do with their friends. Add their responses to the word chart.

Use the word chart to assess children's ability to recognize initial, medial, and final consonants. Children will say the word, point out the initial, medial, or final consonants, and print the letter(s) on the chalk board.

Check children's comprehension of rhyming words; have children find a word on the word chart for which they can give a rhyming word. Ask children to say the word and their rhyming word. Add any new words to the word chart.

Dear Family,

As your child progresses through this unit about friendship, he or she will review the sounds of the consonants. The 21 letters of the alphabet that are consonants are shown below.

● Say the name of each consonant.

Apreciada Familia:

En esta unidad, acerca de la amistad, su niño repasará los sonidos de las consonantes. Las siguientes letras son las 21 consonantes del idioma inglés.

● Pronuncien cada consonante.

The activities on the *Phonics Alive at Home* page are designed to promote active family involvement in developing children's reading and writing skills.

● In this unit, the *Phonics Alive at Home* page features activities related to the unit's "Friends" theme and to the phonics focus on consonants.

● Have children tear out page 6 from their Student Edition. Suggest that they complete the activities at home with family members.

● Throughout Unit 1, encourage children to think about the friends they have and ways in which they can make new friends. Provide opportunities for children to share pictures of friends, stories they have written about friends, and books they have read about friendship.

● As a sign of friendship, have children make welcome cards for new students.

● Read the poem "A Friend" on the reverse side.

● Talk about things friends do together. Tell each other what you like most about a good friend.

● Help your child identify some of the consonants in the poem. Ask what sounds they make.

● Lea al niño la poesía, "A Friend" en la página 5.

● Converse con su niño acerca de lo que hacen los amigos cuando están juntos. Cada uno explique lo que le gusta de un buen amigo.

● Repasen las consonantes que aparecen en la poesía. ¿Cómo suenan?

PROJECT

Ask your child to name some of his or her friends. Together make a list of the names. Underline single consonants in each name. Then choose one friend and write, call, or draw him or her.

Carmela
Omar
Lisa
Jason
Karen

PROYECTO

Pida a su niño nombrar a algunos de sus amigos. Después escriban los nombres. Subrayen las consonantes en cada nombre. Luego, escriban una carta, llamen, o dibujen a uno de los amigos.

LESSON 1: Introduction to Initial, Medial, and Final Consonants—Phonics Alive at Home

ESL Activities

Throughout this unit, ESL activities are referenced. These activities benefit the ESL child in your classroom by providing additional language experiences. Choose the activities that best meet the diverse needs of your class.

For ESL activities related to "A Friend," refer to page 5H.

Take-Home Book

Children and their families will enjoy reading the fold-up book on the *Take-Home Book* page for Unit 1. The book is intended for shared reading and should be sent home with children at any appropriate time during the unit.

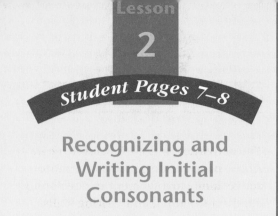
Recognizing and Writing Initial Consonants

Objectives
- To recognize the sounds of initial consonants
- To write initial consonants

Warming Up

Reviewing Consonant Letters
- Write this rhyme on the board:

  Zeke has a pal;
  Her name is Val.
  Max likes to run
  With Gwen for fun.
  Joy and Dan can toss a ball
  And catch it as they jump up tall.

- Read the rhyme together. Call out consonants from the rhyme, and ask volunteers to circle each one every time it appears.

★ *Teaching the Lesson*

- Draw a football on the board. Ask children what letter stands for the beginning consonant sound. Then refer them to the Poetry Poster "A Friend." Read aloud the first line of the poem, and ask children to listen for two other words that begin with the same consonant sound as the one in **football**.

- Hold up each of the following Phonics Picture Cards in mixed order: **bus, cake, door, feet, game, hat, jam, king, mask, net, pig, quilt, red, seal, toys, vine, wave, yo-yo,** and **zebra**. One at a time, ask children to say each initial consonant and print it on the board.

Say the name of each picture. Write the letter or letters that stand for the beginning consonant sound.

| j | m | k | f | z | s | | r | b | qu | h | w | p |

1. football — f
2. jam — j
3. six — s
4. zipper — z
5. moon — m
6. key — k
7. wagon — w
8. heart — h
9. rainbow — r
10. basket — b
11. pencil — p
12. queen — qu

LESSON 2: Recognizing and Writing Initial Consonants   7

Multisensory *Activities*

Auditory ■ Visual

Can't Catch Me
Write the following chant on chart paper, and read it with the class:

  Bobby over the ocean,
  Bobby over the sea,
  Bobby caught a **bunny**,
  But he can't catch me.

Change the name of the child and the animal to two other words that begin with the same consonant, such as **Molly/monkey** or **Tina/turtle**. Then say the chant with the new words.

Auditory ■ Kinesthetic

F Stands for Friend
Materials: Phonics Picture Cards **seal, wave, tub, pig, leaf, fan, game, jam, door, horn**

Give each picture card to a different child. Ask a volunteer to say the name of her or his picture, give the initial consonant, and then find a word that starts with the same sound on the poetry poster. Have children point to the word on the poster and say, for example, "**Seal** and **see** start with **s**."

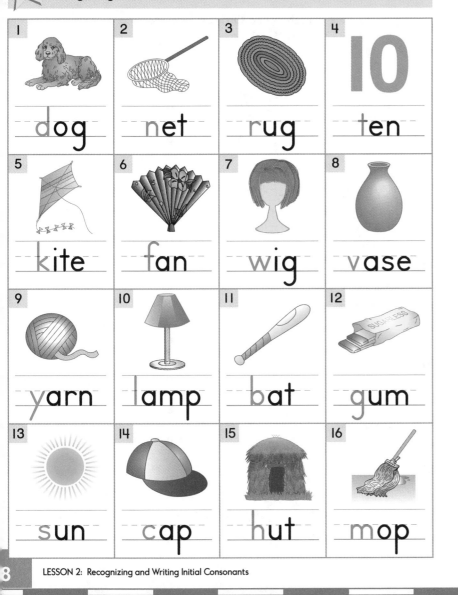

1 d_og	2 n_et	3 r_ug	4 t_en
5 k_ite	6 f_an	7 w_ig	8 v_ase
9 y_arn	10 l_amp	11 b_at	12 g_um
13 s_un	14 c_ap	15 h_ut	16 m_op

LESSON 2: Recognizing and Writing Initial Consonants

8

Multicultural Connection

Write *futbol* on the board. Tell children that **futbol** (FOOT bohl) is the Spanish name for a game played all over the world by children and adults. Ask children to pronounce the word with you. Point out that, although the word sounds like the English word *football*, futbol is really the game of soccer.

Computer Connection

Invite children to learn about the alphabet in Bailey's Book House® (Edmark). Tell them to select the letter-machine graphic and enter a letter of the alphabet. Words that begin with the sound of that letter are displayed on the screen, followed by an animation of those words. For example, for the initial sound of **d**, the screen will display **Dinosaurs dance** and animated dancing dinosaurs.

Practicing the Skill

- Ask children to turn to page 7, and read the directions together. Have them point to each picture as a volunteer identifies it. Complete the first item with the class. Then have children finish the page independently.
- Follow the same procedure for page 8.

Extending the Skill Across the Curriculum

(Language Arts/Social Studies)

Theme Activity

- Ask children what they like to do with their friends, and list responses on the board. Then invite children to use each suggested action word in a sentence and name that word's initial consonant. Model this with a Think Aloud, such as "I like to **paint** pictures with Naomi. **Paint** begins with **p**."
- Read aloud the theme books cited below to initiate further discussion about friendship. Have children scan the books and select words that begin with consonants. Ask them to say other words that have the same initial sounds.

Theme Books

Kellogg, Steven. *Best Friends*. NY: Dial Books for Young Readers, 1986. Friendships among children and animals, with a focus on guide dogs.

King, Larry, L. *Because of Lozo Brown*. NY: Viking Kestrell, 1988. The narrator is afraid to meet the big new boy until he discovers he has nothing to fear.

Recognizing and Writing Final Consonants

Objectives
- To recognize the sounds of final consonants
- To write final consonants

Warming Up

Reviewing Initial Consonants
- Ask volunteers to read these sentences and identify both the repeated initial consonants and the words that begin with them.

  Fay fried five fish over the **fire**.
  Ron rode his **red** bike in the **rain**.
  Yanni's yellow yo-yo is in the **yard**.
  Jan put **jars** of **jelly** in the **jeep**.

- Ask students to make up sentences that have at least three repeated beginning consonants.

★ Teaching the Lesson

Materials: Phonics Picture Cards
- Write this rhyme on the board and read it aloud:

  Ned, Fred, and **Jed,**
  Three friends on a **sled.**

- Ask children to join you in rereading the rhyme. Then circle the **d** in each word, and ask them what consonant sound they hear at the end of **Ned, Fred, Jed,** and **sled.**
- Display the following Phonics Picture Cards: **tub, red, leaf, pig, duck, seal, jam, fan, cap, door, bus, hat,** and **fox.** Invite children to name each picture and identify the final sound. For example, "**Tub** ends with the sound of **b**."

Say the name of each picture. Circle the letter that stands for the ending consonant sound.

#			#			#		
1	web	(b) d t	2	top	(p) m g	3	pig	l b (g)
4	kiss	r (s) f	5	nail	(l) m j	6	foot	(t) d n
7	roof	k h (f)	8	ham	(m) c n	9	star	g (r) p
10	box	t (x) d	11	man	h z (n)	12	hook	w f (k)
13	sled	(d) f k	14	bug	p d (g)	15	bell	r (l) v

LESSON 3: Recognizing the Sounds of Final Consonants

Multisensory *Activities*

Auditory ■ Kinesthetic

Friendly Words
Read aloud these pairs of words: **cup/jeep; cot/mat; sun/pin; bus/jam; tail/bell; web/bib; dog/map; book/milk; fox/six; ram/gum; rug/tag; toad/bug;** and **car/bear.** If the ending sound in each pair is the same, have children clasp their hands together. If the ending sound in each pair is different have them separate their hands. Then ask children to suggest their own word pairs.

Visual ■ Auditory

A Friend at the End
Materials: Poetry Poster "A Friend"

Invite children to look at the Poetry Poster and read the poem aloud together. Then say **man, band, duck, feet,** and **tap.** Ask children to name words in the poem that have the same final consonant sound; for example, "**Man** and **pen** both end with **n**." Challenge children to name other words that end in the same sound.

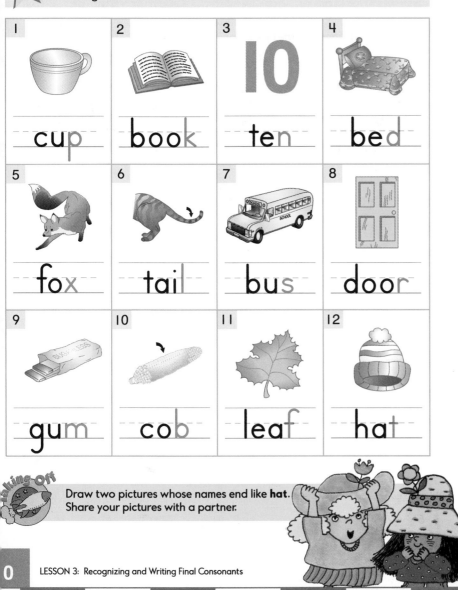

Say the name of each picture. Write the letter that stands for the ending consonant sound.

1 cu**p**	2 boo**k**	3 te**n**	4 be**d**
5 fo**x**	6 tai**l**	7 bu**s**	8 doo**r**
9 gu**m**	10 co**b**	11 lea**f**	12 ha**t**

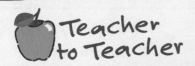

Draw two pictures whose names end like **hat**. Share your pictures with a partner.

0

LESSON 3: Recognizing and Writing Final Consonants

Practicing the Skill

● Invite children to turn to page 9, and read the directions together. Ask children to point to each picture as a volunteer identifies it. Then have children complete the page.

● Read aloud the directions on page 10. Do the first item with the class. Then have children complete the rest. *Taking Off* is an extension activity that children may do on their own.

Extending the Skill Across the Curriculum

(Language Arts/Science)

Theme Activity

● Discuss why people consider pets their friends. Then write *Kinds of Pets* and *What Pets Need* on the board. Ask children for suggestions to list under each heading. Have children circle any final consonants in the words.

● Share the theme book cited below. Choose appropriate words from the book, and have children name their final consonants.

● Encourage children to write and illustrate a story about their pets. Have children without pets write about a pet they would like to have.

● Have children identify words in their stories that begin or end with specific consonants.

📖 **Theme Book**

Sadlier, Marilyn. *Elizabeth and Larry.* NY: Simon and Schuster Books for Young Readers, 1990. A woman and her unusual pet friend.

📁 **Portfolio**

Have children add their stories to their portfolios.

Observational Assessment

Listen carefully when children speak. Note whether they pronounce the initial and final consonants correctly.

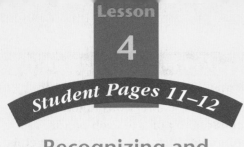

Recognizing and Writing Medial Consonants

Objectives
- To recognize the sounds of medial consonants
- To write medial consonants

Warming Up

Reviewing Consonants
- Read aloud these sets of words: **pal/pony**/bell; **red**/sled/**ran**; **sun**/nut/**sit**; king/**wig/wave**; **lid/lamp**/did; van/**fine/fox**. Have children say the two words that begin with the same initial consonant sound and then name the consonant.
- Follow the same procedure for final consonants. Use **pen/can**/ham; top/**cot/feet**; tail/**leaf/doll**; **web/bib**/wet; ride/**car/deer**; and **dog**/gate/**rug**.

★ *Teaching the Lesson*

- Write the following rhyme on the board:

  Little Miss Muffet sat on a tuffet,
  Eating her curds and whey;
  Along came a spider and sat down
  beside her
  And frightened Miss Muffet away.

- Invite children to join you in a choral reading of the rhyme.
- Substitute for "spider" other animals whose names have medial consonants, such as **tiger, dragon, camel, parrot, kitten,** and **robin.** Have children reread the rhyme using each new animal name.
- Have children identify the medial consonant in each animal's name.

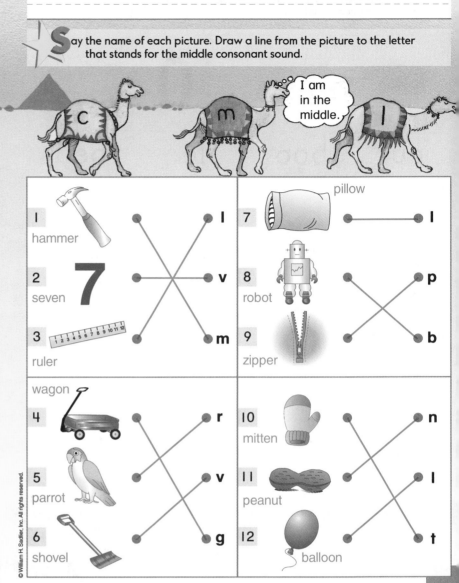

Say the name of each picture. Draw a line from the picture to the letter that stands for the middle consonant sound.

I am in the middle.

1 hammer — l
2 seven — v
3 ruler — m

7 pillow — l
8 robot — p
9 zipper — b

4 wagon — r
5 parrot — v
6 shovel — g

10 mitten — n
11 peanut — l
12 balloon — t

LESSON 4: Recognizing the Sounds of Medial Consonants

Multisensory *Activities*

Visual ■ Kinesthetic

Pickle in the Middle

Materials: construction paper pickles (4" x 1")

Trace and cut out twelve "pickles." Write the words below on the board, and leave space for the middle consonant:

ca(b)in, wa(t)er, se(v)en, ba(c)on, pe(d)al, wa(g)on, sa(l)ad, mo(t)el, tu(l)ip, ro(b)in, le(m)on, pea(n)ut

Have volunteers write each missing letter on a pickle, tape it in place in the word, and then read the word.

Auditory ■ Tactile

Shout It Out

Materials: index cards

Write the following letters on index cards: **b, c, d, g, l, m, n, p, r, t, v.** Distribute the cards. Then say the names of the pictures on pages 11 and 12 of the Student Edition. Ask children to listen for the middle consonant in each word and hold up their index card if it features that letter.

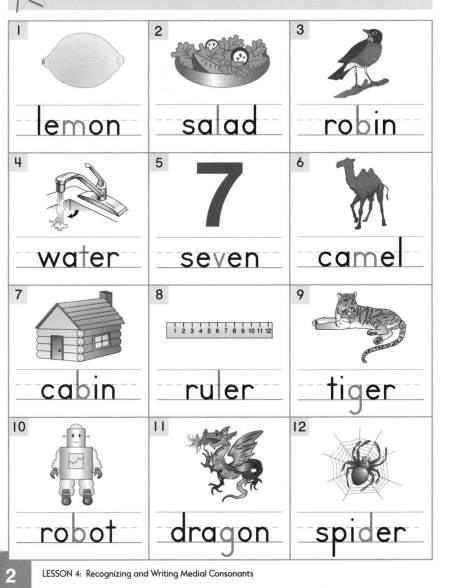

1. lemon
2. salad
3. robin
4. water
5. seven
6. camel
7. cabin
8. ruler
9. tiger
10. robot
11. dragon
12. spider

2 LESSON 4: Recognizing and Writing Medial Consonants

*C*omputer Connection

To reinforce the recognition of initial, medial, and final sounds and the letters that are associated with them, have children play the Sounds game in Phonics® (Dinosoft). For example, have children select "Classroom," "Sounds," and then "Ending Sounds." Philo, the Dino teacher, will display letter cards. Ask children to choose the picture whose name has the same final sound as the sound of the letter on Philo's card.

Practicing the Skill

● Ask children to turn to page 11. Discuss the art, and point out that the letter that stands for the middle consonant sound in **camel** is **m**. Then read aloud the directions, and invite volunteers to identify the pictures. Do the first item with the class. Then have children complete the page independently.

● Work through the first item on page 12 with the class. Then invite children to complete the page.

Extending the Skill Across the Curriculum

(Drama/Art)

Theme Activity

● Reread the Little Miss Muffet rhyme. Replace "spider" with **tiger, dragon, camel, robot, parrot, kitten,** and **robin.** Ask children to imagine that, instead of being frightened, Miss Muffet decided to make friends with these animals.

● Invite children to work in pairs and tell each other what might happen after Miss Muffet makes friends with the animals. You might suggest the following to get children started:

Miss Muffet and her animal friend might go on a trip together and have an adventure, such as climbing a mountain, getting lost in a jungle, taking a hot-air balloon ride, visiting the North Pole, or helping a person or animal in trouble.

● Ask children to act out their stories. Suggest that one child play Ms. or Mr. Muffet and the other play one of the animals.

● You may wish to provide materials for children to make simple costumes, or have them make large name tags for their characters.

Reviewing Initial, Medial, and Final Consonants

Objective
- To write initial, medial, and final consonants

Warming Up

Reviewing Rhyming Words
Write the sentences below on the board. Invite volunteers to read them and identify the rhyming words.

There was a **tag** on the **bag**.
Dan ran toward the **van**.
A little **kitten** slept on a **mitten**.
We have lots of **fun** in the **sun**.
She put a **dragon** in her **wagon**.
The big **pot** was **not hot**.

★ Teaching the Lesson

Materials: Phonics Picture Cards **hat, rug, camel, map, fan, tulip, box, seal, robot, seven, book**; a box

- Draw seven X's on the board, and ask children how many X's you have drawn. Say **seven**, and then ask children what sounds they hear at the beginning, middle, and end of the word. Write **seven** on the board, and ask volunteers to circle **s**, **v**, and **n**.

- Display the Phonics Picture Cards. Have one child hold the box. Ask a volunteer to choose a card, identify its picture, say which consonants are where in the picture name, and put the card in the box. Use a Think Aloud to model this for the children by saying, "I'll put a seven in the box. **Seven** begins with **s**, has a **v** in the middle, and ends with **n**."

Look at the picture clues. Fill in the missing letters in the puzzles.

ACROSS ➡
1
3

DOWN ⬇
1
2

```
¹c  u  ²b
   a     e
   p  ³d  o  l  l
```

ACROSS ➡
4 **7**
5
6

DOWN ⬇
4

```
⁴s  e  v  e  n
 a
⁵l  e  m  o  n
 a
⁶d  o  o  r
```

What seven things would you and your friend put in a backpack? Name each thing, and write the letters that stand for the beginning and ending consonant sounds.

LESSON 5: Reviewing Initial, Medial, and Final Consonants

Multisensory *Activities*

Auditory ■ Tactile

You Decide

Materials: Phonics Picture Cards, index cards

Give each child two index cards. Have children print **B** on one and **E** on the other. As you hold up each picture card, invite volunteers to say the picture name and its initial or final consonant. Direct children to display the **B** if the consonant is at the beginning of the word and the **E** if it is at the end.

Visual ■ Kinesthetic

Fill the Box

Materials: box, classroom objects

Invite children to choose one or two classroom objects to put into a box. Have children make labels for each object and circle the initial, medial, and final consonants on the labels. Then have children work in pairs. Have one partner cover the labels. Have the other identify the consonants in the object's name.

Write the missing letter in each picture name. Then find a rhyming word in the box and write it on the line below.

mug	pedal	pig	foxes	pen	hop	van	hat

1. bat
   hat

2. boxes
   foxes

3. wig
   pig

4. hen
   pen

5. medal
   pedal

6. can
   van

7. rug
   mug

8. pop
   hop

4　LESSON 5: Reviewing Initial, Medial, and Final Consonants

Multicultural Connection

From the library, obtain a children's book that shows a method of writing or an alphabet different from ours. A good book to use is *A to Zen: A Book of Japanese Culture* (Picture Book Studio) by Ruth Wells.

Children who want to correspond with children in another country may write to International Pen Friends, P.O. Box 290065, Brooklyn, NY 11229-0001. Tell children to include their name, address, and countries of interest.

Teacher to Teacher

Have children work in pairs to make up word-search puzzles that provide phonics skills practice. Have them exchange puzzles with other pairs. Use a stopwatch to time children as they solve the word-search puzzles.

Christine Matuszewski
Ramsey, NJ

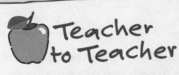

Practicing the Skill

● Draw children's attention to the *Remember* logo at the top of page 13. Read aloud the directions, and ask volunteers to identify the pictures. Have children work in pairs to complete the page.

● Read aloud the directions, and work through the first item on page 14 with the class. Then have children complete the page independently.

Extending the Skill Across the Curriculum

(Language Arts/Social Studies)

Theme Activity

● Display the theme book cited below, and read aloud its title. Ask children what it means to "meet someone halfway." Encourage them to give specific examples. Then read the book to the class.

● Discuss the story and what was most important to the two friends. Reread selected pages, and have children listen for specific consonant sounds.

● Call attention to the friendly letters that Titus and Fuller wrote to each other on the first two pages of the book. Have children write a similar letter to a friend or to a student in another class.

Theme Book

Schindel, John. *I'll Meet You Halfway.* NY: Macmillan, 1993.

Observational Assessment

Scan children's writing to check whether they are applying skills they learned that involve initial, medial, and final consonant sounds.

Portfolio

Have children put their letters into their portfolios. If they choose to mail their letters, you might first make copies for them to keep.

Integrating the Language Arts

Objectives
● To use oral and written language to extend the theme concept
● To demonstrate ability to recognize consonant sounds in context

Background Information

The pictures on page 15 represent children and friendship around the world. The words listed that mean *friend* in different languages are pronounced as follows:

amigo	(ah MEE goh) Spanish
tomodachi	(toh moh DAH chee) Japanese
rafiki	(ra FEE kee) Swahili

★ Teaching the Lesson

● Call children's attention to the pictures on page 15. Ask them what they see in the photos.

● Read aloud and discuss the text on friends. Ask children how the pictures remind them of their own friendships. Encourage children who speak other languages to teach the class another way to say *friend*.

● Call out the position and name of consonant sounds as they appear in selected words in the text. Have children identify the word that contains each letter in the position you specify.

Oral Language Development
Ask children how friends are the same all around the world. Record responses on chart paper.

ESL Activities
Refer to page 5H

 Let's read and talk about friendship.

We're best **buddies** in English.
In Spanish we're **amigos**.
Speak French and call us **amis**.
I'll speak Swahili and call you **rafiki**.
You speak Japanese and call me **tomodachi**.
In any language, we're friends.

How are friends the same all over the world?

LESSON 6: Initial, Medial, and Final Consonants in Context

Reading and Writing Connection

Have children work in four groups. Assign to each group one response from the *Oral Language Development* question (e.g., friends play, learn, work, together; friends help each other). Direct each group to discuss specific examples of its assigned phrase. Then have each child illustrate one example and write a sentence about it. Tell children to circle any initial, medial, or final consonants in their sentences. Display the illustrations on a bulletin board.

Social Studies Connection

Remind children that *amigo* is Spanish for *friend*. Explain that Spanish is a language spoken in many countries. Ask children to name places where they think Spanish is spoken and to find those places on a globe or map.

Point out that Africa is a large continent with many countries and that Swahili is just one language spoken there. Invite children to name other languages spoken in Africa, such as Hausa, Afrikaans, or Yoruba. Encourage the use of reference books.

©William H. Sadlier, Inc. All rights reserved.

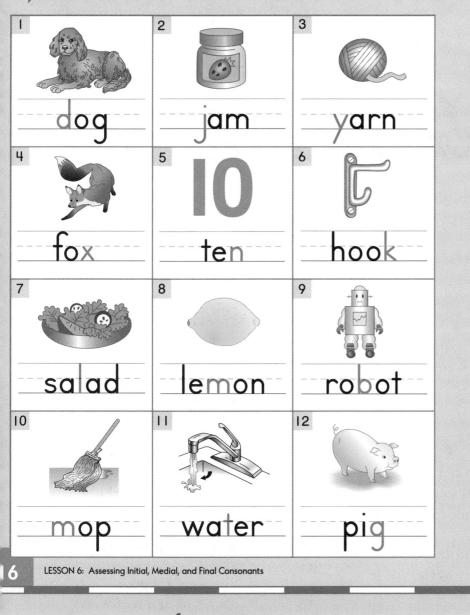

Check-Up Say the name of each picture. Write the letter that stands for the missing sound.

1 do**g**	2 **j**am	3 **y**arn
4 fo**x**	5 **t**en	6 **h**ook
7 sa**l**ad	8 le**m**on	9 ro**b**ot
10 **m**op	11 wa**t**er	12 **p**ig

LESSON 6: Assessing Initial, Medial, and Final Consonants

16

Unit Test The test on page 16 can help you track your class's progress in mastering initial, medial, and final consonants. Before children complete the page, say a few words that contain initial, medial, and final consonants that they have learned. Ask children to identify these consonants. Then read the directions with children and have them complete the page independently.

Observational Assessment Review the observational notes you have made about children's learning and participation in the skills and theme activities presented in this unit. Use these notes to help assess overall performance and progress.

Student Skills Assessment After children have completed the Unit Test, record your evaluation of each child's skills on pages 207–208 of the Student Edition.

Writing Conference Arrange conferences with children to discuss the samples of their work in their portfolios. Encourage children to talk about their writing as you review the samples together. You might write short notes about each child's progress. Add the notes to the child's portfolio, and review them during your next conference.

Group together children who need further consonant instruction for the *Reteaching Activities*. You might then use the alternative assessment methods on page 5C of the Teacher's Edition.

Take Home Book Remind the children to share with their families the *Take-Home Book* page for Unit 1.

Reteaching *Activities*

Climb to the Top
Draw a ladder on the board. Write one of the following words on each rung of the ladder, but omit the first letter of each: **game, vine, lamp, jeep, tub, seal, ball, dig.** Have children "climb" the ladder by saying the words and writing the initial consonants. Then do the same for final consonants. Use words such as **web, cot, roof, map, book, tail, bed,** and **bus.**

Word Search
Assign five of the following letters to pairs of children: **b, d, f, g, k, l** or **m, n, p, r, s, t.** Ask them to look through books to find and then list one word that begins with each of the letters and one word that ends with each. After they have made their lists, have children use the words in sentences and share the sentences with the class.

16

Splish! Splash!

Theme:
*For people, for plants,
for animals—water all around!*

Overview

Unit 2 introduces children to short vowel sounds as they learn about water and the part water plays in their lives.

Objectives

- To enjoy a poem about water
- To recognize short vowel sounds
- To use the short vowel rule to "decode" words
- To rhyme short vowel words
- To read and write short vowel words in context

Thematic Teaching

Elicit what children already know about water, and consider their experiences when selecting activities from the lessons. Provide additional reading material. Display the Poetry Poster "Sampan."

Individual Lessons

Lesson	Skill Focus
7	Introduction to Short Vowels
8	Short Vowel **a** Words and Phonograms
9	Writing Short Vowel **a**
10	Short Vowel **i** Words and Phonograms
11	Writing Short Vowel **i**
12	Short Vowel **o** Words and Phonograms
13	Writing Short Vowel **o**
14	Reviewing and Assessing Short Vowels **a**, **i**, and **o**
15	Short Vowel **u** Words and Phonograms
16	Writing Short Vowel **u**
17	Short Vowel **e** Words and Phonograms
18	Writing Short Vowel **e**
19	Reviewing and Assessing Short Vowels **u** and **e**
20	Connecting Spelling and Writing
21	Integrating the Language Arts

Take-Home Book: *Water's Song*

Curriculum Integration

Spelling A *Spelling Connection* appears in every lesson.

Writing Children write descriptions, captions, fictional stories, group stories, and a brochure on pages 22, 24, 26, 36, 40, 44, and 45.

Science Science-related activities appear on pages 20, 22, 26, 28, and 34.

Music An opportunity for involvement in music appears on page 30.

Optional Learning Activities

Multisensory Activities Visual, auditory, kinesthetic, or tactile skill development is combined with phonics study in every lesson.

Multicultural Connection Children learn about the Nile, the !Kung people, and Incan aqueducts in activities on pages 22, 26, and 34.

Thematic Activities Exciting activities in the *Extending the Skill Across the Curriculum* part of each lesson augment phonics study.

Assessment Strategies

Multiple strategies such as *Observational Assessment,* writing portfolios, written end-of-the-unit assessments, and the *Skills Checklist* at the back of the Student Edition will help you assess children's mastery of phonics skills throughout Unit 2.

Resources

Theme-Related Resources

Down the Drain, 3-2-1 Contact Series. Children's Television Network, 1991.

Ann Grilli. *Wet & Wild: The Wonders of Water.* Castle of Dreams Music, 1990.

Hadithi, Mwenye. *Hot Hippo.* New York: Little, 1986.

Lyon, George Ella. *Come a Tide.* New York: Orchard Books Watts, 1990.

Paraskevas, Betty. *On the Edge of the Sea.* New York: Dial Books Young Readers, 1992.

Patron, Susan. *Dark Cloud Strong Breeze.* New York: Orchard Books, 1994.

Ryder, Joanne. *A House by the Sea.* New York: Morrow, 1994.

Assessment

In Unit 2 children focus on recognizing and writing short vowels. The following are suggestions for evaluating these skills through informal/formal, observational, objective, portfolio, and performance assessments. You may also wish to refer to *Using Technology* for alternative assessment activities.

Informal/Formal Assessment

The tests on pages 17D and 17E assess whether children have mastered the skills of recognizing and writing the short vowels **a, e, i, o,** and **u** as well as short vowel phonograms.

These tools may be used informally at the beginning of the unit to identify a starting point for individual or class instruction or formally at the end of the unit to assess children's progress.

Observational Assessment

Specific opportunities for observation are highlighted in the lesson plans. In addition, there are many opportunities throughout the unit to observe children identifying and writing the short vowels and short vowel phonograms. Other opportunities for observation might include *Spelling Connection, Computer Connection,* and *Theme Activities*. Observe children at different times as they identify each of the short vowels and their phonograms.

Objective Assessment

Use the assessment pages throughout the unit. After completing each assessment page, determine the area(s) in which children would benefit from more instruction; then refer to *Reteaching Activities* found throughout the unit in the Teacher's Edition. After reteaching the skill, reassess children's progress.

Portfolio Assessment

Have children work in five groups, and assign a short vowel to each. Then have the groups scan the poetry pages in this unit to find a poem that features their vowel; for example, short **e** in "At the Shore" on page 37.

Tell each group to read the specific poetry selection and then to brainstorm a list of phonograms for that short vowel. Direct each child in each group to write a poem using as many of the words as possible.

Allow time for children to share their poems with the rest of the group. Tell children to put the poems in their portfolios.

Performance Assessment

Meet with small groups of children. Use the Phonics Picture Cards to assess children's ability to recognize the short vowels. For each short vowel, write out cards with phonograms, such as **am, ag, at, og, op, ot, ug, ut, un, ell, en, ed, ig, it, ill**. Ask children to make up two new words for each phonogram.

Using Technology

To evaluate children's progress, have them complete the *Tech Talk* activities on pages 17K–17L of the Teacher's Edition.

Answer Key				
Page 17D				
1. jam	2. lid	3. dog	4. gas	5. hill
6. rock	7. fan	8. doll	9. milk	10. hat
11. log	12. pin	13. top	14. wig	15. fox
16. mat				
Page 17E				
1. ten	2. bud	3. dog	4. ring	5. lamp
6. rug	7. lock	8. log	9. fin	10. bag
11. pen	12. bat	13. net	14. lid	15. duck

Say the name of each picture. Then write the letter that stands for the vowel sound.

Circle the word that names each picture.

1		tan tin ten	
2		bad bid bud	
3		dig dog dug	
4		ring rang rung	
5		limp lump lamp	
6		rag rug rig	
7		lick luck lock	
8		lag log leg	
9		fin fan fun	
10		bug bag big	
11		pin pen pan	
12		bit but bat	
13		not net nut	
14		lid lad led	
15		deck duck dock	

Game Time

▲▽▲▽▲▽▲▽▲ Phonogram Slides 1–8 ▲▽▲▽▲▽▲▽▲

Blackline Masters 6,7 p.17G,17H

Objective: To read words with short vowel phonograms

Players: individuals or pairs

Materials: scissors

⚙ Duplicate Blackline Masters 6 and 7, and give copies to each child.

⚙ Have children cut out the boxes and the letter slides beneath the boxes. Then have them cut along the dashed lines in front of each phonogram so that the letter slides can be pulled through easily.

⚙ Show children how to display each letter in the opening to make words. Call on volunteers to read aloud words they make.

⚙ Give each child a second set of copies to use at home with their families.

▲▽▲▽▲▽▲ Team Up for Phonograms ▲▽▲▽▲▽▲

Objective: To write words with short vowel phonograms

Players: teams of three or four

⚙ Write a short vowel phonogram on the board. Have teammates work together to make words with that phonogram. Ask one child on each team to record the words.

⚙ After three or four minutes, call out "Stop." Have the teams read aloud their words and cross off their lists those they share with another team. The team with the most words left at the end of the roll call wins the game.

⚙ Continue with other short vowel phonograms, such as **at, ag, in, id, ot, op, ub, ut, ed,** and **ell**.

▲▽▲▽▲▽▲▽▲▽▲▽ Five in a Raft ▽▲▽▲▽▲▽▲▽▲▽▲

Objective: To identify the vowels in short vowel words

Players: groups of five

Materials: chalk or masking tape, vowels written on paper

⚙ Use chalk or masking tape to mark a "raft" on the floor for each group. Invite group members to sit in their raft. Then give each member a large sheet of paper on which is written **a, e, i, o,** or **u** so that each group has a complete set.

⚙ Say a short vowel word such as **fan, cap, land, wax, lid, mitt, fin, dig, rock, job, mop, doll,** **bus, rug, drum, sun, hen, web, vest,** or **net**.

⚙ Tell the groups to decide which vowel is in the word and to have the child with that card stand. Then have the class name the vowel and say the word.

⚙ Continue with other words.

Short Vowel Phonogram Slides 1-4

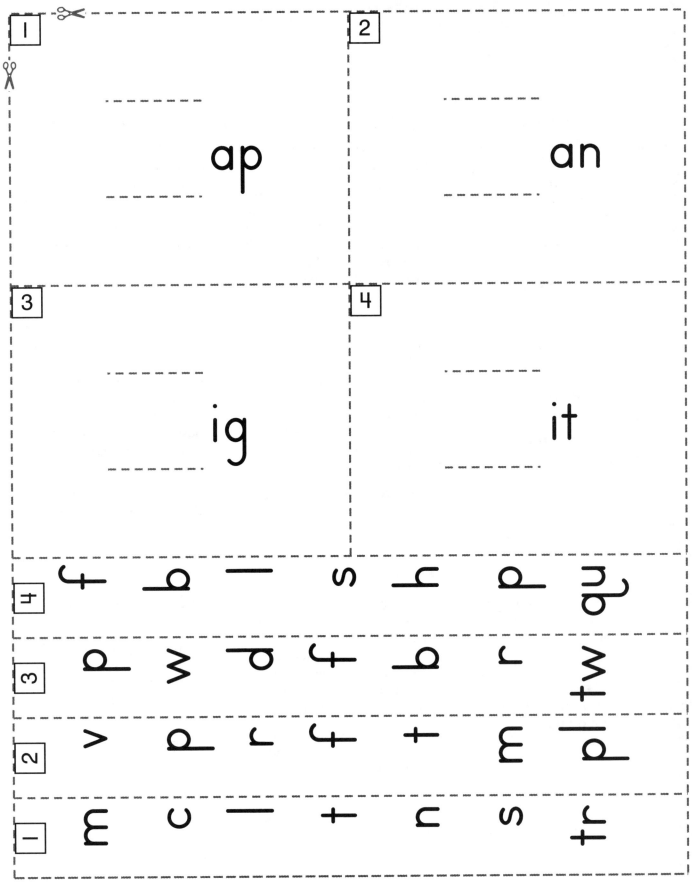

Blackline Master 6: Short Vowel Phonogram Slides 1–4

Short Vowel Phonogram Slides 5-8

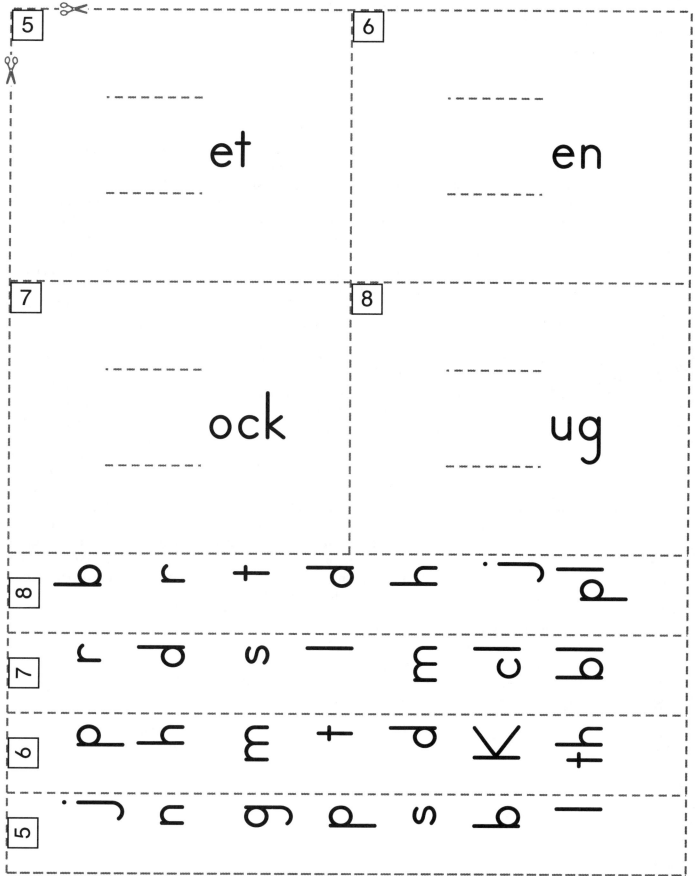

5 6 7 8

et

en

ock

ug

8 b r t d h j pl

7 r d s l m cl bl

6 p h m t d k th

5 j n g p s b l

ESL Activities

Let's Listen *Page 17*

Print the poem in large letters on an experience chart. Read it and act it out with the class. Distribute rhythm instruments. Read the poem aloud again. This time have the children play their instruments each time a noise is indicated in the poem. Call on individuals to identify the noise words. Underline those words, and ask the class to name the vowel sound in each. Have children think of other objects that make the same sounds as those mentioned (e.g., drums tap; sheets flap; children clap; dogs lap). If possible, play a tape of sounds described in the poem.

River Story *Page 17*

Review the poem in terms of sentence and paragraph/verse structure. Introduce and discuss other vocabulary that might be used to describe a river scene. Encourage children to share descriptions particular to their native lands. Then direct attention back to the river scene presented in the poem. Have the class work in small groups to write short stories about the scene. Invite each group to present its story to the class. Then help children edit their work.

Sand Art *Page 19*

Distribute to each child a sheet of posterboard and approximately two cups of sand—assorted colors, if possible. Invite children to draw, color, and cut out pictures of objects whose names contain the sound of short vowel **a**. Have children glue their cutouts onto the posterboard and then partially cover the drawings with sand to make them appear hidden. To vary this activity, you might have children construct their own beach scenes by filling shoe boxes with sand and hiding objects containing the sound of short vowel **a**.

At the Beach *Page 19*

Ask children to bring to class some of their favorite beach items (e.g., pail and shovel, blow-up raft, snorkel). Have each child present his or her beach item to the class and explain why it is a favorite item and how it is used. After the presentations, collect the items, hold them up one at a time, and place them in a large bag. Then remove each item, and ask children whether they remember who owns the item and why it is the owner's favorite.

Find Short i *Page 23*

Recite and act out the poem with the class. Discuss the illustration. Present to the class an experience chart on which the poem is written in large letters. Read the poem together. Hold up a picture of a fish, and use it to introduce the sound of short **i**. Have children find the short **i** words in the poem. Circle those words on the chart.

Friendly Fish *Page 23*

Bring in pictures of fish typically kept in fish tanks. Invite children to describe the fish pictured. Prepare flash cards to introduce the names of the fish. Display the pictures along the chalk ledge. Hold up a flash card and have a child match the name of the fish with its picture. Take the class on a trip to a pet shop or aquarium, and help them find the fish identified in the pictures.

Tom's Adventure *Page 27*

Have children work in groups to write a conclusion to the poem. Tell them to explain what Tom did next and what happened to the fish and the frog.

New Sentences
Page 29

Prepare several sets of flash cards of the short **o** words on pages 27–29. Have the class work in groups, and give one set of cards to each group. Ask the groups to write sentences using the flash-card words. Allow time for each group to present its sentences to the class. Record all the sentences on chart paper, and underline the short **o** words.

Rusty and Dusty
Page 33

Prepare a sentence strip for each sentence in the poem; underline the short **u** words. After reading and discussing the poem and illustration with the class, have children use the sentence strips to retell the events of the poem. Mix up the sentence strips and lean them against the chalkboard. Ask children to close their books; then have them rearrange the sentence strips in the correct order.

Boats of All Kinds
Page 33

Provide children with large, colorful pictures of various types of boats, such as tugboat, steamboat, yacht, and sailboat. Provide appropriate vocabulary, and help children describe the pictures.

Discuss the types of boats and their uses. Then have each child write and illustrate a paragraph describing his or her favorite type of boat.

Spelling Bee Page 35

Conduct a spelling bee with words that contain the sound of short **u**. Have children work in two teams to prepare for and compete in the spelling bee. Give two points for words spelled correctly the first time; give one point for words spelled correctly the second time.

Shore Fun Page 38

Initiate a class discussion about summer vacation and trips to the beach. Organize children's responses in a semantic web on the chalkboard. Then have children work in groups to write short stories about a child's experience at the beach. Ask the groups to illustrate their stories and present them to the class.

Sentence Bee Page 37

On separate index cards, write words that have the sound of short **e**. Include all of those in the poem, as well as several others. Make two identical sets of word cards. Read each word with the class and review the meanings of the words. Have children work in two groups. Give each group a set of cards, and direct children to practice using the words in sentences in preparation for the sentence bee. Then collect the cards and begin the sentence bee. Hold up one card at a time, and have one player on each team write on the board a sentence that contains the word. The first player to write a correct sentence wins a point for her or his team.

A Day at Niagara
Page 45

After discussing the text and illustration on page 45 with the class, together generate a list of things children would like to do at Niagara Falls. Write responses on an experience chart. Ask children to think of an imaginary character to star in a class story about an adventure at Niagara Falls. Once a character has been agreed on, elicit sentences from children one at a time and write the sentences on chart paper to compose the story. Encourage children to illustrate the story on separate paper. Display the illustrations on a bulletin board around the written story.

TECH TALK

Save the Vowels!

Objectives
- To recognize the short vowel sounds for a, e, i, o, u
- To use a writing program such as The Amazing Writing Machine™* to keep a journal and to recognize and write short vowels

Preparation
Read to children excerpts from the book *Fifty Ways You Can Help Save the Planet* (InterVarsity). Then have children brainstorm ways they might conserve, or save, water. Children might say they could shut off water while brushing their teeth, check faucets in the house for leaks, and so on. List the suggestions in a word chart. Ask volunteers to identify and circle the short vowels and then read the words.

One Step at a Time

1 Have children work independently or with a partner.

2 Tell children to use The Amazing Writing Machine™ to begin a journal. The journal-writing part of this program automatically records the day, date, and time notes are entered.

3 Have children keep the journal for at least a week. Ask them to record, on a daily basis, when they use water, how much they use, and how they might use less.

4 Tell children they may use the drawing tools to illustrate all or part of their journals.

5 Direct children to select one way to conserve water. Have them use that idea to write a story convincing other people to do the same.

6 Tell children to illustrate and print their stories.

Class Sharing

Tell children that they are going to have a Water Conservation Day in class. Help them plan different activities. They might include a display of uses of water and ways to conserve it, a skit showing ways people waste water, and a reading of their conservation stories.

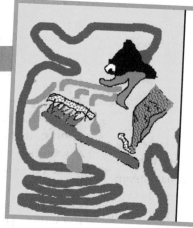

Tuesday, January 2, 1996 10:21 AM This morning I used water to take a shower, brush my teeth, and rinse my cereal bowl.

Pictionary Vowels

Objectives
- To recognize and write words with the short vowel sounds **a, e, i, o, u**
- To use a program such as Kid Phonics™* to produce a vowel pictionary

Preparation Review the short vowel sounds. Write the following words on the board: **ant, six, box, bug,** and **ten.** Have children identify the short vowels, and then ask them to give the rule for short vowels. (If a syllable or word has only one vowel and it comes at the beginning or between two consonants, the vowel is likely to be short.)

One Step at a Time

1 Have children work individually or in small groups. Assign to each child or group a short vowel sound with which to work on Kid Phonics™.

2 Direct children to select "Word Buster" from the Playroom.

3 Have children choose a picture whose name has their short vowel sound. Make sure selections reflect the water theme of the unit. For example, for the short vowel **e,** children might choose a picture of a shell.

4 Tell children to take the picture to the Word Builder. Direct them to spell the word and listen to the audio as the word is spelled aloud.

5 Have children write a sentence that uses their word. Tell them to click on the megaphone to listen to the sentence. Have children make sure the sentence makes sense. Then have them click on OK.

6 If a color printer is available, have children use the crayons on the screen to color the picture. Otherwise, have them print the picture and use real crayons or markers to color it on paper.

Class Sharing

Collect the pages, and combine them into a class Vowel Pictionary. Read the Pictionary to the class. Keep the Pictionary in the Reading Corner for children to refer to throughout the unit.

AUDIO

Drip! Drip!

Help students brainstorm a list of water sounds such as waves crashing, a running stream, water dripping from a faucet, water running in the kitchen sink to get cold, rain, and so on. Write the list of water sounds on chart paper.

Help children tape record some of the different sounds. Then have children listen to the sounds and say "drip, drip" when they hear a sound that is an example of wasting water.

After each "drip, drip," ask volunteers to tape-record their suggestions to stop wasting water. You might want to play this tape at the Water Conservation Day suggested on page 17K.

All referenced software is listed under Computer Resources on page T46.

Literature Introduction to Short Vowels

Objectives
- To enjoy a poem about water
- To identify the vowels **a, i, o, u,** and **e**

Beginning with Literature

- Suggest that children close their eyes and visualize what they hear. Then read aloud the poem "Sampan" on page 17.

- Discuss the illustration on page 17. Explain that a **sampan** is a flat-bottomed Chinese boat propelled by two oars. It has a rudder at the back for steering and often has a sail.

Developing Critical Thinking
Ask a volunteer to read the questions at the bottom of page 17. Encourage children to contribute any ideas or experiences they may have about rivers.

Introducing the Skill

- Tell students that, in this unit, they will learn about vowels. Have a volunteer say each vowel as you write **a, i, o, u,** and **e** on the board.

- Write **lap, net, fins, chop,** and **up** on the board. Say the words together. Call on volunteers to circle the vowel in each word.

Practicing the Skill

Write these words from the poem on the board: **lap, fish, fins, clap, flap, chop, sticks, and, tap, up,** and **brush**. Say the words together. Again read the poem aloud, and ask children to raise their hands when they hear one of the words on the board. Invite a volunteer to point to each word on the poetry poster.

SAMPAN

Waves lap lap
Fish fins clap clap
Brown sails flap flap
Chop-sticks tap tap
Up and down the long green river
Ohe Ohe lanterns quiver
Willow branches brush the river
Ohe Ohe lanterns quiver
Waves lap lap
Fish fins clap clap
Brown sails flap flap
Chop-sticks tap tap

Tao Lang Pee

Critical Thinking Ask children to answer both questions with a calm, woodland setting in mind. Help children to understand
What sights might you see along a river? how the sights and sounds
What sounds might you hear? would change as the seasons change.

LESSON 7: Introduction to Short Vowels

17

Theme Words

The Wonders of Water Show pictures of water scenes such as rivers or waterfalls. For each picture, ask, "Who (or what) is in the picture?" List responses on chart paper. Then ask, "What is happening in the picture?" Add any new words to the list.

Use the list you made to assess children's ability to recognize short vowel sounds. Have children find words with short vowel sounds on the list. Have them say each word and write it on the board. Have children work in small groups. Invite each group to form as many sentences as possible in fifteen minutes, using the words from the list.

Dear Family,

As your child progresses through this unit about water and rivers, she or he will review the short vowel sounds of **a, i, o, u,** and **e.**

● Say the picture names and listen to the short vowel sound in the middle of each word.

Apreciada Familia:

En esta unidad, acerca del agua y los ríos, su niño repasará el sonido corto de las vocales **a, i, o, u, e.**

● Pronuncie el nombre de las cosas en los cuadros y escuche el sonido corto de las vocales en cada palabra.

a	i	o	u	e
map	fin	rod	tug	net

● Read the poem "Sampan" on the reverse side.

● Talk about what it might be like to live on a boat.

● Point out some of the short vowel words in the poem. (**l**a**p, f**i**sh, f**i**ns, cl**a**p, fl**a**p, ch**o**p, st**i**cks, **a**nd, t**a**p, **u**p, br**u**sh**)

● Lea a su niño, "Sampan" en la página 17.

● Hablen sobre como sería vivir en un barco.

● Señalen algunas palabras en la poesía donde el sonido de la vocal es corto como: (**l**a**p, f**i**sh, f**i**ns, cl**a**p, fl**a**p, ch**o**p, st**i**cks, **a**nd, t**a**p, **u**p, br**u**sh**).

PROJECT

On a large sheet of paper, draw a picture of a river. Cut out small pieces of paper in the shape of logs. When your child learns a new short vowel word, have him or her write the word on a log and tape it on the river.

sun
log
fin
bag
pen

PROYECTO

Dibuje un río en un papel grande. Corte pedacitos de papel en forma de tronco. Cuando el niño reconozca una palabra con vocales de sonido corto puede escribirla en un papelito y pegarla en el río.

ESL Activities

ESL activities are referenced throughout this unit. These activities benefit the ESL child in your classroom by providing additional language experiences. Choose the activities that best meet the diverse needs of your class.

For ESL activities related to "Sampan," refer to page 17 I–17J.

Take-Home Book

The Take-Home book for Unit 2, *Water's Song,* found on student pages 211–212, may be enjoyed by children and family members alike. Use this fold-up book to reinforce the phonics skills of short vowels taught in this unit. You may choose an appropriate time to send home this component.

● The *Phonics Alive at Home* page is intended to actively involve families in their children's reading and writing development through activities that apply phonics skills. The *Phonics Alive at Home* on page 18 includes activities related to the unit theme "The Wonders of Water" and to the phonics focus on short vowels.

● Have children tear out page 18 of their books. Ask them to take the page home and complete these activities with family members.

● Encourage children to bring their completed projects to school to share with the class.

● Provide opportunities for children to share pictures they have drawn, books they have read, and stories they have written that deal with water.

● Invite children to bring in photos of places they have visited that were near water. Display these photos on the bulletin board.

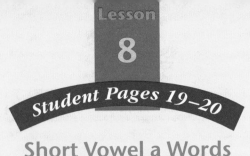
Short Vowel a Words and Phonograms

Objectives
- To identify short **a** words
- To write words with short **a** phonograms

Warming Up

Reviewing Consonants
Materials: Phonics Picture Cards for **lemon, seven, letter, wagon, zipper**.

Display the picture cards. Invite children to name each and write the letter that stands for the initial, medial, or final consonant sound in each name.

★ Teaching the Lesson

- Read aloud the story on page 19. Invite children to name what they see in the sand. List these items on the board. Then read the list with children. Call attention to the short **a** sound in each word.

- Use the word **bat** from the list. Write **at** on the board. Ask what letter should be added to **at** to form the word **bat**. Add the **b**. Then sound and say the word.

- Write **at** beneath **bat**. Ask what letter should be added to form the word **hat**. Add the **h**; then sound and say the word.

- Continue to generate a list of **at** words. Read the list together.

- Help children notice that the words end with the same letters and rhyme. Tell them that a **phonogram** is a vowel or vowel plus a consonant element, as **an** in **van, can, pan,** or **amp** in **camp, lamp, damp**. Point out that **at** is a short **a** phonogram.

ESL Activities
Refer to pages 17I–17J.

19

R ead the story. Underline the short **a** words.

What's in the Sand?

There's lots to see <u>and</u> do in the <u>sand</u>.
<u>Pam</u> watches a <u>crab</u> in the <u>sand</u>.
<u>Jan</u> sees <u>an</u> old <u>map</u> in the <u>sand</u>.
<u>Nat</u> prints his <u>hand</u> in the <u>sand</u>.
<u>Dad</u> finds his <u>cap</u> in the <u>sand</u>.
What <u>can</u> you find in the <u>sand</u>?

LESSON 8: Introduction to Short Vowel **a**   19

Multisensory *Activities*

Visual ■ Kinesthetic

Handprints in the Sand
Materials: construction paper, pencil, scissors

Have children trace around their hands and cut out their handprints. Ask each child to write a short **a** word on his or her handprint. Then collect the handprints, and hide them in the classroom. Invite children to hunt for the handprints and to read the words they find.

Auditory ■ Visual

Memory Match
Materials: index cards

Help children, in pairs, generate a list of words that end in **at, am, ag, an,** and **ap**. Give each pair 10 index cards. Ask them to write two rhyming words for each phonogram, one per card. Have pairs mix the cards, arrange them facedown, and take turns turning up two at a time. If the words on the cards rhyme, the player keeps them. If not, the player puts them back.

Look at and say the phonogram at the top of each box. Then circle the two pictures whose names have that phonogram. Write the words.

1 _ag

bag

crab

tag

tack

bag   tag

2 _am

hand

ram

ant

ham

ram   ham

3 _an

wax

man

can

cap

can   man

4 mask _at

lamp

mat

hat

mat   hat

Write a silly sentence with two rhyming words. Tell what you can take on a raft. For example, "On my raft I can take a **ram** and a **ham**."

LESSON 8: Short Vowel **a** Phonograms

20

Practicing the Skill

● Read aloud the directions on page 19. Have children work in pairs to complete the page.

● Read aloud the directions on page 20. Have children repeat each phonogram after you say it. Then have children complete the page. Invite them to write their silly sentences on a separate sheet of paper.

Extending the Skill Across the Curriculum

(Science/Art)

Theme Activity

Materials: mural paper, markers, writing paper

● Together, talk about the importance of keeping beaches and other recreational areas clean. Introduce the word *pollute* (to make unclean), and discuss how pollution hurts all of us.

● Talk about the kinds of litter that children might see at the beach or other recreational sites. Explain that certain things, such as crabs or shells, belong in the sand; however, people may drop other things—either accidentally or carelessly—in the sand.

● Have children draw a simple beach scene on mural paper. Then have them add in the sand pictures named by words with the sound of short **a** (e.g., **map, can, cap, hat, crab, fan, ant,** (diving) **mask, ham, jam, mat, rag, sack, yam, cat, tag, raft**). Have children label the pictures.

● Staple together five sheets of writing paper for each child. Tell them to use each page for words with a different short vowel sound (**a, e, i, o, u**). Have children begin a word bank using the short vowel words. Whenever children learn a new word, tell them to add it to their word banks. Remind children to refer to these word banks for ideas during writing activities.

Spelling Connection

Read each word and sentence aloud. Then have volunteers spell the words orally or write them on the board.

hat   The tan **hat** is on Jan.
bag   The **bag** has ham in it.
dad   Can **dad** see the cab?
fan   Pam has a **fan** in her class.
map   The **map** is in the car.

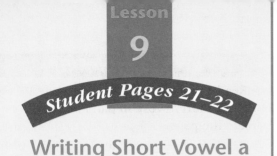

Writing Short Vowel a

Objective
● To read and write short **a** words in context

Warming Up

Reviewing Initial Consonants
Play "consonant round-up." Write all the consonants on the board. Have a child begin by saying the consonant and naming a word that starts with **b**; for example, "**b: ball** starts with **b**." Have that child call on another to name a word that starts with **c**. Continue playing until everyone has a turn.

★ Teaching the Lesson

Materials: Phonics Picture Cards for short **a** words; paper

● On the board write "**Dad and Sam see two crabs in the sand**." Read the sentence with children, and invite a volunteer to underline all the words that have an **a**.

● Have children read aloud the underlined words. Point out that these words have the sound of short **a**. Help children notice that each short **a** word has only one vowel, and that it comes at the beginning of the word or between two consonants.

● Place the picture cards in a bag. Invite volunteers to reach in the bag, take out a card, and write the picture name on the board. Talk about the vowel and its position in the word. Ask children what vowel sound they hear in the words.

● Have children use each short **a** word in a sentence.

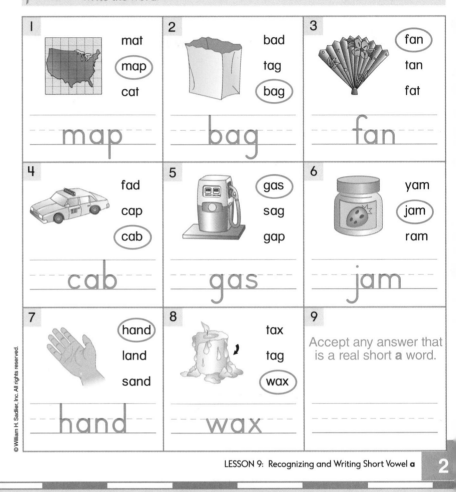

If a syllable or word has only one vowel and it comes at the beginning or between two consonants, the vowel usually has the **short** sound.

Map has the short **a** sound. Circle and write the short **a** word that names each picture. In the last box, draw a picture of a short **a** word. Write the word.

1. mat / (map) / cat — **map**
2. bad / tag / (bag) — **bag**
3. (fan) / tan / fat — **fan**
4. fad / cap / (cab) — **cab**
5. (gas) / sag / gap — **gas**
6. yam / (jam) / ram — **jam**
7. (hand) / land / sand — **hand**
8. tax / tag / (wax) — **wax**
9. Accept any answer that is a real short **a** word.

LESSON 9: Recognizing and Writing Short Vowel **a**   **2**

Multisensory *Activities*

Auditory ■ Kinesthetic

On the River Bank

On the board draw two curvy lines to represent a river. Say a series of short vowel words, such as **tap, fin, ran, bag, net, had, van, lot, yam, cat, bag, sun, fan, wax, map, web, gas, nap, rag,** and **and**. After each, ask children whether the word has a short **a** sound. Invite volunteers to write the short **a** words on the "river bank."

Auditory ■ Visual

Name that Word

Materials: Phonics Picture Cards for short **a** words

Display the picture cards on the chalkboard ledge. Ask children to name each picture. Then have them write short **a** word answers to riddles based on clues such as these:

    Invite me, and I'll come to your
        picnic. (**ant**)
    Use me to hit a ball. (**bat**)
    Use me to move things. (**van**)

Look at the picture. Circle and write the word that completes the sentence.

1	Dad and Sam **pack** lunch.	tack / (pack) / tap
2	They load the **van**.	(van) / yam / man
3	Dad stops for a **map**.	pan / nap / (map)
4	The map leads to the **camp**.	lamp / (camp) / cap
5	Sam sees a **fat** beaver.	fad / pal / (fat)
6	It **has** a flat tail.	pass / hat / (has)
7	It swims very **fast**!	(fast) / sat / cast

LESSON 9: Short Vowel **a** in Sentences

22

Spelling Connection

Read aloud each word and sentence. Then have volunteers spell the words orally or write them on the board.

jam	Pass the **jam** to Tad.
had	Sam **had** a fat cat.
pan	Put the ham in the **pan**.
wag	Lad can **wag** his tail.
cap	Val has a black **cap**.

Multicultural Connection

The Nile River, which flows more than 4,000 miles from the east African highlands to the Mediterranean, is the longest river in the world. Most Egyptians live in the Nile River Valley because most of the rest of Egypt is desert.

Discuss why people live close to rivers. Help them understand that rivers are sources of water used for many purposes, such as drinking water, fishing, irrigation, and transportation.

Practicing the Skill

● Have children turn to page 21. Read aloud the Helpful Hint. Then together read the directions and identify the pictures. Do the first item together before children complete the page. Remind them to draw a picture and write a word in the last box.

● Review the directions on page 22. After children complete the page, read the story with the class.

Extending the Skill Across the Curriculum

(Language Arts/Science)

Theme Activity

● Ask children what they already know about rivers and what they want to know about rivers. Record their responses in a K-W-L chart. Then read aloud the theme book(s) cited below.

● Ask children what they learned about rivers from the theme book(s). Record their responses in the chart.

● Write these short **a** words on the board, and have children use them in sentences about rivers: **raft, dam, ants, map, damp, plants, land**.

● Ask children to write a description of a raft or canoe trip on a river. Post the K-W-L chart for children's reference.

Theme Books

Gilliland, Judith Heide. *River*. Boston: Clarion Books, 1993. Life along the Amazon River is full of amazing plants and animals.

McCauley, Jane R. *Let's Explore a River*. Washington, DC: National Geographic Society, 1988. Ride down the river with a family in a canoe.

Portfolio

Have children add their descriptive writing to their portfolios. Have them identify the words that have the short **a** sound.

22

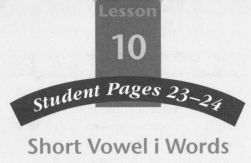

Short Vowel i Words and Phonograms

Objectives
- To identify short **i** words
- To write words with short **i** phonograms

Warming Up

Reviewing Short a
Say these pairs of short vowel words: **pen, pan; wag, wig; hot, hat; tag, tug; cup, cap.** Ask children to write the short **a** word in each pair.

★ *Teaching the Lesson*

- Ask children to listen as you read the poem on page 23. Emphasize words with the sound of short **i**.
- On the board or on chart paper, outline a large fish. Label it **big fish.** Call attention to the short **i** sound in each word.
- Invite children to reread the poem with you. One line at a time, have volunteers name the words with the short **i** sound. Write the words inside the fish outline.
- Ask a volunteer to write the word **big** on the board. Erase the initial **b** and say the phonogram **ig.** Point out that **ig** is a short **i** phonogram.
- Add a **d** to the beginning of **ig.** Together, sound and say the new word, **dig.**
- Erase the initial **d** and substitute **f.** Sound and say the rhyming word.
- Invite volunteers to substitute other initial consonants to form additional rhyming words.

ESL Activities
Refer to pages 17I–17J.

Read the poem. Underline the short **i** words. Then use short **i** words to complete the sentences.

Swish, Swish, Swish

Bill and Jill will never miss
A chance to see the giant fish.
Up and down the big fish swim.
Watch their fins go swish, swish, swish.

What a thrill for Jill and Bill
To see the colorful fish!
In and out the big fish swim.
Watch their fins go swish, swish, swish.

1. Bill and Jill see giant _____fish_____ .

2. The big fish _____swim_____ up and down.

3. The fish swim _____in_____ and out.

4. The fins of the fish go swish, swish, _____swish_____ .

LESSON 10: Introduction to Short Vowel **i**   23

Multisensory *Activities*

Visual ▪ Auditory

Swim to the Sea

Materials: Phonics Picture Cards for short vowel words

Hold up a picture card and ask a child, "Can you swim to the sea?" If the name of the picture is a short **i** word (e.g., **bib**), he or she answers, "Yes, I can swim to the sea with a **bib**"; and then places the card in a pocket chart. At the end of the activity, have volunteers name all the picture cards in the chart.

Visual ▪ Kinesthetic

Go Fish

Materials: bowl, construction-paper fishes, pencils

Give each child a "fish." Assign to each child one short **i** phonogram (**ig, it, in, id, ill,** or **ick**). Have children write a word with their phonogram on each side of the fish. Then place the fish in the bowl. Ask children to close their eyes and "go fish." Have them say the words on the fish they catch, and name other words with the same phonogram.

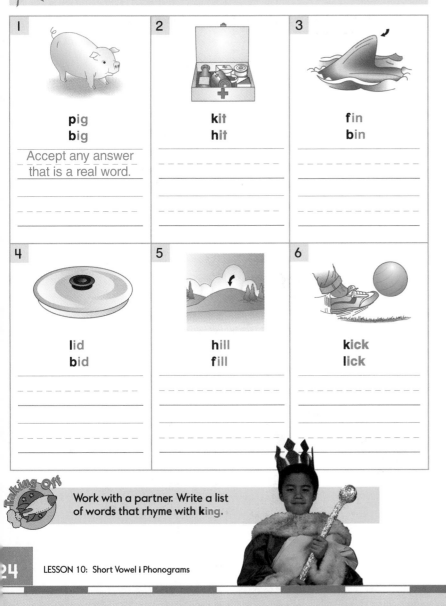

Say the name of each picture. Then read the words. Look at the phonogram in the words and write two more words with that phonogram.

1	2	3
pig **b**ig Accept any answer that is a real word.	**k**it **h**it	**f**in **b**in

4	5	6
lid **b**id	**h**ill **f**ill	**k**ick **l**ick

Work with a partner. Write a list of words that rhyme with **k**ing.

LESSON 10: Short Vowel **i** Phonograms

24

Read the directions on page 23

Practicing the Skill

• Read the directions on page 23 together. Explain that children will use words from the poem to complete the sentences.

• Read aloud the directions on page 24, and model how to complete the first item. Then have children complete both pages.

Extending the Skill Across the Curriculum

(Language Arts/Art)

Theme Activity

• Discuss how people use their senses of sight, hearing, smell, taste, and touch to understand the world around them. Then read aloud the theme book(s) cited below. Have children listen for ways the children in the book(s) use their senses when they are near the sea.

• Make an idea web on chart paper. Write *sea* in a circle in the center of the web. From it, draw five spokes, one for each sense. Have children contribute words that tell what they might see, hear, smell, taste, and feel when near the sea.

• Have children use short **i** words to complete this sentence: "At the **big, big** sea, I can...;" for example, "...I can **pick** up shells."

• Have children illustrate their sentences. Display the illustrations.

Theme Books

Nakawatari, Harutaka. *The Sea and I.* New York: Farrar, Straus, & Giroux, 1992. A Japanese boy waits for his father's return from the sea.

Waddell, Martin. *The Big, Big Sea.* Cambridge, MA: Candlewick Press, 1994. A girl and her mother experience the sea at night.

Portfolio

Have children add their sentences and illustrations to their portfolios.

Spelling Connection

Read aloud each word and sentence. Then have volunteers spell the words orally or write them on the board.

him	Will she go with **him**?
dig	Jim can **dig** in sand.
if	We will not go **if** it rains.
fills	Liz **fills** the cup with milk.
lid	Put a **lid** on the pan.

Computer Connection

Have children use ReadingMaze™ (Great Wave Software). Have them select the Picture⇨Word level. At this level, children will match short **a** or **i** words with pictures. A list of objects to be collected appears at the upper-left of the screen. Have children move through the rooms in the maze to find and collect the objects. Explain that before they can collect an object, children must select the matching word. All objects must be found and collected to advance to the next reading level.

Writing Short Vowel i

Objective
● To read and write short **i** words in context

Warming Up

Reviewing Short Vowel a
Write the consonants on the board. Choose one, and ask a volunteer to name a short **a** word that begins with that consonant. Then have that child call on another child to name a short **a** word that begins with a different consonant. As they are used, circle the consonants so they are not repeated.

★ Teaching the Lesson

● Reread together the poem "Sampan" on page 17. Invite volunteers to point out the words **fish, fins,** and **sticks**. Explain that these words have the sound of short **i**. Help children notice that each short **i** word has one vowel that comes between two consonants.

● Write these sentences on the board:

Kim will **swim** laps.
Link will **drink** some water.
Jill can **fill** the glass.
Lin can **win** the race.
Kip will **rip** the paper.
Nick can **kick** the ball.

Together, read the sentences. Ask volunteers to circle and say the words with short **i** sounds.

● Invite children to pantomime the action of each sentence to show its meaning.

Fin has the short **i** sound. Find the name of each picture. Write the word.

hill	ring	fin	list	bib	six
pink	kiss	milk	rip	lid	mitt

1. fin
2. lid
3. milk
4. bib
5. hill
6. kiss
7. rip
8. pink
9. mitt
10. six
11. ring
12. list

LESSON 11: Recognizing and Writing Short Vowel i 25

Multisensory *Activities*

Visual ■ Kinesthetic

Dish Out Short i
Materials: newspapers, paper plates, scissors, glue

Give each child a paper plate. Have children cut out letters from newspaper headlines. Then have them use the letters to form short **i** words, and glue the words onto the plates. Direct children to exchange plates, read one another's words, and use them in sentences.

Auditory ■ Kinesthetic

To Sip or Not to Sip
Materials: paper cups

Give out paper cups. Say a series of short vowel words such as **mitt, pin, sag, dip, mug, kit, mix, tip, jet, list, plop, fun, wish, bib, gift, dug, net, fill, van,** and **swim**. Invite children to imagine they are taking a sip of water whenever they hear a word with a short **i** sound.

Fill in the circle before the sentence that tells about the picture.

1		● Kit will learn to swim.
		○ Kit will learn to wink.
2		○ She sips her milk fast.
		● She kicks her feet fast.
3		○ Will Kit sit well?
		● Will Kit swim well?
4		● Ms. Hill gives Kit a tip.
		○ Ms. Hill gives Kit a wig.
5		○ Now Kit can sniff like a fish.
		● Now Kit can swish like a fish.
6		● Kit sits down to rest.
		○ Kit rests on a hill.
7		○ Ms. Hill has a list for Kit.
		● Ms. Hill has a gift for Kit.

Draw a picture about swimming. Write one sentence that goes with the picture and one that does not. Ask someone to choose the correct sentence.

LESSON 11: Short Vowel **i** in Sentences

26

Practicing the Skill

● Read aloud the directions on page 25. Together, read the words in the box at the top of the page. Have children identify the pictures. Do the first item together before children complete the page.

● Read the directions on page 26, and model how to do the first item. Suggest that children use phonograms to help them read unknown short **i** words. Have children complete the page. Provide time for them to complete the *Taking Off* activity.

Extending the Skill Across the Curriculum

(Language Arts/Science)

Theme Activity

Materials: magazines, glue, drawing paper

● On the board, write *swimming* and *drinking water* to begin a list of uses of water. Have students brainstorm other uses of water such as washing clothes, dishes, and food; cooking; bathing; watering plants; shelter for water animals and plants; and places for boats to travel.

● Have children find and cut from magazines pictures that show water being used. Have each child glue his or her pictures on a sheet of paper. Then ask children to write sentences that describe their pictures and underline any short **i** words they use.

● Group together pictures that show similar uses of water on a bulletin board for display throughout the unit.

Portfolio

After the unit, return children's work to them to add to their portfolios.

Observational Assessment

Listen for correct pronunciation of short vowel words as children read aloud.

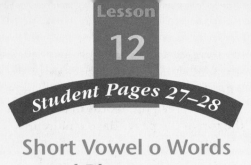

Short Vowel o Words and Phonograms

Objectives
- To identify short **o** words
- To write words with short **o** phonograms

Warming Up

Reviewing Short a and i
Say a series of short **a** and short **i** words, such as **tax, with, sack, hand, brick, list, camp, hid, quit, trip, ant, wish, sag,** and **yam**. Tell children to stand when they hear a short **a** word and to sit when they hear a short **i** word.

⭐ *Teaching the Lesson*

- Have children turn to page 27. Read the poem to children, and invite them to join in as you read it again.
- Ask where the boy in the picture is fishing. Call attention to the short **o** sound in **pond**. Ask children to name words in the poem that have the same vowel sound as **pond**.
- Write **og, ock,** and **op** on the board. Invite children to say each phonogram and find two words in the poem with that same phonogram. Then have volunteers list the words under the appropriate phonogram on the board. Ask volunteers to name and write another rhyming word on each list.
- Review how to blend initial consonants with phonograms to read unfamiliar words.

ESL Activities
Refer to pages 17I–17J.

⭐ **R**ead the poem. Underline the short **o** words. Then use short **o** words to complete the sentences.

At the Pond

Tom went to the pond,
And he sat on some rocks.
He put bait on his rod.
Then he took off his socks.

Tom saw a frog on a log.
He said, "Please don't hop.
You'll scare the fish
If you don't stop."

1. Tom went to the _pond_ .

2. He took off his _socks_ .

3. There was a _frog_ on a log.

4. Tom asked the frog not to _hop_ .

LESSON 12: Introduction to Short Vowel **o**   27

Multisensory *Activities*

Auditory ■ Kinesthetic

Hop in the Pond

Materials: Phonics Picture Cards for short vowel sounds

Set up an imaginary frog pond on the floor. Have a group of children form a circle around the pond. Invite each child, in turn, to pick a picture card and name the picture. Ask the child to hop into the pond if the picture name has a short **o** sound.

Visual ■ Kinesthetic

Sock Match

Materials: sock pattern, paper, crayons, scissors, string, tape

Hang a string clothesline. Have each child trace and cut out two socks. Together, generate a list of words that end in **ot, op, od, og,** and **ock**. Ask children to choose two rhyming words and write one on each sock. Mix the socks on a table. Have children pick two rhyming word socks at a time and hang them on the line.

Look at and say the phonogram at the top of each box. Then circle the two pictures whose names have that phonogram. Write the words.

1 _og
log frog leg lock

log   frog

2 _op
cap mop top ten **10**

top   mop

3 _ot
doll cat cot pot

cot   pot

4 _ock
cob sock rip rock

sock   rock

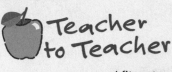

Write a silly sentence with two rhyming words. Tell what you saw at the pond. For example, "At the pond I saw a wet **clock** on a **rock**."

28

LESSON 12: Short Vowel **o** Phonograms

Practicing the Skill

● Ask children to turn to page 27, and read the directions together. Remind children to use words from the poem to complete the sentences. Have children work independently or in pairs to complete the page.

● Have children turn to page 28, and review the directions. Invite volunteers to read the phonograms in blue print. Then have children identify the pictures and complete the page.

● You may wish to have children work in pairs to do the *Taking Off* activity.

Extending the Skill Across the Curriculum

(Mathematics/Science)

Theme Activity

Materials: fish tank or large clear bowl of water; small objects such as a rock, shell, small sponge, pencil, marble, cork, bottle cap, paper clip, plastic cup, piece of wood, and so on

● Display the water-filled tank or bowl and the objects. Invite children to predict whether each object will sink or float in the water. Write their predictions in a chart on the board or on chart paper.

● Have volunteers test each object. Record what happens when each is put into the bowl. Then have children compare their predictions to actual outcomes.

● Have children write each of these short **a** and **i** words on another chart: **bag, cab, can, cap, ham, lamp, pan, rag, van, bib, crib, brick, dish,** and **pig.** Have them predict whether the object would sink or float.

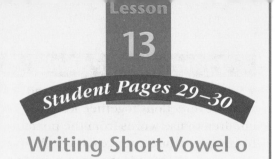

Writing Short Vowel o

Objective
● To read and write short **o** words in context

Warming Up

Reviewing Short Vowel a

On the board write the following short **a** words: **at, bad, bat, dad, fan, fast, fat, had, ham, has, hat, pack, pan, pat, quack, rag, ram, sack, tack, tan, tap,** and **wag.** Ask children to change the **a** to **i** and to read the new words.

★ Teaching the Lesson

Materials: Phonics Picture Cards for short **o** words

● Write this rhyme on the board:

The Seal
Watch him flip,
Watch him **flop**
Into the water
With a **plop**!

● Read the rhyme aloud. Invite a volunteer to underline the words that end in **op.** Point out that these words have the sound of short **o.** Then help children notice that each of these words has one vowel that comes between two consonants.

● Display the picture cards. Ask children to name each picture. Then invite volunteers to write the picture names on the board. Talk about the position of the vowel in each word. Read aloud each word, and ask children what vowel sound they hear. Then have children use each short **o** word in a sentence.

ESL Activities
Refer to page 17I–17J.

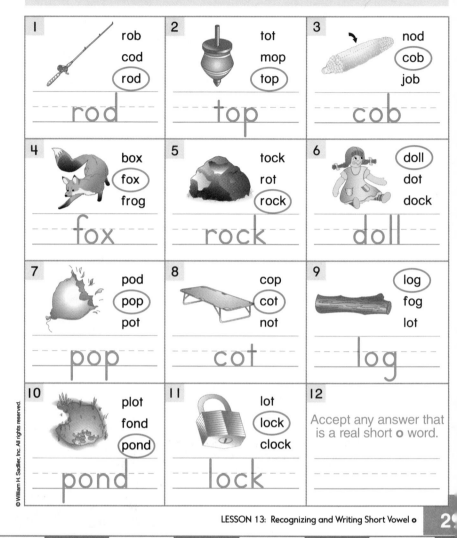

Rod has the short **o** sound. Circle and write the short **o** word that names each picture. In the last box, draw a picture of a short **o** word. Write the word.

1. rob / cod / (rod) rod
2. tot / mop / (top) top
3. nod / (cob) / job cob
4. box / (fox) / frog fox
5. tock / rot / (rock) rock
6. (doll) / dot / dock doll
7. pod / (pop) / pot pop
8. cop / (cot) / not cot
9. (log) / fog / lot log
10. plot / fond / (pond) pond
11. lot / (lock) / clock lock
12. Accept any answer that is a real short **o** word.

LESSON 13: Recognizing and Writing Short Vowel **o**   29

Multisensory *Activities*

Visual ■ Tactile

Beanbag Toss

Materials: beanbag, box, index cards

In advance, write short **o** words on index cards. Have children work in two teams, and alternate between them. Display a card for a team member to read. If the child reads the word correctly, he or she may toss the beanbag into the box. If the beanbag lands in the box, the child's team scores five points.

Visual ■ Kinesthetic

Short o Order

Materials: different-color construction paper, scissors

On strips of different-color paper write sentences such as these:

Don will **jog** to the **pond.**
Spot will go with **Don.**
Spot jumps in with a **plop.**

Cut apart the words in each sentence, and give them to a child to put in order. Have the classmates read each sentence and identify the short **o** words.

Write complete sentences. Put the last three words in order.

1	Mom and Anita	to like golf *like to golf* .
2	Mom hit the ball	a pond into *into a pond* .
3	They saw it land	frog on a *on a frog* .
4	"Mom, don't slip	off rock the *off the rock* ."
5	But Mom	stop not did *did not stop* .
6	She fell in	a with plop *with a plop* !

LESSON 13: Short Vowel **o** in Sentences

Spelling Connection

Read aloud each word and sentence. Then have volunteers spell the words orally or write them on the board.

log	Lots of ants were on the **log**.
got	Don **got** home at noon.
hop	Todd's bunny likes to **hop**.
not	This is **not** a big box.
on	The clock is **on** the desk.

Practicing the Skill

● Ask a volunteer to read the directions on page 29. Help children identify the pictures. Do the first item with the class. Remind children to draw a picture and write a word in the last box to complete the page.

● Read aloud the directions on page 30. Model how to order the words in the first item at the board. After children complete the page, read the story with the class. Ask children to identify the short **o** words in the story.

Extending the Skill Across the Curriculum

(Language Arts/Music)

Theme Activity

● Sing the familiar song "Row, Row, Row Your Boat" with children.

● Change the second and fourth lines of the song to include rhyming short **o** words. (See the examples below.) Write the lines on chart paper, and point to them as you sing.

Row, row, row your boat,
Gently 'round the **rock**,
Merrily, merrily, merrily, merrily,
Now we're at the **dock**.

2nd/ I think I see a **cod**,
4th/ Hurry get your **rod**.

2nd/ I think we'll have to **stop**,
4th/ My little oar went **plop**.

2nd/ Closer to the **log**,
4th/ I thought I saw a **frog**.

2nd/ I'm rowing here with **Bob**,
4th/ We're doing a great **job**.

● Ask children to identify the rhyming words in each verse. Have them make up verses of their own. Advise them to make lists of rhyming words first.

Reviewing and Assessing Short Vowels a, i, and o

Objective
● To review and assess short vowels **a, i,** and **o**

Warming Up

Reviewing Consonants

Have children repeat these tongue twisters and identify the repeated initial consonant.

Pat played with pretty pebbles.
Bill built a blue brick bridge.
Fay fed food to a furry fox.
Duke the dog dug in ditches.
Tiggy tiger tripped on a tree trunk.

★ Teaching the Lesson

Materials: Phonics Picture Cards **ant, bat, ham, hand, tag, van, bib, hill, lid, pin, six, pig, box, doll, log, ox, pot, top**

● Recite this rhyme; then write it on the board:

Listen to the rain drops
    Drip, drip, drip.
Listen to the frogs hop
    Plop, plop, plop.
Listen to the kids swim
    Splash, splash, splash.

● Have children do a choral reading. Form the class into three groups. Have each group read two of the lines. Then have groups read the rhyme loudly and then softly.

● Ask children what vowel sounds they hear in **drip, plop,** and **splash.** Write **short i, short o,** and **short a** on the board. Display each picture card. Have volunteers write the picture names on the board under the correct vowels.

31

Draw a line through three boxes in a row with words or pictures that have the same vowel sound. You can go across, down, or corner-to-corner.

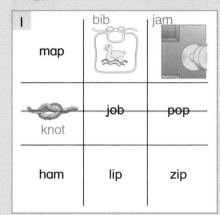

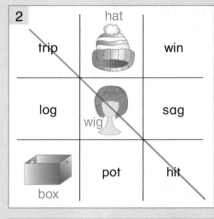

Write a short story. Pretend you're at a fishing pond with a friend. What happens there? Use some of these words in your story: **pal, sand, map, swim, wind, fish, rock, fog, dock.**

Multisensory *Activities*

Visual ■ Tactile

Tic-Tac-Toe We Go

Materials: drawing paper

Have each child draw a large tic-tac-toe grid. Tell children to write a short **a, i,** or **o** word in each block, but to make sure they put three words with the same vowel sound in a row across, down, or diagonally. Have children exchange grids and draw a line through the three words with the same vowel sounds.

Visual ■ Kinesthetic

Vowel Relay

Materials: Phonics Picture Cards for short **a, i,** and **o** words

Have children work in two or more teams. Hold up a Phonics Picture Card. Have teammates take turns writing each letter of the word on the board, in order, until the word is complete. If one player makes a mistake, have the next child correct it. The first team to spell the word correctly scores a point.

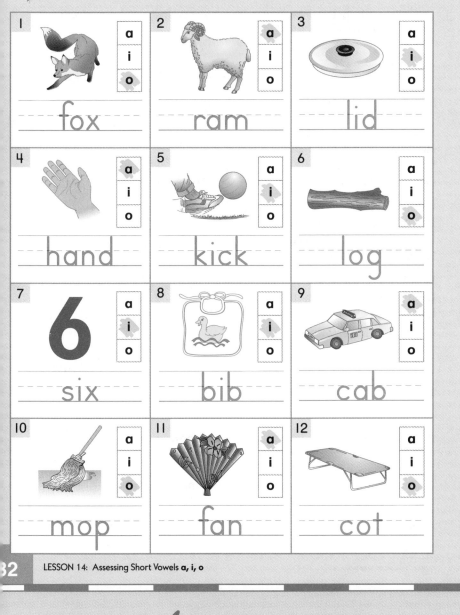

Check-Up Color the box that contains the short vowel sound in each picture name. Write the word.

1. fox — a i **o**
2. ram — **a** i o
3. lid — a **i** o
4. hand — **a** i o
5. kick — a **i** o
6. log — a i **o**
7. six — a **i** o
8. bib — a **i** o
9. cab — **a** i o
10. mop — a i **o**
11. fan — **a** i o
12. cot — a i **o**

LESSON 14: Assessing Short Vowels **a, i, o**

Assessing the Skills

Have children turn to page 31. Read the directions aloud. Do the first item at the board together before assigning the page.

You may wish to have children do the *Taking Off* activity either after they have completed the page or at another convenient time.

The assessment on page 32 can help you evaluate children's progress in mastering the recognition of short vowels **a, i,** and **o**. Before children begin page 32, briefly use the words **map, fin,** and **rod** to review the short vowel sounds. Together, read the directions on the page. Do the first item with the class. Then have children complete the page.

Observational Assessment Review your observational notes on children's learning of and participation in the skill and theme activities throughout the first part of this unit. Use these notes to help assess children's progress.

Student Skills Assessment After children have completed page 32, use the results to fill in the *Skills Assessment* on pages 207–208 in the Student Edition.

Writing Conference Meet with each child to review drawing and writing samples from his or her portfolio. Encourage children to talk about their writing and how it has improved as you review the samples together. Take notes about each child's progress, and use them to help you determine whether the child is applying phonics skills correctly.

Group together for the *Reteaching Activities* children who need further instruction on short vowels **a, i,** and **o**.

Reteaching *Activities*

Pond Hide-and-Seekers
Have children draw a pond or river scene on a sheet of paper. Invite them to hide short vowel **a, i,** and **o** words in the water and among the grass, animals, rocks, and other objects pictured. Then tell children to exchange pictures and challenge their classmates to find the hidden words.

Short Vowel Bingo
Have children fold a sheet of drawing paper into 16 boxes (fold in half four times). On the board write 16 words that are a mixture of short **a, i,** and **o** words. Invite children to write, in any order, one word in each box.

Call out a word from the list. Have children place a counter on the word on their papers. The first child to have markers on four words in a row across, down, or diagonally says, "bingo!"

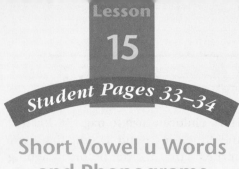

Lesson 15

Short Vowel u Words and Phonograms

Objectives
- To identify short **u** words
- To write words with short **u** phonograms

Warming Up

Reviewing Short o

Write these phrases on the board:

corn on the c___ (**cob**)
shoes and s___ (**socks**)
m___ the floor (**mop**)
l___ the door (**lock**)

Have children complete each with a short **o** word.

★ *Teaching the Lesson*

- Have children turn to page 33. Read aloud the title of the poem, and discuss the illustration. Invite children to listen to you read the poem to the class.
- Point out the short **u** sound in **Tug** in the poem's title. Then invite children to read the poem aloud with you, two lines at a time. Ask volunteers to name the words with the short **u** sound. Write these on the board.
- Write the phonograms **ug, un, ud, uck,** and the word *other* on the board. Help children sort the short **u** words from the poem into each phonogram category. Have volunteers write each word under the appropriate phonogram.
- With children read each category of phonograms and words. Ask volunteers to name and write another rhyming word for each phonogram.

ESL Activities
Refer to pages 17I–17J.

★ **R**ead the poem. Underline the short **u** words. Then use short **u** words to complete the sentences.

Here Comes the Tug!

I have a friend named <u>Rusty</u>.
He has a boat named <u>Dusty</u>.
<u>Up</u> and down the river she <u>runs</u>,
Giving free rides, <u>just</u> for <u>fun</u>.

Oh no, <u>Rusty</u>. What's that <u>thud</u>?
It's poor <u>Dusty</u>, <u>stuck</u> in <u>mud</u>.
<u>Rusty</u>, get the boat to <u>run</u>,
Or we'll sit here in the <u>sun</u>.

Don't <u>fuss</u>, <u>Rusty</u>. We're in <u>luck</u>.
<u>Dusty</u> soon will be <u>unstuck</u>.
Listen and you'll hear a <u>chug</u>.
Aren't you glad to see the <u>tug</u>?

1. Rusty's boat is named ___Dusty___.

2. Dusty went ___up___ and down the river.

3. The boat got ___stuck___ in the mud.

4. The ___tug___ came to help.

LESSON 15: Introduction to Short Vowel **u**

33

Multisensory *Activities*

Auditory ■ Visual

Rhyming Riddles

Materials: Phonics Picture Cards for short **u** words

Have children work in small groups. Give each group a picture card. Ask them to write rhyming riddles. Provide this model:

This word rhymes with **run** and begins with s. (**sun**)

Have groups share their riddles with the class.

Visual ■ Kinesthetic

Under the Rug

Materials: towel, Phonics Picture Cards for short vowel words

Lay the towel on the floor to represent a rug; have children gather around it. Show the picture cards. Have each child, in turn, name a picture. If the name has a short **u** sound, have the child place the card under the "rug." Then have volunteers write the short **u** picture names on the board.

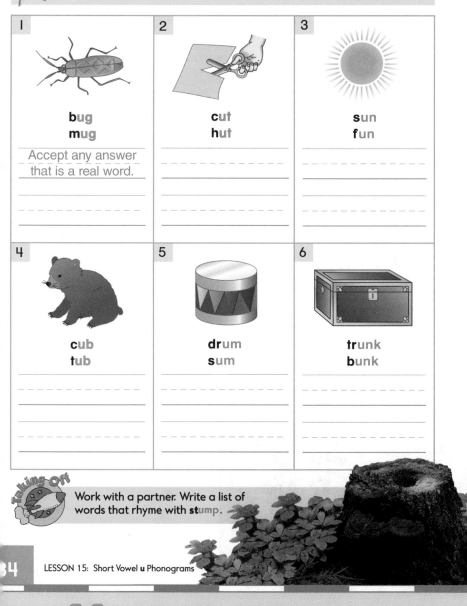

Say the name of each picture. Then read the words. Look at the phonogram in the words and write two more words with that phonogram.

1	2	3
b**ug** m**ug**	c**ut** h**ut**	s**un** f**un**

Accept any answer that is a real word.

4	5	6
c**ub** t**ub**	dr**um** s**um**	tr**unk** b**unk**

Taking Off

Work with a partner. Write a list of words that rhyme with st**ump**.

LESSON 15: Short Vowel **u** Phonograms

34

Multicultural Connection

The Incas, who lived mostly in the Andes mountains of South America, used to bring water down from the mountains by carving channels and basins from stone. The Incas made these stone aqueducts to carry the water from mountain streams to cities and farmlands.

Elicit from children how water comes to them. You might ask, "How does the city get water to your home?" "Where does the water you drink come from?"

Spelling Connection

Read aloud each word and sentence below. Then have volunteers spell the words orally or write them on the board.

cut	Bud **cut** the paper in half.
sun	The **sun** is shining today.
hum	Jud can **hum** a new tune.
us	Please help **us** make lunch.
mug	He drinks milk from a **mug**.

Practicing the Skill

● Ask children to turn to page 33. Invite a volunteer to read the directions. Then read aloud the poem as children follow along. Have them complete the page.

● Review the directions on page 34, and do the first item together. Call attention to the phonograms in blue print. Then have children complete the page.

Extending the Skill Across the Curriculum

(Science/Art)

Theme Activity

● With children, discuss the different places where water can be found in nature, such as rivers, oceans, lakes, ponds, waterfalls, etc. Theme books such as those cited below will make children more aware of water on Earth.

● Share the theme book(s) with the class. Have children identify the vowel sounds as they hear short vowel words in the theme book(s). Invite children to add new short vowel words to their word banks.

Theme Books

Dorros, Arthur. *Follow the Water from Brook to Ocean.* New York: Harper-Collins, 1991. This book tells where flowing water goes.

Stevenson, James. *The Pattaconk Brook.* New York: Greenwillow Books, 1993. A frog and a snail record water sounds.

Observational Assessment
Check students' word banks to see whether they continue to add new words.

16

Student Pages 35–36

Writing Short Vowel u

Objective
- To read and write short **u** words in context

Warming Up

Reviewing Short Vowel a
Share short **a** riddles like these with children. Start each with the phrase "It begins with…

> h and goes on your head." (**hat**)
> r and you dust with it." (**rag**)
> v and you ride in it." (**van**)

★ Teaching the Lesson

- On the board, write "A **duck** with **luck** has **fun** in the **sun**."
- Read the sentence with the class. Have one child underline the words that end with **uck** and another circle the words that end with **un**. Point out that these words have the sound of short **u**. Help children notice that each word has one vowel that comes between two consonants.
- On the board, write the words **mud, runs, gulls,** and **fun**. Have a volunteer read the words aloud. Talk about the vowel and its position in each word. Ask children what vowel sound they hear. (short **u**)
- On the board, write this paragraph, omitting the underlined words.

> Muff <u>runs</u> in the sand. She barks at <u>gulls</u>. She has <u>fun</u> in the sun. She plays in the <u>mud</u>.

Invite children to choose a word from the board to complete each sentence. Then read the story together.

ESL Activities
Refer to pages 17I–17J.

Tug has the short **u** sound. Write the name of each short **u** picture.

1	tug	2	cup
3	sun	4	nut
5	bus	6	rug
7	tub	8	pup
		9	gum
		10	run

LESSON 16: Recognizing and Writing Short Vowel **u**

© William H. Sadlier, Inc. All rights reserved.

Multisensory *Activities*

Auditory ■ Visual
BUNGO

Materials: three-by-three grids, squares of paper

Give three-by-three grids and paper squares to children. Have them write any nine words from page 35 in the spaces in the grid. Then have children play "bungo." Randomly call out the short **u** words. Challenge children to be the first to use the squares to cover three words in a row in any direction.

Auditory ■ Kinesthetic
Jump Over the Mud

Invite a group of children to stand in a line, shoulder-to-shoulder, facing an imaginary mud puddle. Say a series of short vowel words, such as **mud, cuff, sip, hat, but, pen, luck, lot, can,** and **pup**. Invite children to jump over the "mud" when they hear a word that has the sound of short **u**.

Use a word from the box to complete each sentence. Then read the story.

| bumps | gulls | hums | run | stuff |

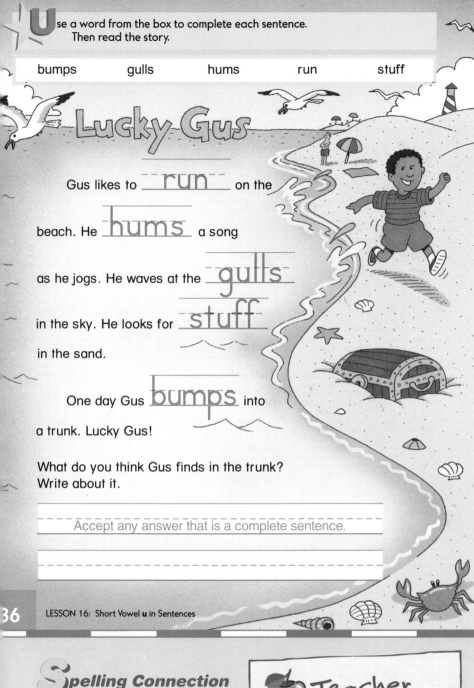

Lucky Gus

Gus likes to __run__ on the

beach. He __hums__ a song

as he jogs. He waves at the __gulls__

in the sky. He looks for __stuff__

in the sand.

One day Gus __bumps__ into

a trunk. Lucky Gus!

What do you think Gus finds in the trunk?
Write about it.

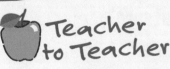

Accept any answer that is a complete sentence.

36 LESSON 16: Short Vowel **u** in Sentences

Spelling Connection

Read aloud each word and sentence below. Then have volunteers spell the words orally or write them on the board.

mud Lad has **mud** on his paws.
dug Bud **dug** in the sand
fun We had **fun** with the pup.
up Gus can jog **up** the hill.
bus Rusty rode the **bus** to school.

Teacher to Teacher

Phonics Cheer

Hip, hip, hooray!
Hip, hip, hooray!
Let's sound and say
the rhyming way.

Hip, hip, hooray!
Hip, hip, hooray!
This fun word game
we all can play.

_Sr. Doloretta Maria
Miami, FL_

Practicing the Skill

● Read aloud the directions on page 35. Help children identify the pictures before they complete the page.
● Ask a child to read aloud the directions on page 36. Remind children to answer the question at the bottom of the page. Then have them complete the page.

Extending the Skill Across the Curriculum

(Language Arts/Social Studies)

Theme Activity

Materials: world map or globe

● Display the map or globe, and identify places with coastlines. Then read aloud the theme book cited below.
● Have children imagine they are at the seashore. Ask what they might see there. List ideas on the board. Have volunteers circle any short **u** words.
● Start a sentence strip with "On my walk, I…." Have children write endings on other sentence strips. Ask them to use at least one short **u** word in each ending, such as "…see a gull in the sky."
● Display the sentence starter with all children's endings on the bulletin board.

Theme Book

Albert, Burton. _Where Does the Trail Lead?_ New York: Simon & Schuster, 1991. A boy makes discoveries about life near the ocean.

Portfolio

Have children add their lists of words from the _Taking Off_ activity on page 34 to their portfolios.

Observational Assessment
Note whether each child participates in activities and how readily each volunteers.

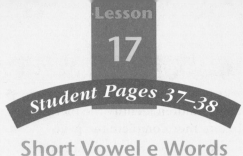

Short Vowel e Words and Phonograms

Objectives
- To identify short **e** words
- To write words with short **e** phonograms

Warming Up

Reviewing Short u

Say a series of short vowel words, such as **tug, rut, drop, nut, spin, hush, wet, judge, map,** and **stump.** Direct children to say "buzz" when they hear words with the sound of short **u.**

★ *Teaching the Lesson*

- Have children turn to page 37. Invite them to look at the pictures as you read the poem aloud. Then read aloud the question "Who gets wet?" Call attention to the short **e** sound in **wet.**

- Ask volunteers to take turns reading each line of the poem. Have the other children raise their hands each time they hear a word with the sound of short **e.**

- Have a child print the word **wet** on the board. Erase the initial **w,** and say the phonogram **et.**

- Add a **p** to **et.** Have children sound and say the word.

- Invite volunteers to substitute other initial consonants to form additional rhyming words. Repeat this activity with other short **e** phonograms, including **ell** and **est.**

ESL Activities
Refer to pages 17I–17J.

R ead the poem. Underline the short **e** words. Then look at the pictures to answer the question.

At the Shore

Kara sells shells.
Sam mends nets.
Tess draws pictures.
Jen walks pets.

Ed sells fresh fish.
Jet takes a nap.
Ben rents rowboats.
Ken gets a snack.

Who gets wet?

Jet gets wet.

LESSON 17: Introduction to Short Vowel e   **37**

Multisensory *Activities*

Visual ■ Kinesthetic

Caught in the Web

Materials: poster board, markers, index cards, tape

Draw a large spider web on poster board, and write each of these words on a card: **bed, tub, fed, hut, end, get, led, stop, let, met, fix, peck, rest, set, jam, land, tell, west, him,** and **yes.** Have children choose a card and read the word. Have them tape the card on the web if the word has the short **e** sound and outside the web if it does not.

Visual ■ Auditory

In the Net

Materials: Phonics Picture Cards for short vowel words, paper bag

Draw crossing lines on a paper bag to represent a net. Place the bag on a table, and have children gather around it. Show the cards. Have each child, in turn, name a picture and, if the name has the short **e** sound, place that card in the "net." Then have children write the short **e** picture names and underline the phonograms.

Say the name of each picture. Look at the phonogram in the picture name and write another word with that phonogram.

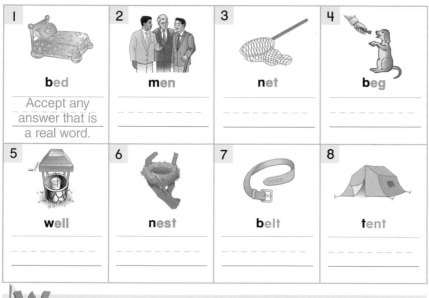

1 **b**e**d**	2 **m**e**n**	3 **n**e**t**	4 **b**e**g**
Accept any answer that is a real word.			

5 **w**e**ll**	6 **n**e**st**	7 **b**e**lt**	8 **t**e**nt**

Write a word with a short **e** phonogram to answer each question.

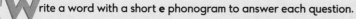

9. What names a color and rhymes with **bed**? red

10. What names a number and rhymes with **men**? ten

11. What gives you water and rhymes with **bell**? well

12. What holds your pants up and rhymes with **melt**? belt

LESSON 17: Short Vowel **e** Phonograms

Spelling Connection

Read aloud each word and sentence below. Have volunteers spell the words orally or write them on the board.

red	Peg has a **red** tent.
get	Let me **get** you some milk.
pen	Ted writes with a black **pen**.
yes	**Yes**, Fred sells pretty shells.
leg	My cat has one white **leg**.

Computer Connection

Have children explore the Vowel Pond in Reader Rabbit® 2 Deluxe (The Learning Company) to review the short vowel sounds of **e**. In the Vowel Pond, the vowel is displayed on Reader Rabbit's raft. Instruct children to click on Reader Rabbit's raft to hear the sound of the short vowel and then to choose the fish that displays a word with the same vowel sound.

Practicing the Skill

● Ask children to turn to page 37. Review the directions. You might have volunteers read aloud each line of the poem as others identify the appropriate picture. Then have children complete the page.

● Read aloud the directions for each activity on page 38. Tell children that the words they read and write at the top of the page will help them answer the questions at the bottom. Remind children that words that end with the same phonogram rhyme.

Extending the Skill Across the Curriculum

(Art/Language Arts)
Theme Activity
Materials: shoeboxes, tinfoil, transparent wrap, tissue paper, modeling clay, toothpicks, craft sticks

● Reread the poem on page 37. Discuss things to see and do at the seashore. List them on the board.

● Give out the art materials, and invite small groups or pairs of children to make a diorama of the seashore.

● Have children share their dioramas with the class. As children tell about their seashore scenes, list the objects they have used that have the sound of short **e**.

● Display children's dioramas around the room for all to enjoy.

Writing Short Vowel e

Objective
● To read and write short **e** words in context

Warming Up

Reviewing Short Vowel o
Ask "yes/no" questions like these:

Can a **fox** jump over a **rock**?
Is a **rod** the same as a **cot**?
Does a **box** have a **top**?
Can a **hog** play **golf**?

Invite children to answer each question; then to name and spell the short **o** words.

★ Teaching the Lesson

● On the board, write this rhyming couplet:

Snail, snail, in your **shell**,
You just sit there for a **spell**.

Read the rhyme with children. Have a child point out the words that end with **ell**. Tell children these words have the sound of short **e**. Help them notice that each short **e** word has one vowel that comes between two consonants.

● Write these sentences on the board:

A snail has a **shell**.
A bird has a **nest**.
A spider has a **web**.
A lion has a **den**.
A pig has a **pen**.

Together, read the sentences. Then call on volunteers to circle and say the words with the short **e** sound.

● Invite each child to draw a picture that shows the meaning of one of the sentences.

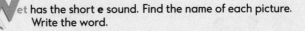

Wet has the short **e** sound. Find the name of each picture. Write the word.

well	vest	web	wet	desk	leg
jet	ten	hen	belt	sled	egg

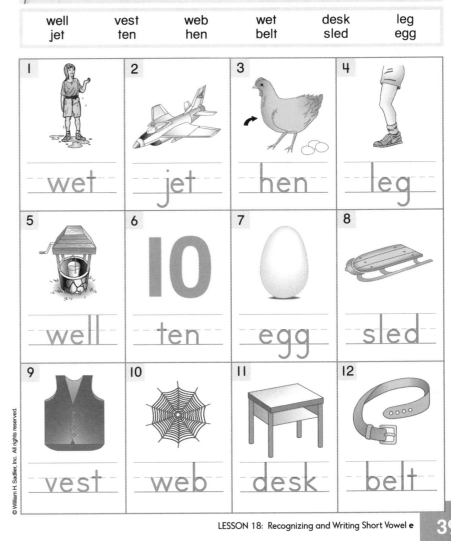

1. wet
2. jet
3. hen
4. leg
5. well
6. ten
7. egg
8. sled
9. vest
10. web
11. desk
12. belt

LESSON 18: Recognizing and Writing Short Vowel **e**

39

Multisensory *Activities*

Auditory ▪ Kinesthetic

Tent for Rent

Materials: construction paper

Have children work in pairs. Have each child fold a sheet of paper in half to make a "tent." Assign to each child a different short **e** phonogram to print on the outside of his or her tent. Then have children write words that end with that phonogram on the inside. Ask partners to exchange tents, read the words, and add other rhyming words.

Kinesthetic ▪ Visual

Wishing Well

Materials: container, index cards

Label the container "Wishing Well." Have children write short **e** words from pages 39 and 40 on index cards, one word per card. Ask them to place the cards facedown in a pile. Then tell them to choose a card, read the word, and use it in a sentence. Children may then make a wish and put the card into the wishing well.

1.
- ○ Ming wears a dress.
- ● Ming wears a vest.

2.
- ● She goes on deck.
- ○ She goes to bed.

3.
- ○ Chen helps fix the desk.
- ● Chen helps mend the net.

4.
- ● Ming gets ten fish.
- ○ Ming gets six eggs.

5.
- ○ They sell the last nest to Jen.
- ● They sell the best fish to Jen.

6.
- ● The rest are fed to the gulls.
- ○ The rest are led to the tent.

7.
- ● Ming and Chen get wet.
- ○ Ming and Chen go to the vet.

Taking Off

Draw a picture of Ming and Chen. Write one sentence that goes with the picture and one that does not. Ask someone to choose the correct sentence.

40

LESSON 18: Short Vowel **e** in Sentences

Spelling Connection

Read aloud each word and sentence below. Then have volunteers spell the words orally or write them on the board.

egg	A hen laid an **egg**.
met	Jeff **met** Peg at school.
bed	Jed went to **bed** at ten.
tell	Please **tell** me a story.
men	The **men** went west.

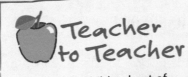

Teacher to Teacher

Provide each child a sheet of paper with a short vowel word on it. Write a different word for each child. Direct children to write a rhyming word on the paper. Then have them illustrate the rhyming pair of words; for example, **wet pet**.

Sr. Marianne Therese Somerville, NJ

Practicing the Skill

● Together read the directions and the words in the box at the top of page 39. Ask what vowel sound children hear in each word. Then have them complete the page.

● Read aloud the directions on page 40. Do the first item with the class. You might have children work in pairs to complete the page and do the *Taking Off* activity.

Extending the Skill Across the Curriculum

(Language Arts/Art)
Theme Activity
Materials: drawing paper, crayons

● Have children tell what they know about fishing. Then read aloud the theme book(s) cited below.

● Have children make a class album about an imaginary fishing trip. Ask each child to draw a picture of one event on such a trip.

● Write these phrases on the board: **best** fishing **vest; mend** the **net; eggs** in a **nest; get wet; went west;** spider **web; set** up a **tent; end** of the trip; **met** a pal; **fell** in the water; **let** the fish go; took a **rest;** and **kept shells.** Read the phrases with the class. Encourage children to refer to them to write captions for their pictures.

📖 Theme Books
Kidd, Nina. *June Mountain Secret.* New York: HarperCollins, 1991. Nina and her dad fish for trout.

Kovacs, Deborah and Shattuck, William. *Moonlight on the River.* New York: Viking, 1993. Striking charcoal illustrations of two brothers fishing at night.

📁 Portfolio
Have children include their fishing pictures and captions in their portfolios. Encourage them to circle any short **e** sound words in their captions.

Reviewing and Assessing Short Vowels u and e

Objective
● To review and assess short vowels **u** and **e**

Warming Up

Reviewing Short Vowel i
Materials: Phonics Picture Cards **pig, lid, six, pin, hill, bib, swim**

Display the picture cards. Invite children, in turn, to name each picture, and write a list of rhyming words on paper. Have volunteers say and spell their words for you to write them on the board.

★ Teaching the Lesson

● Write this rhyme on the board:

Rub a **dub dub**.
Who's that in the **tub**?
Chet with a **pet**.
Ken with a **hen**.
Chuck with a **duck**.
They all **get stuck**.

Read the rhyme with children. Invite volunteers to underline the short **u** words and circle the short **e** words.

● On a sentence strip, write this scrambled sentence:

in the mud. Shel fell

Display the strip as you read it to children. Ask what is wrong with the sentence. Then cut the words apart. Challenge volunteers to reorder the words to make a sentence.

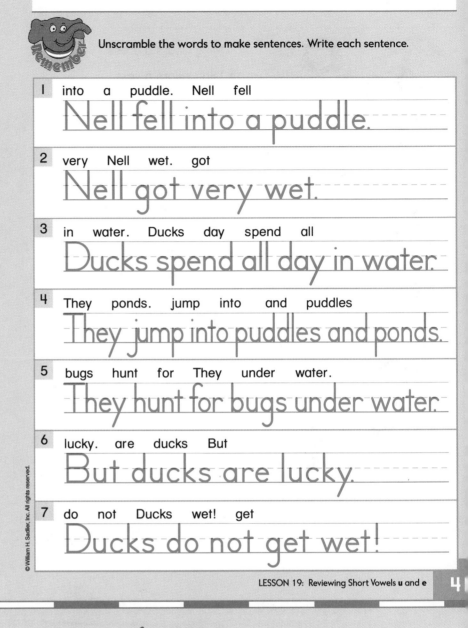

Unscramble the words to make sentences. Write each sentence.

1 into   a   puddle.   Nell   fell

Nell fell into a puddle.

2 very   Nell   wet.   got

Nell got very wet.

3 in   water.   Ducks   day   spend   all

Ducks spend all day in water.

4 They   ponds.   jump   into   and   puddles

They jump into puddles and ponds.

5 bugs   hunt   for   They   under   water.

They hunt for bugs under water.

6 lucky.   are   ducks   But

But ducks are lucky.

7 do   not   Ducks   wet!   get

Ducks do not get wet!

LESSON 19: Reviewing Short Vowels **u** and **e**   4

Multisensory *Activities*

Visual ■ Kinesthetic

Making Sense
Materials: index cards, envelopes

Write each word of a sentence on an index card. Scramble the cards and put them in an envelope. Have children work in pairs to put the words in order. Use sentences such as these:

Jud has a pet hen.
Nell plays in the mud.
Ducks do not get wet.
The bug went under the rug.

Visual ■ Auditory

Ducks and Hens
Draw a tic-tac-toe grid on the board. Divide the class into two teams: ducks and hens. Alternating team members, have ducks write short **u** words in the grid squares, while hens write short **e** words. The first team to write three words in a row in any direction wins.

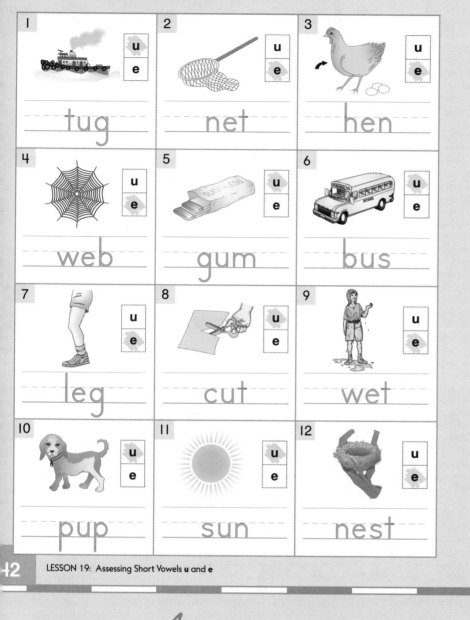

Check-Up Color the box that contains the short vowel sound in each picture name. Write the word.

1. u / **e** — tug	2. u / **e** — net	3. u / **e** — hen
4. u / **e** — web	5. **u** / e — gum	6. **u** / e — bus
7. u / **e** — leg	8. **u** / e — cut	9. u / **e** — wet
10. **u** / e — pup	11. **u** / e — sun	12. u / **e** — nest

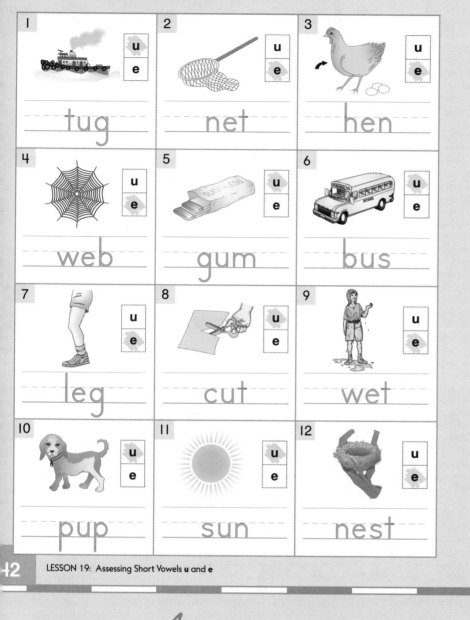

42

LESSON 19: Assessing Short Vowels **u** and **e**

Reteaching *Activities*

Rhyme Around

Materials: Phonics Picture Cards for short **u** and short **e** words

Review short **u** and **e** phonograms and words. Have children form a circle. Hand a child a Phonics Picture Card. Ask him or her to name the picture and pass the card to the next child, who must name a rhyming word. Continue around the circle; allow children to say "pass." When the children run out of rhyming words, begin again with another card.

Shape and Sort

Materials: pipe cleaners or yarn, glue, construction paper, crayons

Assign to each child a short **u** or short **e** word. Invite children to print their word, and then shape and glue a pipe cleaner or piece of yarn over the **u** or **e**. Have children exchange papers and read one another's words as they trace the vowel with their fingers. Then have them sort the words by vowel sound.

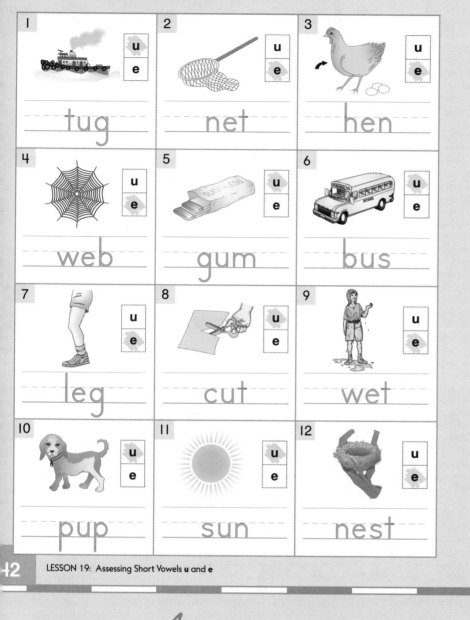

Assessing the Skills

Read the directions aloud on page 41, and do the first item together. If children have trouble unscrambling a sentence, suggest they write each word on a separate piece of paper and reorder the words concretely. Then have them write the sentence on the page.

The assessment on page 42 can help you evaluate children's progress in mastering the recognition of short vowels **u** and **e**. Before children begin page 42, use the words **tug** and **net** to review these short vowel sounds. Then together read the directions on the page. Do the first item with the class. Then have children complete the page.

Observational Assessment Review the observational notes you made on children's learning of and participation in the skill and theme activities in Unit 2. Use these notes to help assess children's progress.

Student Skills Assessment After children have completed page 42, use the results to fill in the *Skills Assessment* on pages 207–208 in the Student Edition.

Writing Conference Meet with each child to review drawing and writing samples from his or her portfolio. Encourage children to talk about their writing and how it has improved as you review the samples together. Take notes about each child's progress. Use the notes to help you determine whether the child is applying phonics skills correctly.

Group together for the *Reteaching Activities* children who need further instruction on short vowels **u** and **e**.

42

Lesson 20

Connecting Spelling and Writing

Objectives
- To say, spell, sort, and write short vowel words
- To write a story using spelling words

Warming Up

Reviewing Consonants

Write several consonants on the board. Invite volunteers to write below them as many words starting with those consonants as they can.

★ Teaching the Lesson

Materials: index cards

- Write this rhyme on the board:

  Chug a **lug**! **Chug** a **lug**!
  I'm **glad** to see the **tug**.

- Read the rhyme together. Invite a volunteer to point out the words with the short **u** sound. Ask another child to point out the word with the short **a** sound.

- Have children write each vowel (**a, i, o, u,** or **e**) on an index card.

- Say each spelling word on page 43. Ask a volunteer to repeat each word, spell it, and say the word again. Have children hold up the card for the vowel sound they hear as each word is said.

- Invite volunteers to use each spelling word in a sentence.

Practicing the Skill

Together read the directions and the spelling list on page 43. Do the first item with children. Then have them complete the page.

Spell and Write Say and spell each word in the box. Then write each word under the short vowel sound in its name.

| big |
| cut |
| ran |
| ten |
| got |
| tug |
| let |
| did |
| fox |
| has |

1 Short a
ran
has

2 Short i
big
did

3 Short o
got
fox

4 Short u
cut
tug

5 Short e
ten
let

LESSON 20: Connecting Spelling and Writing **43**

Multisensory *Activities*

Auditory ■ Tactile

Water Words

Materials: lined paper

Have each child make five columns on lined paper and label them: **short a, short i, short o, short u,** and **short e.** Tell children to listen for the short vowel sound in each word. Then say each spelling word. Invite children to write the word under the correct short vowel label. Have children exchange papers and check one another's work.

Auditory ■ Kinesthetic

Spell Hop

Materials: poster board, marker, masking tape

Print each vowel on a sheet of poster board, and tape the sheets to the floor. Have children form a line. Call out the spelling words. Invite children, in turn, to spell the word and hop to the letter that represents the sound in the word.

The pictures tell a story. Draw a picture to show what happens next. Then write a sentence to go with each picture. Use one or more of your spelling words.

| big | cut | ran | ten | got | tug | let | did | fox | has |

1

_____
_____
_____
_____
_____
_____

2

_____
_____
_____
_____
_____
_____
_____

3

_____
_____
_____
_____
_____
_____
_____

LESSON 20: Connecting Spelling and Writing

Spelling Connection

Have the class work in two or three teams. On separate large flash cards, write each spelling word with the letters scrambled. Have a child from each team come to the board to unscramble the letters and write the word. The first person to write the word correctly gets a point for his or her team.

The Writing Process

Tell children that they will write sentences that tell a story. Point out that every story has a beginning, a middle, and an end. Together read the directions on page 44.

Brainstorm Discuss the pictures, which represent the beginning and middle of the story. Encourage children to share their ideas for a story ending.

Write Have each child draw a picture to show what happens next. Then have children write drafts of their story sentences on sheet of paper.

Revise Remind children to be sure their sentences tell about the pictures before they write the sentences on the page.

Publish After children complete the page, invite them to share their sentences. You may want to have children underline the spelling words in their sentences.

Extending the Skill

Have children use the pictures on page 44 to write dialogue. Ask what children think the tugboat captain might say in each of the first two pictures. Have children draw speech balloons on a sheet of paper and write the captain's words in the balloons. Then have children imagine they are captains and share their dialogue with classmates.

Portfolio

Children may wish to add their drawings and stories to their portfolios.

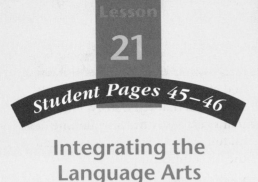

Integrating the Language Arts

Objectives
- To use oral and written language to extend the theme concept
- To demonstrate ability to recognize short vowel sounds in context

Background Information

- There are really two waterfalls along the Niagara River: Horseshoe Falls on the Canadian side, and the American Falls in the United States. Horseshoe Falls is slightly shorter, but it is more than twice as wide as the American Falls. Visitors may go into tunnels behind Horseshoe Falls, where they can watch the water from underneath the falls! Not all the water in the Niagara River flows over the falls. Some of it is directed through pipes and used for electricity for the surrounding areas.

★ Teaching the Lesson

- Have children look at the pictures on page 45 and identify what they see. Ask volunteers to read the captions. Ask any child who has visited Niagara Falls to share his or her experiences.
- Read the text aloud. Then ask for volunteers to reread each of the sentences.
- Challenge children to skim the text to find short vowel words.

Oral Language Development
Invite children to answer the question: If you visited Niagara Falls, what would you like to do there?

ESL Activities
Refer to pages 17I–17J.

Look and Learn Let's read and talk about Niagara Falls.

Welcome to Niagara Falls. These falls are in New York and in Canada. Do you want to see the top? Visit the tower on the New York side. Watch the water rush down with a crash.

Would you like a closer look? Put on a raincoat and take a boat ride on the *Maid of the Mist*. But don't get upset if you get wet!

If you visited Niagara Falls, what would you do there?

LESSON 21: Short Vowels in Context **45**

Reading and Writing Connection

- Provide children with encyclopedias and books about Niagara Falls. For more information, write to The Niagara Falls Convention & Visitors Bureau, 345 Third Street, Niagara Falls, NY 14303; or call Niagara County Tourism: 1-800-338-7890.
- Have children make a travel brochure to persuade people to visit Niagara Falls and to show all the things people can do there.

Mathematics Connection

- Horseshoe Falls is about 160 feet high. To help children better understand this, take them outdoors or into a long hallway and, together, mark off 160 feet. Assign a 10-foot length for each child to measure and then mark with tape or chalk.
- If you live near tall buildings, have children count 16 stories high. This is about 160 feet—the height of the Canadian Niagara Falls.

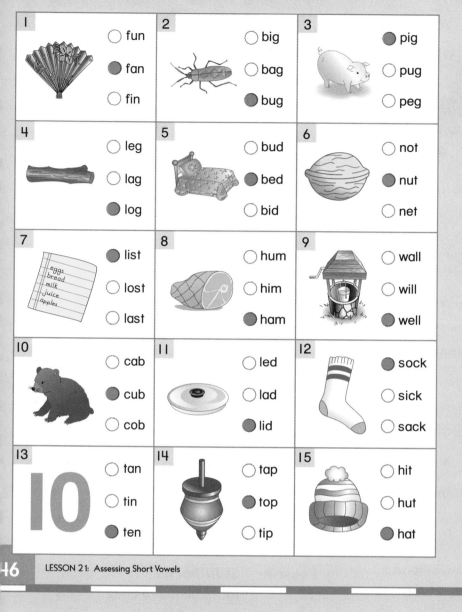

1. ○ fun ● fan ○ fin

2. ○ big ○ bag ● bug

3. ● pig ○ pug ○ peg

4. ○ leg ○ lag ● log

5. ○ bud ● bed ○ bid

6. ○ not ● nut ○ net

7. ● list ○ lost ○ last

8. ○ hum ○ him ● ham

9. ○ wall ○ will ● well

10. ○ cab ● cub ○ cob

11. ○ led ○ lad ● lid

12. ● sock ○ sick ○ sack

13. ○ tan ○ tin ● ten

14. ○ tap ● top ○ tip

15. ○ hit ○ hut ● hat

LESSON 21: Assessing Short Vowels

Reteaching *Activities*

Over the Falls

● Have children draw a picture of a waterfall on large construction paper. List the following short vowel words on the board: **can, mat, bag, jam, hill, lid, pig, fin, rod, dog, got, fox, sun, cup, rug, nut, ten, jet, fell,** and **web.**

● Have partners listen to each other read the words. If children read the words correctly, have them write the words in their waterfalls.

Drip, Drop

● Draw five clouds on white construction paper. Cut them out, and write a vowel on each.

● Cut out 20 raindrop shapes, each large enough for children to write a word on.

● Dictate a short vowel word from the list below. Have one child write the word on a raindrop, a second child match it to the correct cloud, and a third child glue it in place. Use these words: **map, bat, tag, wax, big, rip, pin, six, log, cob, hot, job, fun, hut, up, bus, net, hen, well,** and **fed.**

Assessing the Unit

Unit Test The assessment on page 46 helps you evaluate children's progress in mastering the recognition of short vowels. Before children complete the assessment on page 46, review the short vowel words **map, fin, rod, tug,** and **net.** Ask volunteers to identify each vowel. Demonstrate how to mark answers by filling in the circles before the correct word. Together, read the directions. Then have children complete the assessment.

Observational Assessment Review your observational notes on children's learning of and participation in the skill and theme activities of Unit 2. Use these notes to help assess children's overall performance and progress.

Student Skills Assessment After children have completed the assessment on page 46, use the results, along with any observations you noted during the unit, to fill in the *Skills Assessment* on pages 207–208 in the Student Edition.

Writing Conference Meet with children throughout Unit 2 to review samples from their portfolios. Encourage children to talk about their writing and how it has improved as you review the samples together. Invite them to evaluate their work by asking what they do better now than they did at the beginning of the unit. Take notes about each child's progress. Use these and previous notes to help you evaluate children's writing and to determine whether the child is applying phonics skills correctly.

Add your notes to each child's portfolio. Review them during your next conference.

Group together for the *Reteaching Activities* children who need further short vowel instruction.

Take-Home Book Remind children to complete at home the *Take-Home Book* page for Unit 2.

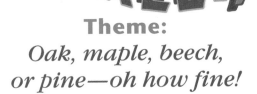

PLANNING RESOURCE

EARTH, TREES, and ME

Theme:
*Oak, maple, beech,
or pine—oh how fine!*

Overview

Unit 3 presents long vowel sounds, which children learn as they explore the topic of trees.

Objectives

- To enjoy a poem about trees
- To recognize long vowel sounds **a, i, o, u**, and **e**
- To use the long vowel rule to "decode" words
- To rhyme and spell long vowel words
- To read and write long vowel words in context

Thematic Teaching

Display pictures and reading material on trees. Read *The Giving Tree* by Shel Silverstein (Harper Children's Books) to the class. Consider children's experiences and knowledge about trees when selecting activities from the lessons.

Display the Poetry Poster "Trees," and refer to it throughout the unit.

Individual Lessons

Lesson	Skill Focus
22	Introduction to Long Vowels
23	Long Vowel **a**
24	Long Vowel **i**
25	Long Vowel **o**
26	Reviewing and Assessing Long **a, i,** and **o**
27	Long Vowel **u**
28	Long Vowel **e**
29	Reviewing and Assessing Long Vowels **u** and **e**
30	Connecting Spelling and Writing
31	Integrating Language Arts

Take-Home Book: *Tree Leaves and Seeds*

Curriculum Integration

Spelling A *Spelling Connection* appears in most lessons.

Writing Children write letters and stories on pages 54, 64, and 65.

Science Science-related activities appear on pages 50 and 58.

Social Studies Activities involving social studies are on pages 52, 54, and 58.

Art An opportunity for creativity through art appears on page 60.

Optional Learning Activities

Multisensory Activities Every *Multisensory Activity* appeals to either visual, auditory, tactile, or kinesthetic learning styles.

Multicultural Connection Material that enriches understanding other cultures is provided in activities on pages 52 and 58.

Thematic Activities The *Extending the Skill Across the Curriculum* feature of each lesson emphasizes the unit theme across various disciplines.

Assessment Strategies

Multiple strategies such as *Observational Assessments,* writing portfolios, written end-of-the-unit assessments, and the *Skills Checklist* at the back of the Student Edition will help you assess children's mastery of phonics skills throughout Unit 3.

Resources

Volumes of Poems by Harry Behn
Crickets and Bullfrogs and Whispers of Thunder. Orlando, FL: Harcourt, 1984.

Cricket Songs. New York: Harcourt, 1964.

More Cricket Songs. New York: Harcourt, 1971.

Theme-Related Resources
B, Billy. *Billy B Sings About Trees.* Do Dreams Music, 1981.

Ehlert, Lois. *Red Leaf, Yellow Leaf.* Orlando, FL: Harcourt Brace, 1991.

A Walk in the Rainforest. The Young Naturalist Foundation, 1990.

Assessment

In Unit 3 children focus on recognizing and writing the long vowels. The following are suggestions for evaluating these skills through informal/formal, observational, objective, portfolio, and performance assessments. You may also wish to refer to *Using Technology* for alternative assessment activities.

Informal/Formal Assessment

The test on page 47D assesses whether children have mastered identifying and writing the long vowels **a, e, i, o,** and **u** and long vowel phonograms. This tool may be used informally at the beginning of the unit to identify a starting point for individual or class instruction or formally at the end of the unit to assess children's progress.

Observational Assessment

Specific opportunities for observation are highlighted in the lesson plans. In addition, there are many opportunities throughout the unit to observe children identifying and writing the long vowels and long vowel phonograms. Other opportunities for observation might include *Multisensory Activities*. Observe children at different times as they identify each of the long vowels and their phonograms.

Objective Assessment

Use the assessment pages throughout the unit. After completing each assessment page, determine the area(s) in which children would benefit from more instruction; then refer to *Reteaching Activities* found throughout the unit in the Teacher's Edition. After reteaching the skill, reassess children's progress.

Portfolio Assessment

Bring in a bonsai tree or show children pictures of a bonsai. Tell children that it is a tree dwarfed, or made small, by cutting its roots and branches. Explain to children that this art form began in China more than 1,000 years ago.

Have children compare the trees in their environment to the bonsai. Then ask them to imagine they are little trees. Direct children to write a story about how they feel about being a little tree.

Give children these starter sentences:

> "Today I am still the littlest tree on the block. The big trees hide the sun from me."

Have children complete their stories. Tell children to underline all the long vowel words in their stories. Have them place the stories in their portfolios.

Performance Assessment

Tell children that they will review the long vowel words by playing tic-tac-toe. Direct nine children to place their chairs in the front of the room in tic-tac-toe fashion and to stand behind the chair formation. Provide five sheets of posterboard marked "X" and five marked "O." Have the rest of the class work in two teams—Xs and Os. Alternate giving a spelling word to a child on each team. Children must say the word, spell it, and say it again. If the word is spelled correctly, he or she directs one of the nine children to sit in a chair and hold up the appropriate letter sheet. The first team to get three in a row earns one point. Continue playing the game until all the words have been reviewed.

Using Technology

To evaluate children's progress, have them complete the *Tech Talk* activities on pages 47I–47J of the Teacher's Edition.

Answer Key

Page 47D

1. rain   2. beads   3. tube
4. coat   5. nine   6. jeep
7. cube   8. tape   9. robe
10. like   11. fruit   12. rake
13. snow

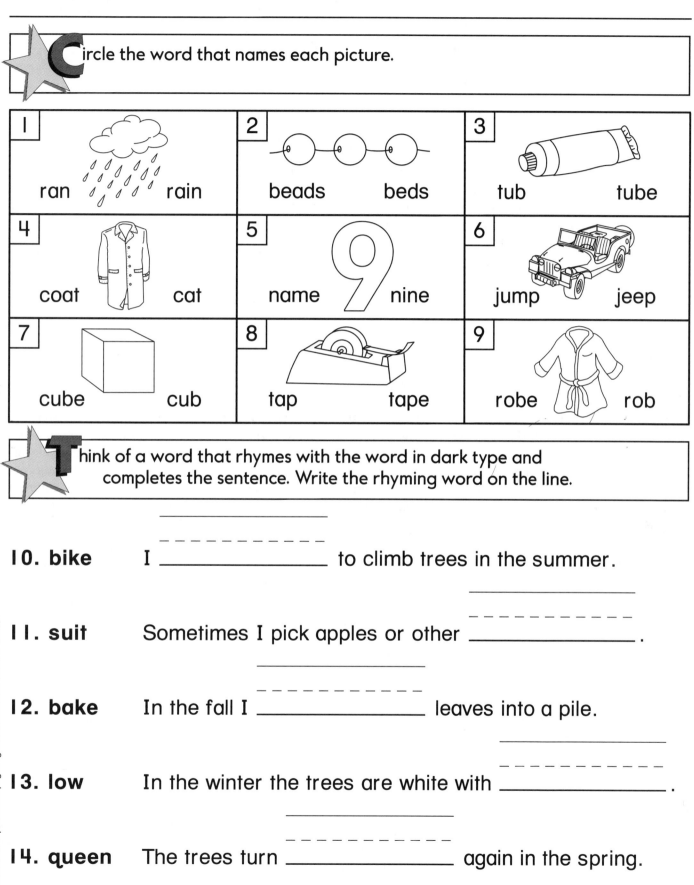

Circle the word that names each picture.

1		2		3	
ran	rain	beads	beds	tub	tube
4		5		6	
coat	cat	name	nine	jump	jeep
7		8		9	
cube	cub	tap	tape	robe	rob

Think of a word that rhymes with the word in dark type and completes the sentence. Write the rhyming word on the line.

10. bike   I _____ to climb trees in the summer.

11. suit   Sometimes I pick apples or other _____.

12. bake   In the fall I _____ leaves into a pile.

13. low   In the winter the trees are white with _____.

14. queen   The trees turn _____ again in the spring.

Game Time

▲▽▲▽▲▽▲▽▲▽▲▽ Phonogram Flaps ▽▲▽▲▽▲▽▲▽▲▽▲

Blackline Master 9 p. 47F

Objective: To make and read words with long vowel phonograms

Players: individuals

Materials: scissors, stapler

❋ Duplicate Blackline Master 9 and distribute copies. Have children cut out each phonogram box and each letter at the bottom.

❋ Tell children to stack all the number 1 letter cards together and staple them to the left edge of the number 1 phonogram box in front of the letters **ake**.

❋ Call on volunteers to lead the class in blending the letter on each flap with the phonogram to read the words.

❋ Have children match up letters and phonograms 1 through 6 in the same way.

❋ Encourage them to make additional phonogram flaps.

▲▽▲▽▲▽▲▽▲▽▲▽ Out on a Limb ▽▲▽▲▽▲▽▲▽▲▽▲

Blackline Master 10 p. 47G

Objective: To read words with long vowel sounds

Players: pairs

Materials: buttons, scissors, number cube

❋ Duplicate Blackline Master 10 and give a copy to each child. Have children cut out the word boxes at the bottom. Then give each child a button to use as a marker, and give each pair a number cube.

❋ Tell partners to take turns rolling the number cube and moving their markers the corresponding number of spaces on their game sheets.

❋ Explain to children that after each move they must replace their marker with a cutout word whose vowel sound matches that of the space on which they have landed. Tell them the object is to fill the entire tree with words by moving forward and backward along the palm leaves.

❋ Players who land on spaces that already have words must stay there until their next turn. The first player to fill his or her tree wins the game.

▲▽▲▽▲▽▲▽▲▽ Ring Around the Tree ▽▲▽▲▽▲▽▲▽▲

Objective: To spell long vowel words

Players: whole class or small groups

Materials: long vowel word cards

❋ Make long vowel word cards for words such as: **may, gray, nail, mail, make, came, leaf, eat, seed, tree, tie, pie, side, five, coat, home, row, tune, blue,** and **fruit.**

❋ Choose one child to be a "tree"; have the rest of the class stand in a circle around the tree.

❋ Privately show the tree a word card, and have him or her point a "limb" at a classmate and say the word so that the chosen child can try to spell it. If the child spells the word correctly, he or she becomes the tree; otherwise the original tree may point a limb at another classmate.

Long Vowel Phonogram Flaps

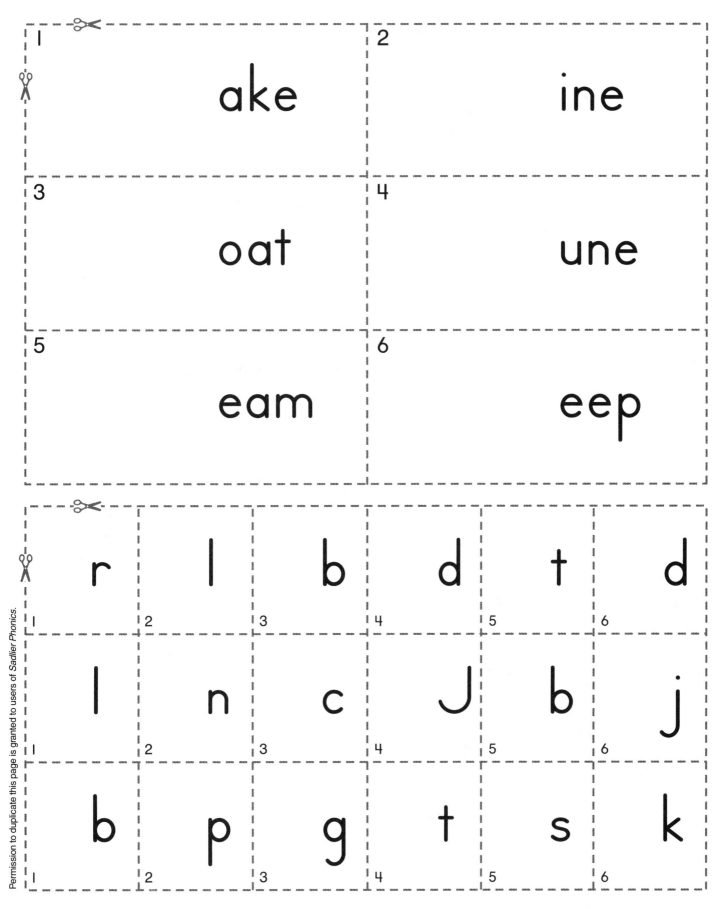

1 ake

2 ine

3 oat

4 une

5 eam

6 eep

r 1 l 2 b 3 d 4 t 5 d 6

l 1 n 2 c 3 J 4 b 5 j 6

b 1 p 2 g 3 t 4 s 5 k 6

Out on a Limb

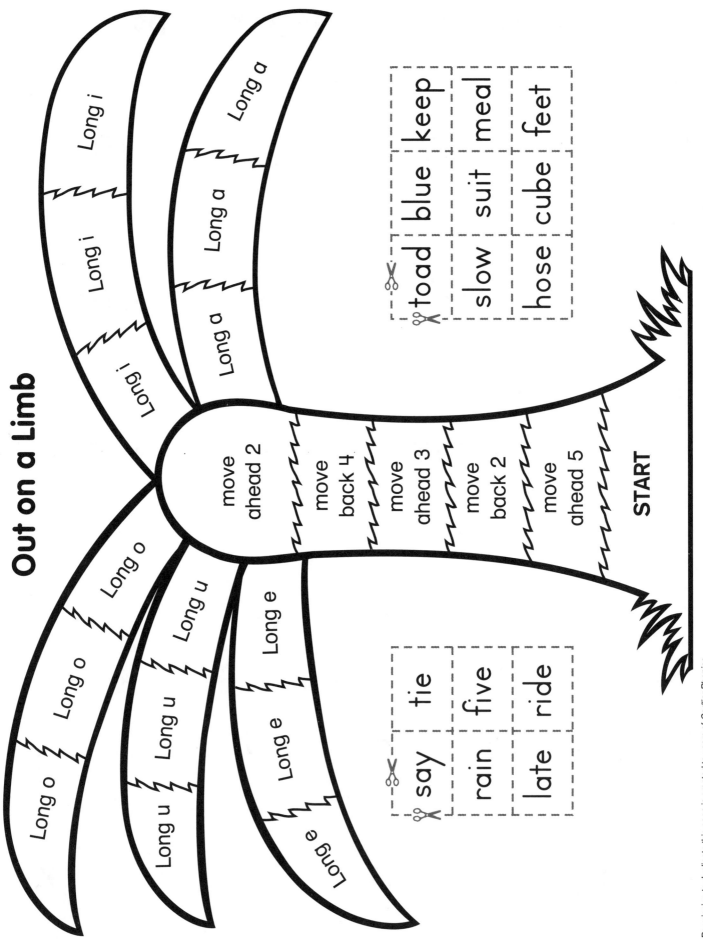

Long i · Long i · Long i

Long a · Long a · Long a

Long o · Long o · Long o

Long u · Long u · Long u

Long e · Long e · Long e

move ahead 2

move back 4

move ahead 3

move back 2

move ahead 5

START

toad	blue	keep
slow	suit	meal
hose	cube	feet

say	tie
rain	five
late	ride

ESL Activities

My Family Tree
Page 47

Make copies of a tree outline, and distribute them to the class. Initiate a discussion of family members; write useful vocabulary on the board. Explain the layout of a family tree. Draw a simple model on the board. Then have each child use family photos or illustrations, and the outline to make a personal family tree. Tell children that family members included on their tree do not have to be related by blood.

Friendly Trees
Page 47

Ask children to name uses for trees. Then have each child draw, color, and cut out a tree leaf. Have children write on the leaf one of the uses for trees. Some children might want to draw lines on the leaves to make writing easier. Draw a large outline of a tree on a bulletin board, and post the leaves on and around it.

At the Lake
Page 49

On a bulletin board, display a large mural of a lake and surrounding area. Remind children that **lake** has the sound of long **a**. Prepare cutout drawings and magazine pictures of items and seasonally dressed people that may or may not be found in the lake scene. You might include pictures of a toad, a child dressed in a skiing outfit, a cactus plant, a pine tree, and a dishwasher. Hold up the pictures one at a time. Ask children to name or describe each picture and say whether it belongs in the lake scene. Have the children post appropriate pictures in or around the lake.

What Do You See?
Page 59

Help the class brainstorm a chalkboard list of words with the sound of long **e**. Tell children to focus on words that can be drawn. Then invite the class to make a mural depicting the long **e** words. At the top of the mural write *What do you see?* Have one child pose the question to another. Direct the second child to respond in a complete sentence and then to pass the question on to a third child. Continue the pattern through the entire class. Encourage students to describe, as well as name, what they see and in what part of the picture they see it. For example: "I see a yellow **bee** in the middle of the picture."

Special Trees
Page 64

Provide large, colorful pictures of trees indigenous to various countries around the world (e.g., umbrella pines of Italy, evergreens of Germany). Try to include trees from children's native lands. Initiate a class discussion about the trees—their characteristics, uses, place of origin, and so on. On chart paper, list similarities and differences as children name them. Distribute craft materials, such as crepe paper, construction paper, pipe cleaners, and glue, and encourage children to make their favorite type of tree.

TECH TALK

Name That Tree

Objectives
- To recognize long vowel sounds in context
- To use E-mail and encyclopedia software such as Compton's Multimedia Encyclopedia

Preparation
Display books related to the topic of trees. Read *The Giving Tree* by Shel Silverstein (HarperCollins) to children. Write **tree** on the board, and ask children to identify the word's long vowel sound. Then write the names of trees with long vowel sounds. Some examples include **oak, spruce, maple, pine,** and **cedar.** Ask children to identify the long vowels.

One Step at a Time

1 Have children work independently or in small groups. Direct children to choose and research one of the trees listed on the board or another tree with a long vowel sound.

2 Tell children to use the multimedia encyclopedia to conduct their research. If your class is on-line, have children send E-mail messages to different areas of the United States to learn what kinds of trees are in those areas.

3 Explain to children that they might include in their reports the name of the tree, where it grows, the structure of the tree, the type of leaf it has, its importance as a resource, and any unusual feature of the tree.

4 Have children use a word-processing program to write their reports. Then have them either use a paint program, such as Flying Colors™*, to make an illustration of the tree and/or its leaf, or print the report and illustrate it with crayons or markers.

Class Sharing

Help children prepare a display titled "Trees with Long Vowel Names." You might help them draw large outlines of the trees they have chosen to research. Display these or the illustrated print-outs around the classroom. Then have children prepare to present the information about their particular trees. Remind children to include any information they might have received through E-mail. Invite another class for the presentations.

Fishing for Long Vowels

Objectives

- To use a program such as Reader Rabbit® 2 Deluxe* to review short and long vowel sounds
- To use a program such as Kid Pix® Studio* to review short and long vowel words

Preparation

Read *The Big Tree* by Bruce Hiscock (Macmillan), about all the changes in a tree in 200 years, or another book about trees. Have children identify words from the story that have long vowels. Write these words on the board. Then have children identify the words that have short vowels, and write these on the board as well.

One Step at a Time

1 Have children work independently or in small groups to use Reader Rabbit® 2 Deluxe (or a similar program). Tell them to choose Level 2 for long vowels. Then have children complete the activity by following Reader Rabbit's directions.

2 Direct children to do the same to review short vowels.

3 Have children use Kid Pix® Studio or another paint program to write a long vowel word, decorate it, and print it. Then have children cut the word into puzzle pieces. Give each child a number to put on the back of each of their puzzle pieces; for example, Pattie uses the numeral 1, Karen uses the numeral 2, and so on.

4 Have children do the same for a short vowel word.

Class Sharing

Laminate the puzzle pieces, and place each word in an envelope or a bag. Place these in the Reading Corner. Have children put the puzzle pieces together to make a word. Tell them to read the word and identify the long or short vowel.

Sing Along

AUDIO

Play the cassette *Billy B Sings About Trees* by Billy B. Have children select one of the songs they especially like. Write its lyrics on the board. Call on volunteers to say the words and identify the short and long vowels.

Help children learn the song, and tape record them singing it. Then have children do a choral reading of the poem "Trees." Tape record the reading. You might use these recordings when children give their presentations on different kinds of trees.

All referenced software is listed under Computer Resources on page T46.

Literature Introduction to Long Vowels

Objectives
- To enjoy a poem about trees
- To identify long vowel sounds

Starting with Literature

- Read aloud the poem "Trees" on page 47 while the class is among actual trees, if possible.

- Reread the poem, and have children join in. Have them listen for the rhymes and get a sense of the poem's rhythm.

- Ask children what trees provide for the world. List their ideas on chart paper.

Developing Critical Thinking
Use the questions at the bottom of the page to help children become more aware of the importance of trees. Ask children what can be done to help protect trees.

Introducing the Skill

Say the words **shade, tree, pine, grow,** and **fruit.** After each word ask children to repeat the vowel sound they hear. Help them understand that the sound of the vowel in each word is also the vowel's name. Explain that these sounds are called *long vowel* sounds.

Practicing the Skill

- Read "Trees" again slowly. Have children raise their hands when they hear a word with a long vowel sound. Then have them repeat the word. Invite a volunteer to write the words on the board.

- Explain that in some long vowel words, two or more letters make the long sound, such as **ee** in **trees.**

TREES

Trees are the kindest things I know,
They do no harm, they simply grow

And spread a shade for sleepy cows,
And gather birds among their boughs.

They give us fruit in leaves above,
And wood to make our houses of,

And leaves to burn on Hallowe'en,
And in the Spring new buds of green.

They are the first when day's begun
To touch the beams of morning sun,

They are the last to hold the light
When evening changes into night,

And when a moon floats on the sky
They hum a drowsy lullaby

Of sleepy children long ago . . .
Trees are the kindest things I know.

Harry Behn

(1) Trees give us oxygen.
(2) Respect a tree's growth by not pulling on branches or carving on its trunk.

Critical Thinking
In what other ways are trees kind? (1)
What can you do to be kind to trees? (2)

LESSON 22: Introduction to Long Vowels

47

Theme Words

Earth, Trees, and Me Reread the poem "Trees" with the class. Discuss the topic, and elicit from children what things or ideas they associate with trees, such as descriptions of trees, kinds of trees, and products made from trees. List responses on chart paper. Then ask, "What do you like about trees?" Add the new words children name to the list. (Use and add to the list throughout the unit.)

At the end of the unit, use the theme words to assess children's ability to recognize and spell words with long vowel sounds. Have children point to words on the list that contain long vowels. Then have children say the words and write them on the board. You may then wish to invite children to use words from the list to tell stories about trees.

Dear Family,

As your child progresses through this unit about trees and nature, he or she will review the long vowel sounds of **a, i, o, u,** and **e.**

● Say the picture names and listen to the long vowel sounds. Long vowels say their own names.

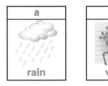

a	i	o	u	e
rain	vine	snow	fruit	leaf

● Read the poem "Trees" on the reverse side.

● Talk about different ways that trees help us.

● Point out some of the long vowel words in the poem. (**trees, know, grow, shade, sleepy, fruit, leaves, make, green, beams, floats**)

Apreciada Familia:

En esta unidad, acerca de la naturaleza, su niño repasará los sonidos largos de las vocales **a, i, o, u, e.**

● Pronuncie el nombre de las cosas y escuche el sonido largo de las vocales. El sonido largo es como el nombre de la vocal.

● Lea la poesía "Trees" en la página 47.

● Hable con su niño sobre cómo los árboles nos ayudan.

● Señalen algunas palabras donde el sonido de la vocal es largo como: (**trees, know, grow, shade, sleepy, fruit, leaves, make, green, beams, floats**).

PROJECT

Make a word tree from a small branch that has fallen off a tree. Fill an empty can with dirt or clay, and put the branch in the can so that it stands up. Then have your child draw leaves and cut them out. He or she can write new long vowel words on the leaves and attach them to the tree.

PROYECTO

Haga un árbol de palabras. Consiga una ramita de un árbol. Llene una lata de tierra o barro para sostener la rama. Haga que el niño dibuje hojas y las recorte. A medida que el niño vaya aprendiendo palabras donde el sonido de las vocales es largo, puede escribirlas en las hojas y atarlas al árbol con un cordón.

LESSON 22: Introduction to Long Vowels—Phonics Alive at Home

ESL Activities

Opportunities for ESL activities are provided throughout this unit. These activities benefit the ESL students in your classroom by providing additional language experiences. Choose the activities that best meet the diverse needs of your students.

For ESL activities related to "Trees" refer to page 49H.

Take-Home Book

Include family members in class-related activities by sending children home with a book of their own. The fold-up book *Tree Leaves and Seeds*, which can be found in the Student Edition on pages 213–214, is for shared reading enjoyment.

The book will encourage children to apply their newly learned long vowel phonics skills to the theme of trees. Use the Take-Home Book to conclude the unit, or send it home with children at another appropriate time.

● *Phonics Alive at Home* is intended to involve families in their children's development in reading and writing through activities that apply phonics skills.

● The *Phonics Alive at Home* page for this unit presents activities related to the theme "Earth, Trees, and Me." The activities also relate to the phonics focus on long vowels.

● Have children tear out the *Phonics Alive at Home* page from their books. Tell children to take the page home and complete the activities with family members.

● Invite children to share their completed word trees (or photos of them) with classmates. You may wish to make a word-tree display on the bulletin board.

● Encourage children to ask family members questions about trees, including the names of trees they see around their homes and on the way to school. Have children draw and label pictures of these trees or their leaves.

● Provide opportunities for children to share books about trees they have read, as well as their writing about and illustrations of trees.

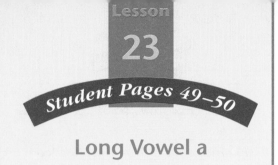

Lesson 23

Student Pages 49–50

Long Vowel a

Objectives

- To identify long **a** words
- To write words with long **a** phonograms
- To read and write long **a** words in context

Reviewing Short a

Display Phonics Picture Cards for short **a** words. Invite children to say and write each picture name.

★ Teaching the Lesson

- On the board write: **Gail likes to play in the shade of the tree.** Read the sentence together. Then invite a volunteer to underline all the words that contain the letter **a**. Have children say the underlined words. Point out that these words have the sound of long **a**.

- On the board write the phonogram **ail**. Ask what letter should be added to **ail** to form the word **Gail**. Add the **G**. Then sound and say the word, and have children repeat it. Write **ail** beneath **Gail**. Ask what letter should be added to form the word **hail**. Add the **h**, sound and say the word, and have children repeat it. Continue to generate a list of **ail** words. Read the list together. Ask which letters make the long **a** sound. Repeat the activity for long **a** phonograms **ay** and **ade**.

- Help children see that each long **a** phonogram has two vowels. Explain that the sound of first vowel (**a**) is its name; the second vowel (**i**, **y**, or **e**) is silent.

ESL Activities

Refer to page 47H.

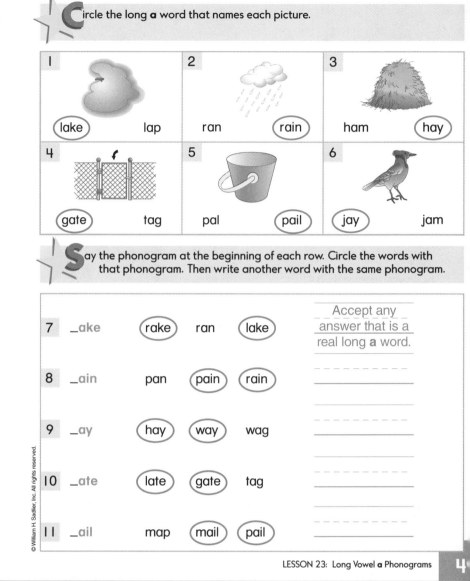

Circle the long **a** word that names each picture.

| 1 | lake / lap | 2 | ran / **rain** | 3 | ham / **hay** |
| 4 | **gate** / tag | 5 | pal / **pail** | 6 | **jay** / jam |

Say the phonogram at the beginning of each row. Circle the words with that phonogram. Then write another word with the same phonogram.

7	_ake	**rake** ran **lake**	Accept any answer that is a real long **a** word.
8	_ain	pan **pain** **rain**	
9	_ay	**hay** **way** wag	
10	_ate	**late** **gate** tag	
11	_ail	map **mail** **pail**	

LESSON 23: Long Vowel **a** Phonograms

Multisensory *Activities*

Visual ■ Tactile

Sort the Mail

Materials: Phonics Picture Cards for short **a** and long **a** words, two boxes labeled "Long **a**" and "Lost Mail"

Place the cards facedown in a pile. Have a child choose a card, say its name, and write the name on the board. Direct children to "mail" cards with long **a** words by placing them in the "Long **a**" box and to place other cards in the "Lost Mail" box.

Auditory ■ Tactile

Fade-Away Vowels

On the board write the words **grain, may, pane, cape, rail, bake, ray, shade, pain,** and **play.** Say each word, and have children repeat it. Then ask a volunteer to name the vowel that is heard and the vowel that is silent. To emphasize that the silent vowel is not heard, have the volunteer lightly trace over it with his or her finger to make it fade.

If there are two vowels in a one-syllable word, the first vowel is usually **long** and the second vowel is silent. There are different ways to spell long vowels.

Lake, **rain**, and **hay** have the long **a** sound. Color the raindrops that have long **a** words.

Raindrops: ame, pave, gain, wait, way, cab, late, tan, ail, may, mat, say, tap, make, lane

Circle and write the word that completes each sentence.

1. Fay likes to __paint__ on rainy days. (paint) pan

2. She paints a picture of the __gray__ sky. grass (gray)

3. She also likes to make things with __clay__ . clam (clay)

4. She makes a horse with a long __mane__ . man (mane)

5. One day she __may__ take art classes. (may) mat

LESSON 23: Recognizing and Writing Long Vowel **a**

Spelling Connection

Read aloud each word and sentence below. Invite a volunteer to spell the word orally. Ask another volunteer to write it on the board.

wait   I will **wait** near a tree.
way   A tree is in the **way**.
came   Sap **came** from a tree.
rain   **Rain** fell on the ground.
rake   Did you **rake** the leaves?

Computer Connection

Invite children to learn about the letters of the alphabet through rhyme and object/word associations in The Book of Shadowboxes: A Story of the ABC's (EduQuest). Have children select the A–Z menu icon from the opening screen, choose the vowel **a**, and then choose who will read the rhyme. After the rhyme is read, have children identify objects (in a shadowbox) whose names appear in the rhyme. Then have children select the Treasure Hunt icon to find other objects that contain the sound of long **a**.

Practicing the Skill

• Read the first set of directions on page 49, and identify the pictures. Then read aloud the second set of directions. Do several items with the class. Have children complete the page.

• Review the *Helpful Hint* on page 50. Then read the first set of directions together, and have children color the appropriate raindrops. Ask a volunteer to read the second set of directions. Then have children complete the page.

Extending the Skill Across the Curriculum

(Science/Social Studies)

Theme Activity
Materials: large cards

• To start a discussion about trees ask, "How does a tree begin?" and "What happens to leaves in the fall?" Help children see that, like trees, they too change as they grow. Then read aloud the theme book cited below.

• Write each of these sentences from the theme book below on a large card:

The **maple** tree grew from seed.
War started the **same** spring.
Paul Revere **made** his famous ride.
Rain helped the tree **make** sugar.
Leaves **lay** on the ground.
The **nation** grew larger.
There were now 28 **states**.
Sap **came** in the spring to **awaken** closed buds.
Heavy wet **flakes** fell one **day**.
Snow **made** the branches break.

• Write "Changes in a Maple Tree" and "Changes in U.S. History" on the board. Have children sort the cards into these two categories. Then have them read the sentences aloud and identify each long **a** word.

Theme Book
Hiscock, Bruce. *The Big Tree*. New York: Atheneum, 1991. Two hundred years of changes in a tree and the U.S.

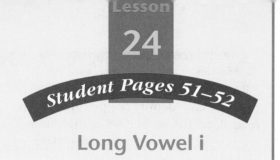

Long Vowel i

Objectives

- To identify long **i** words
- To write words with long **i** phonograms
- To read and write long **i** words in context

Warming Up

Reviewing Short i

On the board write **ill, it, im, in,** and **ip.** Ask children to list five short **i** words for each phonogram.

★ Teaching the Lesson

- On chart paper write the lyrics below. Have children sing them to the "Kookaburra" melody.

    Kookaburra sits in the old **pine** tree,
    Wishing for the **pie** that he can see.
    Smile, kookaburra, **smile,** kookaburra.
    Fine your **life** must be.

Call attention to the long **i** sound in **pine.** Then reread each line, and have volunteers say and underline the long **i** words.

- Write **pine** on the board. Erase the **p,** and read the long **i** phonogram **ine.** Add **f** to the beginning of **ine.** Sound and say the word together. Continue to substitute initial consonants to form rhyming words. Repeat the activity with the word **pie.**

- Ask what letters make the long **i** sound in **pine** and **pie.** Point out that each word has two vowels; the first vowel (**i**) says its name and the second (**e**) is silent.

Circle the word that names each picture. Color the pictures whose names have the long **i** sound.

1		2		3	
	vase		time		kiss
	van		(tie)		kite
	(vine)		tin		kid
	vane		tame		(kit)

4		5		6	
	(pie)		fine		lame
	pop		fame		(lime)
	pink		five		lane
	pack		(fin)		land

Say each phonogram. Then read the words. Write another word with the same phonogram. Accept any answer that is a real word.

7	8	9	10
_ine	_ie	_ime	_ide
vine	tie	dime	hide
dine	lie	time	side
_____	_____	_____	_____
_____	_____	_____	_____
_____	_____	_____	_____

Taking Off

Work with a partner. Write a list of words that rhyme with **bike.**

LESSON 24: Long Vowel **i** Phonograms

5

Multisensory *Activities*

Auditory ■ Tactile

Pick a Lime

Materials: Phonics Picture Cards for short **i** and long **i** words, basket or bag labeled "Limes"

Tell children to imagine they are picking limes from a tree. Invite them to take a picture card and say its name. Direct them to put the card in the basket if it has the same vowel sound as **lime.** You may also wish to have children sort the long **i** words in the basket into two groups: i___e and ie.

Visual ■ Kinesthetic

Fly to the Hive

Materials: oaktag, marker, index cards, tape

On index cards write long **i** words such as **hide, ripe, side, pine, tie, bike, dime, nine, ride, hive, lie, bite, fine, five,** and **kite** and short **i** words such as **lip, trip, kit, hit,** and **big.** Outline a large beehive on oaktag. Have each child pick a card and read the word. If it is a long **i** word, have the child attach the card to the hive.

Vine and **tie** have the long **i** sound. Change each word to a long **i** word by adding a final **e**.

1 kit	2 rip	3 pin	4 fin
kite	ripe	pine	fine

5 rid	6 dim	7 hid	8 bit
ride	dime	hide	bite

Use a word from above to complete each phrase.

9. ride a bike

10. fly a kite

11. nickel and dime

12. a fine day

13. a ripe plum

14. a pine tree

15. hide and seek

16. a big bite

LESSON 24: Recognizing and Writing Long Vowel **i**

52

Spelling Connection

Read aloud each word and sentence below. Invite a volunteer to spell the word orally. Ask another volunteer to write it on the board.

tie   I will **tie** my apron.
time   It is **time** to pick apples.
vine   Grapes grow on a **vine**.
ripe   I picked the **ripe** fruit.
fine   I did a **fine** job.

Multicultural Connection

Explain that many people who pick fruit are migrant workers, who move to different farms to find work. Tell children that some migrant workers come from other countries, such as Mexico. Then read aloud a book about Cesar Chavez, such as *Cesar Chavez and La Causa* by Naurice Roberts (Children's Press). Talk with children about some of the difficulties migrant workers must overcome. Ask children what they might do in the same situations.

Practicing the Skill

● Review both sets of directions, the pictures, and the phonograms on page 51. Then have children complete the page.

● Have children work in pairs and take turns printing words that rhyme with **bike** between the spokes in *Taking Off*.

● Go over the directions at the top of page 52. Then have children complete the exercise. Read aloud the second set of directions. Have children use the long **i** words they made in the first exercise to complete the phrases.

Extending the Skill Across the Curriculum

(Social Studies/Drama)

Theme Activity

● Talk with children about orchards and fruit trees. Ask children who have picked fruit from trees to tell about their experience. Then read aloud the theme book cited below.

● Explain that some people's jobs involve growing and picking fruit. Help children develop a list of questions they might ask someone who has such a job. For example:

What **time** do you start picking fruit?
How do you know when the fruit is **ripe**?
What do you **like** about picking fruit?

Write the questions on the board.

● Have pairs of children act out the questions and answers. Then have volunteers list on the board the long **i** words they heard in the answers.

Theme Book

Slawson, Michele B. *Apple Picking Time*. New York: Crown Publishing Group, 1994. A day of apple picking.

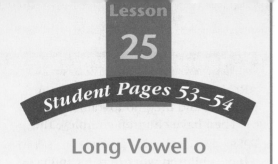

Lesson 25

Student Pages 53–54

Long Vowel o

Objectives
- To identify long **o** words
- To write words with long **o** phonograms
- To read and write long **o** words in context

Warming Up

Reviewing Short e

Invite children to write rhyming sentences that include words with short **e** phonograms. Provide this example: **Bess** and **Ben fed the hen**.

★ Teaching the Lesson

- On the board write this rhyme:

  Mary, Mary, quite contrary,
  How does your garden **grow**?
  "I use a **hose**,
  So the water can **soak**
  My pretty white **rose**
  And my brand new **oak**."

Read the rhyme together. Call attention to the long **o** sound in **grow**. Then ask children to name other words in the poem that have the same vowel sound.

- On the board write **ow, oak,** and **ose**. Focus on each long **o** phonogram in turn. Invite children to say each phonogram and to point to rhyming words with the same phonogram in the poem. (Remind children that **how** does not rhyme with **grow**.) List the words beneath the appropriate phonogram. Elicit other rhyming words for each phonogram, and add them to the list.

- Call attention to the letters that make the long **o** sound in **grow, soak,** and **hose**. Help children see that **soak** and **hose** each have two vowels; the sound of first vowel (**o**) is its name; the second vowel (**a** or **e**) is silent.

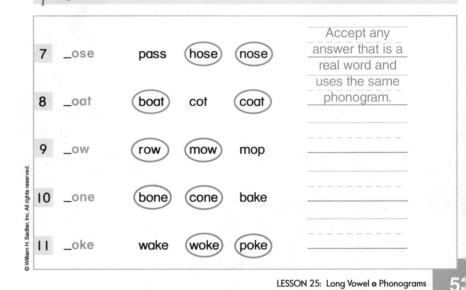

Circle the long o word that names each picture.

| 1 | raise / rise / **rose** | 2 | bat / **boat** / bone | 3 | snail / **snow** / slow |
| 4 | **road** / robe / rod | 5 | can / cane / **cone** | 6 | **smoke** / smile / snake |

Say the phonogram at the beginning of each row. Circle the words with that phonogram. Then write another word with the same phonogram.

7	_ose	pass	**hose**	**nose**
8	_oat	**boat**	cot	**coat**
9	_ow	**row**	**mow**	mop
10	_one	**bone**	**cone**	bake
11	_oke	wake	**woke**	**poke**

Accept any answer that is a real word and uses the same phonogram.

LESSON 25: Long Vowel **o** Phonograms

53

Multisensory *Activities*

Visual ■ Auditory

The Old Oak Tree

Materials: construction paper, scissors, tape

From construction paper, make three tree trunks and fifteen branches. On each branch write one of these words: **coat, loaf, road, foam, soap, row, tow, bow, low, grow, bone, cone, hole, home,** or **note**. Label the tree trunks o___e, oa, and ow. Then invite each child to choose a branch. Have the child say the word and tape the branch to the appropriate trunk.

Visual ■ Kinesthetic

Soap on a Rope

Materials: construction paper, yarn, hole punch, crayons

Cut construction paper into rectangles about the size of a bar of soap. Give each child a "soap bar." Invite children to write their favorite long **o** word on the bar. Then have them punch holes in the bars, thread yarn through to form large loops, and wear the bars as necklaces. Encourage children to read each other's soap-on-a-rope words.

Rose, boat, and snow have the long **o** sound. Color the stones that have long **o** words.

home | low | dock | soak | note | sock

roam | block | woke | tone | doll | hose

blow | foam | stop | zone | rode | rock

The underlined word in each sentence does not make sense. Write a long **o** word from the box that would make sense.

| bow | cone | rose | toad | rope | loaf |

1. I have ice cream in a <u>cane</u>.   cone

2. Joe tied the boat with a <u>rake</u>.   rope

3. Ben has a <u>lime</u> of bread in a bag.   loaf

4. Mike put a <u>bike</u> on the gift.   bow

5. A red <u>ride</u> grows in the garden.   rose

6. Mom saw a <u>tide</u> jump in the lake.   toad

LESSON 25: Recognizing and Writing Long Vowel **o**

Spelling Connection

Read aloud each word and sentence below. Ask a volunteer to spell the word orally. Have another volunteer write the word on the board.

soap   Rosa washed with **soap**.
note   Joan wrote a **note** to Moe.
low   One tree branch was **low**.
rope   José tied knots in the **rope**.
boat   The old **boat** can float.

Teacher to Teacher

Display a large map of the world on the bulletin board. As you work through the unit on long vowel sounds, have children find the continents, countries, and bodies of water whose names have the long vowel sound they are studying. Invite children to list the names and mount the list next to the map.

Deborah Scigliano
Pittsburgh, PA

Practicing the Skill

● Read aloud the two sets of directions on page 53, and identify the pictures and phonograms together. Have children complete the page.

● Ask children how **rose, boat,** and **snow** are alike. (They all have the sound of long **o**.) Then review both sets of directions on page 54, and have children complete the page.

Observational Assessment
*Note how readily children recognize the various long **o** phonograms.*

Extending the Skill Across the Curriculum

(Language Arts/Social Studies)

Theme Activity
● Read aloud the theme books cited below. Then write these phrases on the board: **hole** in the tree; **home for** us, **old oak** tree, **grows** tall, along the **road, hope** to keep our **home, know** what is right, when the wind **blows,** and when the **snow** falls. Read aloud each phrase, and have volunteers identify the long **o** word(s).

● Tell children to imagine they are animals who live in trees that are about to be cut down. Have them write "letters to the editor" telling why their homes should be saved. Encourage children to use phrases from the list.

● Ask volunteers to share their letters with the class.

Portfolio
Have children place their letters to the editor in their portfolios.

Theme Books
Cherry, Lynne. *Great Kapok Tree: A Tale of the Amazon Rain Forest.* San Diego, CA: Harcourt Brace Jovanovich, 1990. A rain forest.

Butterworth, Nick. *One Blowy Night.* Boston: Little, Brown, 1992. A park keeper relocates animals.

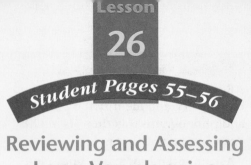

Lesson 26

Student Pages 55–56

Reviewing and Assessing Long Vowels a, i, o

Objective
- To review and assess long vowels **a, i, o**

Warming Up

Reviewing Short u

On the board write phrases such as these:

> stuck in the **mad**
> **hem** a little tune
> **tag** on the rope

Call on children to change the vowel in one word in each phrase to short **u** so that it makes sense.

★ Teaching the Lesson

Materials: Phonics Picture Cards for long **a**, long **i**, and long **o** words

- Display the picture cards in random order on the chalk ledge. Tell children they will use long **a**, long **i**, and long **o** words to build a nonsense sentence. Demonstrate by placing the card for **lake** on another part of the chalk ledge. Say, "There is a **lake**." Then place the **toad** picture card on the ledge next to the lake. Say, "There is a **toad** in the **lake**."

- Ask a volunteer to add a third picture and expand the sentence; for example, "There is a **tie** on the **toad** in the **lake**." Have children continue to build the sentence until all the picture cards have been used.

- Invite volunteers to write the name of each picture on the board.

Observational Assessment
Note how well children make up phrases to expand the sentence.

Look at the picture. Then follow the directions below.

Directions
1. Color the lake blue.
2. Draw a road by the lake.
3. Circle the boat.
4. Color the pine tree green.
5. Draw a box around the kite.
6. Color each rose yellow.
7. Color the pail gray.
8. Draw a hole for the mole.
9. Draw a line over the stone.
10. Make an X on the hive.
11. Color the toad brown.
12. Draw a tail on the fox.

Lesson 26: Reviewing Long Vowels **a, i, o**   55

Multisensory *Activities*

Visual ■ Tactile

Pine Tree Puzzle
Materials: green construction paper, scissors, marker

Draw a triangular pine tree on the paper, and cut it into three horizontal parts. In each part write long vowel **a, i,** or **o** words with the same phonogram (e.g., **take/cake/lake**). Then cut the words apart. Have a small group of children piece the tree together by distinguishing spelling patterns and long vowel sounds.

Visual ■ Kinesthetic

Stone's Throw
Materials: mural paper, marker, beanbag

Divide mural paper into large squares. Write a long **a, i,** or **o** word from pages 55 and 56 in each square and a point value next to each word. Tape the mural paper to the floor. Then invite children to take turns tossing a beanbag at the words. Children score points by reading the word in the square on which the beanbag lands.

55

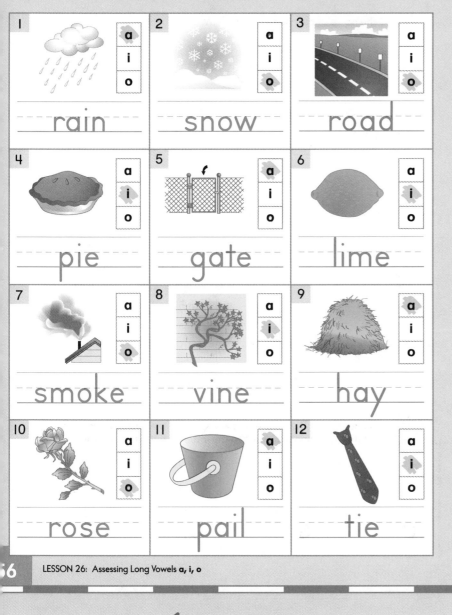

Check-Up Color the box that contains the long vowel sound in each picture name. Write the word.

1. **a i o** — rain	2. **a i o** — snow	3. **a i o** — road
4. **a i o** — pie	5. **a i o** — gate	6. **a i o** — lime
7. **a i o** — smoke	8. **a i o** — vine	9. **a i o** — hay
10. **a i o** — rose	11. **a i o** — pail	12. **a i o** — tie

LESSON 26: Assessing Long Vowels **a, i, o**

Assessing the Skills

Check-Up Read aloud the instructions at the top of page 55. Then call on volunteers to read the numbered directions at the bottom of the page. Have children complete the picture as directed. For page 56, review the long vowel phonograms, and have volunteers give examples of each. Then read the directions together and have children complete the page.

Observational Assessment Observe which children are having difficulty using the correct phonogram for a particular word. Discuss with them the possible reasons for their difficulties. Make notes for use in reteaching.

Student Skills Assessment Record your observations of each child on the checklist on pages 207–208 of the Student Edition.

Writing Conference Together review each child's writing portfolio. Encourage the child to talk about how his or her writing has improved since your last conference and where he or she is experiencing difficulty. Use your *Writing Conference* notes to help you determine whether the child is correctly applying phonics skills.

Group together children who need further instruction on long vowels **a, i,** and **o** for the *Reteaching Activities*.

Reteaching *Activities*

Tell Me What to Do

On the board write long **a, i,** and **o** words from pages 49–56. Invite children to the board to mark a word according to your directions. Say, for example, "Circle **cave**," or "Underline **hive**." Continue by asking children to give their classmates similar directions.

Trace the Vine

Materials: yarn, index cards, stapler

Staple a long piece of yarn to a bulletin board in a swirled pattern to represent a vine. On index cards write long **a, i,** and **o** words from pages 49–56, and staple the cards along the vine as if they were leaves. Remind children that long vowels say their names. Then invite children to work in pairs to say the words as they trace the vine from beginning to end.

Long Vowel u

Objectives
- To identify long **u** words
- To write words with long **u** phonograms
- To read and write long **u** words in context

Warming Up

Reviewing Short Vowels

On the board write these sets of words: **got, top,** nap; **van, pin, past;** bug, **well, jet; ship, gift,** rock; and **fun,** went, **mug.** Read them aloud. Have volunteers circle the words in each set that have the same vowel sound.

★ Teaching the Lesson

Materials: Phonics Picture Cards **mule, blue, fruit, June**

- Display the picture cards, and ask children to name each picture. Call attention to the long **u** sound in each word.

- Read aloud the paragraph below, but leave out the words in parentheses. Have children complete each sentence by choosing the correct picture card.

    It was a warm day in (**June**). The sky was (**blue**). Sue went for a long ride on her (**mule**). When she got back, she ate a juicy (**fruit**).

- On the board write **une, ue, ule,** and **uit.** Have volunteers read each phonogram and write a word with that phonogram beneath each one. Ask others to name and write rhyming words.

- Call attention to the two vowels that make the long **u** sound in each word on the board. Point out that the sound of the first vowel (**u**) is also its name; the second vowel (**e** or **i**) is silent.

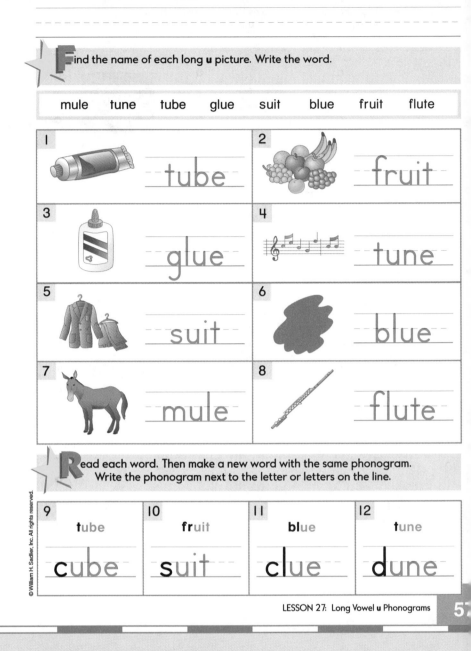

Find the name of each long **u** picture. Write the word.

| mule | tune | tube | glue | suit | blue | fruit | flute |

1. tube
2. fruit
3. glue
4. tune
5. suit
6. blue
7. mule
8. flute

Read each word. Then make a new word with the same phonogram. Write the phonogram next to the letter or letters on the line.

9. **t**ube	10. **fr**uit	11. **bl**ue	12. **t**une
cube	**s**uit	**c**lue	**d**une

LESSON 27: Long Vowel **u** Phonograms

57

Multisensory *Activities*

Visual ■ Kinesthetic

Juicy Fruit

Materials: orange construction paper circles, crayon, tape

On the board draw a tree, and list long **u** words such as **blue, fruit, mule,** and so forth. Distribute the paper circles. Assign to each child a long **u** word to write on his or her "orange." Have children tape their oranges to the tree. Invite children to "pick" an orange by reading the word and identifying its vowel sound.

Visual ■ Tactile

Glue Clues

Materials: paper, clay, crayons, glue

Distribute materials, and assign to each child a long **u** word. Have children write their words on paper. Then have them shape and glue rolled clay over the letters that stand for the **u** sound. Invite children to exchange papers and read one another's words as they trace the clay letters with their fingers.

Tube, fruit, and blue have the long **u** sound. Complete each sentence by choosing two long **u** words that make sense.

1

fruit cube juice

Sue makes __fruit__ __juice__.

2

mule dune cute

Joe rides a __cute__ __mule__.

3

fuse flute tune

June plays a __tune__ on a __flute__.

4

huge tuba rule

Duke plays a __huge__ __tuba__.

5

suit clue blue

Luke gets a new __blue__ __suit__.

6

due use ruler

Nina likes to __use__ a __ruler__.

LESSON 27: Writing Long Vowel **u**

Spelling Connection

Read aloud each word and sentence below. Call on a volunteer to spell the word orally. Have another volunteer write the word on the board.

mule June rode on a **mule**.
suit Luke wore a brown **suit**.
blue Sue wears a **blue** cap.
use Please **use** the back door.
cube Tammy put an ice **cube** in her lemonade.

Multicultural Connection

● The saguaro (sa-WAHR-oh), or giant cactus, which grows in the southwestern United States and in Mexico, resembles a tree. Mature plants may grow to 60 feet. For hundreds of years, Native Americans have harvested the saguaro's fruit to make jams.

● You may wish to read aloud from the book *Desert Giant: The World of the Saguaro Cactus* by Barbara Bash (Little, Brown & Company). Encourage children to find out what trees nearby provide fruit for jams, jellies, and preserves.

Practicing the Skill

● Together review the directions, pictures, and phonograms on page 57. Then have children complete the page.

● Ask children how the words **tube, fruit,** and **glue** are alike. (They all have the sound of long **u**.) Then read the directions at the top of page 58. Do the first sentence together. Have children complete the page.

Extending the Skill Across the Curriculum

(Language Arts/Science)

Theme Activity

● In the center of a sheet of chart paper, draw a simple tree. Use it as the focal point of a concept map about the uses of trees. Start the map with things children have already talked about, such as giving shade. Then share the theme books cited below.

● Elicit additional ideas for the concept map, such as wood; paper; shelter; the **fruit** grown on several kinds of trees; and the **juice** made from that fruit.

● Display the map, and encourage children to add to it when they discover new uses for trees.

● On the board write the sentence starter "In the shade of the huge oak tree…," and these long **u** words: **juicy, tune, cube, flute, juice,** and **prune.** Have children use the words to complete the sentence; for example:

…June ate a **juicy prune**.
…Sue played a **tune** on her **flute**.
…Luke put an ice **cube** in his **juice**.

Theme Books

Brenner, Barbara, and May Garelick. *The Tremendous Tree Book*. Honesdale, PA: Boyels Mills Press, 1992. The tree, one of the most useful plants on Earth.

Gackenbach, Dick. *Mighty Tree*. San Diego: Harcourt Brace Jovanovich, 1992. A story of three trees.

Lesson 28

Student Pages 59–60

Long Vowel e

Objectives
- To identify long **e** words
- To write words with long **e** phonograms
- To read and write long **e** words in context

Warming Up

Reviewing Short i
Read aloud the sentences given below. Have children name and spell the short **i** words they hear:

Liz will dig holes for **six** trees.
The **big pig** stepped on a **fig**.
Jill hid the **gift in** a box.
Did Rick fill the cup **with milk**?

★ Teaching the Lesson

- Together reread the first stanza of the poem "Trees" (page 47). Call attention to the long **e** sound in **green**.

- Have a volunteer write the word **tree** on the board. Erase the initial **tr** and read aloud the phonogram **ee**.

- Add a **b** to **ee**. Ask children to sound and say the word. Then invite volunteers to substitute other initial consonants to form additional rhyming words. Repeat this activity with the words **seat** and **jeep**.

- Call attention to the letters that make the long **e** sound in each word. Then help children to see that each word has two vowels. Point out that the sound of the first vowel (**e**) is also its name; the second vowel (**e** or **a**) is silent.

ESL Activities
Refer to page 49H.

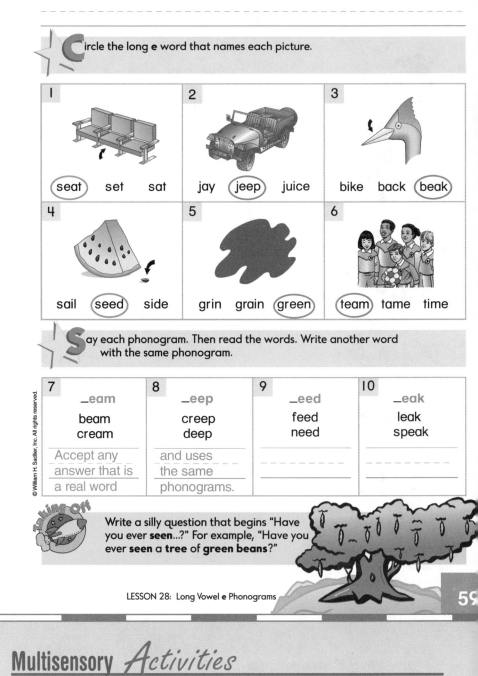

Circle the long **e** word that names each picture.

1. (seat) set sat
2. jay (jeep) juice
3. bike back (beak)
4. sail (seed) side
5. grin grain (green)
6. (team) tame time

Say each phonogram. Then read the words. Write another word with the same phonogram.

7. _eam
   beam
   cream
   Accept any answer that is a real word

8. _eep
   creep
   deep
   and uses the same phonograms.

9. _eed
   feed
   need

10. _eak
    leak
    speak

Taking Off Write a silly question that begins "Have you ever **seen**...?" For example, "Have you ever **seen** a **tree** of **green beans**?"

LESSON 28: Long Vowel **e** Phonograms

59

Multisensory *Activities*

Visual ■ Auditory

Do You Hear Long e?
Materials: Phonics Picture Cards for short **e** and long **e** words

Display the picture cards one at a time, and ask children to name each. If the name has the long **e** sound, have them write it on a sheet of paper. Have children read their word lists. Record correct words on the board. Help children to see that two spelling patterns—**ee** and **ea**—have the sound of long **e**.

Visual ■ Kinesthetic

Falling Leaves
Materials: red, yellow, and orange construction paper; leaf patterns; scissors; pencils; tape

Have children trace and cut out construction paper leaves and write a long **e** word on each. Encourage them to use words not used in the previous activity. Have children put their leaves in a pile. Invite each child to pick a leaf, read the word, and mount the leaf to the bulletin board.

59

Seat and **jeep** have the long **e** sound. Write a long **e** word to answer each question.

1. What part of your foot rhymes with **feel**? heel

2. What kind of insect rhymes with **see**? bee

3. What part of a plant rhymes with **reed**? seed

4. What kind of animal rhymes with **real**? seal

5. What part of a bird rhymes with **leak**? beak

6. What part of a month rhymes with **peek**? week

Change the vowel in each word to **ea** to write a new word. Read the new long **e** word.

7 not	8 bat	9 trot
neat	beat	treat
10 mat	11 stem	12 drum
meat	steam	dream

LESSON 28: Writing Long Vowel **e**

60

Spelling Connection

Read aloud each word and sentence below. Have a volunteer spell the word orally. Ask another volunteer to write the word on the board.

leaf	Pete found a red **leaf**.
seed	An acorn is a **seed**.
week	We spent a **week** at camp.
bee	A **bee** flew out of the hive.
jeans	My **jeans** are dark blue.

Computer Connection

Invite children to explore Downtown Sounds in Read, Write, & Type!™ (The Learning Company) to help them associate sounds with letters and identify sounds in words. Vexor the Virus steals and hides letters, and children are asked to rescue the letters by identifying the pictures whose names contain their sound. Throughout the game children are asked to identify initial, medial, and final sounds of the hidden letter.

Practicing the Skill

● Review the directions, pictures, and phonograms on page 59. Do the first item in each exercise with the class. Then have children complete the page.

● Direct children's attention to *Taking Off*. Read aloud the sample silly question. Then invite children to make up their own questions.

● Ask children how the words **seat** and **jeep** are alike. (They both have the sound of long **e**.) Then review the directions on page 60, and have children complete the page.

Extending the Skill Across the Curriculum

(Language Arts/Art)
Theme Activity

Materials: construction and writing paper, crayons, scissors, glue

● Use the theme book cited below to help generate ideas for leaf art. Then have children cut out varied leaf patterns. Invite children to use their leaves to make pictures of animals.

● Write this poem on chart paper:

> **See** the **leaves**?
> They're yellow, red, and **green**.
> I put them on my paper
> And made a pretty **scene**.
> **See** the face?
> And legs and tail and **feet**?
> No, it's not **real**,
> But don't you think it's **neat**?

Read the poem together. Ask children to identify the long **e** words. Then have them copy the poem and attach it to the back of their leaf animals.

 **Theme Book**

Sohi, Morteza E. *Look What I Did with a Leaf!* New York: Walker, 1993. Animals that can be made from leaves.

Observational Assessment
*Note whether children are able to read long **e** words in context.*

Lesson 29

Student Pages 61–62

Reviewing and Assessing Long Vowels u and e

Objective
● To review and assess long vowels **u** and **e**

Warming Up

Reviewing Consonants
Materials: Phonics Picture Cards **ham, hat, cap, cup, fan, fox, six, sun, jam, jet**.

Mix the picture cards on a table. Ask children to sort them by the initial consonant sounds of their names. Have them say each picture name and stress the initial consonant sound. Then have children sort the cards by the final consonant sounds of the names and say the names again, stressing the sound of the final consonant.

★ Teaching the Lesson

● Write sentences with long **u** and long **e** words on sentence strips. For example:

> **Miss Reed** has **tea** with her **meal**.
> **June eats fruit** under a **tree**.
> **Sleepy Lee** plays a **flute** in her **dream**.

● Read each sentence together. Call on volunteers to find and circle the long **u** words and the long **e** words.

● Cut each sentence into three parts, as on page 61. Elicit children's ideas for recombining the parts to form new sentences. Ask volunteers to read the new sentences to classmates.

Observational Assessment
Note how well children are able to identify long u and long e words.

Combine words from boxes 1, 2, and 3 to write sentences. How many different sentences can you write?

1	2	3
Sweet Sue	plays the flute	on a dune.
Queen Jean	rides a mule	each June.
Mr. Green	plants a tree	on the street.

Accept any answer that combines words from boxes 1, 2, and 3 that make a sentence.

LESSON 29: Reviewing Long Vowels **u** and **e**   **61**

Multisensory *Activities*

Visual ■ Auditory

I'll Give You a Clue
Materials: Phonics Picture Cards for long **u** and long **e** words

Display the picture cards on the chalk ledge. Tell children to look and listen as you provide clues to the name of each picture. For example:

> This stubborn animal has the long **u** sound. (**mule**)
> This car has the long **e** sound. (**jeep**)

Have children write the picture names on paper.

Visual ■ Kinesthetic

Blue or Green
Materials: blue and green construction paper

Have children work in pairs. Give each pair a sheet of blue and of green paper. Demonstrate how to fold the blue paper into thirds and the green paper in half, one part for each phonogram. Have children write long **u** words on the blue paper and long **e** words on the green. Then have children share their words.

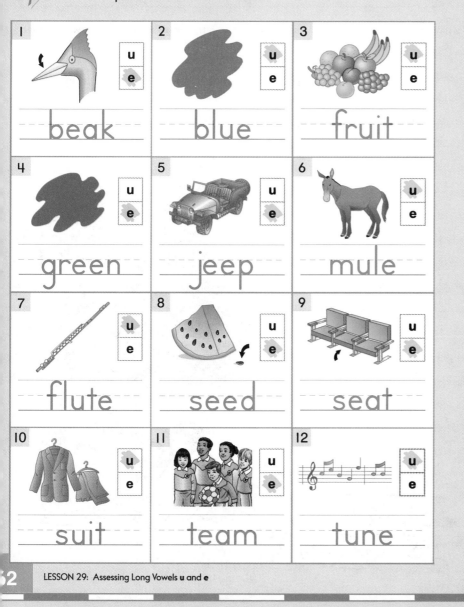

1 | u / e | beak
2 | u / e | blue
3 | u / e | fruit
4 | u / e | green
5 | u / e | jeep
6 | u / e | mule
7 | u / e | flute
8 | u / e | seed
9 | u / e | seat
10 | u / e | suit
11 | u / e | team
12 | u / e | tune

LESSON 29: Assessing Long Vowels **u** and **e**

Assessing the Skills

Check-Up Read the directions at the top of page 61. Ask volunteers to read the words in boxes 1, 2, and 3. Together choose words from each box to make up a sentence. Have children complete the page. Then, together, identify the pictures on page 62. Review the different spellings and phonograms for the long vowel sounds, and have children complete the page.

Observational Assessment Note how well children choose the correct phonogram for a word.

Student Skills Assessment Record your observations of each child on the checklist on pages 207–208 of the Student Edition.

Writing Conference Review the writing each child has placed in her or his portfolio. Invite the child to talk about how her or his writing is improving and where she or he is experiencing difficulty. Take notes on each child's progress. Use these notes to help you determine how well children are applying phonics skills.

Group together children who need further instruction on long **u** and long **e** for the *Reteaching Activities*.

Reteaching *Activities*

Keep the Beat

Materials: Phonics Picture Cards for long **u** words and long **e** words

On the board write the words **tube** and **jeep**. Tell children to use these key words to help them remember the sounds of long **u** and long **e**. Then display the picture cards, and invite volunteers to name each picture. Tell children to pretend to play a flute when they hear a long **u** sound and beat a drum when they hear a long **e** sound.

Tree of Vowels

Materials: oaktag, marker, index cards, tape

On index cards write long **u** and long **e** words used in the lessons on pages 57–62. On the board or chart paper, draw the outline of a tree with two main branches. Label one branch "Long **u** Words," and the other branch "Long **e** Words." Invite each child to pick a card, say the word, and attach the card to the correct branch.

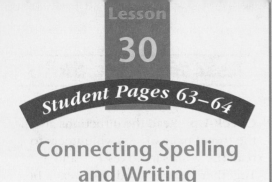
Connecting Spelling and Writing

Objectives
● To say, spell, sort, and write long vowel words
● To write a list using spelling words

Warming Up

Reviewing Long Vowel Phonograms

Materials: Phonics Picture Cards **hay, lake, pail, pie, kite, boat, rose, snow, blue, fruit, June, jeep, team**

Display the picture cards, and ask volunteers to name them. Have children write a rhyming word for each name.

★ *Teaching the Lesson*

● Say, "Let's **eat** a snack under the apple **tree**." Ask children which words have a long vowel sound.

● Write **eat** and **tree** on the board. Invite a volunteer to underline the letters that make the long **e** sound.

● Write each spelling word from page 63 on the board, leaving the vowels blank. Then say each word. Have children repeat the word, spell it, and say it again. Ask volunteers to identify the vowel sound and fill in the missing letters on the board.

● Invite children to use each spelling word in a sentence.

Practicing the Skill

Together read the directions and the list of spelling words on page 63. Have a volunteer explain where to write **home**, the first word on the list. (under "Long o")

Spell and Write Say and spell each word in the box. Then write each word under the long vowel sound in its name.

home	1 Long **a**	2 Long **i**	3 Long **o**
may	may	five	home
five	make	pie	coat
tune			
tree	4 Long **u**		
coat	tune		
fruit	fruit		
eat	5 Long **e**		
pie	tree		
make	eat		

LESSON 30: Connecting Spelling and Writing   **63**

Multisensory *Activities*

Visual ■ Tactile

Spell with Tiles

Materials: small oaktag squares, envelopes, markers

Have children work in pairs, and give each pair an envelope with 38 squares. Tell children to write a letter on each square as needed to spell all the spelling words. Have partners take turns saying and spelling the words aloud. Then ask them to mix the squares and take turns choosing squares to reconstruct the words.

Visual ■ Tactile

Seed Words

Materials: seeds, paper, glue sticks

Assign to each child a spelling word. Distribute materials. Have children write their words, trace the letters with glue sticks, and then sprinkle seeds on the glue. After the glue dries, have children run their fingers over the letters as they say, spell, and say the words. Ask children to trade words and repeat the procedure.

home	may	five	tune	tree	
coat	fruit	eat	pie	make

Things To Do

hum a tune

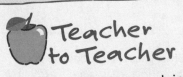

64 LESSON 30: Connecting Spelling and Writing

The Writing Process

Tell children that they will be writing a list of things to do. Explain that some lists are helpful for keeping track of things and that other lists are just for fun. Together read the directions and the spelling words on page 64.

Brainstorm Tell children to imagine they are in the picture at the top of the page. Elicit ideas for things to do under an apple tree. Encourage children to be imaginative and have fun making the list.

Write Have children write drafts of their lists on paper.

Revise Direct children's attention to the sample list item. Tell them to make sure each item on their lists has an action word such as **hum**. Remind them to check the spelling of each word. Then have children write the final version on the page.

Publish After children complete their lists, invite them to read their favorite item to classmates. Then have children underline the spelling words in their lists.

Extending the Skill

Have children work in small groups to make other lists. Invite each group to choose a topic of its own or to use one of the following: favorite fruits, favorite animals, or favorite trees. Have each group choose one person to serve as the recorder and one as the reader. Invite children to share and compare their completed lists.

Portfolio

Have children add their lists to their Portfolios.

ESL Activities
Refer to page 49H.

Spelling Connection

Have children work in pairs. Give each pair ten index cards, and tell them to write one spelling word on each card. Have children shuffle the cards and place them facedown on a desk or table. Invite partners to alternate turning up two cards at a time and then saying and spelling the words. If the words have the same vowel sound, the child keeps the cards. If not, he or she puts them back facedown on the table.

Teacher to Teacher

Have children hold letter cards in the correct order to form short vowel words, such as kit, rat, or fin. Have a child with the silent letter **e** tiptoe up to change each short vowel word to a long vowel word. Together say, spell, and say each word again.

*Sr. Margaret Eileen
Reading, PA*

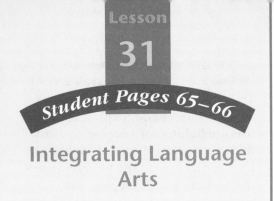

Integrating Language Arts

Objectives

• To use oral and written language to extend the theme concept

• To demonstrate the ability to recognize long vowel sounds in context

Background Information

General Sherman is the name of a giant sequoia tree in California. It is the largest tree on Earth and also one of the oldest living things, probably between 3,000 and 4,000 years old. The area where General Sherman and other sequoias grow is Sequoia National Park.

★ Teaching the Lesson

• Invite children to look at the pictures on page 65. Ask what they think is unusual about the trees.

• Invite volunteers to read the text aloud. Suggest that children demonstrate just how big General Sherman is by having 25 of them join hands to form a circle. Ask children what part of the tree is as big as the circle they have formed. (the trunk)

• Have children scan the text on page 65 for any long vowel words. Ask children to underline them and to identify any that have the same spelling pattern.

Oral Language Development

Use the question at the bottom of the page to prompt discussion about the great size of the giant sequoias and the awesomeness of nature. Invite students to think about how the General Sherman giant sequoia got so big.

Let's read and talk about a tree named General Sherman.

Did you ever hug a tree? Could you reach all the way around? Not if you hugged General Sherman! General Sherman is the name of a giant sequoia tree. It is the biggest giant sequoia in California. In fact, it is the biggest tree in the world. General Sherman's trunk is very, very wide. It would take about 25 children holding hands to make a circle around this huge tree.

How would you feel standing next to General Sherman in a forest of giant sequoia trees?

LESSON 31: Long Vowels in Context   **65**

Reading and Writing Connection

Supply children with books about giant sequoia trees, such as *Trees* by Illa Podendorf (Children's Press) and *Discovering Trees* by Douglas Florian (Charles Scribner's Sons).

Invite children to write a story in which they imagine that General Sherman can talk. Tell them to think about what the tree might say. Perhaps they might like to explore some of the things the tree might have seen over the years. Encourage children to base their stories on facts they have learned about the giant tree.

Social Studies Connection

Sequoia trees and Sequoia National Park are named after a Cherokee leader, Sequoyah. Between 1809 and 1821, he developed the first alphabet and system of writing for the Cherokee language.

Invite students to explore what it would be like if they could not write their ideas on paper. Ask how this would change the way they learn in school.

Check-Up Fill in the circle next to the word that names the picture.

1				2				3		
	○ van				● glue				○ hat	
	○ vane				○ clue				● hay	
	● vine				○ glum				○ hand	

4				5				6		
	○ said				○ snail				● tube	
	● seed				○ slow				○ tub	
	○ see				● snow				○ tune	

7				8				9		
	○ lack				○ pine				○ bet	
	○ late				● pie				○ beat	
	● lake				○ pane				● boat	

Underline all the words that have a long vowel sound. Then circle **Yes** or **No** to answer each question.

10. Is a <u>jeep</u> the <u>same</u> as a jet?	Yes	(No)
11. Can a <u>goat</u> paint a <u>gate</u>?	Yes	(No)
12. Can a <u>seal</u> swim in the <u>sea</u>?	(Yes)	No
13. Is a <u>peach</u> a fruit?	(Yes)	No
14. Is a <u>cape</u> a big cap?	Yes	(No)
15. Can you <u>hide</u> a <u>flute</u> in a <u>lime</u>?	Yes	(No)
16. Is a <u>dime</u> the <u>same</u> as a <u>vine</u>?	Yes	(No)
17. Can you put <u>ice</u> <u>cream</u> in a <u>cone</u>?	(Yes)	No

66   LESSON 31: Assessing Long Vowels

Assessing the Unit

Unit Test Review the different spellings for each long vowel sound and elicit examples of each. Then read aloud the directions on page 66. Have children identify the pictures in the first exercise. Demonstrate on the board how to mark the correct answers. For the second exercise make sure children understand that they are to underline all long vowel words in each sentence and circle **Yes** or **No**.

Observational Assessment Review the notes you have made throughout this unit. Use the notes to help assess students' progress and decide whether reteaching is necessary.

Student Skills Assessment Use the *Check-Up* on page 66 and your observations to record your evaluation of each child's skills on the checklist on pages 207–208 of the Student Edition.

Writing Conference Meet with each child to discuss a sample of writing from his or her portfolio. Encourage the child to talk about the writing and to compare it to what he or she has done in the past. Make notes about signs of progress, and include these notes in the child's portfolio. Also use the notes to help you assess whether the child is applying phonics skills in his or her writing. Encourage the child to edit the writing sample after your conference.

Group together children who need further instruction on long vowels for the *Reteaching Activities*. You may wish to use the alternative assessment methods on page 49C of the Teacher's Edition.

Take-Home Book Remind children to complete at home the *Take-Home Book* page for Unit 3.

Reteaching *Activities*

Take It to the Bank
Write long vowel words on small index cards. Include all the different spellings of each vowel sound. Have children work in pairs to sort the cards according to vowel patterns. Then invite children to choose at least one word for each long vowel spelling and add it to their word banks. Have children make flash cards for the new words. Direct them to practice the words with their partners.

Tree Slides
Materials: oaktag, scissors, crayons

Draw and cut out several tree shapes with large trunks. Make two vertical slits, one to two inches apart, high on the trunks. Write long vowel words on long strips of oaktag that will fit through the slits. Put similar spelling patterns on each strip (e.g., **oa** words on one and **o___e** words on another). Have children slide the strips through the openings and read each long vowel word as it appears.

PLANNING RESOURCE

IN THE City

Theme:
*Uptown, downtown,
all around the city!*

Overview

Unit 4 presents soft and hard **c** and **g** sounds and consonant blends as children explore the concept of a city.

Objectives

- To enjoy a poem about the city
- To recognize and write soft and hard **c** and **g** sounds
- To use soft and hard **c** and **g** words in context
- To spell words with soft and hard **c** and **g** and consonant blends.
- To recognize and write words with **l**-, **r**-, and **s**-blends in context

Thematic Teaching

Elicit what children already know about the concept of **a** city. Consider children's experiences and prior knowledge when selecting activities, and provide extra reading material for the class.

Display the Poetry Poster "City Street," and refer to it throughout the unit.

Individual Lessons

Lesson	Skill Focus
32	Introduction to Variant Consonant Sounds and Blends
33	Recognizing and Writing Soft and Hard **c**
34	Recognizing and Writing Soft and Hard **g**
35	Reviewing Soft and Hard **c** and **g**
36	Recognizing and Writing **l**-Blends
37	Recognizing and Writing **r**-Blends
38	Recognizing and Writing **s**-Blends
39	Recognizing and Writing Final Blends
40	Reviewing Consonant Blends
41	Connecting Spelling and Writing
42	Integrating Language Arts

Take-Home Book: *City Beat*

Curriculum Integration

Spelling   A *Spelling Connection* appears in most lessons.

Writing   Children write letters, descriptions, captions, and observations on pages 70, 78, 80, 84, 86, and 87.

Math   Involvement in mathematics is fostered through activities on pages 72 and 76.

Social Studies   Activities involving social studies are found on pages 70, 76, 84, and 87.

Science   Science-related activities appear on page 78.

Optional Learning Activities

Multisensory Activities   Every lesson includes activities that appeal to visual, auditory, tactile, or kinesthetic learning styles.

Multicultural Connection   Children celebrate city living in activities that emphasize cultural diversity on pages 70, 78, 80, and 82.

Thematic Activities   *Extending the Skill Across the Curriculum* in each lesson reinforces thematic activities.

Lois Lenski

Lois Lenski grew up at the turn of the century in a small town in Ohio. Although she became interested in art in the third grade, drawing paper was scarce, so Lenski drew on the backs of used envelopes her father would throw away. She traced pictures of flowers from catalogs and painted them in watercolors. Lenski began her career as an artist, but later in her professional life she wrote stories to accompany her artwork.

Author's Corner

Assessment Strategies

Multiple strategies such as *Observational Assessments,* writing portfolios, written middle- and end-of-the-unit assessments, and the *Skills Checklist* at the back of the Student Edition will help you assess children's mastery of phonics skills throughout Unit 4.

Resources

Works by Lois Lenski
Little Airplane. Cowboy Small. New York: McKay, 1980.

Little Auto. New York: McKay, 1980.

Little Farm. New York: McKay, 1980.

Assessment

In Unit 4 children focus on recognizing and writing variant consonant sounds and consonant blends. The following are suggestions for evaluating these skills through informal/formal, observational, objective, portfolio, and performance assessments. You may also wish to refer to *Using Technology* for alternative assessment activities.

Informal/Formal Assessment

The tests on pages 67D, 67E, and 67F assess children's mastery of the skill of recognizing and writing variant consonant sounds and consonant blends.

These tools may be used informally at the beginning of the unit to identify a starting point for individual or class instruction or formally at the end of the unit to assess children's progress.

Observational Assessment

Specific opportunities for observation are highlighted in the lesson plans. *Multisensory Activities* offers additional chances for observation.

Objective Assessment

Use the assessment pages throughout the unit. Determine the area(s) in which children would benefit from more instruction; then refer to *Reteaching Activities* found throughout the unit in the Teacher's Edition. Finally, reassess children's progress.

Portfolio Assessment

Display pictures, photographs, or postcards of cities around the world. Then have children name things they would like in a perfect city. List their responses on the board.

Invite children to work in small groups to write a story about the perfect city. Tell groups that each child should write about one part of the city, such as the traffic, stores, or parks. Remind children to follow the five steps they have learned for writing a story. Direct them to underline any words with blends they have learned in this unit.

Have children add their stories to their portfolios.

Performance Assessment

Invite children to write a speech to welcome a visitor from another country. Tell children to name their city: **c** City, **g** City, **l**-blend City, **r**-blend City, or **s**-blend City. Explain that everything in each city is connected with its name.

Model this description:

> Welcome to **c** City. It is very easy to find your way around our city because the names of all of the streets begin with **c**. I live on **Cedar** Street. My friend lives on **Candy** Lane.

Make sure children use the five writing steps.

Using Technology

Have children complete the activities on pages 67K–67L of the Teacher's Edition.

Answer Key

Page 67D
1. Hard **c** 2. Soft **c** 3. Hard **c** 4. Soft **c** 5. Hard **c** 6. Soft **c**
7. gym 8. gem 9. giraffe 10. game 11. gull 12. dragon

Page 67E
1. spoon 2. prize 3. flag 4. screen 5. bride 6. smoke
7. blocks 8. grill 9. slide 10. trains 11. street 12. glide
13. driving

Page 67F
1. mask 2. hand 3. lamp 4. king 5. fist 6. quilt
7. ant 8. gift 9. gold 10. nest 11. milk 12. pink
13. tent

Say the name of each picture. If the word has the soft **c** sound, circle **Soft c**. If the word has the hard **c** sound, circle **Hard c**.

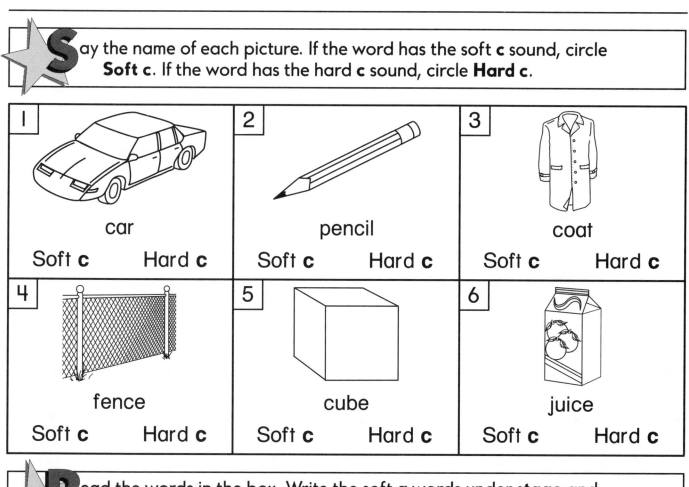

1	car	2	pencil	3	coat
	Soft **c**　　Hard **c**		Soft **c**　　Hard **c**		Soft **c**　　Hard **c**

4	fence	5	cube	6	juice
	Soft **c**　　Hard **c**		Soft **c**　　Hard **c**		Soft **c**　　Hard **c**

Read the words in the box. Write the soft **g** words under **stage** and the hard **g** words under **goat**.

gym	game	gull	gem	giraffe	dragon

stage

7. _____

8. _____

9. _____

goat

10. _____

11. _____

12. _____

Circle the blend that begins each picture name. Then write the blend beneath the picture to complete the word.

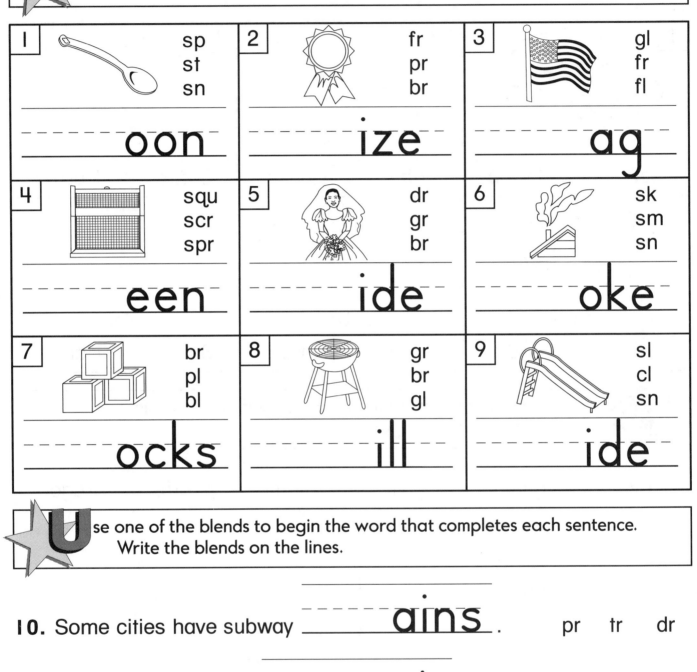

1. sp / st / sn — **oon**	2. fr / pr / br — **ize**	3. gl / fr / fl — **ag**
4. squ / scr / spr — **een**	5. dr / gr / br — **ide**	6. sk / sm / sn — **oke**
7. br / pl / bl — **ocks**	8. gr / br / gl — **ill**	9. sl / cl / sn — **ide**

Use one of the blends to begin the word that completes each sentence. Write the blends on the lines.

10. Some cities have subway _____ **ains** .   pr   tr   dr

11. Tracks run under the _____ **eet** .   spr   scr   str

12. The trains _____ **ide** along the tracks.   gl   cl   bl

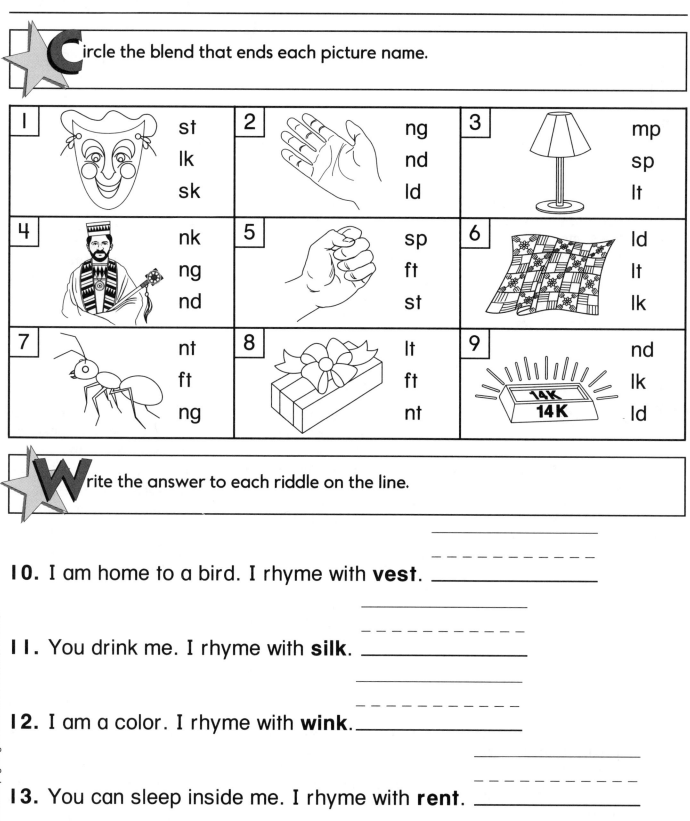

Circle the blend that ends each picture name.

1	st lk sk	2	ng nd ld	3	mp sp lt
4	nk ng nd	5	sp ft st	6	ld lt lk
7	nt ft ng	8	lt ft nt	9	nd lk ld

Write the answer to each riddle on the line.

10. I am home to a bird. I rhyme with **vest**. _____

11. You drink me. I rhyme with **silk**. _____

12. I am a color. I rhyme with **wink**. _____

13. You can sleep inside me. I rhyme with **rent**. _____

14. I march in a parade. I rhyme with **sand**. _____

Game Time

▲▽▲▽▲▽▲▽▲▽▲▽▲ Skyscraper Blends ▲▽▲▽▲▽▲▽▲▽

Blackline Master 14 p.67H

Objective: To match pictures to words that have the same initial consonant blends

Players: pairs

Materials: glue, construction paper, scissors

❂ Duplicate Blackline Master 14 and give a copy to each pair. Have children glue the page onto construction paper and cut out the cards. Encourage them to color the pictures.

❂ Tell partners to mix up the cards and each take half. Explain that the object of the game is to build

an unusual skyscraper by one player after the other laying down a card.

❂ Tell children they can build up, down, or to either side, as long as they match a picture to a word, or a word to a picture, with the same initial blend.

▲▽▲▽▲▽▲▽▲▽▲▽ Around the Block ▽▲▽▲▽▲▽▲▽▲▽

Blackline Master 15 p.67I

Objective: To read words with soft and hard c and g

Players: pairs

Materials: posterboard, glue, scissors, crayons

❂ Duplicate Blackline Master 15 and give a copy to each pair. Have children glue the paper onto posterboard and cut out the number squares and then place them facedown in a pile. Tell each player to cut out and color a tennis-shoe game marker as well.

❂ Direct partners to play the game as follows:

1. Players alternate picking a number card and moving that number of spaces on the board.

2. Players read the word on which they land and identify its **c** or **g** sound as soft or hard.

3. If the player responds correctly, he or she stays on the space. If not, the player must move back to her or his previous space.

4. The first player to "walk around the block" wins.

▲▽▲▽▲▽▲▽▲▽▲▽▲ Street Signs ▽▲▽▲▽▲▽▲▽▲▽▲

Objective: To identify final consonant blends in words

Players: whole class arranged in rows

❂ Give each row a street name with an ending blend. You might use **Ca**mp Street, W**es**t Street, Ba**nk** Street, Go**ld** Street, Ki**ng** Street, and Mi**nt** Street.

❂ Tell each "street" of children to stand when they hear you say a word that has the same ending blend as the name of their street.

❂ Say words with ending blends that match the streets you have chosen. You might say **jump, ramp, lamp, best, cast, fist, sink, trunk, tank, held, fold, sold, rent, went, sent, sing, long,** and **ring.**

❂ Play again, with the focus on beginning blends.

Skyscraper Blends

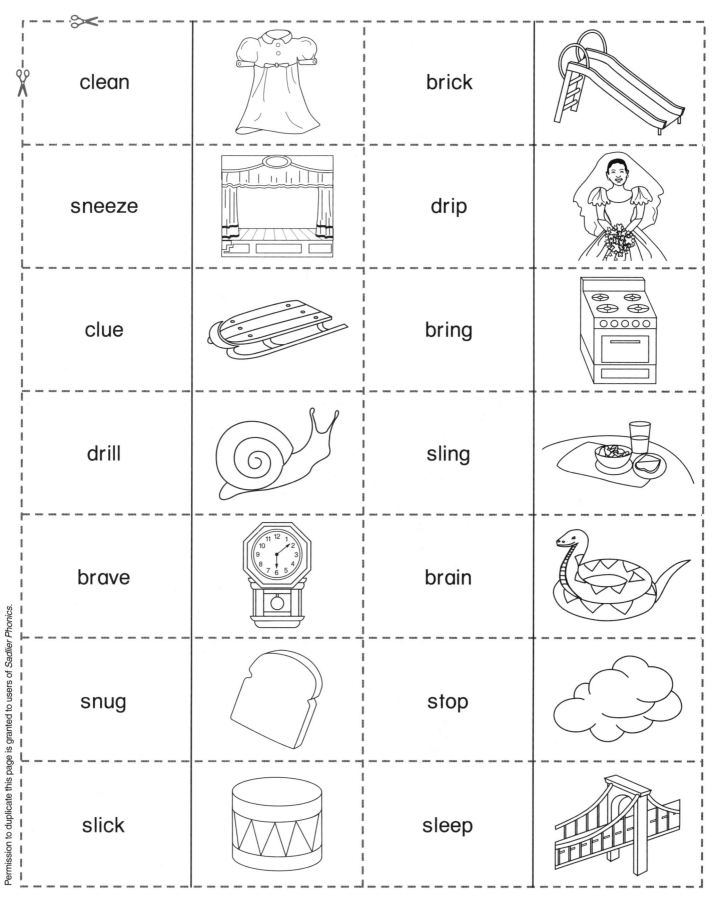

clean		brick	
sneeze		drip	
clue		bring	
drill		sling	
brave		brain	
snug		stop	
slick		sleep	

Around the Block

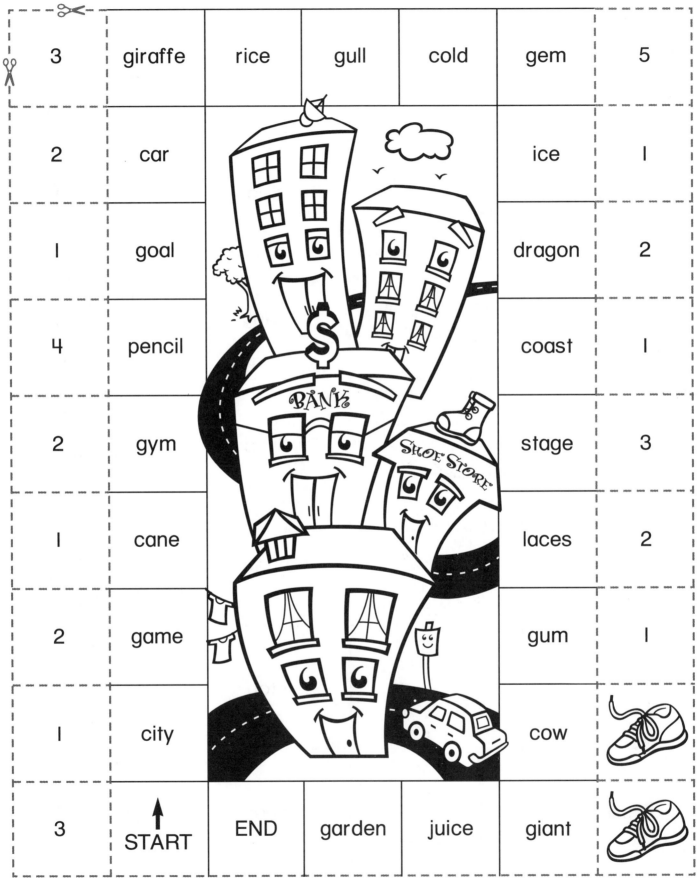

3	giraffe	rice	gull	cold	gem	5
2	car				ice	1
1	goal				dragon	2
4	pencil				coast	1
2	gym				stage	3
1	cane				laces	2
2	game				gum	1
1	city				cow	
3	↑ START	END	garden	juice	giant	

E S L Activities

Big Town, Small Town
Page 67

Present two pictures to the class: one, a bustling city scene; the other, a tranquil country scene. Invite children to discuss the similarities and differences between a big city and a small town. Provide craft materials, and have children make dioramas of city or country scenes. You might follow this up with a class reading of Aesop's fable about a city mouse and a country mouse.

Sounds of the City
Page 67

Direct each child to make a posterboard sign that illustrates a stanza of the poem. Possible illustrations include: a car honking (extended lines may be used for noise); a truck filled to the brim; a whistle blowing; red and green traffic lights. Recite the poem together, and have children raise their signs as the appropriate stanzas are read. You might also provide rhythm instruments and noisemakers to embellish the reading.

Winter Fun
Page 70

Have children work in groups. Direct each group to prepare a brief skit about Celia and Carrie. Tell them to include a choreographed dance on the ice pond. Have the groups present their skits to the class.

Word Scrambles
Page 85

Use the words in the box on page 85 to make a list of twelve scrambled words. Have children work in groups, and give each group a copy of the scrambled word list. The first group to unscramble the words correctly wins.

You're the Author
Page 87

Have children work in pairs. Direct each pair to write a paragraph about what might be happening inside one of the buildings illustrated or where one of the cars might be going. Allow time for children to share their work with the class.

Our City
Page 87

Initiate a class discussion on the layout of your city. Divide the city into four or five sections, and have children name the principal buildings, monuments, structures, streets, fields, and so forth in each section. Record the information on the board or on chart paper. Then have children work in groups to depict the city on strips of scroll paper. Assign one section to each group, and tell them to draw and color their section's prominent features. Arrange the different strips together to form a mural map of the city. To extend the activity, you might have children take photos of principal sites and then attach the photos to the appropriate locations of the mural.

TECH TALK

The Missing Blends

Objectives
- To review r-, s-, l-blends and initial and final blends
- To use a program such as Microsoft® Fine Artist* to review consonant blends

Preparation
Read *Taxi: A Book of City Words* by Betsy Maestro (Houghton Mifflin). Have children identify words that are about the city. Add them to the Theme Words chart. Then ask children to name the blends that they recognize.

One Step at a Time

1. Have the class work independently or in small groups. Have children on Microsoft® Fine Artist go straight to the Painting Studio to "paint something new."

2. Ask children to look at the Theme Words chart. Review the different kinds of blends. Tell children to choose one of the blends and make an animated illustration depicting words that contain the blend.

3. Direct children to think of words that contain their blend. Then tell them to use the stamps and drawing and paint tools to depict one or more of the blend words. Encourage children to use moving stamps and characters for which they can add comic balloons.

4. Have children add one or more comic balloons that include the blend, a blend word, and a sentence using the featured blend word. For a stamp of a child playing baseball, a comic balloon might read: "**pl/playing: Playing** baseball is fun."

5. Have children print their completed illustrations and then cover the speech balloons with self-sticking notepaper.

Class Sharing

Have children work in small groups. Tell each child to present his or her illustration to the group, who then will guess the covered blend words and sentences. Then tell the presenter to lift the notepaper and read the text.

You might display the illustrations on a bulletin board or in the Reading Corner for children to use to practice reading blends.

City Movies

Objectives

● To recognize and write words with the soft and hard c and g sounds

● To use E-mail, encyclopedia software, and a word-processing/paint program to produce a play about cities

Preparation

Reread the text on page 87. Have students read words and identify each soft and hard c and g. Then ask volunteers to locate New York, Los Angeles, Chicago, Houston, and Philadelphia on a map. Explain that millions of people live in these cities. Tell children that they are going to learn how these cities are the same and different. Then allot specific on-line time for the class.

One Step at a Time

1 Have children work in five groups. Assign a different city to each group.

2 Have children brainstorm what they want to learn about each city, such as the kind of weather, kinds of transportation, type of land (hilly, flat), and so on. List these on the board.

3 Encourage children to E-mail requests for information to young people in other cities or to use the multimedia encyclopedia to research information.

4 Have each group use a program with writing and graphics tools, such as Kid Works™ 2*, to write a report on its assigned city. Tell children to include pictures and/or charts.

5 Have children print their illustrated reports.

Class Sharing

Give children time to rehearse presenting their reports. Then have each group give its presentation. Ask the class to name the cities' similarities and differences. List these on the board. You might invite parents to attend the presentations.

A New York Tour

Show the video *My New York* (Spoken Arts). Have children name the different places to visit in New York. List each place and things to do there on the Theme Words chart.

Have children work in small groups. Give each group the name of a place in New York. Tell each group to write a short play about visiting that place. Help children write dialogue for each person in the group. Allow time for rehearsals.

Have one child be a "tour guide" and announce each place to visit. Then have each group perform its play. Videotape the performances. Invite other classes to the show!

All referenced software is listed under Computer Resources on page T46.

Literature Introduction to Variant Consonant Sounds and Blends

Objectives
- To enjoy a poem about cities
- To identify soft and hard **c** and **g**
- To identify consonant blends

Starting with Literature

Recite the poem "City Street" on page 67. Ask children what they see in the illustration. Then together recite the poem. Ask children what sounds they hear on the streets where they live.

Developing Critical Thinking
Use the questions at the bottom of page 67 to engage children in a discussion about how their community compares with the one in the poem.

Introducing the Skill

- Write **cars, city, go,** and **gem** on the board. Have a child underline the c's and g's. Say the words together. Explain that **c** and **g** each make a soft and a hard sound.

- Write **stop** and **honk** on the board. Have students say the words and name the underlined consonants. Explain that two or three consonants sounded together so that each is heard, like **st** in **stop**, is called a *blend*.

Practicing the Skill

- Invite children to scan the poem for words that have a **c**. Have them say each word.

- Ask children to list from the poem five words that have consonant blends. Encourage them to share their lists.

CITY STREET

Honk—honk—honk!
Beep—beep—beep!
Hear the noise
Of city street.

Cars race fast,
Trucks bump past;
Creeping slow
The buses go.

Green turns red,
A sudden stop;
Up the hand
Of traffic cop.

Whistle shrill—
All is still;
Sudden hush—
The people rush.

Red turns green,
Then on again;
Cars race fast,
Trucks bump past.

Lois Lenski

Critical Thinking
How is the place where you live like this busy city?
How is it different?

LESSON 32: Introduction to Variant Consonant Sounds and Consonant Blends

67

In the City Reread the poem "City Street" to the class. Show assorted pictures of cities at different times of day and during different seasons. Ask students to name some distinctive features of a city. Write responses on a word chart that will be utilized and added to throughout this unit.

At the end of the unit, the word chart will be helpful for assessing children's ability to recognize the soft and hard sounds of **c** and **g** and initial and final consonant blends. Children may refer to the word chart as they write sentences about a visit to a city and describe their experiences there. Similarly, the display pictures will be extremely helpful for children unfamiliar with a city setting.

Dear Family,

As your child progresses through this unit about cities, she or he will learn about the two sounds of **c** and **g** and about consonant blends. A **consonant blend** is two or three consonants sounded together in a word so that each letter is heard.

- Read the words below. Listen to the sounds of the letters that are underlined.

Apreciada Familia:

En esta unidad sobre las ciudades, su niño aprenderá los dos sonidos de las letras **c** y **g** y sobre combinación de sonidos de las consonantes. Una **combinación de sonido** se forma cuando dos o más consonantes están juntas pero cada una tiene su propio sonido al pronunciar la palabra.

- Lean las siguientes palabras. Escuchen el sonido de las letras subrayadas.

Soft c	Hard c		Soft g	Hard g		Consonant Blends	
<u>c</u>ity	<u>c</u>ar		<u>g</u>ym	<u>g</u>o		<u>pl</u>ay	re<u>nt</u>

- Read the poem "City Street" on the reverse side.
- Talk about the city scene.
- Point out the consonant sounds in these words from the poem: soft **c** (**c**ity, ra**c**e); hard **c** (**c**ars, **c**op); hard **g** (**g**o); consonant blends (**h**o**nk**, **st**reet, fa**st**, **tr**ucks, bu**mp**, **cr**eeping, **sl**ow, **gr**een, **st**op, ha**nd**, **tr**affic).

- Lean la poesía "City Street" en la página 67.
- Hablen de la escena en la ciudad.
- Señalen los sonidos de las consonantes en estas palabras de la poesía: **c** suave (**c**ity, ra**c**e); **c** fuerte (**c**ars, **c**op); **g** fuerte (**g**o); combinación de consonantes (**h**o**nk**, **st**reet, fa**st**, **tr**ucks, bu**mp**, **cr**eeping, **sl**ow, **gr**een, **st**op, ha**nd**, **tr**affic).

PROJECT

Make a city skyscraper with your child. Use index cards or rectangular pieces of paper for the bricks. When your child learns a new word with soft or hard **c** or **g** or with a consonant blend, have him or her write the word on a brick and add it to the building.

sink
brick
skate / plane
game / giant
bag / stage
cent / nice
came / cube

PROYECTO

Junto con el niño hagan un rascacielos. Use tarjetas 3X5 o pedazos de papel para los ladrillos. Cuando el niño aprenda una palabra nueva con sonidos suave o fuerte de la **c** o la **g**, o de combinación, pídale escribir la palabra en un ladrillo y pegarlo al edificio.

LESSON 32: Introduction to Variant Consonant Sounds and Consonant Blends—Phonics Alive at Home

Phonics Alive at Home

- The *Phonics Alive at Home* page is intended to get families actively involved in their children's reading and writing development through activities that apply phonics skills. In this unit the page includes activities related to the theme of cities and to the phonics focus on consonant sounds and consonant blends.

- Have children tear page 68 from their books, and suggest that they complete the activities at home with family members.

- Encourage children to bring to class pictures of special places in their neighborhood to share with the class.

- Provide opportunities for children to share books they have read about cities, as well as any photos, drawings, or writings they may have produced on the subject.

- Ask children to take notes or keep an informal journal about things they see and do in their city or town. If children live in a rural area, have them tell or write about times they have gone into a downtown area or traveled to a city. Children may also enjoy bringing in related newspaper articles or magazine pictures about city life.

ESL Activities

ESL activities are referenced throughout this unit. These activities benefit the ESL child in your classroom by providing additional language experiences. Choose the activities that best meet the diverse needs of your class.

For ESL activities related to "City Street," refer to page 67J.

Take-Home Book

In keeping with the city theme of Unit 4, we encourage children to read and reread to family members *City Beat*, found on pages 215–216 of the Student Edition. This fold-up book will also reinforce the consonant blend phonics skills taught in this lesson. You may use this take-home component as a culminating activity, or send it home at another appropriate time during the unit.

33

Student Pages 69–70

Recognizing and Writing Soft and Hard c

Objectives
- To recognize soft and hard **c** sounds
- To write soft and hard **c** words

Warming Up

Reviewing Initial Consonants
- Write this rhyme on the board:

  Stop, look, and listen
  Before you cross the street.
  Use your eyes, use your ears,
  Then use your feet!

- Read the rhyme together as a class. Then say, one word at a time, **library, fountain, subway, car,** and **bus,** and ask students to identify words in the poem that begin with the same sounds.

★ Teaching the Lesson

- Reread with the class "City Street" from the poetry poster. Ask volunteers to point to the words **cars** and **cop** in the poem. Elicit from children that these words begin with the same sound. Tell them it is called a *hard c* sound.

- Focus on the word **city** in the poem. Elicit that **city** begins with the letter **c** but with a different sound than **cars** and **cop.** Tell children that the **c** in **city** is a *soft c* that sounds like the sound of **s.** Focus children's attention on the rule in the Helpful Hint box on page 69. Ask them how this rule applies to **city.**

- Invite children to follow along as you read "The Cold Day" on page 70. Direct them to raise their hands when they hear hard **c** words. Then challenge children to find the soft **c** words.

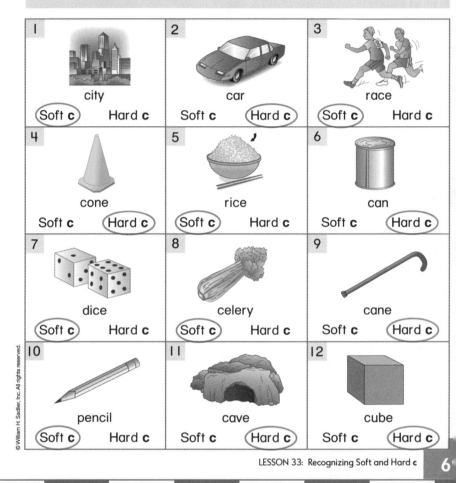

C usually has the soft sound when it is followed by **e, i,** or **y.**

City has the soft **c** sound. **Car** has the hard **c** sound. Say the name of each picture. Circle **Soft c** if the word has the soft **c** sound. Circle **Hard c** if it has the hard **c** sound.

1 city — (Soft c) Hard c	2 car — Soft c (Hard c)	3 race — (Soft c) Hard c
4 cone — Soft c (Hard c)	5 rice — (Soft c) Hard c	6 can — Soft c (Hard c)
7 dice — (Soft c) Hard c	8 celery — (Soft c) Hard c	9 cane — Soft c (Hard c)
10 pencil — (Soft c) Hard c	11 cave — Soft c (Hard c)	12 cube — Soft c (Hard c)

LESSON 33: Recognizing Soft and Hard **c**

6

© William H. Sadlier, Inc. All rights reserved.

Multisensory *Activities*

Auditory ■ Tactile

Soft and Hard c's

Materials: cardboard, tracing paper

Make one large **c** on cardboard and another on tracing paper. Tape both to the board, and elicit from the class that **cardboard** has the hard **c** sound and **tracing** has the soft **c.** Then say the following words, and have volunteers write each under the letter that represents its **c** sound: **cart, nice, place, cement, coin, can, police, corner, car, fence, city,** and **colorful.**

Visual ■ Auditory

City c's

Write the following tongue twister on the board: "Cindy Carns carefully sat on a cement curb counting colorful cabs." Challenge children to copy the sentence on paper and to repeat it several times. Have them circle words that have a soft **c** sound and underline those with a hard **c** sound. Then encourage children to write their own **c** tongue twisters to share with the class.

69

Read the story. Underline the hard **c** words.
Write the soft **c** words below.

The Cold Day

It was a <u>cold</u> day. <u>Carrie</u> <u>called</u> her friend Celia. "I'm going ice skating," <u>Carrie</u> said. "<u>Can</u> you <u>come</u>?"

The two friends walked to the pond in the center of the city. They skated to <u>music</u> and made up a dance. <u>Carrie's</u> face was red from the wind. "It's time to go," she said. "Let's race."

At home <u>Carrie's</u> mom made them a <u>cup</u> of hot <u>cocoa</u>. "This is the best place to be on a <u>cold</u> day," <u>Carrie</u> said.

Celia   ice

center   city

dance   face

race   place

LESSON 33: Recognizing and Writing Soft and Hard **c**

0

Spelling Connection

Read aloud the words and sentences below. After each sentence, have volunteers spell the featured word or write it on the board.

cap	Juan is wearing a baseball **cap**.
car	A red **car** is on the street.
city	Lee lives in a big **city**.
nice	Be **nice** to your friends.
coat	Where is my blue **coat**?

Multicultural Connection

Background Information All over the world, people's livelihoods are often dictated by whether they live in the city or country. In the country, people might tend to the land and animals; in the city, high-rise buildings, noise, and crowded streets point toward different ways of earning a living.

Activity Ask children first to imagine life in a large city and then life on a farm in the countryside. Have them share ideas and draw pictures of where they would prefer to live.

Practicing the Skill

● Review the Helpful Hint and read the directions on page 69. Do the first item together; then have children complete the page.

● Remind children that they have already read the story on page 70. Go over the directions; then have children complete the page.

Extending the Skill Across the Curriculum

(Language Arts/Social Studies)

Theme Activity

● Write **city** and **country** on the board. Have children identify each word's beginning sound and discuss where they prefer to live.

● Read to the class the theme book(s) cited below. List on the board "city" and "country" words children name from the reading. Include **office, traffic, cathedral, tractor, cows,** and **space,** and ask children which sound of **c** is in each.

● Direct children to write letters inviting and persuading a friend in the country to visit the city. Have them circle any hard **c** words and underline any soft **c** words used.

Theme Books

Provensen, Alice and Martin. *Town & Country.* NY: Crown, 1984. Life in a big city and scenes on a farm.

Gray, Nigel. *A Country Far Away.* NY: Orchard, 1989. Parallel lives in an African village and a Western city.

Observational Assessment
Check children's letters, not for spelling, but for ability to discriminate between soft and hard c words.

Portfolio
Have children add their letters to their portfolios.

ESL Activities
Refer to page 67J.

Lesson 34

Recognizing and Writing Soft and Hard g

Objectives
- To recognize soft and hard **g** sounds
- To write soft and hard **g** words

Warming Up

Reviewing Soft and Hard c

Say these words, one at a time: **city, cement, cabs, faces, celebrations, music, coffee, tacos, popcorn, cider,** and **cool**. Have volunteers identify the soft **c** or hard **c** sound in each.

★ Teaching the Lesson

- Write on the board: "Going to Gary's, I saw a giant gas station, a huge bridge, and some girls playing a game of tag."
- Read the sentence aloud; then invite a volunteer to underline the words **going, Gary's, gas, girls, game,** and **tag.** Elicit from the class that these words all have the same sound of **g.** Tell children that this sound is called the *hard g* sound.
- Have another volunteer circle the words **giant, huge,** and **bridge.** Elicit from the class that the **g** sound in these words is different than that in the underlined words. Tell them that this sound is called the *soft g* sound and is the same as the sound of **j.**
- Share with children the Helpful Hint on page 71. Then ask them to find in the sentence on the board words with a **g** sound that can be explained by this rule. Make sure children realize that there are exceptions to the rule, such as **girl** and **get.**

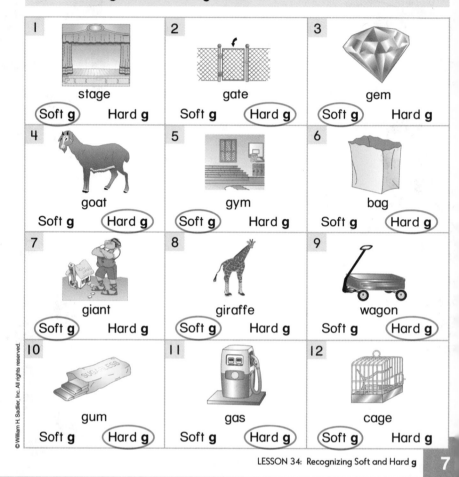

G usually has the soft sound when it is followed by **e, i,** or **y.**

Stage has the soft **g** sound. **Gate** has the hard **g** sound. Say the name of each picture. Circle **Soft g** if the word has the soft **g** sound. Circle **Hard g** if it has the hard **g** sound.

1 stage	2 gate	3 gem
(Soft g) Hard g	Soft g (Hard g)	(Soft g) Hard g
4 goat	5 gym	6 bag
Soft g (Hard g)	(Soft g) Hard g	Soft g (Hard g)
7 giant	8 giraffe	9 wagon
(Soft g) Hard g	(Soft g) Hard g	Soft g (Hard g)
10 gum	11 gas	12 cage
Soft g (Hard g)	Soft g (Hard g)	(Soft g) Hard g

LESSON 34: Recognizing Soft and Hard **g**   7

Multisensory *Activities*

Visual ■ Kinesthetic

Jump-Rope Rhymes

Write on the board and recite the following jump-rope rhyme:

> My name is Gordon,
> And my wife's name is Ginny,
> We come from Geneva,
> Where we sell gum!

Have children identify the soft and hard **g** words that they hear. Then invite them to jump in place as they recite the rhyme and substitute their own initial **g** words for the last word in each line.

Auditory ■ Tactile

Green Means Go

Materials: green paper strips

Call attention to the use of "green" and "red" in "City Street." Elicit from children that a green traffic light means go and red means stop. Give each child a strip of green paper. Tell students to wave their green strips only when they hear a word with a hard **g** sound. Then say these words, one at a time: **gum, gentle, leg, bug, page, good, gum,** and **wagon.**

Read the movie titles on the posters. Underline the hard **g** words. Write the soft **g** words.

Gigi
Gentle
Giraffe

Giant
Gym

Gina
Magic

Make a movie poster. Write the title of a make-believe movie and draw a picture to go with it. In the title, use one soft **g** word and one hard **g** word.

LESSON 34: Recognizing and Writing Soft and Hard **g**

Spelling Connection

Read aloud the words and sentences below. After each sentence have volunteers spell the featured word or write it on the board.

game Will you play a **game** of tag with me?

huge There are **huge** buildings in the city.

gas Where is the **gas** station?

gym I went to the **gym** to play basketball.

goal My **goal** is to visit cities around the world.

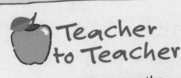

Teacher to Teacher

Draw two skyscrapers on the board. Use horizontal lines to indicate floors. Have the class work in two teams; assign each team a building. Direct players to alternate writing on each floor soft and hard **c** or **g** words. Tell children each correct word advances the building's elevator one floor. The first team to reach the top wins!

S. Marianne Therese Somerville, NJ

Practicing the Skill

- Review the Helpful Hint and the directions on page 71. Then have the class complete the page.

- Explain the directions on page 72. After children complete the page, challenge them to make their own movie posters, as suggested in *Taking Off*.

Extending the Skill Across the Curriculum

(Math/Art)

Theme Activity

Materials: boxes, construction paper, tape, scissors, markers, glue

- Ask children to name different kinds of buildings found in cities, such as museums, apartments, and office buildings. Make a class list on the board, and add to it after you read the theme book(s) cited below.

- Have each child work with a partner to make a model of one of the buildings on the board. Give each pair a box. Tell children to tape construction paper around their box and then to draw in windows and doors to make it look like a building. Have them give their building an initial **g** name and post it on the model.

- Line up the buildings to indicate streets in "**G** City," and secure them to a large piece of chart paper. Have volunteers label the streets with soft and hard **g** names. Ask children to identify the **g** sound in each.

- Use the buildings to solve math problems. For example: How many buildings are on Gem Street and Golf Lane? Which has more windows: Ginny's Cafe or Giant Shoes? Invite students to make up their own problems.

Theme Books

Maestro, Betsy. *Taxi: A Book of City Words.* Boston: Clarion, 1989. A taxi ride builds city vocabulary.

Florian, Douglas. *City Street.* NY: Greenwillow, 1990. Vibrant street scenes captioned with rhymes.

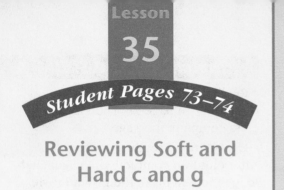

Lesson 35

Reviewing Soft and Hard c and g

Objectives
● To recognize the sounds of soft and hard **c** and **g**
● To write soft and hard **c** and **g** words

Warming Up

Reviewing Rhyming Words
Show the class Phonics Picture Cards in sets of three, such that two picture names in each set rhyme. Invite children to name the pictures and identify the rhyming words. Use these cards: **cake, bike, rake; pen, ten, van; bug, tag, rug; suit, fruit, boat; tree, green, bee; king, ring, igloo; box, six, ox; toad, hand, band; jam, ham, hat.**

★ Teaching the Lesson

● Call children's attention to the illustrations on page 73. Ask them what activities are shown in the pictures and which activities they like the best.

● Call attention to the *Remember* logo at the top of the page, and ask children what it means. Have one volunteer read the directions aloud, and ask another to read the words in the box below the directions.

● Demonstrate how to complete the poem by writing this example on the board:

  Garth came to the park to play (tag).
  Later he collected trash in a bag.

Ask children to complete the rhyme using one of the following words: **hopscotch, tag, music.** Then ask a volunteer to circle the hard **c** and hard **g** words in the couplet.

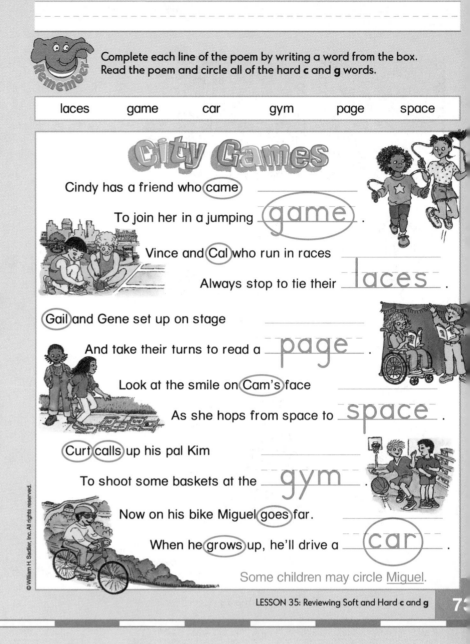

Complete each line of the poem by writing a word from the box. Read the poem and circle all of the hard **c** and **g** words.

laces	game	car	gym	page	space

City Games

Cindy has a friend who (came) _____
To join her in a jumping (game).
Vince and (Cal) who run in races
Always stop to tie their laces.
(Gail) and Gene set up on stage
And take their turns to read a page.
Look at the smile on (Cam's) face
As she hops from space to space.
(Curt) (calls) up his pal Kim
To shoot some baskets at the gym.
Now on his bike Miguel (goes) far.
When he (grows) up, he'll drive a (car).

Some children may circle Miguel.

LESSON 35: Reviewing Soft and Hard **c** and **g**   73

Multisensory *Activities*

Auditory ■ Kinesthetic

Simon Says Circle Game
Play a version of Simon says. Tell children to follow only those directions that contain words with a soft **c** or **g**. Give directions like these:

  Take two **giant** steps to the right.
  Call your name.
  Hop in **place**.
  Gently touch the floor.
  Point to a **shoelace**.
  Giggle softly.
  Make a funny **face**.

Tactile ■ Visual

Building Giant Skyscrapers
Materials: markers, colored paper strips, shelf paper, tape

Have children work in small groups. Distribute small, colored paper strips to each group. Give children five minutes to write on separate strips words with a soft or hard **c** or **g** sound. Then invite the groups to tape the strips, one above another, onto a long stretch of shelf paper to make floors of a "**c** and **g** skyscraper."

73

Check-Up Circle the words in each list that have the same **c** or **g** sound as the picture name.

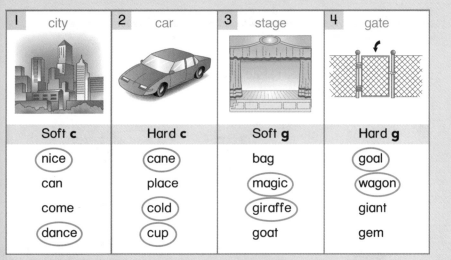

1 city	2 car	3 stage	4 gate
Soft c	**Hard c**	**Soft g**	**Hard g**
(nice)	(cane)	bag	(goal)
can	place	(magic)	(wagon)
come	(cold)	(giraffe)	giant
(dance)	(cup)	goat	gem

Write **S** beside each word that has the sound of soft **c** or **g**. Write **H** beside each word that has the sound of hard **c** or **g**.

5 cup H	6 center S	7 page S	8 gate H
9 gull H	**10** face S	**11** ice S	**12** car H
13 gym S	**14** cage S	**15** gas H	**16** cube H
17 race S	**18** fence S	**19** game H	**20** gentle S

LESSON 35: Assessing Soft and Hard **c** and **g**

Reteaching *Activities*

I Spy c's and g's

Have children work in two teams. Allow each team five minutes to search the classroom for items whose names contain the sound of soft or hard **c** or **g**. Have them list the items on paper. Encourage children to refer to pictures in books and on posters, as well as to actual objects in the room. The team with the most items listed wins.

Soft or Hard

Allow time for each child to find one small object that is hard and another that is soft. Tell children to hold up their hard objects when they hear you say a word with a hard **c** or **g**, and their soft objects when they hear a word with a soft **c** or **g**. Say words such as: **car, gentle, place, gum, city, leg, page, corner, pencil, coin, goat**, and **nice**.

Recognizing and Writing l-Blends

Objectives
- To recognize the sounds of **l**-blends
- To write words with **l**-blends

Warming Up

Reviewing Initial Consonants

Materials: Phonics Picture Cards

- Write this rhyme on chart paper:

  The busy downtown is booming
  With cars beep-beeping and zooming.
  Can you hear the loud honks and toots
  Of cabs and buses on their routes?

Recite the rhyme with the class.

- Show, one at a time, picture cards **balloon, cap, horn, leaf, red, toys,** and **zipper**. Have students name the pictures and identify words in the rhyme that have the same initial sound.

★ Teaching the Lesson

Materials: Phonics Picture Cards

- Write this sentence on the board:
  Slowly Blake climbed up the slippery slide at the playground.

Have a volunteer read the sentence aloud.

- Circle each initial **l**-blend. Tell the class that the circled letters form initial consonant blends. Explain that a blend is two or three consonants sounded together so that the sound of each letter can still be heard. Have children read the Helpful Hint definition of a consonant blend at the top of page 75 and apply it to the words on the board.
- Hold up the following picture cards one at a time: **block, glass, clap, blue, plane,** and **cloud**. Invite children to say the picture name and to identify the **l**-blend in each name.

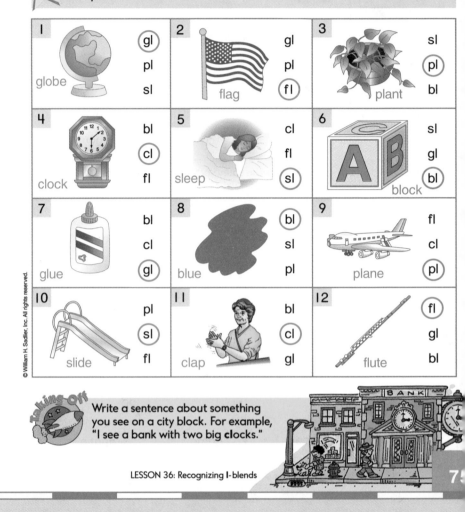

A **consonant blend** is two or three consonants sounded together in a word so that each letter is heard.

Globe begins with the **l**-blend **gl**. Circle the **l**-blend that begins each picture name.

1 globe — (gl) pl sl	2 flag — gl pl (fl)	3 plant — sl (pl) bl
4 clock — bl (cl) fl	5 sleep — cl fl (sl)	6 block — sl gl (bl)
7 glue — bl cl (gl)	8 blue — (bl) sl pl	9 plane — fl cl (pl)
10 slide — pl (sl) fl	11 clap — bl (cl) gl	12 flute — (fl) gl bl

Write a sentence about something you see on a city block. For example, "I see a bank with two big **cl**ocks."

LESSON 36: Recognizing l-blends

75

Multisensory *Activities*

Auditory ■ Kinesthetic

City Sounds Clapping

Write the word **clap** on the board, and ask children to identify the consonant blend. Tell children to clap their hands when they hear you say a word with an **l**-blend. Then say a list of sounds heard in a city; for example, **blare, beep, honk, slam, clank, hum, shout, clash, screech, crack, whistle, blast, crash, clomp, blip, slosh,** and **squeal**.

Visual ■ Auditory

City Riddles

On the board write **flag, cloud, glass,** and **black**. Have volunteers circle the **l**-blends. Tell children to use the words to answer the following riddles:

Windows are made of me. What am I? (**glass**)
I fly in front of city hall. What am I? (**flag**)
I am the color of night. What am I? (**black**)
I am something you see in the sky. What am I? (**cloud**)

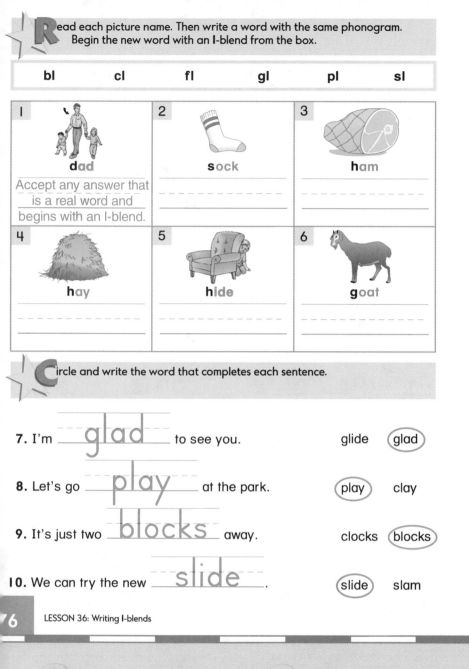

Read each picture name. Then write a word with the same phonogram. Begin the new word with an **l**-blend from the box.

bl	cl	fl	gl	pl	sl

1	2	3
dad	**s**ock	**h**am
Accept any answer that is a real word and begins with an l-blend.		

4	5	6
hay	**h**ide	**g**oat

Circle and write the word that completes each sentence.

7. I'm ___glad___ to see you.   glide   (glad)

8. Let's go ___play___ at the park.   (play)   clay

9. It's just two ___blocks___ away.   clocks   (blocks)

10. We can try the new ___slide___.   (slide)   slam

76

LESSON 36: Writing l-blends

Spelling Connection

Read each word and sentence aloud. Then have a volunteer spell the words or write them on the board.

block We drove around the **block**.
floor On what **floor** is your apartment?
glad I am **glad** I live in a city.
plant There is a **plant** growing by the sidewalk.
clock The **clock** tower is tall.

Computer Connection

Invite children to sharpen their spelling and vocabulary skills by playing Spell Dodger!™ (Arcadia Productions). Before children begin, select the game difficulty and word level for each child. Then direct children to collect letter tokens and solve spelling problems on Spell Dodger! Once children have collected all the letter tokens, they can move on to the next level and test their skill at catching falling letters to spell words.

Practicing the Skill

- Review the definition at the top of page 75. Ask volunteers to read the directions and identify the pictures. Do the first item together.
- Read aloud the directions on page 76. Ask children what word is formed when the phonogram **ow** is added to the first blend at the top of the page. (**blow**) Do the first item; then read aloud the remaining directions.
- Have children complete both pages. Tell them not to do the *Taking Off* activity on page 75 until after they have finished all other exercises.

Extending the Skill Across the Curriculum

(Social Studies/Math)

Theme Activity
Materials: mural paper

- Invite students to share experiences they have had shopping in a department store. Explain that some department stores have many floors.
- Draw the outline of a skyscraper on mural paper. Divide it into four floors, labeled Toys, Clothing, Kitchen Gear, and Florist. Ask children to name items that could be purchased on each floor.
- Read the following **l**-blend words, and ask volunteers to write each on its proper floor: **blocks, gloves, flowers, plates, blouses, blender, blooming plants, blue jeans, glasses, plastic planes, plaid pants, clown games, clay pots,** and **fluffy slippers.** Say the words with the class, and circle the blends.
- Use the department store setting for consumer-math problems such as: If Freida has sixty cents and she spends thirty cents on a plant, how much will she have left?

Observational Assessment
*As students say **l**-blend words, observe whether they are blending the consonants together yet still pronouncing the sound of each.*

76

Recognizing and Writing r-Blends

Objectives
● To recognize the sounds of **r**-blends
● To write words with **r**-blends

Warming Up

Reviewing I-Blends
● Write the word **pay** on the board. Beneath it, write the word **play**, and underline the blend **pl**. Elicit from children that the two words rhyme.

● List on the board: **back, fat, side, pan, boom, favor, sick, bow,** and **cub**. Have children read the words aloud. Then ask volunteers to say and write an **l**-blend rhyme for each.

★ Teaching the Lesson

Materials: Phonics Picture Cards
● Have children turn to the poem "City Street" on page 67. Call volunteers to the poetry poster to point to the words **trucks, creeping, green,** and **traffic** as you say them. Explain that these words begin with **r**-blends—consonants sounded with the consonant **r**. Have volunteers print the words on the board and circle the **r**-blends.

● Write **br, cr, dr, fr, gr, pr,** and **tr** on the board. Tell children that each pair of letters is an **r**-blend. Display the following picture cards one at a time: **brush, drum, grapes, prize, train, fruit,** and **truck**. Invite children to say the picture names and identify the **r**-blends.

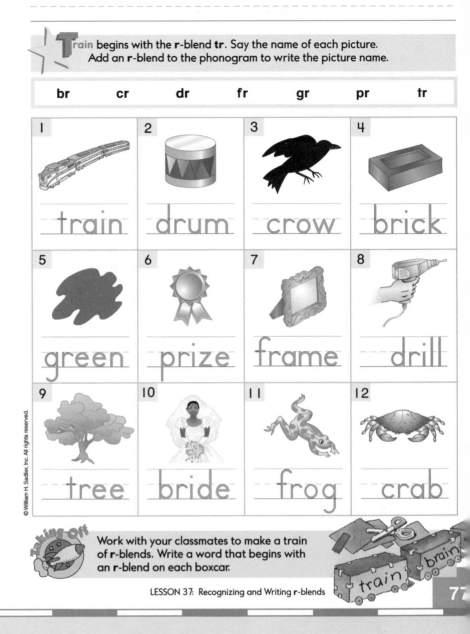

Train begins with the **r**-blend **tr**. Say the name of each picture. Add an **r**-blend to the phonogram to write the picture name.

br	cr	dr	fr	gr	pr	tr

1. train
2. drum
3. crow
4. brick
5. green
6. prize
7. frame
8. drill
9. tree
10. bride
11. frog
12. crab

Taking Off Work with your classmates to make a train of **r**-blends. Write a word that begins with an **r**-blend on each boxcar.

LESSON 37: Recognizing and Writing **r**-blends

77

Multisensory *Activities*

Visual ■ Kinesthetic

Great Groceries

Write **grocery** on the board and have children identify the blend. Ask children to think of grocery items that have **r**-blends in their names. List responses on the board. The list might include **bread, corn, grapefruit, pretzels,** and **crackers**. Have each student select a word and draw a picture of it. Tell students to label their pictures and circle the **r**-blends.

Auditory ■ Kinesthetic

Rollicking r-Blends

On chart paper write these words:

Drive, drive, drive the truck
Briskly down the street.
Carefully, carefully, carefully, carefully,
Braking with my feet.

Have volunteers circle the **r**-blends. Then sing the lyrics with the class to the tune of "Row, Row, Row Your Boat." Encourage students to pantomime driving a truck as they sing.

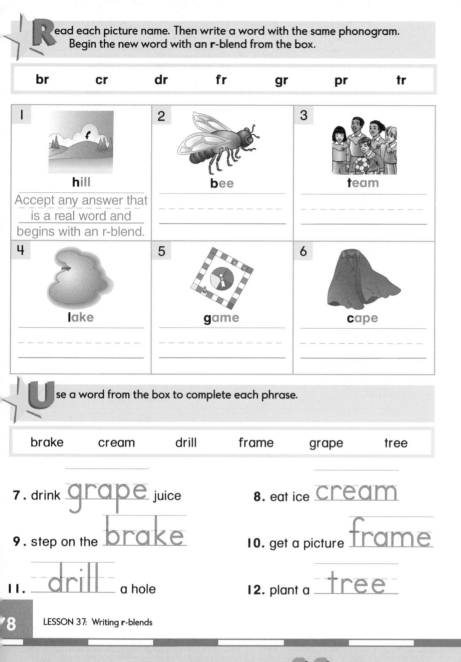

Read each picture name. Then write a word with the same phonogram. Begin the new word with an **r-blend** from the box.

br	cr	dr	fr	gr	pr	tr

1. hill

Accept any answer that is a real word and begins with an r-blend.

2. bee

3. team

4. lake

5. game

6. cape

Use a word from the box to complete each phrase.

brake	cream	drill	frame	grape	tree

7. drink grape juice

8. eat ice cream

9. step on the brake

10. get a picture frame

11. drill a hole

12. plant a tree

LESSON 37: Writing r-blends

78

Spelling Connection

Read each word and sentence aloud. Then have volunteers spell the words or write them on the board.

truck	The **truck** inched down the crowded street.
brick	There is a **brick** wall around the playground.
gray	The sky is **gray** and cloudy.
friend	I like playing in the park with my **friend** Brian.
grapes	Keiko bought some **grapes** at the market.

Multicultural Connection

Materials: Away from Home by Anita Lobel (Greenwillow), globe or atlas

Invite students to look at paintings of cities around the world in the picture book *Away from Home*. Challenge them to scan the pictures for objects whose names have r-blends. Then suggest that students work in pairs to locate some of the cities on a globe or in an atlas.

Practicing the Skill

● Read aloud the directions and consonant blends at the top of page 77. Ask what two consonant sounds are heard in each blend. Then invite volunteers to identify the pictures, and do the first item together.

● Have children turn to page 78. Call on volunteers to tell, in their own words, what to do in each section.

● Have children complete the exercises on both pages. Then have them do the *Taking Off* activity on page 77.

Extending the Skill Across the Curriculum

(Language Arts/Science)

Theme Activity

● Help children identify their five senses: touch, sight, smell, taste, and hearing. Then read the theme books cited below about using senses.

● Reread parts of the books, and ask students to raise their hands when they hear an **r-blend**.

● Take the class on a walk around the school grounds. Have children work in four groups; ask one student in each group to be a recorder. Tell two groups to concentrate on what they see, the other two on what they hear.

● Back in the classroom, encourage children to compare findings. Make a class observation list, and ask volunteers to circle **r-blends**.

● Have students write a paragraph on what they observed or heard. Encourage them to use **r-blend** words.

Theme Books

Jakobsen, Kathy. *My New York.* NY: Little, Brown, 1993. Becky writes to her friend in the country.

Komaiko, Leah. *My Perfect Neighborhood.* NY: HarperCollins, 1990. A humorous walk in a city.

Portfolio

Have students add their paragraphs to their portfolios.

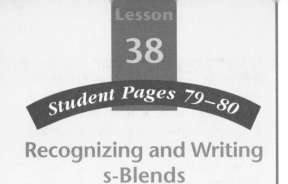

Recognizing and Writing s-Blends

Objectives
- To recognize the sounds of **s**-blends
- To write words with **s**-blends

Warming Up

Reviewing l-Blends and r-Blends
Materials: Phonics Picture Cards, blue and brown construction paper

- Cut a large blue flower and a brown triangle from construction paper. Tell children that **blue** and **flower** begin with **l**-blends, and **brown** and **triangle** begin with **r**-blends.

- Distribute picture cards **block, clap, glass, drum, grapes, prize, train, fruit, green, tree, truck,** and **brown**. Have students sort the pictures by blend.

★ Teaching the Lesson

- Ask children to turn to the poem "City Street" on page 67. Then call volunteers to the poetry poster, and have them point to the words **street, slow, stop,** and **still**. Explain that these words begin with **s**-blends; that is, **s** and one or two other letters sounded together.

- Write **scr, sl, sm, sn, sp, spr, squ, st,** and **str** on the board. Tell children that these are **s**-blends.

- Display on the chalk ledge the following picture cards: **screen, sled, smell, snail, spoon, spray, squirrel, star, swim, strawberry, snow, smoke,** and **screw**. Invite students to name the pictures and identify the **s**-blends. Then ask children to name other words that begin with **s**-blends, and list these on the board.

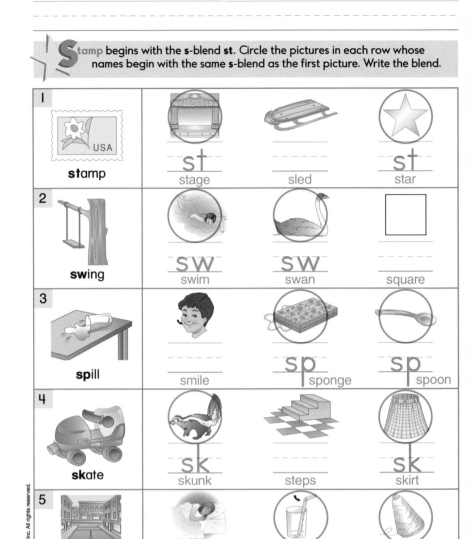

Stamp begins with the **s**-blend **st**. Circle the pictures in each row whose names begin with the same **s**-blend as the first picture. Write the blend.

1. stamp — st stage — sled — st star
2. swing — sw swim — sw swan — square
3. spill — smile — sp sponge — sp spoon
4. skate — sk skunk — steps — sk skirt
5. street — sleep — str straw — str string

LESSON 38: Recognizing and Writing **s**-blends

79

Multisensory *Activities*

Auditory ■ Kinesthetic

Stand or Sit?
Write **stand** and **sit** on the board and read the words aloud. Ask children to identify the word with the **s**-blend. Direct them to stand each time they hear you say an **s**-blend. Then say these "city" words:

smog	store	sidewalk
sewer	super	skyscraper
steel	smoke	siren
speed	street	subway
statue	sun	space
stairs	sounds	special

Visual ■ Kinesthetic

Act It Out
Write the following **s**-blend action words on chart paper:

stumble	slide	swim
sway	skip	snap
sniff	stir	spin
sneeze	sleep	spill
sweep	steer	stamp

Help the class read the words, and invite volunteers to circle the **s**-blends. Then call on students to pantomime a word while the class guesses the action and names the blend.

Write a word with an **s-blend** to answer each question.

sc	sm	sn	squ	spr

1. What tells your weight and rhymes with **tale**? scale

2. What sound made by a mouse rhymes with **beak**? squeak

3. What crawls in the grass and rhymes with **rake**? snake

4. What means "not large" and rhymes with **tall**? small

5. What comes after winter and rhymes with **wing**? spring

Circle and write an **s-blend** to complete the word in each sentence.

6. A big truck sweeps the city street. (str) sw sl

7. Brushes scrub the street clean. sc (scr) sn

8. The truck also sprays water. st (spr) spl

9. Watch out for the splash! sl sp (spl)

LESSON 38: Writing **s-blends**

 **S**pelling Connection

Read aloud each word and sentence. Then have volunteers spell the words or write them on the board.

skate   Would you like to **skate** with me?

swing   Imani likes to **swing** in the park.

square   There is a **square** sign over the shoe store.

smell   Do you **smell** the bread from the bakery?

sky   The **sky** is blue and clear today.

 **M**ulticultural Connection

Materials: Subway Sparrow by Leyla Torres (FS&G)

Read aloud *Subway Sparrow*, a story about a bird trapped in a New York subway train. Ask children to tell how strangers overcame language and age barriers to help the bird. Talk about different languages students hear where they live and about language-based misunderstandings. Write **sparrow** on the board, and circle the **s-blend**. Then reread the story, and have students find other **s-blends**.

Practicing the Skill

- Have volunteers read aloud the directions on page 79 and identify the pictures. Do the first item together. Be sure children circle the pictures of the **stage** and **star**, as well as write the blend **st** beneath each.

- Read aloud the directions on page 80, and together do the first item in each section. Then have children complete pages 79 and 80.

Extending the Skill Across the Curriculum

(Language Arts/Art)

Theme Activity

Materials: paper, yellow and black crayons, toothpicks, globe

- Ask students what causes day and night. Use a globe to explain that as the earth turns, the part of the earth facing the sun has day while the part turned away has night.

- Read to the class about night and day in cities. Use the theme books cited below.

- Ask the class to name **s-blend** words from the oral reading. List these on the board.

- Have each student color an entire sheet of paper first with yellow crayon and then with black over the yellow.

- Direct students to use a toothpick to scratch the outline of city buildings against the night sky. Tell them also to scratch out descriptive captions that include **s-blend** words, such as those listed on the board.

Theme Books

Greenfield, Eloise. *Night on Neighborhood Street.* NY: Dial, 1991. Poetic portraits of urban night.

Tresselt, Alvin. *Wake Up, City!* NY: Lothrop, Lee & Shepard, 1990. A city at daybreak.

Portfolio

Have students add their drawings and captions to their portfolios.

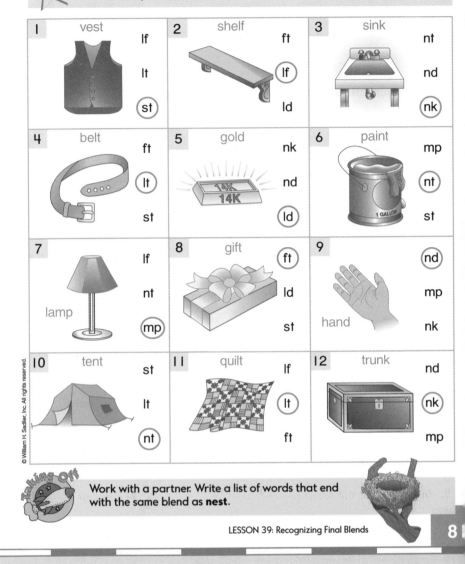

Lesson 39

Recognizing and Writing Final Blends

Objectives
- To recognize the sounds of final blends
- To write words with final blends

Warming Up

Reviewing Initial Blends
- Outline three skyscrapers on the board. Label them: **l**-blends, **r**-blends, and **s**-blends.
- Distribute Phonics Picture Cards **block, clap, glass, plane, grapes, prize, train, fruit, green, screen, smell, smoke,** and **screw**. Have students identify pictures and initial blends and place the cards under the appropriate buildings.

★ Teaching the Lesson

Materials: Phonics Picture Cards

- Focus children's attention on the "City Street" Poetry Poster. Recite the poem and have a volunteer point to the words **honk, fast, past, hand,** and **bump** as you say them. Have the class write the words on paper and circle the blends while a volunteer does the same on the board. Explain that these words have final consonant blends.

- Display, one at a time, picture cards **band, desk, giant, lamp, list, ring, sink, gift, king, mask, nest, quilt,** and **hand**. Invite children to say each picture name and identify its final consonant blend, while volunteers write the words on the board and circle the final blends.

Observational Assessment
Evaluate students' understanding of final blends. Ask, "How do you know when a word has a final blend?"

Vest ends with the consonant blend **st**. Circle the blend that ends each picture name.

1 vest	2 shelf	3 sink
lf / lt / **(st)**	ft / **(lf)** / ld	nt / nd / **(nk)**
4 belt	5 gold	6 paint
ft / **(lt)** / st	nk / nd / **(ld)**	mp / **(nt)** / st
7 lamp	8 gift	9 hand
lf / nt / **(mp)**	**(ft)** / ld / st	**(nd)** / mp / nk
10 tent	11 quilt	12 trunk
st / lt / **(nt)**	lf / **(lt)** / ft	nd / **(nk)** / mp

Work with a partner. Write a list of words that end with the same blend as **nest**.

Multisensory *Activities*

Auditory ■ Visual

Listen for the Final Blend
Materials: index cards

Write **st, nt, mp, nk, ng, nd,** and **lk** on separate index cards. Give a card to every child. Direct children to hold up their card when they hear a word with a blend that matches it. Say words associated with cities; for example:

ramp	hydrant	restaurant
honk	building	pavement
chalk	sidewalk	newsstand
bang	bump	playground

Visual ■ Tactile

See the Street Signs
Materials: crayons, paper

Ask children to read the street signs on the poetry poster. Then write on the board: **playground, parking, keep left, railroad crossing, bump, people working, dead end,** and **no smoking**. Have volunteers read the words and phrases aloud and circle the final blends. Then have children draw their own street signs.

Write a word with the same phonogram.

1 **v**est *Accept any answer that is a real word.*	2 **b**ump	3 **m**elt	4 **l**ift
5 **c**old	6 **w**ent	7 **b**end	8 **b**unk
9 **st**amp	10 **dr**ink	11 **st**and	12 **tw**ist

Use a word from the box to complete each sentence.

stand	went	best	drink

13. Last week Mom and I ___went___ to a street fair.

14. First we stopped at a fresh fruit ___stand___.

15. Then we got grape juice to ___drink___.

16. We had the ___best___ time together!

FRESH FRUIT

LESSON 39: Writing Final Blends

Spelling Connection

Read each word and sentence aloud. Then have volunteers spell the words or write them on the board.

best Where is the **best** place to play jump rope?

honk Please do not **honk** your horn.

song What **song** would you like to sing?

gift I made a **gift** for my friend's birthday.

walk Would you like to take a **walk** around the block?

Multicultural Connection

Materials: books cited below

Share multicultural city songs, chants, rhymes, and games. *Street Rhymes Around the World* edited by Jane Yolen (Boyds Mills) is a collection of 32 rhymes from 17 nations. Each rhyme is presented in its native language and English. *Hopscotch Around the World* by Mary D. Lankford (Morrow Jr) contains 19 hopscotch games from 16 countries. Complete game rules are given, as well as information on various cultural backgrounds.

Practicing the Skill

● Read aloud the directions on page 81. Ask what two consonant sounds are heard in the blend at the end of the word **vest**. Then have children emphasize each final blend as they identify the pictures.

● Call attention to the phonograms in blue on page 82. Point out that many phonograms have final blends. Go over each set of directions, and together do the first item in each section.

● Have children complete both pages. Then explore *Taking Off* on page 81.

Extending the Skill Across the Curriculum

(Language Arts/Music)

Theme Activity

● Have children turn to "City Street" on page 67. Ask them to name the sound words mentioned in the poem, such as **honk, beep, whistle,** and **hush.** Ask for examples of other sounds that can be heard in cities. Then read about city sounds in the theme books cited below.

● On the board list sounds from the readings as children name them. Include sounds with final blends.

● Have children work in small groups. Ask each child to choose a city sound to imitate in a distinctive pitch and rhythm. Then direct each group to sing a city song by having all members make their sounds at the same time. Remind children not to shout, so that all individual sounds may be heard. Allow one group at a time to "perform" for the class.

Theme Books

Brown, Craig McFarland. *City Sounds.* NY: Greenwillow, 1992. Farmer Brown enjoys the sounds of the city as he drives his truck.

Emberley, Rebecca. *City Sounds.* NY: Little, Brown, 1989. Sounds—of morning, of traffic, of subways, in parks, and more.

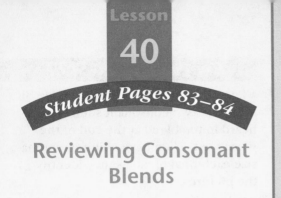

Reviewing Consonant Blends

Objective
- To review initial and final consonant blends

Warming Up

Reviewing Soft and Hard c and g

On the board write groups of words with soft and hard **c** and **g**, as follows:

> city, cars, race, ice
> goat, bag, giant, gate
> wagon, gym, giraffe, stage
> cone, cave, cube, center

Have children read aloud each group of words, and tell which word doesn't belong and why.

★ Teaching the Lesson

Materials: Phonics Picture Cards for initial and final blends, paper bag

- Recite with the class "City Street" on page 67. On the board write the headings "Initial Blend" and "Final Blend." Then have volunteers reread each stanza, and have other children name the words with blends and write them under the appropriate headings.

- Put the initial blend picture cards in a bag. Have children choose a card, name the picture and blend, and then name another word that begins with the same blend.

- Repeat the procedure for words with final blends.

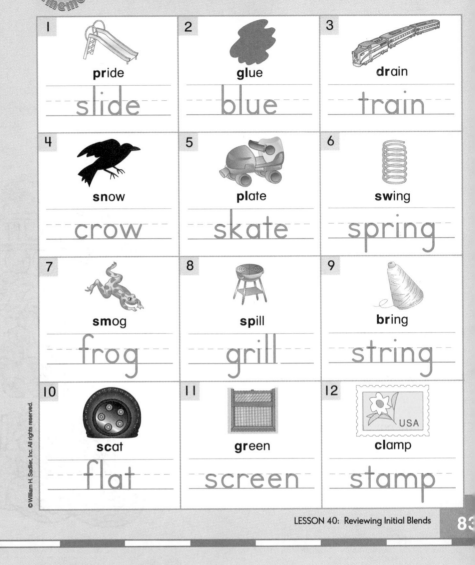

Look at the picture and read the word. Change the blend to write the word that names the picture.

1 **pr**ide — slide	2 **gl**ue — blue	3 **dr**ain — train
4 **sn**ow — crow	5 **pl**ate — skate	6 **sw**ing — spring
7 **sm**og — frog	8 **sp**ill — grill	9 **br**ing — string
10 **sc**at — flat	11 **gr**een — screen	12 **cl**amp — stamp

LESSON 40: Reviewing Initial Blends

83

Multisensory *Activities*

Auditory ■ Visual

It Begins Like…

Display the Phonics Picture Cards for initial and final blends on the chalk ledge. Tell children to refer to the pictures for answers to riddles such as these:

> It begins like **square** and names a frisky animal. (**squirrel**)

> It rhymes with **damp** and gives off light. (**lamp**)

Have children write their answers on paper and underline the blends.

Visual ■ Kinesthetic

Playground Blends

On the board list playground words with blends (e.g., **play, sand, grass, jump, slide, friend, glide, swim, fast, skate, clap, swing**). Have each child fold a sheet of paper into four columns headed "l-blend," "r-blend," "s-blend," and "final blend." Ask children to sort the words on the board and write them in the correct columns. Challenge children to find words that can be listed in more than one column.

Write the name of each picture in the puzzle. Then read the shaded letters down to find the answer to the question.

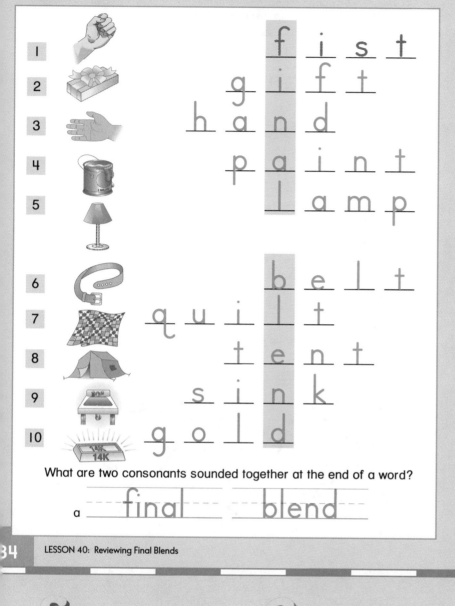

1. f i s t
2. g i f t
3. h a n d
4. p a i n t
5. l a m p
6. b e l t
7. q u i l t
8. t e n t
9. s i n k
10. g o l d

What are two consonants sounded together at the end of a word?

a final blend

LESSON 40: Reviewing Final Blends

Spelling Connection

Read each word and sentence aloud. Then have volunteers spell the words or write them on the board.

slide	Ari likes to **slide** in the park.
green	Grass is **green** and so are leaves.
spring	Robins return in the **spring**.
bank	We put money in a **bank**.
bump	Sometimes trucks **bump** into cars.

Computer Connection

Invite children to ride Ernest the Engine to the Word Mine to build consonant blend words in Reader Rabbit®2 (The Learning Company). First, select "Levels" from the train station and change the activity level to "Beginning blend words." Then instruct children to select "Word Mine." Tell them to look at the beginning blend on the mining cart and choose a word-ending on a crystal that could combine with the blend to form a word. Explain to children that forming three words earns them a crystal.

Practicing the Skill

- Go over the directions and pictures on page 83. Then have children complete the page.
- Review the directions and picture names on page 84. Then have children work in pairs to complete the puzzle.

Extending the Skill Across the Curriculum

(Social Studies/Language Arts)

Theme Activity
- Share these definitions:
    city (urban area): a place to live and work that has many people and many neighborhoods
    suburb (suburban area): a place to live and work that is just outside a city
    town: a place to live and work that has fewer people and fewer neighborhoods than a city
    country (rural area): a place to live and work that has a lot of land but fewer people than a suburb or town.

Then have children discuss the kind of community in which they live. Ask what they like best about living there.

- Share one of the theme book adaptations of Aesop's fable "The Town Mouse and the Country Mouse" (see citations below). Then discuss the story. Ask children whether they would rather be a town or a country mouse.

- Have children write either their own version of the fable or a review of it. Tell them to underline in their writing words that have consonant blends.

Theme Books
Stevens, Janet. *The Town Mouse and the Country Mouse.* NY: Holiday House, 1987.

Wallner, John. *City Mouse-Country Mouse.* NY: Scholastic, 1988.

Portfolio
Have children add their fables to their portfolios.

Connecting Spelling and Writing

Objectives
- To say, spell, sort, and write words with consonant blends
- To write a stage plan using spelling words

Warming Up

Reviewing Long and Short Vowels

Direct children to sort Phonics Picture Cards for long and short vowel names by type of vowel. Have them name and explain the groupings used.

★ Teaching the Lesson

- Write this rap on the board:

  We'll do a **play**
  About our **street**.
  Help set the **stage**;
  Help keep the beat.

Chant it with the class. Have children point out the words that begin or end with a blend. List these on the board. Then say, spell, and repeat each word with children. Call on volunteers to underline and name each blend.

- Repeat the process with the remaining spelling words from the list on page 85.

Observational Assessment
Note which blends pose the most difficulties.

Practicing the Skill

Have children read aloud the directions and the spelling words on page 85. Then have them complete the page.

ESL Activities
Refer to page 67J.

85

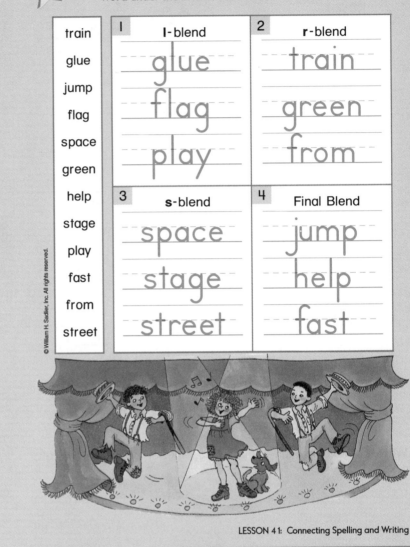

Spell and Write Say and spell each word in the box. Then write each word under the blend in its name.

train	1 **l**-blend	2 **r**-blend
glue	glue	train
jump	flag	green
flag	play	from
space		
green	3 **s**-blend	4 Final Blend
help	space	jump
stage	stage	help
play	street	fast
fast		
from		
street		

© William H. Sadlier, Inc. All rights reserved.

LESSON 41: Connecting Spelling and Writing 85

Multisensory *Activities*

Auditory ■ Kinesthetic

Blend Sort
Materials: four index cards per child

Give out index cards and have children label them "l-blend," "r-blend," "s-blend," and "final blend." Tell children to hold up the appropriate card for each kind of blend they hear. Then say each spelling word and ask volunteers to repeat the word, spell it, and say it again.

Visual ■ Kinesthetic

Picking Pairs
Materials: Phonics Picture Cards for consonant blends

Choose two picture cards for each blend. Shuffle the cards and place them facedown on a table. Have children come to the table in pairs, turn over two cards, and name both the pictures and the blends. If the blends match, have the partners keep the cards. If not, have them replace the cards, and invite the next pair to take a turn.

Spell and Write Join the stage crew for a class play called "City Streets."
Plan the scenery and the sound effects. Write what you will see
and hear on the stage. Use two or more of your spelling words.

train	glue	jump	flag	space	green	
help	stage	play	fast	from	street	

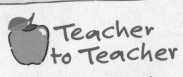

Scenery: What You Will See

_____

_____

_____

_____

_____

_____

_____

Sound Effects: What You Will Hear

_____

_____

_____

_____

_____

_____

_____

_____

86   LESSON 41: Connecting Spelling and Writing

Spelling Connection

Have children match spelling words
from page 85 with other words
linked to them in meaning. You
might use these pairs of associated
words:

    track, whistle (**train**)
    red, yellow (**green**)
    lane, road (**street**)
    paste, tape (**glue**)
    run, hop (**jump**)
    out of, off (**from**)

Some answers may vary.

Teacher to Teacher

Draw a large umbrella on the
board. Invite students to draw
raindrops above the umbrella
and to write within each drop a
word with an **r**-blend. Then draw
a star, and ask students to print
inside each point a word with an
st-blend.

Marie Leahy
Maple Shade, NJ

The Writing Process

Invite children to write a stage plan for
a class play called "City Streets." Tell
them that a stage plan explains what is
seen and heard on stage. Select a volunteer to read aloud the directions on
page 86.

Brainstorm Talk about what is seen
and heard on city streets. Ask questions
like these to prompt discussion: Are
the buildings tall or short? Is the traffic
fast or slow? Are the sidewalks empty
or crowded? What honks and beeps?
What clangs? What other noises might
be heard? Encourage children to share
ideas of what should be seen and
heard in the play.

Write Have children write drafts of
stage plans on paper. Tell them to follow the layout on page 86 and to use
phrases if they wish.

Revise Remind children to make sure
they have put each item in the right
category and have included at least two
spelling words. Circulate and spot check
work as children write their revised
stage plans on page 86.

Publish Have children underline
spelling words used in their stage plans.
Then invite class sharing.

Extending the Skill

Invite children to put on a scene from
the play "City Streets." Together, write
a more detailed class plan that specifies
who the characters are and what will
happen. Then have some children refer
to their own stage plans to make appropriate scenery. Encourage others to
improvise and practice dialogue and
still other students to provide sound
effects. Then bring the class together
to perform.

📁 Portfolio
Children may wish to add their stage
plans to their portfolios.

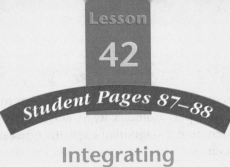

Integrating Language Arts

Objectives
- To use oral and written language to extend the theme
- To demonstrate recognition of soft and hard **c** and **g** and initial and final blends

Background Information

In the United States, more people live in cities than in rural areas. People live in cities for many reasons. There are more jobs, museums, plays, movies, sporting events, and stores in cities. Many people like the bustling activity in cities and the variety of cultures. The five most populous cities in this country are New York City, Los Angeles, Chicago, Houston, and Philadelphia.

★ Teaching the Lesson

- Have a volunteer read the text on page 87. Invite children to tell what they see in the pictures.
- Have children imagine they are one of the pedestrians in the photo. Ask where they are going and what they hear and see.
- Direct children to reread the text to find the soft and hard **c** and **g** words and the words with blends. Have them organize these words under the headings "hard **c**," "soft **c**," "hard **g**," "soft **g**," "initial blend," and "final blend."

Oral Language Development
Challenge children to describe how things might have looked and sounded to the photographer.

ESL Activities
Refer to page 67J.

Look and Learn — Let's read and talk about city streets.

The buildings are tall. They look like giants in the sky. The people look small as they hurry by. The cement sidewalks are always crowded, and there's lots of noise. Cars move fast. Buses stop and go. Horns blow. Sirens scream. Brakes screech. City streets are busy places.

What do these pictures tell about the city? Tell how things look. Tell how things might sound.

LESSON 42: Variant Consonant Sounds and Consonant Blends in Context   87

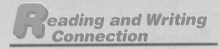

Reading and Writing Connection

Have children choose and illustrate one part of city life. Tell them to refer to the photos on page 87, the poem on page 67, and books read throughout this unit. Direct children to print captions beneath their illustrations, and to include and highlight soft and hard **c** and **g** words and words with blends.

Bind the illustrations into a class book. Encourage children to sign the book out and take it home to share with their families.

Social Studies Connection

Materials: street map, sketching materials

Show children a street map. Elicit from them that people use maps to find their way around. Then ask children to draw and label a simple picture map of an imaginary city block, as if they were looking down on the street. Suggest that they first draw and label the street, and then the buildings along the street.

Encourage children to include and circle soft and hard **c** and **g** words and words with blends.

Check-Up Fill in the circle next to the blend that begins the picture name.

1 plane ○ pr ○ bl ● pl	2 street ○ squ ● str ○ spr	3 crab ● cr ○ cl ○ gr
4 skate ○ sl ● sk ○ cl	5 globe ○ gr ○ cl ● gl	6 swing ○ sm ○ sn ● sw
7 tree ● tr ○ str ○ dr	8 slide ● sl ○ st ○ sp	9 brick ○ gr ○ dr ● br

Circle the word that fits each clue.

10. You can run water in this.	(sink)	sift	wink
11. You can use this when you camp.	west	(tent)	test
12. You can find a bird in this.	vest	(nest)	bent
13. You can hold things with this.	hunk	damp	(hand)
14. You can put things in this.	(trunk)	tramp	bunk
15. You can put this on a desk.	last	land	(lamp)
16. You can give this to someone.	sift	gust	(gift)
17. You can use this to hold up your pants.	(belt)	melt	best

LESSON 42: Assessing Initial and Final Blends

Reteaching *Activities*

Blend Bingo

Materials: blank bingo grids, small plastic or paper chips

Give small chips and a blank four-square by four-square bingo card to each child. Tell children to fill the squares with 16 of these blends: **bl, cl, fl, pl, br, cr, dr, fr, gr, pr, tr, sk, sl, sm, sn, sp, st, sw, ng, lt, nt, mp, nk,** and **ft.** Say words with blends, and have students cover the blends they hear. Continue until a student covers an entire row, bingo style.

City Poetry

Materials: chart paper

Write this rhyme on chart paper:

Splish, splash go the ducks.
Vroom, vroom go the trucks.
Clang, clang goes the crane.
Click, clack goes the train.
Swoosh, swoosh goes the fan.
Honk, honk goes the van.

Have the class recite the rhyme. Then ask them to find words in the rhyme that have the same blend as each of these words: **traffic, crowd, swim, clock, split, sing,** and **rink.**

Assessing the Unit

Unit Test The assessment on page 88 will help you observe your students' progress toward mastering initial and final blends. Have students read with you the directions for the first part of page 88. Then have them complete the assessment.

Observational Assessment Review the notes you have recorded about children's learning and participation throughout this unit. Use these notes to assess children's overall performance and progress concerning initial and final blends.

Student Skills Assessment After children have completed the assessment on page 88, use the results—along with your observational notes—to complete the skills checklist on Student Edition pages 207–208.

Writing Conference Meet with individual children to discuss writing samples they have added to their portfolios during this unit. Encourage children to talk about their writing as you review the samples together. Take specific notes about each child's work and self-evaluation. Use these and previous notes to help assess children's overall writing and successful application of phonics skills. Add the notes to the child's portfolio, and review them during your next conference.

Group together students who need further instruction regarding initial and final blends, and help them complete the *Reteaching Activities*. You might then use the alternative assessment methods on page 67C of the Teacher's Edition.

Take-Home Book Remind children to complete the *Take-Home Book* page for Unit 4 at home.

PLANNING RESOURCE

Going Places

Theme:
North, South, East, or West—
Going places is the best!

Overview

Unit **5** introduces children to compound words, two-syllable words, **y** as a vowel, consonant digraphs, and **r**-controlled vowels through the theme "Going Places."

Objectives

- To enjoy a poem about a museum
- To recognize and write compound and two-syllable words
- To recognize and write words with **y** as a vowel
- To recognize, write, and spell words with consonant digraphs
- To recognize, write, and spell words with **r**-controlled vowels

Thematic Teaching

Ask children what places they have visited or want to visit. Consider their experiences when selecting activities.

Display the Poetry Poster "Museum Door," and refer to it throughout the unit.

Individual Lessons

Lesson	Skill Focus
43	Introduction to Consonant Digraphs and **r**-Controlled Vowels
44	Compound Words
45	Recognizing Two-Syllable Words
46	Recognizing and Writing **y** as a Vowel
47	Assessing Compound Words and **y** as a Vowel
48	Recognizing Initial Consonant Digraphs **th, sh, wh,** and **ch**
49	Recognizing Final Consonant Digraphs **ck, th, sh,** and **ch**
50	Recognizing Consonant Digraphs **kn** and **wr**
51	Connecting Spelling and Writing
52	Reviewing Consonant Digraphs
53	Recognizing and Writing **ar**-Words
54	Recognizing and Writing **or**-Words; Reviewing **ar**-Words
55	Recognizing and Writing **er-, ir-,** and **ur**-Words
56	Reviewing **er-, ir-,** and **ur**-Words
57	Connecting Spelling and Writing
58	Integrating the Language Arts

Take-Home Book: *Magic Carpet Ride*

Lee Bennett Hopkins

Author's Corner

Lee Bennett Hopkins grew up poor, but he didn't know it. As a "city kid" he enjoyed playing in front of open fire hydrants on hot days. A favorite teacher taught Hopkins to love reading and the theater. When he became a teacher himself, Hopkins found out that he loved poetry, too. Now he's best known for writing and collecting poems.

Curriculum Integration

Spelling A *Spelling Connection* appears in most lessons.

Writing Children write original impressions and song lyrics, dates of events, descriptions, and a letter on pages 94, 102, 106, 110, 114, 116, 118, and 119.

Social Studies Activities that build on social studies concepts appear on pages 92, 104, and 119.

Science Children connect phonics and science through the activity on page 116.

Music An opportunity to foster music enrichment appears on page 102.

Optional Learning Activities

Multisensory Activities Every lesson includes activities that appeal to various learning styles—visual, auditory, tactile, or kinesthetic.

Multicultural Connection Children celebrate cultural diversity in activities on pages 100 and 112.

Thematic Activities The *Extending the Skill Across the Curriculum* aspect of each lesson enhances thematic activities.

Assessment Strategies

Multiple strategies such as *Observational Assessment,* portfolios, written middle- and end-of-the-unit assessments, and the *Skills Checklist* at the back of each Student Edition will help you assess children's mastery of phonics skills throughout Unit 5.

Resources

Works by Lee Bennett Hopkins
Best Friends. New York: Harper, 1986.

Ring Out, Wild Bells: Poems about Holidays and Seasons. Orlando, FL: HarBrace, 1992.

Theme-Related Resources
Disney Travel Songs. The Walt Disney Company, 1994.

Kroll, Virginia. *Masai and I.* Old Tappan, NJ: S&S Children's Books, Four Winds, 1992.

My Little Island. GPN/WNED-TV, 1987.

Assessment

In Unit 5 children focus on recognizing and writing compound words, **y** as a vowel, consonant digraphs, and **r**-controlled vowels. The following are suggestions for evaluating these skills through informal/formal, observational, objective, portfolio, and performance assessments. You may also wish to refer to *Using Technology* for alternative assessment activities.

Informal/Formal Assessment

The tests on pages 89D, 89E, 89F, and 89G assess children's mastery of the skills of recognizing and writing compound words, **y** as a vowel, consonant digraphs, and **r**-controlled vowels. These tools may be used informally at the beginning of the unit to identify a starting point for individual or class instruction or formally at the end of the unit to assess children's progress.

Observational Assessment

Specific opportunities for observation are highlighted in the lesson plans and occur throughout the unit. *Multisensory Activities* offers additional chances for observation.

Objective Assessment

Use the assessment pages throughout the unit. Determine the area(s) in which children would benefit from more instruction; then refer to *Reteaching Activities* found throughout the unit in the Teacher's Edition. Finally, reassess children's progress.

Portfolio Assessment

Review "What is this place?" found on page 93 in *Teaching the Lesson*. Invite children to write statements about different places. Have them illustrate their answers. Then have children paste their statements on one side of a sheet of construction paper and their illustrated answers on the other side.

Tell children to work in small groups to identify the places. Then have them add the sentences to their portfolios.

Performance Assessment

Set up stations for the skills taught in this unit (e.g., compound words, two-syllable words, **y** as a vowel, initial consonant digraphs, final consonant digraphs, and **ar-**, **or-**, **er-**, **ir-**, and **ur-**words).

At each station display a laminated sheet of words or Phonics Picture Cards with directions. For example, at the compound word station, have a list of compound words with directions asking children to write the individual, smaller words that make each compound. Explain to children that they will take their answer sheet and proceed from station to station to complete each task.

Using Technology

Have children complete the activities on pages 89M–89N of the Teacher's Edition.

Answer Key

Page 89D
1. sidewalk 2. pinecone 3. snowflake 4. tiptoe 5. shoebox
6. raincoat 7. weekend 8. fireplace 9. suitcase 10. mailbox
11. popcorn 12. peanut 13. cupcake 14. baseball 15. butterfly
16. goldfish 17. sunset 18. beanbag 19. sailboat 20. herself
21. beehive 22. grapefruit 23. treetop 24. windmill

Page 89E
1. sky, dry 2. puppy, twenty, pony 3. sunny, penny, baby
4. why, fly 5. angry, windy 6. my 7. many 8. baby 9. very
10. fly 11. shy

Page 89F
1. whale 2. chin 3. knot 4. wrist 5. shell 6. thimble
7. whiskers 8. knight 9. ship 10. tooth 11. truck 12. brush
13. bench 14. dish 15. lock

Page 89G
1. car 2. purse 3. bird 4. water 5. turtle 6. horn 7. card
8. barn 9. shirt 10. Yes 11. No 12. No 13. No 14. No 15. No

Draw a line from a word in the first column to a word in the second column to make a compound word.

1	side ●	● flake	9	suit ●	● box	
2	pine ●	● toe	10	mail ●	● corn	
3	snow ●	● walk	11	pop ●	● case	
4	tip ●	● cone	12	pea ●	● nut	
5	shoe ●	● coat	13	cup ●	● fish	
6	rain ●	● end	14	base ●	● ball	
7	week ●	● place	15	butter ●	● cake	
8	fire ●	● box	16	gold ●	● fly	

Match words in the first column with words in the second column to make compound words. Write the words on the lines.

sun	bag		bee	fruit
bean	boat		grape	hive
sail	self		tree	mill
her	set		wind	top

17. _____

18. _____

19. _____

20. _____

21. _____

22. _____

23. _____

24. _____

L In each row circle the words that have the same sound of **y** as the first word.

1	sky	dry	funny	by	story
2	rainy	puppy	twenty	try	pony
3	city	cry	sunny	penny	baby
4	my	candy	why	berry	fly
5	very	angry	fry	sly	windy

U Use a word from the box to complete each sentence.

many	shy	baby	fly	my	very

6. Last week _____ family went to the zoo.

7. There were so _____ animals there!

8. I saw a tiny _____ chimp.

9. I took a picture of a _____ tall giraffe.

10. Then I saw some birds too big to _____ .

11. I learned that pandas are quite _____ .

Fill in the circle next to the consonant digraph that begins each picture name.

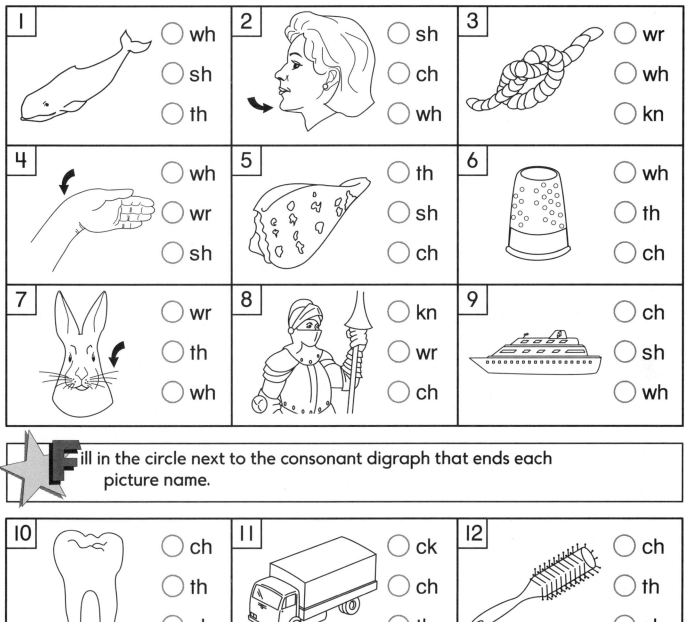

1. ○ wh ○ sh ○ th

2. ○ sh ○ ch ○ wh

3. ○ wr ○ wh ○ kn

4. ○ wh ○ wr ○ sh

5. ○ th ○ sh ○ ch

6. ○ wh ○ th ○ ch

7. ○ wr ○ th ○ wh

8. ○ kn ○ wr ○ ch

9. ○ ch ○ sh ○ wh

Fill in the circle next to the consonant digraph that ends each picture name.

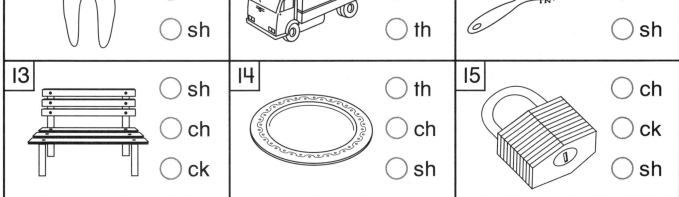

10. ○ ch ○ th ○ sh

11. ○ ck ○ ch ○ th

12. ○ ch ○ th ○ sh

13. ○ sh ○ ch ○ ck

14. ○ th ○ ch ○ sh

15. ○ ch ○ ck ○ sh

Circle the word that names the picture.

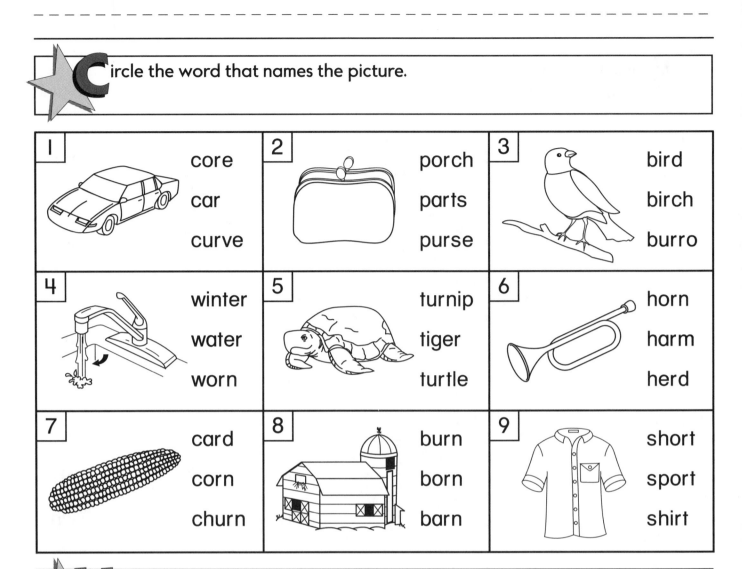

1 core / car / curve	**2** porch / parts / purse	**3** bird / birch / burro
4 winter / water / worn	**5** turnip / tiger / turtle	**6** horn / harm / herd
7 card / corn / churn	**8** burn / born / barn	**9** short / sport / shirt

Underline words that have **ar**, **or**, **er**, and **ur**.
Then circle **Yes** or **No** to answer each question.

10. Is a turkey smaller than a burro?	Yes	No
11. Can a shark drive a car?	Yes	No
12. Is a thorn the same as a horn?	Yes	No
13. Can you serve butter on a harp?	Yes	No
14. Is a shirt like a bird?	Yes	No
15. Can you surf on a porch?	Yes	No

Game Time

▲▽▲▽▲▽▲▽▲▽▲▽▲▽Suitcases to Go▲▽▲▽▲▽▲▽▲▽▲▽▲▽

Blackline Master 20 p.89I

Objective: To make compound words by joining two smaller words

Players: individuals or pairs

Materials: scissors

❂ Duplicate Blackline Master 20 and give a copy to each child. Have children cut out the suitcases. Then have them match words on the suitcases to make compound words.

❂ If children are working in pairs, give each pair only one blackline master. Tell each partner to take a set of suitcases that look alike.

Then direct one player to put down a suitcase and the other player to place one of his or her suitcases beside it to make a compound word. Tell players to alternate laying down first words.

❂ Have individuals or partners use each compound word in a sentence.

▲▽▲▽▲▽▲▽▲▽▲▽▲▽ That's the Ticket! ▽▲▽▲▽▲▽▲▽▲▽▲▽▲

Blackline Master 21 p.89I

Objective: To identify consonant digraphs for given pictures

Players: pairs

Materials: construction paper, glue, scissors, paper bag

❂ Duplicate Blackline Master 21 and give a copy to each pair. Have children glue the page onto construction paper and cut out the "tickets."

❂ Tell each partner to choose an A or B ticket to use as a marker. Have partners put their 1 through 4 tickets into a paper bag.

❂ Direct each pair to take turns drawing a number and moving

that number of spaces toward the roller coaster. Tell them to name the picture on which they land and identify the beginning or ending digraph. The winner is the player who gets to the roller coaster first.

❂ To vary the game, have children name another word that begins or ends with each digraph.

▲▽▲▽▲▽▲▽▲▽▲▽▲▽In the Right Place▽▲▽▲▽▲▽▲▽▲▽▲▽▲

Blackline Master 22 p.89K

Objective: To make sentences that have words with r-controlled vowels

Players: individuals or pairs

Materials: construction paper, glue, scissors

❂ Duplicate Blackline Master 22 and give a copy to each child. Have children glue the page to construction paper and cut out the sentence parts.

❂ Show children how to compose a sentence by putting together a 1, a 2, and a 3 card.

❂ Direct children to use all the words to make sentences and then read their sentences to a partner.

❂ Invite children to rearrange parts 1, 2, and 3 to make some silly sentences.

Suitcases to Go

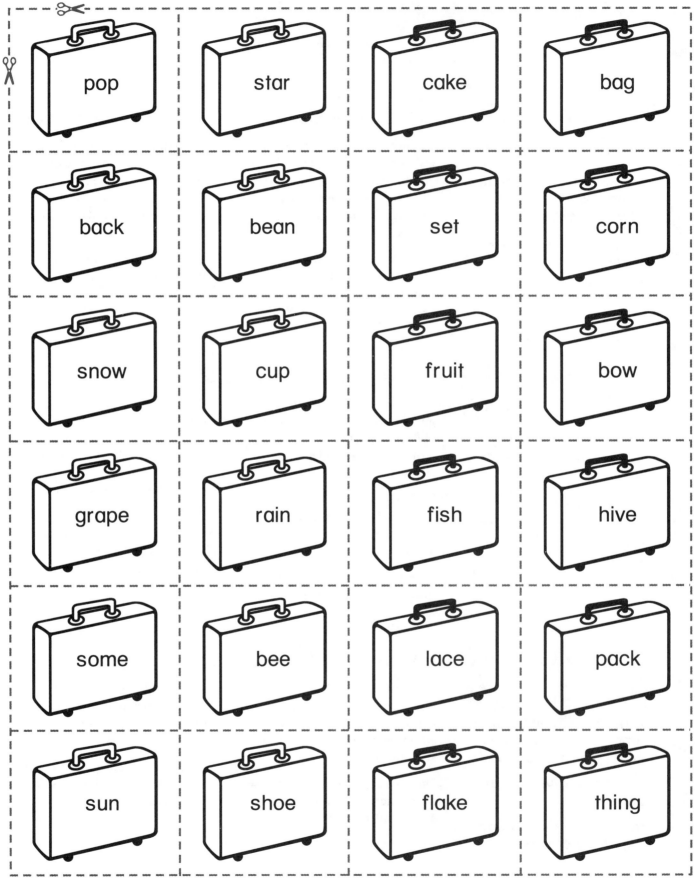

pop · star · cake · bag

back · bean · set · corn

snow · cup · fruit · bow

grape · rain · fish · hive

some · bee · lace · pack

sun · shoe · flake · thing

That's the Ticket!

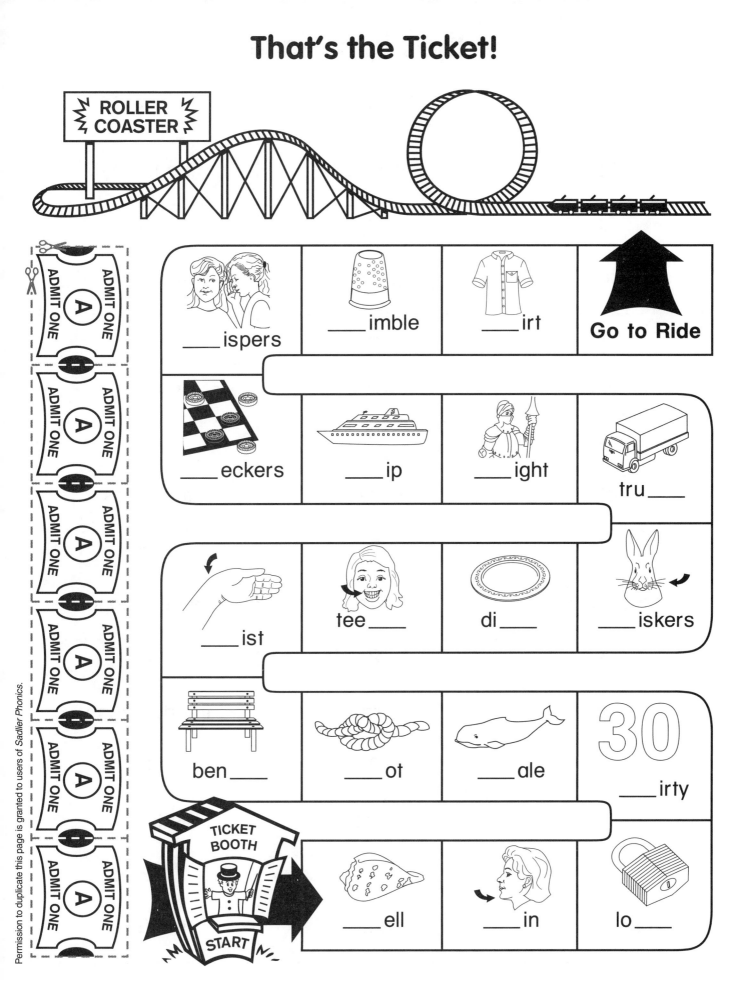

ROLLER COASTER

____ispers

____imble

____irt

Go to Ride

____eckers

____ip

____ight

tru____

____ist

tee____

di____

____iskers

ben____

____ot

____ale

30
____irty

TICKET BOOTH

START

____ell

____in

lo____

ADMIT ONE A (×7)

In the Right Place

1	2	3
Clark	serves	the turkey.
1	2	3
Barb	sorts	the corn.
1	2	3
Father	wore	the shirt.
1	2	3
Mother	marks	the cards.
1	2	3
Her sister	tore	the newspaper.
1	2	3
Kurt	turns	the doorknob.
1	2	3
Cory	stirs	the turnips.
1	2	3
My brother	waters	the fern.

E S L Activities

Treasures of Egypt
Page 89

Have children work in groups. Provide each group with interesting pictures of several different Egyptian artifacts. Ask each group to imagine how the objects were used by their owners and to write a short story about at least one of the objects. Provide reference books, and have children look up the real use of the objects. Invite each group to present its story and facts to the class.

Flash of the Past
Page 89

Prepare pictures of the items mentioned in the poem. Recite the poem, and hold up each picture as it is mentioned. Then have the class recite the poem as you hold up the pictures. Mix up the pictures and ask, "What do you see?" as you hold up each picture again. Call on volunteers to respond. Provide art materials and have children draw or construct models of their favorite ancient treasures.

Friends from Space
Page 102

Help children turn the "Earth Visit" narrative into a skit. Have them select roles, including that of narrator, and devise simple costumes and props.

Fun on Earth
Page 102

Have children work in pairs to list five other things Earth visitors might do on Earth to entertain themselves. Then have children present their lists to the class.

Cartoon Fun
Page 115

Have children work in groups. Make a blackline enlargement of the illustration, and give each group a copy. Direct the groups to write captions for the clerk, girl, boy, woman, parrot, turtle, rabbit, and frog to reveal what they might be saying or thinking.

Young Botanists
Page 115

Show the class various pictures of cut flowers and flowering plants. Discuss the physical characteristics of the plants, their care requirements, and where they are most often grown. Display the pictures on the chalk ledge, and write the names of the plants on index cards. Read the names with the class. Then mix up the cards, and invite children to match each name with its picture.

Are You Listening?
Page 119

Select phrases from the passage for dictation. Read the phrases one at a time in random order, and have children copy the words they hear. Then have children work in pairs to review their work. Call on volunteers to write the phrases on the board, and have children make final corrections. Then help the class put the phrases in the proper order.

Freedom Means...
Page 119

Discuss the concept of freedom. Write pertinent words and expressions on the board. Then have children work in groups to compose a paragraph that tells what freedom means to them. Suggest that group members take turns adding sentences to the composition.

TECH TALK

Compound It!

Objectives
- To help students recognize that a compound word is made by joining two smaller words
- To use a program such as Reader Rabbit® 2 Deluxe* to review compound words
- To use a drawing program to make pictures of compound words

Preparation Review what a compound word is. On the board write word pairs such as **water** and **melon,** and **boat** and **house.** Ask volunteers to combine two words to write a compound word.

One Step at a Time

1. Have children work in small groups to use Reader Rabbit® 2 Deluxe to review compound words.

2. Direct children to choose "Word Mine." Tell them to click on Level 1-Compound Words.

3. Have children make new words. Be sure children identify the compound words and the two smaller words that make up the compound words.

4. Assign to each group one of the smaller words, such as **water.** Direct the groups to brainstorm compound words that have the assigned words as one part; for example, **watermelon** or **rainwater.** Tell children to use a drawing program such as Microsoft® Fine Artist* to make pictures of compound words that contain assigned words.

5. Tell children to enter the Painting Studio and access the paint tools. Have them divide the screen in half vertically, depict and write both words, and then print the compound-word pictures. Have children repeat the procedure for each word they brainstormed.

Class Sharing

Have each group mount its word pictures on mural paper and present its word list to the class. Challenge volunteers to name other words, such as **waterfall,** for each original word part.

On a separate part of the mural paper, write the title "Going Places." Ask volunteers to identify the words that tell about going places. Move these words under the title.

North, South, East, or West!

Objectives
- To write a story using two-syllable words
- To use a writing and paint program such as Kid Works™ 2*

Preparation
Read *The Moon Was the Best* by Charlotte Zolotov (Greenwillow) or *A Visit to Washington, D.C.* by Jill Krementz (Scholastic). If anyone in the class has been to Washington, D.C., ask him or her to tell about it. Ask other children to tell about places they have visited.

Write *Paris* on the board. Ask children how many vowel sounds they hear. On the board write one- and two-syllable words from the stories, and have children name the number of vowel sounds they hear for each word.

One Step at a Time

1. Have children work independently or in small groups.

2. Write the following on the board:

   I would like to go to _____. I would like to see _____ there. It would be fun to _____.

3. Have the class complete the sentences on the computer. Have children on Kid Works™ 2 use the Story Writer feature. Tell them they may add more sentences.

4. Guide children to select "Story Illustrator" to access the paint tools. Encourage them to draw features of the places they would like to visit.

Direct children to store illustrations in "Picture Box" in the Story Writer feature.

5. Tell children to select "Story Writer" to retrieve their illustrations and add them to their sentences.

6. Have children print their illustrated sentences. Tell them to circle the one-syllable words and underline the two-syllable words.

Class Sharing

Allow time for children to share their illustrated sentences about places they would like to visit. Be sure children explain to the class which words have one syllable and which have two.

Name That Skill!

Review the concepts studied in this unit, including compound words, consonant digraphs, **r**-controlled vowels, and two-syllable words. List these on chart paper.

Have children work in small groups. Tell them to look for different items in the classroom that might represent a phonics concept; e.g., **chalk** has the consonant digraph **ch**. Have children find the items and discuss with their group how each represents a phonics concept.

Videotape children's explanations. Make sure each child contributes.

All referenced software is listed under Computer Resources on page T46.

Literature Introduction to Consonant Digraphs and r-Controlled Vowels

Objectives
- To enjoy a poem about a museum
- To identify words with consonant digraphs and r-controlled vowels

Starting with Literature

- Ask children to tell about a time they went to a museum and to describe some of the things they saw. Explain that they can enjoy *and* learn from museum treasures, such as artwork and displays related to history or science.

- Have children imagine they are in a museum like the one illustrated on page 89. Then read aloud "The Museum Door," both alone and with the class.

Developing Critical Thinking
Encourage thoughtful answers to the questions at the bottom of the page.

Introducing the Skill

Tell the class that in this unit they will learn: (1) two small words can be put together to make one *compound* word; (2) two-syllable words can be distinguished from one-syllable words; (3) **y** can sometimes act as a vowel; (4) two consonants together can make a new sound; (5) an **r** after a vowel changes the vowel sound.

Practicing the Skill

Have children name from the poem words with vowels followed by **r**. (**art, armor, cart, dinosaur**) Then have volunteers locate **knights** and **throne**. Identify **kn** and **thr** as consonant digraphs.

THE MUSEUM DOOR

What's behind the museum door?

Ancient necklaces,
African art,
The armor of knights,
A peasant cart;

Priceless old coins,
A king's ancient throne,
Mummies in linen,
And a dinosaur bone.

Lee Bennett Hopkins

Critical Thinking
What would you most like to see in a museum? Why?
How might a museum visit help you to learn?

LESSON 43: Introduction to Compound Words, **y** as a Vowel,
Consonant Digraphs, and **r**-controlled Vowels

Theme Words

Going Places To stimulate children's curiosity about going places, invite the class to ride your "magic carpet." For each "ride," describe a famous place in greater and greater detail until children can identify the place. On a word chart, record descriptive words associated with famous or interesting places. Keep this word chart periodically or continuously on display to emphasize the unit's theme.

Utilize and expand the word chart throughout the unit. It can be a helpful tool for assessing children's ability to recognize compound words, two-syllable words, **y** as a vowel, consonant digraphs, and **r**-controlled vowels. For future review, you might draw a five-car train on the board and label each car with one of the skills taught. Then ask children to name theme words that could be "carried" by each car.

Dear Family,

As your child progresses through this unit about going places, he or she will learn more about words, letters, and sounds. Read the definitions and examples together.

compound word: word made up of two or more smaller words (**raincoat, baseball**)

words with y as a vowel: words in which **y** has the sound of long **i** or long **e** (**fly**, **city**)

consonant digraph: two consonants together that stand for one sound (**chin**, **tooth**)

words with ar, or, er, ir, ur: words in which **r** gives the vowel a new sound (**barn**, **corn**, **fern**, **bird**, **turn**)

- Read the poem "The Museum Door" on the reverse side.
- Talk about museums or other interesting places you have visited.

Apreciada Familia:

En esta unidad, acerca de los paseos, su niño continuará aprendiendo sobre letras, palabras y sonidos. Juntos lean las definiciones y los ejemplos.

palabras compuestas: aquellas formadas por dos o más palabras (**raincoat, baseball**).

y con sonido de vocal: palabras en las que la **y** tiene el sonido largo de la **i** o la **e** (**fly**, **city**).

consonantes digrafas: dos consonantes juntas que producen un solo sonido (**chin**, **tooth**).

palabras con ar, or, er, ir, ur: palabras donde la letra **r** da a la vocal un nuevo sonido (**barn**, **corn**, **fern**, **bird**, **turn**).

- Lea la poesía, "The Museum Door" en la página 89.
- Hablen de los museos u otros lugares interesantes que hayan visitado.

PROJECT

Have your child make a map of an imaginary town that she or he would like to visit. Together make up place names for the map from new words your child learns. Help your child label the map. Then "stroll" around town together.

PROYECTO

Pida al niño dibujar el mapa de un pueblo imaginario el cual le gustaría visitar. Con las nuevas palabras busquen nombres para el mapa. Ayude al niño a rotular el mapa. Después caminen juntos por el pueblo.

LESSON 43: Introduction to Compound Words, **y** as a Vowel, Consonant Digraphs, and **r**-controlled Vowels—Phonics Alive at Home

---

ESL Activities

ESL activities are referenced throughout this unit. These activities benefit the ESL child in your classroom by providing additional language experiences. Choose the activities that best meet the diverse needs of your class.

For ESL activities related to "The Museum Door," refer to page 89L.

Take-Home Book

Children may enjoy reading the Unit 5 Take-Home Book, *Magic Carpet Ride*, with their families. This fold-up book, on pages 217–218, culminates the theme on interesting places while encouraging children to apply newly learned phonics skills regarding consonant digraphs, two syllable words, and **r**-controlled vowels. You might choose to conclude the unit with this take-home component or send it home at another appropriate time during the unit.

- The *Phonics Alive at Home* page is intended to get families actively involved in their children's reading and writing development through activities that apply phonics skills.
- In this unit the page features a concise explanation of the phonics focus on compound words, two-syllable words, **y** as a vowel, consonant digraphs, and **r**-controlled vowels. Activities are related to the unit theme of "Going Places" and include a guide for discussion and a creative project.
- Have children tear *Phonics Alive At Home* page 90 out of their books. Encourage them to take the page home to discuss and complete with their families.
- Ask children to bring their completed projects to school and present them to the class.
- Provide ample opportunities for children to share their thoughts, writing, and drawings related to places they have visited or would like to visit.
- Ask children to bring to class photos or pictures of places they have gone with their families. Post these pictures on a bulletin board beneath the title "Places We Go" or "Places We Visit."

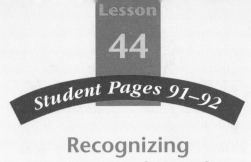
Recognizing Compound Words

Objective
● To recognize and write compound words

Warming Up

Reviewing Soft and Hard c
Draw two suitcases on the board. Label one "Soft **c**" and the other "Hard **c**." Then list these words between the suitcases: **can, rice, cone, juice, cube, ice, pencil, cage, lace, cap, cup, cake, cent,** and **cookies**. Ask students to determine the sound of **c** for each word and draw a line from the word to the correct suitcase.

★ Teaching the Lesson

Materials: flash cards, red and blue markers, scissors

● Write this sentence on the board: "Sue spent the weekend with her grandmother on a **houseboat**." Have children read the sentence together. Ask them which word is made up of two smaller words. Then circle each small word in **houseboat**. Explain that the two small words make up a new word called a *compound word*.

● On flash cards, write the first half of each of the following compound words in blue marker; write the second half in red: **jellyfish, raincoat, without, windmill, watermelon, treetop, pancake, beanbag, fireplace, airplane, daylight, baseball,** and **mailbox**. Cut each card between the two small words.

● Give one half-card to each child. Tell children with blue words to find their red word partners. Then have the pairs read aloud their compound words.

A **compound word** is made up of two or more smaller words.

The compound word **starfish** is made up of **star** and **fish**. Combine a word from Box 1 with a word from Box 2 to name each picture. Write the compound words.

Box 1			Box 2		
back	pea	rain	ball	corn	nut
base	play	star	bow	fish	pack
mail	pop	wind	box	mill	pen

1. starfish
2. popcorn
3. mailbox
4. peanut
5. backpack
6. rainbow
7. baseball
8. playpen
9. windmill

LESSON 44: Recognizing and Writing Compound Words 9

Multisensory *Activities*

Visual ■ Tactile

Postcards from a Friend
Materials: construction paper in two different light colors

Have children work in small groups; assign each group five compound words. Distribute postcard-size pieces of the colored paper so that children can write the first part of each compound word on one color and the second on the other. Have groups exchange cards and put together one another's compound words.

Visual ■ Kinesthetic

Climb the Beanstalk
Materials: mural paper, index cards, tape

On mural paper draw a twelve-leaf beanstalk. On index cards write **ant-hill, beanbag, mask, crisp, street, bedroom, campfire, paint, dog-house, slippers, flashlight, popcorn, train, sandbox, sunset, grapefruit, tiptoe,** and **butterfly**. Have children choose cards, read aloud the compound words, and then tape them to the leaves.

Make compound words. Draw a line from each word in the first column to a word in the second column.

1	bean	side	9	day	cake
2	tea	bag	10	pan	weed
3	in	coat	11	sea	fruit
4	rain	cup	12	grape	dream
5	row	self	13	suit	case
6	sand	flake	14	bee	way
7	snow	boat	15	week	end
8	him	box	16	run	hive

Combine each word with a picture name and write the compound word.

17 ant	anthill	20 cake	cupcake
18 set	sunset	21 man	frogman
19 pine	pinecone	22 tree	treetop

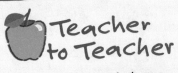

If you could go **anywhere**, where would you go? Write about a place you would like to visit.

LESSON 44: Recognizing and Writing Compound Words

2

Read aloud the Helpful Hint and directions at the top of page 91.

Practicing the Skill

● Read aloud the Helpful Hint and directions at the top of page 91. Do the first item with the class. Then have children complete the page.
● Go over the directions and first item for each section on page 92. Then have children complete the page.
● Utilize *Taking Off* at any time.

Extending the Skill Across the Curriculum

(Language Arts/Social Studies)

Theme Activity
Materials: world map, drawing paper, crayons

● Share the theme books cited below. Have the class listen for what children in the stories see, especially those things named by compound words.

● Display a world map. Have children choose a place they would like to visit and imagine what they might see along the way as they travel there. Tell children to think in particular of things named by compound words. On chart paper list examples, such as **sailboat, starfish, lighthouse, steamship, seashell, rainbow, blackbird, dragonfly, butterfly,** and **grasshopper**.

● Have children illustrate one of the compound-word sights and include the word in a caption.

● Bind the pages into a class book titled "Along the Road to Anywhere."

Theme Book
Field, Rachel. *A Road Might Lead to Anywhere*. New York: Little, Brown & Co., 1990. A road to many places.

Stock, Catherine. *Where Are You Going Manyoni?* New York: Morrow Junior Bks., 1993. A girl walks miles to school in rural Africa.

Observational Assessment
Note whether children mistakenly write compound words as two separate words.

Spelling Connection

Read aloud the words and sentences below. Invite volunteers to spell each word orally or write it on the board.

sailboat   The **sailboat** glided on the water.
beanbag   We played a game with a **beanbag**.
sunset   What a beautiful **sunset**!
sandbox   Put the pail in the **sandbox**.
outside   The **outside** air is warm.

Teacher to Teacher

On the bulletin board, draw a large kite with a string and a tail. Have each student think of a compound word, write it on a paper bow, and attach the bow to the kite's tail.

*S. Margaret Eileen
Reading, PA*

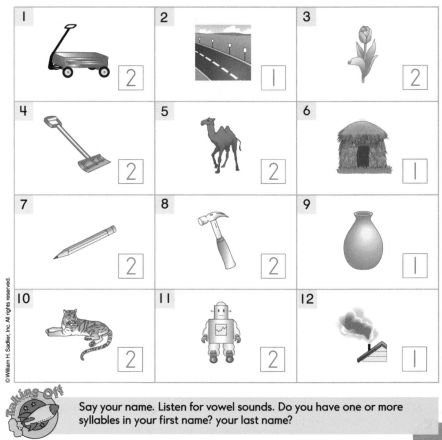

Lesson 45

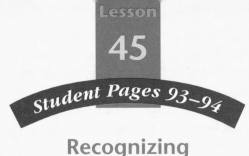

Student Pages 93–94

Recognizing Two-Syllable Words

Objectives
- To recognize two-syllables words
- To write two-syllable words in sentences

Warming Up

Reviewing Short a and Long a
Materials: index cards

Draw the outline of two large faces on the board. Write "Short **a**" above one and "Long **a**" above the other. On index cards, write these words: **trade, crab, flake, main, tag, snail, camp, play, tack,** and **face.** Hold up each card, and have a volunteer read it and identify the **a** sound. Then have the student draw a mouth, eye, nose, or other feature on the corresponding face.

★ Teaching the Lesson

- Ask children, "What is this place?" after saying each of these clues:

  It has big buildings and busy streets. (**city**)

  It is a place with trees where you play with others. (**park**)

  You see clowns, elephants, and acrobats here. (**circus**)

  You go here to see all kinds of animals. (**zoo**)

- Write each answer on the board. Clap once for each syllable as you say each word. Repeat the words, and have children clap out the syllables with you. Then read aloud the Helpful Hint on page 93 to stress the relationship between syllable and vowel sound.

- Clap out syllables for other one- and two-syllable words until children feel comfortable recognizing the number of syllables in the words.

A **syllable** is part of a word that has a vowel sound. Words can have one, two, or more syllables.

The word **road** has one syllable. The word **wagon** has two syllables. Say the name of each picture. Listen for the vowel sounds. Write 1 or 2 for the number of vowel sounds you hear.

1. `2`
2. `1`
3. `2`
4. `2`
5. `2`
6. `1`
7. `2`
8. `2`
9. `1`
10. `2`
11. `2`
12. `1`

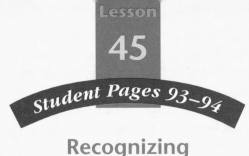

Say your name. Listen for vowel sounds. Do you have one or more syllables in your first name? your last name?

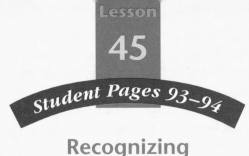

LESSON 45: Recognizing Two-Syllable Words

93

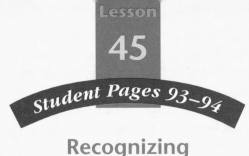© William H. Sadlier, Inc. All rights reserved.

Multisensory *Activities*

Auditory ■ Kinesthetic

Jump Once, Jump Twice

Ask the class to stand. Tell children to jump in place once if they hear you say a one-syllable word and twice if they hear two syllables. Then say these words: **hammer, bake, wagon, train, painting, yellow, stamp, sister, brother, pen, paper, book, country, horse, friend, travel, spend, poster, glove, sailboat, goldfish, trunk, queen,** and **sweater.**

Auditory ■ Tactile

Give Us a Hand

Invite children to think of objects in the room that have one- or two-syllable names. Ask a child to say the name of his or her object. Tell the class to raise one hand if the name has one syllable and both hands if it has two syllables. Encourage children to count the syllables by clapping their hands softly or tapping their hands on their legs.

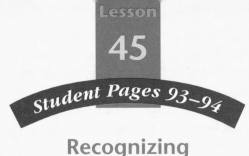

93

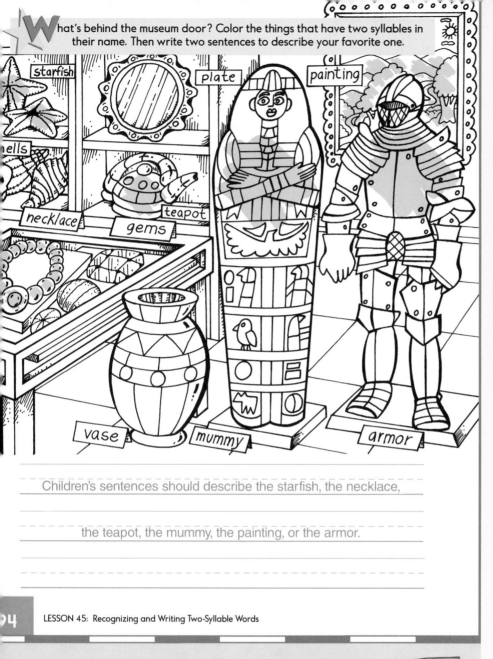

What's behind the museum door? Color the things that have two syllables in their name. Then write two sentences to describe your favorite one.

starfish
plate
painting
shells
necklace
teapot
gems
vase
mummy
armor

Children's sentences should describe the starfish, the necklace,

the teapot, the mummy, the painting, or the armor.

LESSON 45: Recognizing and Writing Two-Syllable Words

Spelling Connection

Read aloud the words and sentences below. Invite volunteers to spell each word orally or write it on the board.

wagon	Carlos has a red **wagon**.
tulip	The **tulip** is a spring flower.
camel	A **camel** lives in the desert.
sister	My **sister** is seven years old.
poster	Keisha has a **poster** on her wall.

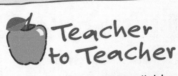

Teacher to Teacher

To have children "feel" syllables, ask them to place the backs of their hands under their chins and then say the word. The number of times they feel their chin drop is usually the same as the number of syllables in the word.

Mildred A. Levesque
Fall River, MA

Practicing the Skill

● Review the Helpful Hint on page 93. Ask a volunteer to read aloud the directions. Then go over the example item, and have children complete the page. Turn to page 94 before exploring *Taking Off* at the bottom of this page.

● Have a volunteer read aloud the directions and point out one two-syllable object on page 94. Then have children color and write their sentences.

Extending the Skill Across the Curriculum

(Language Arts/Art)
Theme Activity
Materials: paints, brushes, paper

● Ask children to think of beautiful things they have seen (e.g., flowers in a neighbor's garden, animals at a zoo, sunsets, rainbows). You might share the theme books cited below to spark children's imaginations.

● Invite children to paint a picture of something beautiful.

● Help children set up an "art museum" in a corner of the classroom that others may visit. Display the paintings there.

● Compile a class list of objects in the paintings. Ask children to identify the one- and two-syllable words.

● Encourage children to write about how their pictures make them feel.

Theme Books
Radin, Ruth Yaffe. *High in the Mountains*. New York: Macmillan, 1989. A child describes a day spent near Grandpa's mountain house.

Zolotow, Charlotte. *The Moon Was the Best*. New York: Greenwillow, 1993. A mother shares memories of Paris with her daughter.

Portfolio
Have children put their paintings and writing in their portfolios.

Recognizing and Writing y as a Vowel

Objectives
- To recognize the sounds of **y** as long **i** and **y** as long **e**
- To read and write words with **y** as a vowel in context

Warming Up

Reviewing Short i and Long i
Ask children to repeat each sentence below after you. Call on volunteers to identify the words with long **i** and short **i** sounds.

Mike slid on the **thick ice.**
Nick will split the **lime pie.**
Can **Kim hide five pink pigs?**
Did Jill pick up the **kite line?**
Kim likes to make **thin slices.**

★ Teaching the Lesson

- Write this rhyme on the board:

  I have a **lucky penny,**
  It's **shiny,** bright, and new.
  I **try** to never spend it,
  So I keep it in **my** shoe.

- Read the rhyme with the class. Circle **lucky, penny,** and **shiny,** and ask children to listen to the sound **y** makes as you reread each word. Elicit that the **y** has the long **e** sound. Then repeat the procedure with **try** and **my.** Elicit that the **y** in these words has the long **i** sound.

- You may wish to explain that **y** at the end of a two-syllable word usually has the sound of long **e,** and **y** at the end of a one-syllable word usually has the sound of long **i.**

Sometimes **y** has the sound of long **i.** Sometimes it has the sound of long **e.**

The **y** in **fly** has the long **i** sound. The **y** in **city** has the long **e** sound. Say the name of each picture. Circle **Long i** if the **y** has the long **i** sound. Circle **Long e** if it has the long **e** sound.

1 fly	2 city	3 penny
(Long i) Long e	Long i (Long e)	Long i (Long e)
4 cry	5 forty	6 sky
(Long i) Long e	Long i (Long e)	(Long i) Long e
7 bunny	8 candy	9 twenty
Long i (Long e)	Long i (Long e)	Long i (Long e)
10 dry	11 pony	12 daisy
(Long i) Long e	Long i (Long e)	Long i (Long e)

LESSON 46: Recognizing **y** as a Vowel 95

Multisensory *Activities*

Auditory ■ Kinesthetic

Bunny Hop, Fly Around
Materials: Phonics Picture Cards **cry, bunny, fry, strawberry, sky, thirty, cherry**

Have children form a circle around you. Hold up the picture cards for volunteers to name. If the **y** in the word sounds like long **e,** have the child say "bunny" and have the class hop around the circle. For long **i,** have the child say "fly" and have the class flap their arms and "fly" around the circle.

Visual ■ Auditory

Penny a Point
Materials: pennies, word cards

Prepare word cards for **cry, twenty, happy, my, any, easy, by, candy, city, sky, sly, money, only, lady, many,** and **sixty.** Have children work in two teams. Alternating between teams, hold up a card and have a player read the word and tell the sound of **y.** Give out pennies for correct responses. The team with more pennies after all cards have been shown wins.

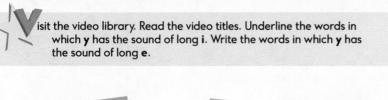

Visit the video library. Read the video titles. Underline the words in which **y** has the sound of long **i**. Write the words in which **y** has the sound of long **e**.

Henny	Penny
Poppy	Ruby
Copycat	Ugly

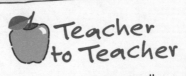

Make up a title for a video or a book. Try to use one or two words with **y** as a vowel.

LESSON 46: Recognizing and Writing **y** as a Vowel

96

Spelling Connection

Read aloud the words and sample sentences below. Invite volunteers to spell each word orally or write it on the board.

penny	Molly has a lucky **penny**.
my	Where is **my** hat?
only	Sly has **only** ten cents.
try	Sally will **try** to win the race.
many	There are **many** people on the bus.

Teacher to Teacher

Have children work in small groups to build a story from the sentence starter "I spy...." Tell them to use words ending in **y** that sounds like long **i** to make sentences. For example, "I spy a **fly** and then **try** to **cry** 'oh **my**.'" Have each group record its story and share it with the class. Children might also make hilarious illustrations for their stories.

Virginia E. Hill
Newtown, PA

Practicing the Skill

- Read aloud the Helpful Hint and directions on page 95. Do the first two items with the class. Then have children complete the page.
- Have volunteers read aloud the directions and video titles on page 96. Ask the class to name one title for each of the two vowel sounds of **y**. Then have children complete the page.
- Invite the class to exercise their imaginations by "Taking Off" at the bottom of page 96.

Extending the Skill Across the Curriculum

(Language Arts/Study Skills)

Theme Activity

- Arrange to take your class on a tour of the local or school library. Before visiting, inquire about the library's shelving system, and then review with children how to use the alphabet to help locate books. Also check whether the library has in circulation the books shown as video titles on page 96. In lieu of these, identify and inquire about other age-appropriate titles that include words in which **y** is a vowel. Assign to each child, or pairs of children, one or two available books.
- As part of the tour, ask the librarian to show the class how to locate a title that has not been assigned. Then ask children to find their assigned title(s).
- You may wish to have children check out the books, read them, and give oral reports telling what a book was about and what they liked best about it.
- Each child might also compile from her or his book(s) a list of words that have **y** as a vowel and sort those words according to the specific vowel sound of **y** (i.e., long **i** sound, long **e** sound).

96

Lesson 47

Reviewing Compound Words and y as a Vowel

Objectives
● To review compound words and **y** as a vowel
● To assess compound words and **y** as a vowel

Warming Up

Reviewing Short o and Long o
Materials: Phonics Picture Cards
boat, log, box, rose, snow, doll, ox, smoke, pot, toad, top, toe, fox, block

Display the **boat** and **log** picture cards on the chalk ledge. Have a volunteer identify the vowel sounds in both words. Then show the other picture cards. Have volunteers name each picture and place it next to the card on the chalk ledge (**boat** or **log**) whose vowel sound matches its own.

★ Teaching the Lesson

● On the board write the following story; leave blank the second half of each compound word.

> Last **week(end)** we went camping. We pitched our tent on an **ant(hill)**. We sang songs around the **camp(fire)**. It made me feel like a **cow(boy)**. The next morning we ate **pan(cakes)**. I like camping **out(side)**.

● Read the story with the class, and together complete the compound words.

● Review the Helpful Hint on page 95. On the board write **why, hobby, sky, fly, sleepy, sandy, cry, rocky, windy, why,** and **pony.** Point to each word, and have children write **e** or **i** on paper to identify the sound of the **y**.

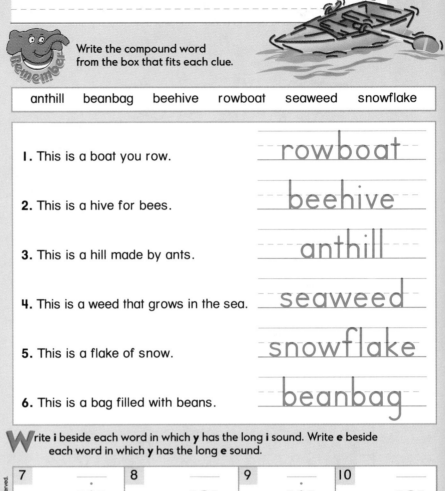

Write the compound word from the box that fits each clue.

| anthill | beanbag | beehive | rowboat | seaweed | snowflake |

1. This is a boat you row. — **rowboat**

2. This is a hive for bees. — **beehive**

3. This is a hill made by ants. — **anthill**

4. This is a weed that grows in the sea. — **seaweed**

5. This is a flake of snow. — **snowflake**

6. This is a bag filled with beans. — **beanbag**

Write **i** beside each word in which **y** has the long **i** sound. Write **e** beside each word in which **y** has the long **e** sound.

7	8	9	10
fly __i__	city __e__	try __i__	daisy __e__

11	12	13	14
candy __e__	penny __e__	dry __i__	why __i__

LESSON 47: Reviewing Compound Words and **y** as a Vowel

Multisensory *Activities*

Visual ■ Tactile

Jigsaw Anyone?
Materials: scissors, duplicating master

Make a duplicating master of compound words with a jagged "jigsaw puzzle" line between the two parts of each word. Have children work in small groups, and give each group a copy. Direct the groups to cut along the jigsaw lines, mix up the separated words, and piece them together again. Have the class read aloud each compound word.

Visual ■ Kinesthetic

Be Happy, Don't Cry
Materials: paper, scissors, word cards

Have each child cut out two large circles. Ask children to draw a **happy** face on one circle and a face with tears, for **cry**, on the other. Flash y-as-vowel word cards for volunteers to read. If the **y** in the word sounds like long **e**, have children hold up their **happy** faces, and say, "Be happy." If the **y** sounds like long **i**, have them hold up their sad faces and say, "Don't **cry**."

Check-Up Make compound words. Draw a line from each word in the first column to a word in the second column. Write the new word.

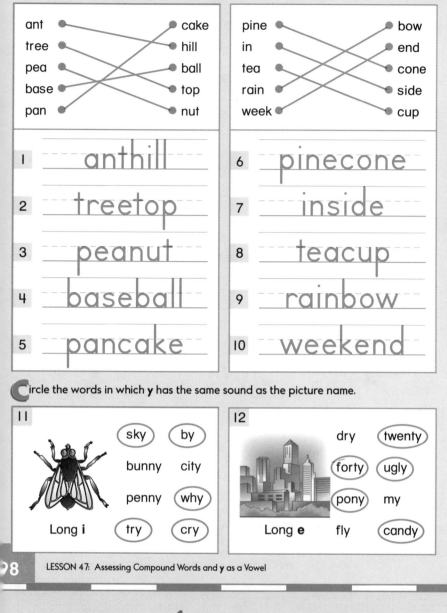

	first	second
	ant	cake
	tree	hill
	pea	ball
	base	top
	pan	nut

1. anthill
2. treetop
3. peanut
4. baseball
5. pancake

	first	second
	pine	bow
	in	end
	tea	cone
	rain	side
	week	cup

6. pinecone
7. inside
8. teacup
9. rainbow
10. weekend

Circle the words in which **y** has the same sound as the picture name.

11. Long **i**
- sky
- by
- bunny
- city
- penny
- why
- try
- cry

12. Long **e**
- dry
- twenty
- forty
- ugly
- pony
- my
- fly
- candy

LESSON 47: Assessing Compound Words and y as a Vowel

98

Reteaching *Activities*

Together Forever
Materials: red and blue markers, index cards

On index cards, write in red: **pop, back, wind, base, bean, him, tip, play rain**, and **tree**. On the other cards, write in blue: **corn, pack, mill, ball, bag, self, toe, pen, bow**, and **top**. Group the cards by color and display them on the chalk ledge. Have children combine words from each group to make compound words.

City or Sky?
Materials: index cards, tape

On the board draw city buildings beneath a cloudy sky. On index cards write **rainy, twenty, sunny, windy, lobby, lucky, money, party, try, why, sty, buy, dry, sly**, and **my**. Invite children to take turns picking cards and saying the words. If the **y** in the word has the long **i** sound, have the child tape the card in the **sky**. If the **y** has the long **e** sound, have the child tape the card in the **city**.

Assessing the Skills

Check-Up Have children look at the *Remember* and *Check-Up* logos on pages 97 and 98, and ask what each logo means. Then go over the directions for both sections on each page. Make sure children understand the directions before having them complete the pages.

Observational Assessment Review all observational notes you recorded during the first part of this unit. Use the notes to help you assess individual student progress and to help you decide whether reteaching is necessary at this point.

Student Skills Assessment Use the checklist on Student Edition pages 207–208 to record your observations of each child.

Writing Conference Talk with each child about his or her portfolio samples. Encourage children to talk about their writing both in terms of creative expression and as a reflection of their phonics skill mastery, particularly regarding one- and two-syllable words. Make notes about each child's progress. Have children make notes as well and add the notes to their portfolios.

Group together students who need further instruction and who seem to have similar weaknesses. Then complete the *Reteaching Activities*.

Recognizing Initial Consonant Digraphs th, sh, wh, and ch

Objectives
- To recognize initial consonant digraphs **th, sh, wh,** and **ch**
- To rhyme and write words with **th, sh, wh,** and **ch**

Warming Up

Reviewing Soft g and Hard g
Write **game, gem, giant, gate, magic, gym, wagon,** and **goat** on the board. Have volunteers underline the soft **g**'s and circle the hard **g**'s. Challenge children to use as many of the words as possible in sentences to answer the question, "Where are you going?"

★ Teaching the Lesson

Materials: Phonics Picture Cards **thirty, wheat, sheep, chair, shorts, cherry**

- Write these sentences on chart paper:
  Charley chases Champ around the cherry tree.
  Whiskers naps on wheat stalks in the wheelbarrow.
  Theo thanks father for the thermos.
  Sheila shops for shoes and shirts.

- Together read the sentences aloud. Have children name the repeated sound in each sentence. Then underline the consonant digraphs, and introduce the concept of a consonant digraph as two consonants that stand for one sound.

- Hold up each picture card, and have children name the picture and beginning consonant digraph.

A **consonant digraph** is two consonants together that stand for one sound.

Thumb begins with the consonant digraph **th**. Circle the consonant digraph that begins each picture name.

1 thumb — (th) sh wh	2 shell — ch th (sh)	3 wheel — (wh) ch th
4 chain — sh wh (ch)	5 whale — th sh (wh)	6 chick — (ch) th sh
7 think — wh sh (th)	8 sheep — (sh) wh ch	9 wheat — th ch (wh)
10 shovel — ch th (sh)	11 thorn — wh ch (th)	12 cheese — sh wh (ch)

Taking Off
Work with your classmates to list **thirteen** words that begin with consonant digraphs.

Multisensory *Activities*

Auditory ■ Kinesthetic

Thumbs Up for th!
Direct children to give a thumbs-up sign if they hear you say a word that begins with the **th** sound. Tell them to give a thumbs-down sign if they hear a different beginning digraph and to be prepared to identify it. Then say words such as **thimble, white, chair, think, sheep, whale, thirsty, shop, thirteen, throat, shake, wheel, child, chain, ship, whisper, this, check, thick,** and **shell.**

Visual ■ Tactile

Think and Choose
Materials: large construction paper, crayons, glue, scissors

Have children fold paper into four "boxes" and depict **cherry, shoe, wheel,** and **thirty,** each in a separate box. On another sheet have them copy and cut out **think, three, thank, then, shade, sheep, shelf, ship, whale, what, wheat, while, chain, chick, chin,** and **chop.** Have them glue each word in the box depicting its digraph.

★ **C**ircle and write the word that completes each sentence.

1. Do you know _where_ the president lives? (where) what

2. _Shall_ I give you a hint? (Shall) Chill

3. George Washington _chose_ the place. chase (chose)

4. But he didn't have a _chance_ to live there. change (chance)

5. It is painted _white_. (white) wheat

6. I _think_ it's a good place to visit. thing (think)

7. Let me _show_ you Washington, D.C. chow (show)

★ **C**hange the beginning digraph and write a rhyming word. Use **th, sh, wh,** or **ch.**

8 **ch**in	9 **ch**eep	10 **sh**op	11 **wh**ine
Accept any answer that is a real word	and begins with a digraph.		
12 **sh**ip	13 **ch**eat	14 **wh**y	15 **th**ick

LESSON 48: Writing Initial Consonant Digraphs **th, sh, wh, ch**

Spelling **Connection**

Read aloud the words and sentences below. Invite volunteers to spell each word orally or write it on the board.

where **Where** are you going?
there We will be **there** soon.
what **What** did you put in the box?
chop Did you **chop** down the tree?
shade Trees give us **shade.**

Multicultural **Connection**

Tell the class that in 1791, George Washington chose the location for what would become the city of Washington, D.C. Explain that the city was modeled after Paris, France, by Pierre-Charles L'Enfant, a French engineer, and that Benjamin Banneker—a scientist, mathematician, and former slave—helped to survey the land and plan the city. Show children a map of Washington, D.C. Help them locate the buildings that were mentioned in *Extending the Skill.*

Practicing the Skill

- Go over the Helpful Hint and directions at the top of page 99. Then have children complete the page.
- Have children work in small groups on the *Taking Off* activity to prepare for page 100.
- Go over the directions for both sections on page 100. Then have children complete the page.

Extending the Skill Across the Curriculum

(Language Arts/Social Studies)
Theme Activity
Materials: map of United States; pictures of Washington, D.C.

- Locate on a map and discuss Washington, D.C. Then read aloud the theme book(s) cited below.
- Give out copies of the text below; leave out the underlined words.

The President lives in the White House in Washington, D.C. The tallest building in the city is the Washington Monument. It was built in honor of our first president, George Washington. A wall with the names of service men and women killed in the Vietnam War serves as the Vietnam Veterans Memorial. Nearby is the Lincoln Memorial, named after Abraham Lincoln. The Jefferson Memorial honors the third U.S. president, Thomas Jefferson.

- Together read the paragraphs and fill in the missing monuments.
- Encourage children to use words with **th, sh, wh,** and **ch** to write about why they would like to visit Washington, D.C.

📖 **Theme Books**
Krementz, Jill. *A Visit to Washington, D.C.* New York: Scholastic, 1986. A boy takes us on a tour of his city.

Steins, Richard. *Our National Capital.* Highland Park, NJ: Mill Brook Press, 1994. D.C. history.

Recognizing Final Consonant Digraphs ck, th, sh, and ch

Objectives
- To write words with final consonant digraphs **ck, th, sh, ch**
- To use words with consonant digraphs in context

Warming Up

Reviewing Short u and Long u
Read aloud the riddles below. Tell children that each answer has a short **u** or long **u** sound.

I'm like a long-eared horse. (**mule**)
I might be a pear or a peach. (**fruit**)
I protect you from rain. (**umbrella**)
I can be used like paste. (**glue**)

Have children write each answer on the board and name the **u** sound.

★ Teaching the Lesson

Materials: Phonics Picture Cards **teeth, fish, bench, lock**

- Have children identify each picture. Write each name on the board, and circle the consonant digraph. Discuss how the letters of digraphs such as **th, sh, ch,** and **ck** make a new sound when paired together.

- Write this story on chart paper:
  Ri**ck** and I walked nor**th** along a pa**th**. We headed for **th**e bea**ch** to ca**tch** some fre**sh** fi**sh**. As we sat on a ro**ck** and ate a sna**ck**, I saw **wh**at looked like a di**sh** in the sky. It landed on a big bu**sh**. **Wh**at was it?

- Read the story aloud, and have volunteers circle the final consonant digraphs.

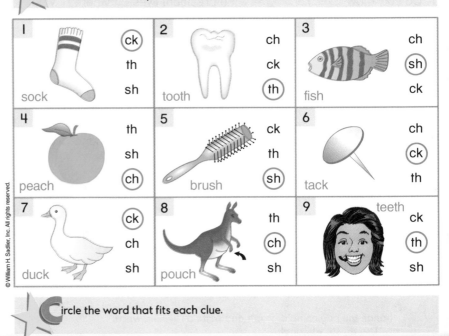

Sock ends with the consonant digraph **ck**. Circle the consonant digraph that ends each picture name.

1 sock — (ck) th sh	2 tooth — ch ck (th)	3 fish — ch (sh) ck
4 peach — th sh (ch)	5 brush — ck th (sh)	6 tack — ch (ck) th
7 duck — (ck) ch sh	8 pouch — th (ch) sh	9 teeth — (ck) th sh

Circle the word that fits each clue.

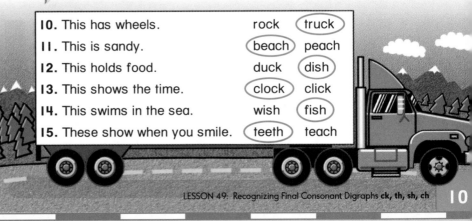

10. This has wheels.	rock	(truck)
11. This is sandy.	(beach)	peach
12. This holds food.	duck	(dish)
13. This shows the time.	(clock)	click
14. This swims in the sea.	wish	(fish)
15. These show when you smile.	(teeth)	teach

LESSON 49: Recognizing Final Consonant Digraphs **ck, th, sh, ch**

10

Multisensory *Activities*

Auditory ■ Tactile

Which Sandwich?

Materials: paper, scissors, tape

Have children draw and cut out eight paper "bread slices" and write **ck, th, sh,** and **ch,** each on two slices. Then direct them to write each word you say on a slice labeled with that word's final digraph. Say **block, snack, thick, rich, bunch, much, fresh, wish, fish, fifth, both,** and **with.** Then have the class make "sandwiches" by taping together same-digraph slices.

Visual ■ Kinesthetic

Mars to Earth

Materials: mural paper, index cards, tape

On opposite ends of mural paper, draw circles to represent Earth and Mars. On index cards, write words with consonant digraphs from student pages 99–102. Have children go from Mars to Earth by reading the word cards, identifying the digraphs, and taping the cards in a path between the two "planets."

Read the story. Then answer the questions.

Earth Visit

"Let's take a trip," said Chid-Chid.
"Where to?" asked Shub-Shub.
"To Earth," said Whicky-Whacky.
They left a note that said "Be back soon!"
and their spaceship took off with a swish.

Thirteen hours later, they were on a
beach on Earth. They swam like fish,
they played Earth games, and they
munched Earth snacks.

They each got something to remember
their trip. Chid-Chid got an Earth rock,
Shub-Shub got a beach ball, and
Whicky-Whacky got a juicy peach.

1. What did Chid-Chid, Shub-Shub, and Whicky-Whacky
do at the beach?

They swam like fish, played Earth
games, and munched Earth snacks.

2. What did Chid-Chid get to remember the trip?

Chid-Chid got an Earth rock.

3. What would you get to remember a day at the beach?

Accept any reasonable response.

02 LESSON 49: Writing Final Consonant Digraphs **ck, th, sh, ch**

Spelling Connection

Read aloud the words and sentences
below. Invite volunteers to spell each
word orally or write it on the board.

tack	Hang the picture with a **tack**.
sock	I keep my marbles in a **sock**.
bench	We sat on a **bench** to rest.
fish	Chad likes to catch **fish**.
path	The **path** led to the beach.

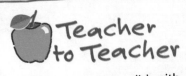

Teacher to Teacher

Obtain a transparency disk with
a spinner, and label each segment
of the spinner with a consonant
digraph. Invite three players at a
time to take turns spinning. Give
each player one minute to name
as many words as possible that
have the digraph sound on which
the spinner lands. Record and tally
the words to determine a winner.

Mary Catherine Murphy
Honolulu, HI

Practicing the Skill

- Read aloud the directions for both
sections on page 101. Ask volunteers
to explain how they would do the first
item in each section. Then have children complete the page independently
or in pairs.

- With the class, read aloud the story
on page 102. Then have children work
in pairs to answer the questions.

Extending the Skill Across the Curriculum

(Language Arts/Music)

Theme Activity

- Together reread "Earth Visit" on page
102. Then invite children to sing "She'll
Be Coming Round the Mountain."

- On chart paper write these variations
of the lyrics:

> They'll be riding in a space **craft**
> **when** they come.
> She'll be eating **cheese** and **cherries**
> for her **lunch**.
> He will **munch** upon some **chowder**
> at the **dock**.
> They'll be **churning through the**
> water in **their ship**.
> She'll be **whistling** to the **children**
> on **the shore**.
> He'll be carrying a **chicken** in his
> **truck**.

- Have children underline the words
with beginning or final consonant
digraphs. Encourage them to sing their
favorite lines. Then have them compose and sing new lines of their own.

Observational Assessment
Note how frequently children use
words with consonant digraphs in
their writing.

📁 **Portfolio**
Have children place the lyrics they
wrote in their portfolios.

ESL Activities
Refer to page 89L.

Lesson 50

Student Pages 103–104

Recognizing Consonant Digraphs kn and wr

Objectives
- To recognize consonant digraphs **kn** and **wr**
- To write consonant digraphs **kn** and **wr** in sentences

Warming Up

Reviewing Short e and Long e
On the board write **bet, fed, hat, lap, met, red, sat, sped, stem, ten,** and **step**. Have the class read the words. Challenge pairs of children to make long **e** words by adding only one letter to each word on the board. (**beet** or **beat, feed, heat, leap, meet** or **meat, reed** or **read, seat, speed, steam, teen, steep**)

★ Teaching the Lesson

Materials: Phonics Picture Cards **knot, knee, wreath, wren**

- Knock on your desk. Ask the class what they hear. Elicit the word **knock**, and write it on the board. Say the word, and circle the **kn**. Help children realize that **kn** makes the same sound as **n** and that the **k** in the digraph **kn** is silent.
- Write the word **wrote** on the board. Say **wrote** several times, and use it in a sentence. Circle the **wr**. Elicit that **wr** makes the same sound as **r** and that the **w** in the digraph **wr** is silent.
- Display the picture cards. Have children identify the picture names and write them on the board. Ask volunteers to circle the consonant digraph in each word.

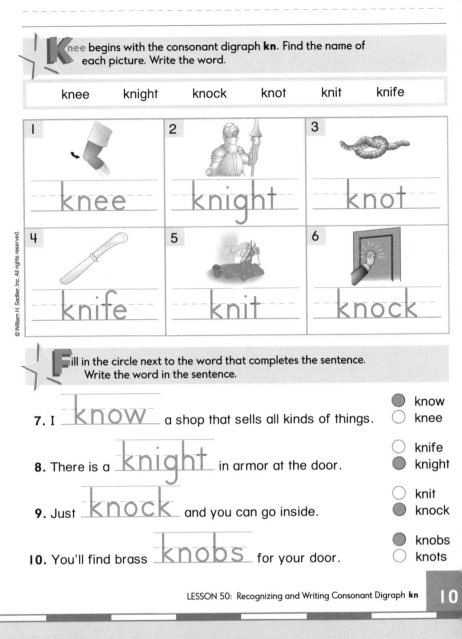

Knee begins with the consonant digraph **kn**. Find the name of each picture. Write the word.

| knee | knight | knock | knot | knit | knife |

1	2	3
knee	knight	knot
4	5	6
knife	knit	knock

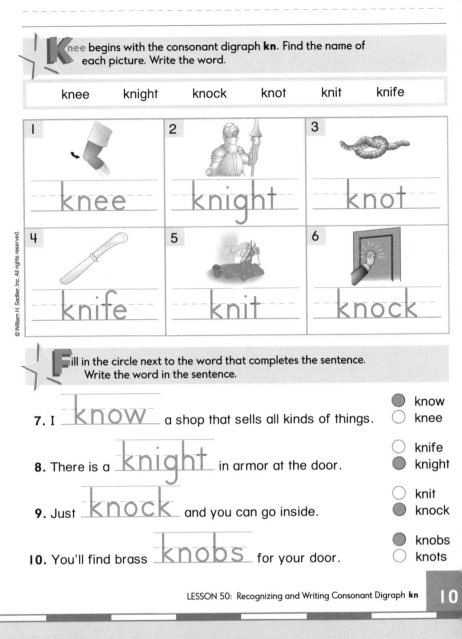
Fill in the circle next to the word that completes the sentence. Write the word in the sentence.

7. I ___know___ a shop that sells all kinds of things. ● know ○ knee

8. There is a ___knight___ in armor at the door. ○ knife ● knight

9. Just ___knock___ and you can go inside. ○ knit ● knock

10. You'll find brass ___knobs___ for your door. ● knobs ○ knots

LESSON 50: Recognizing and Writing Consonant Digraph **kn**   10

Multisensory *Activities*

Visual ■ Auditory

Quick Flash

Materials: **kn** and **wr** word cards

Have children line up in pairs. Flash a word card for the pair at the front of the line to read. Have the child who first reads the word correctly go to the end of the line to play again. Have the other child return to his or her desk. Continue in this way until you run out of cards or players.

Kinesthetic ■ Auditory

Stepping Stones to the Gym

Materials: **kn** and **wr** word cards

Use **kn** and **wr** word cards to mark a path on the floor to an area designated as the "gym." Have children, one at a time, walk the path by saying each word before they step on it. Vary the words occasionally. When all children have had a turn, invite those who made it to the "gym" to lead the class in exercises.

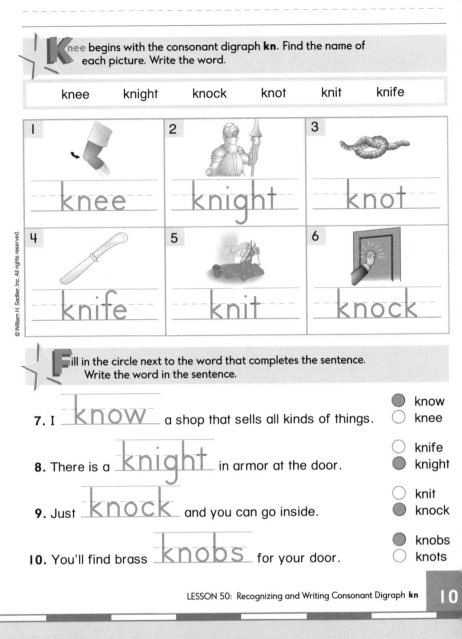

103

© William H. Sadlier, Inc. All rights reserved.

Wrist begins with the consonant digraph **wr**. Circle and write the word that names each picture.

1
rip
(wrist)
wish

wrist

2
which
reach
(wrench)

wrench

3
whip
(wrap)
ripe

wrap

4
(write)
white
wheat

write

5
read
(wreath)
with

wreath

6
rent
went
(wren)

wren

Write a **wr**-word from above to complete each sentence.

7. You ___write___ a letter.

8. You ___wrap___ a gift.

9. You hang a ___wreath___ on a door.

10. You use a ___wrench___ to fix things.

11. You wear a watch on your ___wrist___.

04

LESSON 50: Recognizing and Writing Consonant Digraph **wr**

Spelling Connection

Read aloud the words and sentences below. Invite volunteers to spell each word orally or write it on the board.

knot Tanya has a **knot** in her shoelace.

knock I heard a **knock** at the door.

wrap Omar used blue paper to **wrap** the gift.

write Martin can **write** his name.

wrist Anita wears a bracelet on her **wrist**.

Computer Connection

Have children use Sound It Out Land™ 2 (Conexus) to explore with Sing-Along Sam the phonetic sounds of consonant digraphs and blends. Invite children first to listen to Sam's song and note the different digraphs and blends in the lyrics depicted. Then have children themselves choose the pictures that identify the featured words.

Practicing the Skill

Ask a volunteer to read aloud the directions for both sections on page 103. Do the first item in each section with the class. Then have children work in pairs to complete the page. Do the same for page 104.

Extending the Skill Across the Curriculum

(Social Studies/Art)

Theme Activity

Materials: posterboard, markers, crayons

● Ask children what they know about knights. Then read aloud the theme book cited below.

● On chart paper, write the story below; leave blanks for the underlined words. Then write the missing words in a scrambled list on the board.

If you had traveled in Europe hundreds of years ago, you might have seen soldiers on horseback. These soldiers were called <u>knights</u>. Sometimes they competed at jousting—a sport in which two knights tried to <u>knock</u> each other off their horses. They <u>wrapped</u> their <u>bodies</u> in metal suits of armor. Metal gloves protected their <u>knuckles</u> and <u>wrists</u>. Hinges in the leg armor allowed them to bend their <u>knees</u>. Many people wrote stories about knights. What do you <u>know</u> about them?

● Read the story aloud. Have children fill in the blanks and identify the digraphs.

● Explain that knights painted signs on their shields to show who they were. Then invite children to design their own shields on posterboard.

📖 **Theme Book**

Dann, Geoff, and Chris Gravett. *Knight.* New York: Knopf Books for Young Readers, 1993. Colorful pictures of armor and shields.

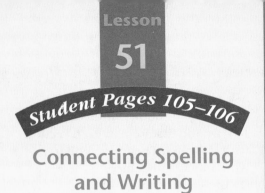

Connecting Spelling and Writing

Objectives
- To say, spell, sort, and write words with consonant digraphs
- To write a speech using spelling words

Warming Up

Reviewing Two-Syllable Words
Say one-syllable and two-syllable words, such as **beanbag, armor, ant, pine, bunny,** and **mummies**. Have children clap once for each syllable they hear.

★ Teaching the Lesson

- Invite children to turn to page 105 and read the billboard at the bottom of the page. Ask them to name the word on the sign that has a consonant digraph and to underline the digraph in their books. (**PEACH**)

- Have children work in pairs to review the spelling words listed on the page. Direct one child in each pair to read a spelling word; then have the other say the word, spell it, and say it again. Have children take turns reading and spelling.

- Ask children to name the spelling words that have the consonant digraph heard in each of these words: **when, rea<u>ch</u>, tee<u>th</u>, <u>sh</u>eep, <u>wr</u>ist, <u>kn</u>ob,** and **ro<u>ck</u>**. Have volunteers write each spelling word response on the board and circle its consonant digraph.

Practicing the Skill

Have children read the directions and the spelling words on page 105. Ask a volunteer to tell how to sort the words by digraph. Then have children complete the page.

Spell and Write Say and spell each word in the box. Then write each word under the digraph in its name. Circle the digraph in each word.

thorn
truck
chose
wrote
peach
why
knee
show
black
wash
both
what

1 **th**	2 **sh**	3 **wh**
thorn	show	why
both	wash	what

4 **ch**	5 **ck**
chose	truck
peach	black

6 **kn**	7 **wr**
knee	wrote

WELCOME TO PEACH COUNTRY

LESSON 51: Connecting Spelling and Writing 10

Multisensory *Activities*

Visual ■ Kinesthetic

Take a Tile
Materials: 12 index cards, 12 envelopes, box

Write each spelling word on an index card; leave extra space between letters. Cut each word into its individual letters, and put the letters in an envelope. Place all the envelopes in a box. Invite children, working individually or in pairs, to choose an envelope and arrange the letters to spell the spelling word.

Auditory ■ Kinesthetic

Spell It With Digraphs
Materials: consonant digraph cards

Give each child a card with **th, sh, wh, ch, ck, kn,** or **wr** written on it. Tell children to listen for the digraph on their card as you say each spelling word. Direct children who hear their digraph to come forward, say the word, spell it, and say the word again. When each word has been spelled, have children exchange digraphs, and continue.

Be a tour guide. Welcome a visitor to your favorite place and tell about it. Write what you would say. Use one or more of your spelling words.

| thorn | truck | chose | wrote | peach | why |
| knee | show | black | wash | both | what |

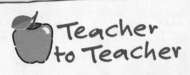

Welcome to

LESSON 51: Connecting Spelling and Writing

Spelling Connection

Write each of the following in big letters on separate sheets of construction paper: **a, b, c, e** (make two), **h, k, l, n, o, p, r, s, t, u, w,** and **y.** Choose a spelling word, and use magnets or tape to fasten its letters to the board, facedown and in order. Have the class work in three teams. Direct the teams to take turns guessing letters in the word. When a team guesses a correct letter, turn it over and let that team either select another letter or guess the word to win the game.

Teacher to Teacher

On the board, make simple drawings to illustrate words with consonant digraphs (e.g., **wheel, choo-choo** train, **ship, knot, thermometer, wristwatch, truck**). Have children write the picture's name within each drawing, and underline the digraph.

*Marie Leahy
Maple Shade, NJ*

The Writing Process

Tell children they are going to write a speech as if they were a tour guide welcoming a visitor to their favorite place. Then have them read the directions on page 106.

Brainstorm Ask children to tell about their favorite places. Encourage them to talk about favorite neighborhood places, as well as the best places to go to for a trip. Ask children what they most enjoy about each place and what they would like to tell others about it.

Write Have children choose one place to write about as if they were a tour guide welcoming a visitor. Encourage them to write first drafts of their speeches on paper.

Revise Ask children to make sure they mentioned what visitors would enjoy doing and seeing in the children's favorite places. Then invite them to write their final drafts in the space provided on page 106.

Publish Invite children to give their speeches as if they were greeting visitors to their favorite places. After the presentations, have children go back and underline the spelling words they used in their speeches.

Extending the Skill

Children may enjoy writing a tourist's guide to the school or neighborhood. Have children work in small groups, and ask each group to choose one place to describe. Direct the groups to write and illustrate a paragraph describing their places. Compile children's work in a book, and display it in the classroom or school library.

Portfolio

Children may wish to add their speeches to their portfolios.

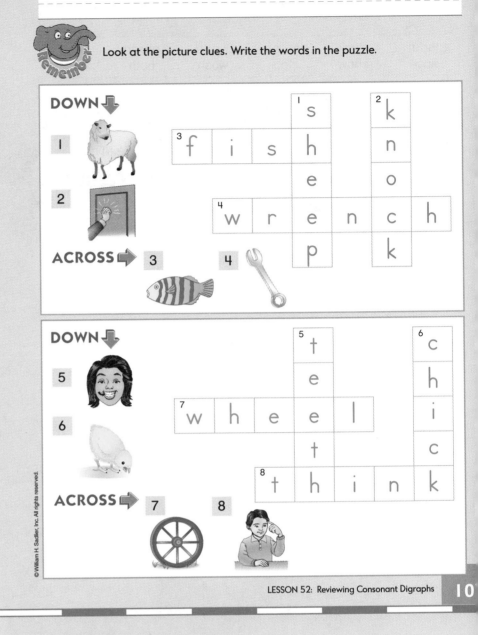

Lesson 52

Reviewing Consonant Digraphs

Objectives
- To use words with consonant digraphs in a crossword puzzle
- To identify beginning and final consonant digraphs

Warming Up

Reviewing Compound Words
Say the first part of a compound word, and give a clue for the second part. Have children name the compound word. You might use the following:

star/animal with fins (**fish**)
butter/annoying insect (**fly**)
sand/cardboard container (**box**)
note/something to read (**book**)
bean/sack (**bag**)
oat/breakfast or lunch (**meal**)
tip/a part of your foot (**toe**)
snow/corn cereal (**flakes**)

★ Teaching the Lesson

Say the tongue twisters below, and challenge children to repeat them. Have volunteers identify the consonant digraph they hear most often in each.

Thirsty Thea thought her **thermos** was in **Thebes.**
Shawn shopped for **shirts** in **Shanghai.**
Chuck chased a **chicken** in **Charleston.**
Why did **Whiskers whimper** in **Wheeling?**
Rick's **tru**ck got **stu**ck on a ro**ck** in Com**st**o**ck.**
A **Knight** bought a **knife** and a **knapsack** in **Knoxville.**
A **wren wriggled** on a **wreath** in **Wrigley.**

Look at the picture clues. Write the words in the puzzle.

DOWN ⬇

ACROSS ➡

3 fish
4 wrench

(puzzle grid: s, k / f i s h / n / e o / w r e n c h / p k)

DOWN ⬇

ACROSS ➡

7 wheel
8 think

(puzzle grid: t, c / e h / w h e e l / t i / t h i n k c)

LESSON 52: Reviewing Consonant Digraphs **10**

Multisensory Activities

Auditory ■ Tactile

Knock or Shake
Materials: shakers or other rhythm instruments

Give shakers to half the class, and tell the other half their signal will be to knock on their desks. Direct children to shake or knock if they can identify the digraph in a word you say. Then say words with consonant digraphs from student pages 99–106. Alternate between "shakers" and "knockers" to have students name the digraphs.

Visual ■ Kinesthetic

Picture This
Materials: drawing paper, crayons

Have children work in seven groups. Assign **th, sh, wh, ch, ck, kn,** or **wr** to each group. Tell the groups to draw a picture of an object whose name contains their digraph and to write around it other words that contain that digraph. Display the digraph pictures, and encourage children to practice reading all the words.

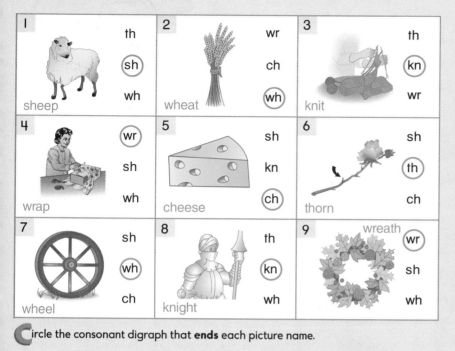

1. sheep — th, (sh), wh
2. wheat — wr, ch, (wh)
3. knit — th, (kn), wr
4. wrap — (wr), sh, wh
5. cheese — sh, kn, (ch)
6. thorn — sh, (th), ch
7. wheel — sh, (wh), ch
8. knight — th, (kn), wh
9. wreath — (wr), sh, wh

Circle the consonant digraph that **ends** each picture name.

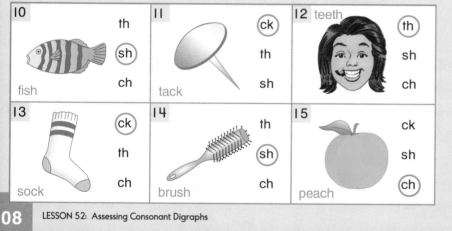

10. fish — th, (sh), ch
11. tack — (ck), th, sh
12. teeth — (th), sh, ch
13. sock — (ck), th, ch
14. brush — th, (sh), ch
15. peach — ck, sh, (ch)

08 LESSON 52: Assessing Consonant Digraphs

Reteaching *Activities*

Think, Check, and Show
Materials: index cards

On separate index cards write words with consonant digraphs. Give a few cards to each child. Have one child read a word aloud. Direct the rest of the children to hold up any of their own cards that have words with the same consonant digraph. Invite the children, one at a time, to say the words and name the consonant digraph.

On the Consonant Digraph Road
Materials: Phonics Picture Cards for words with consonant digraphs, mural paper, envelopes, markers

Draw a road on mural paper, and write the names of cities from *Teaching the Lesson* along the road. Tape a large envelope under each city. Have children, one at a time, choose a picture card, name it, and "travel" along the road to put the card in the envelope of the city with the same digraph.

Assessing the Skills

Check-Up Review with the class how to complete a crossword puzzle. Then have children turn to page 107 and identify the pictures. You might have them work in pairs to complete the page.

Have the class turn to the assessment on page 108. Read aloud the directions, and have volunteers identify the pictures. Emphasize to children that they should look for beginning digraphs at the top of the page and final digraphs at the bottom.

Observational Assessment Review any observational notes you have taken since the last assessment. Use them to help you decide which children can benefit most from reteaching.

Student Skills Assessment Use the checklist on Student Edition pages 207–208 to record your observations of each child's progress.

Writing Conference Meet with children individually to review their writing. Use your notes and children's comments to determine whether each child can discriminate between different consonant digraphs. Encourage each child to set a goal for improvement to be reached before the next conference.

Group together children who need further instruction. Then complete the *Reteaching Activities*.

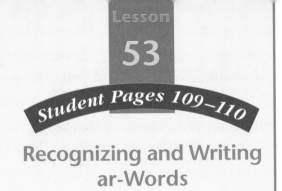

Recognizing and Writing ar-Words

Objectives

- To recognize the sound of **ar**
- To write **ar**-words in context
- To rhyme **ar**-words

Warming Up

Reviewing s-Blends

Read aloud each sentence below. Direct children to write on paper each **s**-blend they hear. Then check answers.

A **star** is **sparkling** in the **sky**.
Spring flowers have a **sweet smell**.
The **snow** made the **streets slick**.
We **swam** and **splashed** in the **stream**.
A **squirrel scratched** the **stump**.
The **snake's skin** has **stripes**.

★ Teaching the Lesson

- Invite children to sing "Old MacDonald." Then change the lyrics to introduce **ar**-words. Write **farm, barn, star, car,** and **harp** on the board. Point to each word as you sing it in the verse below.

  Old MacDonald had a **farm**,
  E-I-E-I-O.
  And on his farm he had a **barn**,
  E-I-E-I-O.

Sing the verse again. This time substitute into the third line: he saw a **star**; he drove a **car**; he played a **harp**.

- Ask volunteers to underline the letters that make the **ar** sound in each word on the board. Tell children that **r** after a vowel gives the vowel a new sound.

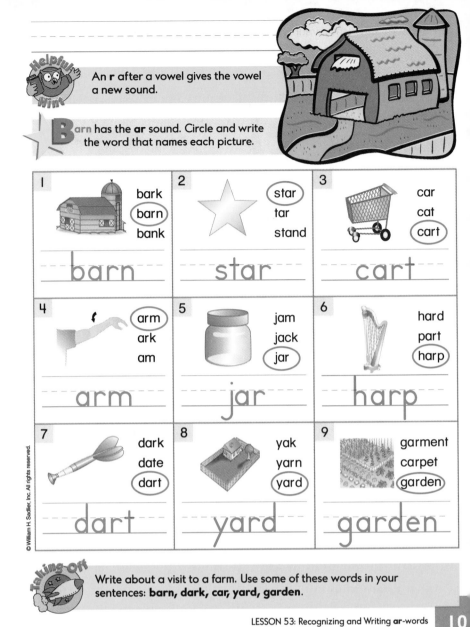

Helpful Hint: An **r** after a vowel gives the vowel a new sound.

★ **B**arn has the **ar** sound. Circle and write the word that names each picture.

1	bark (**barn**) bank **barn**	2	(**star**) tar stand **star**	3	car cat (**cart**) **cart**
4	(**arm**) ark am **arm**	5	jam jack (**jar**) **jar**	6	hard part (**harp**) **harp**
7	dark date (**dart**) **dart**	8	yak yarn (**yard**) **yard**	9	garment carpet (**garden**) **garden**

Taking Off: Write about a visit to a farm. Use some of these words in your sentences: **barn, dark, car, yard, garden**.

LESSON 53: Recognizing and Writing **ar**-words

10

Multisensory Activities

Auditory ■ Visual

Art in the Cart

Recite "The Museum Door" from the Poetry Poster. Ask children to name the **ar**-words that rhyme. (**art, cart**) Then write **barn, far, park, car,** and **arch** on the board. Have children use them to complete these rhymes:

There's a **jar** in the (**car**).
I hear a **bark** in the (**park**).
I dropped **yarn** in the (**barn**).
The **star** is very (**far**).
They **march** under the (**arch**).

Visual ■ Kinesthetic

Stars Above the Barn

Materials: yellow paper stars, markers, mural paper

Draw a barn on mural paper, and write each of these **ar**-words on a yellow paper star: **farm, apart, harm, sharp, march, chart, charm, spark, yarn, large, start, bark, harp, car, arm,** and **jar**. Have children, one at a time, read aloud a star word and then tape it above the barn.

Use a word from the box to complete each sentence.

far	dark	farm	hard	bark	barn

1. Is it __hard__ to milk a cow?

2. Ask Mrs. Martin! She lives on a __farm__.

3. It is not __far__ from my house.

4. There are many animals in the __barn__.

5. Sparky the dog likes to __bark__ at the cows.

6. Sometimes I visit until it gets __dark__.

Write a rhyming word.

7 harm	8 star	9 yard
Accept any answer that is a real word.		
10 lark	11 yarn	12 dart

10

LESSON 53: Writing **ar**-words

Spelling Connection

Read aloud the words and sentences below. Invite volunteers to spell each word orally or write it on the board.

barn   The cows are in the **barn**.
star   The sun is really a **star**.
farm   Barb owns a chicken **farm**.
dark   The moon was bright in the **dark** sky.
large   Cows are **large** animals.

Computer Connection

Have children improve their word-building skills by exploring the Word Mine in Reader Rabbit® 2 (The Learning Company). Direct children to make compound words by selecting beginning or ending word crystals. For example, given the word ending **bow**, children would select the **rain** crystal to build the word **rainbow**. Challenge children to collect as many crystals as they can in the Word Mine.

Practicing the Skill

● Have volunteers read aloud the directions and the Helpful Hint and identity the pictures on page 109. Then have children complete the page.

● Go over the directions for both sections on page 110. Encourage children to use trial and error if they are unsure about the sentence completions at the top of the page. You might have them work in pairs to complete the page.

Extending the Skill Across the Curriculum

(Language Arts/Math)

Theme Activity

● Ask children to tell what they know about farm life. Encourage them to share actual experiences or talk about books or stories they have read. Then read aloud the theme book cited below.

● Help children generate a list on the board of events from the book. Include **ar**-words whenever possible; for example:

The sky was still **dark** when the rooster crowed.

At sunset the sky turned **scarlet**.

● On the board write A.M. and P.M. Explain that A.M. refers to the time from midnight to noon, and P.M. from noon to midnight. Then have children guess the time for each event listed. Start them off by saying, for example, "The sky was still dark when the rooster crowed. It might have been about 5:00 A.M."

● Have children choose a favorite event to write about and illustrate.

Theme Book

Tresselt, Alvin. *Sun Up*. New York: Lothrop, Lee & Shepard, 1991. A day on a farm.

Portfolio

Have children put their sentences in their portfolios.

Lesson 54

Student Pages 111–112

Recognizing and Writing or-Words and Reviewing ar-Words

Objectives
- To recognize and write **or**- and **ar**-words in context
- To rhyme **ar**- and **or**-words

Warming Up

Reviewing r-Blends

Write **br, cr, dr, fr, gr, pr,** and **tr** on the board. Ask children to answer each riddle below with an **r**-blend word and identify each blend. Preface each of the following by saying, "It rhymes with."

...log, but can hop; (**frog**)

...sail, but is a path; (**trail**)

...head, but you eat it; (**bread**)

...team, but is whipped; (**cream**)

...gum, but you hit it with sticks; (**drum**)

...pain, but cereal is made from it; (**grain**)

...dune, but it's a dried fruit. (**prune**)

★ Teaching the Lesson

Materials: Phonics Picture Cards **horn** and **corn**

- Recite "Little Boy Blue" with the class. Hold up the **horn** and **corn** picture cards. Isolate and say the sound that **or** makes in those words. Then repeat the words, with emphasis on the **or** sound.
- On the board, write **cork, sport, shore,** and **thorn** in one column and **born, fork, port,** and **store** in another. Together read the words aloud. Then have volunteers draw lines to match the rhyming words.

111

Corn has the **or** sound. Find the name of each picture. Write the word.

| acorn | cord | core | cork | corn | fork |
| forty | horn | horse | porch | thorn | torch |

1. corn
2. torch
3. cord
4. fork
5. horse
6. porch
7. horn
8. cork
9. thorn
10. core
11. acorn
12. forty

LESSON 54: Recognizing and Writing **or**-words

111

Multisensory *Activities*

Auditory ■ Kinesthetic

Horses or Marchers

Have children stand in a circle. Tell children to trot in place like a **horse** if they hear you say a word with the **or** sound and to **march** in place if they hear the **ar** sound. Then say **core, yarn, dark, corn, sharp, thorn, acorn, chart, forty, torch, large,** and **dart.**

Visual ■ Auditory

For the Corner or the Jar

Materials: empty plastic jar, slips of paper

On separate slips of paper write: **barn, card, darts, march, hard, yard, spark, shark, arm, lark, cord, horn, horse, porch, born, sport, form, score, torn,** and **shore.** Direct each child to choose a word and put it in the **jar** if it has an **ar** sound, or on the **corner** of the table if it has an **or** sound.

Draw a line from each word in the first column to a rhyming word in the second column.

1	park	•	• tar	9	farm	•	• worn
2	scar	•	• porch	10	form	•	• charm
3	sore	•	• spark	11	born	•	• yarn
4	torch	•	• more	12	barn	•	• storm
5	dark	•	• thorn	13	start	•	• mark
6	arm	•	• shore	14	pork	•	• stork
7	score	•	• harm	15	short	•	• smart
8	torn	•	• bark	16	shark	•	• sport

Circle all the **ar**-words. Underline all the **or**-words. Then circle **Yes** or **No** to answer each question.

17. Can a (park) path be <u>short</u>?	(Yes) No
18. Can a <u>horse</u> play a (harp)?	Yes (No)
19. Can you buy a (scarf) in a <u>store</u>?	(Yes) No
20. Is a <u>fork</u> the same as a <u>torch</u>?	Yes (No)
21. Can a (shark) throw (darts)?	Yes (No)
22. Is an <u>acorn</u> made of (yarn)?	Yes (No)
23. Can a <u>stork</u> play (cards)?	Yes (No)
24. Can a dog (bark) and (snarl)?	(Yes) No
25. Does <u>corn</u> have <u>thorns</u>?	Yes (No)
26. Can you read a <u>story</u> in the <u>morning</u>?	(Yes) No

12   LESSON 54: Reviewing **ar**-words and **or**-words

Spelling Connection

Read aloud the words and sentences below. Invite volunteers to spell each word orally or write it on the board.

corn	I like to eat sweet **corn**.
porch	Carmela has a swing on her front **porch**.
short	Marco got his hair cut **short**.
more	Art picked **more** oranges than Omar.
thorns	The rose bush has many sharp **thorns**.

Multicultural Connection

Explain that the Amish lead simple lives and avoid using modern conveniences. For example, they have neither electricity nor running water in their homes; they dress plainly; they often live on farms and travel by horse and buggy to nearby places.

Help children make a list of the advantages and disadvantages of horse-and-buggy transportation.

Practicing the Skill

● Read aloud the directions on page 111, and have volunteers name the pictures. Do the first item with the class. Then assign the page. Suggest that children check off each word in the list after they use it.

● Go over the directions for both sections on page 112. Demonstrate how to do the first item in each section. Then have children complete the page.

Extending the Skill Across the Curriculum

(Language Arts/Art)

Theme Activity

Materials: drawing paper, crayons, markers

● Invite children to use their imaginations to "armchair-travel." To set the scene, explain that in some parts of our country, mainly in Pennsylvania and Ohio, people called the Amish live simple lives very different from most of ours. Then read aloud the theme book cited below about life in an Amish family. As you read the story, point out the **ar**- and **or**-words.

● Ask children to draw an autumn picture of their favorite scene from the story. Tell them to include and label objects whose names have the sounds of **ar** or **or**, such as **farmhouse, barn, jar, yard, horse, corn, porch,** and **acorns**.

Theme Book

Mitchell, Barbara. *Down Buttermilk Lane.* New York: Lothrop, Lee & Shepard, 1993. An Amish family travels by buggy to shop in the village.

Observational Assessment

*As children label their pictures, observe who may be having difficulty distinguishing between the sounds of **ar** and **or**.*

Student Pages 113–114

Recognizing and Writing er-, ir-, and ur-Words

Objectives
● To recognize the sound of **er, ir,** and **ur**
● To write **er-, ir-,** and **ur**-words in context

Warming Up

Reviewing l-Blends
Write **bl, cl, fl, gl, pl,** and **sl** on the board. Invite children to think of **l**-blend words that belong with the following pairs:

grow, green (**plant**)
sky, white (**clouds**)
shirt, arm (**sleeve**)
cover, bed (**blanket**)
colorful, blossoms (**flowers**)
map, Earth (**globe**)

★ Teaching the Lesson

● Write these rhymes on the board:
Birdie, birdie, in the tree,
Did I hear you **chirp** at me?
Turtle, turtle, near the gate,
Hurry, hurry don't be late.
Mermaid, mermaid in the sea,
Will you **serve** the whale his tea?.

● Read the rhymes aloud with the class. Remind children that a vowel followed by **r** makes a new sound. Then have volunteers underline the **ir-, ur-,** and **er**-words. Lead children to generalize that **ir, ur,** and **er** often stand for the same sound.

● Write **turn, first, purple, fern, third, circus, spider, summer,** and **fur** on the board. Ask volunteers to read the words and circle the letters that stand for the **er** sound.

The **er** in **fern**, the **ir** in **bird**, and the **ur** in **turtle** make the same sound. Sort the words. Write the **er**-words under **fern**, the **ir**-words under **bird**, and the **ur**-words under **purse**.

burn	chirp	clerk	curb	dirt	first
girl	her	herd	nurse	perch	serve
surf	term	third	thirty	turkey	turn

1 fern	2 bird	3 purse
clerk	chirp	burn
her	dirt	curb
herd	first	nurse
perch	girl	surf
serve	third	turkey
term	thirty	turn

Write a silly sentence with an **er**-word, an **ir**-word, and a **ur**-word. For example, "At the **turkey** farm, I saw **thirty birds** on one **perch**."

LESSON 55: Recognizing and Writing **er**-words, **ir**-words, and **ur**-words

---

Multisensory *Activities*

Visual ■ Kinesthetic

Circle Game
Materials: posterboard; flash cards with **er-, ir-,** and **ur**-words from pages 113-114

Have children sit in a circle. Write **er, ir,** and **ur** on separate sheets of posterboard. Give the signs to three children to hold up. Flash a word card. Have a volunteer read the word and say, for example, "**Turkey** has **ur,**" and then take over holding up the appropriate sign. Repeat the process.

Visual ■ Tactile

Three-Ring Circus
Materials: tape, paper, scissors

On the board draw an outline of a circus tent with three large rings below it. Write **ir, er,** and **ur** in the rings. Have children work in three groups, one group for each ring. Direct each group to cut out small "circus balls" and write a word with their group's vowel sound on each. Have children tape the balls in the correct rings and read the words.

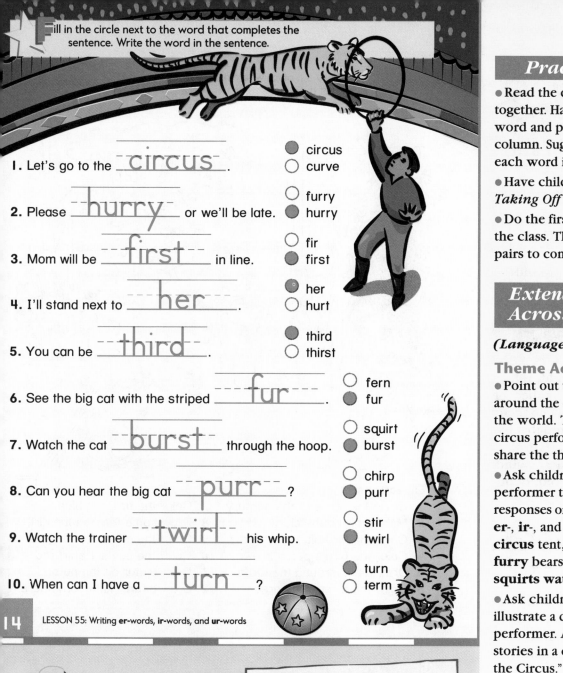

Fill in the circle next to the word that completes the sentence. Write the word in the sentence.

1. Let's go to the **circus** .
- ● circus
- ○ curve

2. Please **hurry** or we'll be late.
- ○ furry
- ● hurry

3. Mom will be **first** in line.
- ○ fir
- ● first

4. I'll stand next to **her** .
- ● her
- ○ hurt

5. You can be **third** .
- ● third
- ○ thirst

6. See the big cat with the striped **fur** .
- ○ fern
- ● fur

7. Watch the cat **burst** through the hoop.
- ○ squirt
- ● burst

8. Can you hear the big cat **purr** ?
- ○ chirp
- ● purr

9. Watch the trainer **twirl** his whip.
- ○ stir
- ● twirl

10. When can I have a **turn** ?
- ● turn
- ○ term

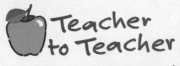

14

LESSON 55: Writing **er**-words, **ir**-words, and **ur**-words

Spelling Connection

Read aloud the words and sentences below. Invite volunteers to spell each word orally or write it on the board.

curb	I rode my bike over the **curb**.
nurse	The **nurse** works in the hospital.
shirt	My blue **shirt** has long sleeves.
third	Kurt sits in the **third** row.
winter	Snow falls in the **winter**.

Teacher to Teacher

Draw a large jar on posterboard and mount it on a bulletin board. Each time a student learns a new **ar-**, **er-**, **ir-**, or **ur-** word have him or her write it on a "marble" made from construction paper and put it into the jar.

*S. Margaret Eileen
Reading, PA*

Practicing the Skill

● Read the directions on page 113 together. Have children identify the key word and picture at the top of each column. Suggest that children check off each word in the box as they write it.

● Have children work in pairs to do the *Taking Off* activity.

● Do the first item on page 114 with the class. Then have children work in pairs to complete the page.

Extending the Skill Across the Curriculum

(Language Arts/Social Studies)

Theme Activity

● Point out that many circuses travel around the country and even around the world. Talk about circuses and circus performers with the class. Then share the theme book cited below.

● Ask children what kind of circus performer they would like to be. List responses on chart paper. Try to include **er-**, **ir-**, and **ur-**words, such as: **trailer, circus** tent, tightrope **walker, tigers, furry** bears, **juggler,** a **flower** that **squirts water, purple,** and **curtain**.

● Ask children to write about and illustrate a day in the life of a circus performer. After sharing, compile the stories in a class book titled "A Day at the Circus."

Theme Book

Garland, Michael. *Circus Girl*. New York: Dutton Children's Books, 1993. A family works in the circus.

Portfolio

Have children include their circus stories in their portfolios.

Observational Assessment

Non-visual learners may confuse the spellings of er, ir, and ur. Check children's writing to see who needs practice with these combinations.

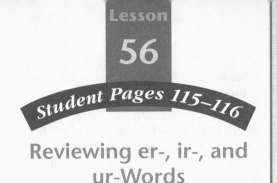

Lesson 56

Reviewing er-, ir-, and ur-Words

Objectives
- To follow directions that include words with **er, ir,** and **ur**
- To write a story using **er-, ir-,** and **ur**-words

Warming Up

Reviewing Final Blends

Have each child write either **ld, nd, mp, ng, nk, nt, sk,** or **st** on a sheet of paper. Invite children to hold up their papers when they hear a word that has their blend. Then say **toast, stamp, gold, bring, trunk, paint, desk, wind, long, frost, pink, camp, sold, bent, disk,** and **find.**

★ Teaching the Lesson

Materials: Phonics Picture Cards **fern, bird, purse**

- Display the picture cards on the chalk ledge and write the picture names in random order on the board. Have volunteers match each picture with its name and circle the **er, ir,** or **ur.**
- Write these directions on separate sentence strips:

1. Circle the name of a plant.
2. Draw a box around the name of an animal.
3. Draw a star over another name for pocketbook.

- Display the sentence strips. Then ask volunteers to read each strip and follow the direction on it.

ESL Activities
Refer to page 89L.

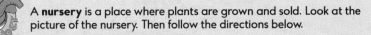

A **nursery** is a place where plants are grown and sold. Look at the picture of the nursery. Then follow the directions below.

Directions

1. Circle the name of the nursery.
2. Make an X on the clerk.
3. Color the bird blue and yellow.
4. Color the bird's perch brown.
5. Draw a box around the turtle.
6. Color the turnip tops green.
7. Color the fir trees blue.
8. Draw some ferns in the dirt.
9. Color the girl's skirt purple.
10. Color the boy's T-shirt red.
11. Draw a star on the purse.
12. Draw a furry kitten anywhere.

LESSON 56: Reviewing **er**-words, **ir**-words, and **ur**-words

---

Multisensory *Activities*

Visual ■ Tactile

Artistic Words

Materials: construction paper

Have children trace their hands to draw a **turkey** (fingers are the tail feathers), a **flower** with five petals, and a **fir** tree. On the board write **purple, turn, nurse, curl, clerk, perch, corner, paper, fern, dirt, bird, shirt, girl,** and **third.** Tell children to write **ur**-words on the turkey's tail, **er**-words on the flower petals, and **ir**-words on the fir tree.

Auditory ■ Tactile

Vowel + r Match

Materials: index cards; Phonics Picture Cards **fern, letter, zipper, bird, thirty, shirt, purse, turtle**

Write the name of each picture card on a separate index card. Then give one of the cards to each child. Have a child with a picture card hold it up and say the picture name. Direct children with word cards to hold up their card and read it if they think it has a matching word.

115

Write a story about visiting a nursery. Circle the **er**-words, **ir**-words, and **ur**-words that you use. Use some of the words in the box.

birch	bird	chirp	clerk	dirt	fern
first	nursery	perch	purple	serve	turn

NURSERY

LESSON 56: Reviewing **er**-words, **ir**-words, and **ur**-words

Spelling Connection

Read aloud the words and sentences below. Invite volunteers to spell each word orally or write it on the board.

dirt   Don't get **dirt** on your new clothes.
perch   The parrot sat on a **perch**.
corner   Kirk planted a tree near the **corner** of the house.
purple   **Purple** flowers are my favorite.
bird   A **bird** made a nest in the tree.

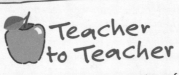
Teacher to Teacher

Have partners play a variation of tic-tac-toe. Instead of drawing X's and O's in the tic-tac-toe grid, have children choose to write **ar**-, **er**-, **ir**-, **or**-, or **ur**-words.

Peggy O'Toole
Haddonfield, NJ

Practicing the Skill

Materials: blue, yellow, brown, green, purple, and red crayons

● Read aloud the directions at the top of page 115. Have children name and point out what they see in the illustration. Then go over the twelve directives at the bottom of the page. You may wish to pause after each while children follow it.

● Ask children to tell what might go on at a nursery. List children's ideas on chart paper. Then read aloud the directions at the top of page 116. Supply extra paper for children who may want to write longer stories.

Extending the Skill Across the Curriculum

(Language Arts/Science)
Theme Activity
Materials: potting soil, plastic cups, seeds and/or potato or sweet potato eyes, plant cuttings

● If possible, plan a field trip to a nursery. Alternatively, invite a nursery worker to speak to the class, and supply pictures for reference.

● Discuss the importance of nurseries and the kinds of things that workers do there—planting and caring for flowers, vegetables, and trees; selling plants and gardening supplies.

● Try to work **er**-, **ir**-, and **or**-words into the discussion, and write them on the board as they come up.

● Make a classroom nursery. You might plant cuttings, seeds, or potato and sweet potato eyes in plastic cups. When the plants are large enough, have children take them home, or donate them to a shelter or nursing home.

Portfolio
Remind students to put their stories from page 116 in their portfolios.

Connecting Spelling and Writing

Objectives
- To say, spell, sort, and write words with **r**-controlled vowels
- To write a letter using spelling words

Warming Up

Reviewing y as a Vowel
Share riddles about words with **y** as a vowel; for example, "It follows fifty-nine." (**sixty**)

★ *Teaching the Lesson*

Materials: index cards

- On the board write: "I saw a **herd** of wild ponies." Read aloud the sentence. Ask which word has the **er** sound.
- Together say and spell **herd**; then say the word again. Have a child underline the letters that stand for the **er** sound.
- List the remaining spelling words from page 117. Say each word with children; then spell and repeat it.
- Have children work in groups to write each word on an index card and then sort the words by vowel sound.
- Ask each group to explain how the words were sorted.

Observational Assessment
Listen to children's explanations of how they sort words for clues to their thinking processes.

Practicing the Skill

Have children turn to page 117. Call on a volunteer to read aloud the directions and the spelling words. Ask why **er**-words, **ir**-words, and **ur**-words are listed in the same column. (They all stand for the same sound.)

117

Spell and Write Say and spell each word in the box. Then write each word under the correct heading.

	1	**2**	**3**
clerk	**er**-words	**or**-words	**ar**-words
start	clerk	store	start
purse	her	before	far
store	herd	horse	
first	**ir**-words		
her	first		
before	girl		
turn	**ur**-words		
far	purse		
horse	turn		
girl			
herd			

PHOTOS

LESSON 57: Connecting Spelling and Writing

Multisensory *Activities*

Visual ■ Kinesthetic

Buy a Word
Materials: construction paper, scissors, crayons, index cards

Write each spelling word on an index card. Have children write **ar, or, er, ir,** and **ur** on dollar-bill shaped pieces of paper. Then set up a "word store." Appoint a "clerk" to read a spelling word on an index card. Invite a "customer" to buy the word by spelling it and handing the clerk a bill with its **r**-controlled vowel sound.

Tactile ■ Visual

Cornmeal Words
Materials: cornmeal, box or pan

Cover the bottom of a box or pan with cornmeal. Have children take turns dictating the spelling words and writing them in the cornmeal with their fingers. Encourage children to say the name of each letter as they write it.

Write a letter to a friend. Tell about a trip that you have taken or would like to take. Use one or more of your spelling words.

clerk	start	purse	store
first	her	before	turn
far	horse	girl	herd

Dear _____ ,

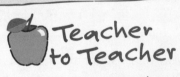
You'll never guess where I went!

Your friend,

The Writing Process

Tell children that they are going to write a letter about a trip they have taken or would like to take. Then have children read the directions on page 118. Call attention to the proper location of the date, greeting, and closing of a letter.

Brainstorm Have the class brainstorm a list of places they have visited or would like to visit. Encourage children to share their experiences.

Write Tell children they may write their letters to anyone they wish. Have them write drafts of their letters on sheets of paper.

Revise Ask children to make sure they have told what they liked best about their real or imaginary trip. Remind them to check spelling and punctuation before they write their final versions in the space provided on page 118.

Publish Invite children to share their letters with classmates. You might have children go back and underline the spelling words they used in their letters.

Extending the Skills

Model how to address an envelope. Then invite children to address envelopes to the people who are to receive their letters. You may wish to provide made-up addresses for children to use.

Portfolio

Have children add their letters to their portfolios.

Spelling Connection

Write a spelling word on the board. Have children cover their eyes as you erase the letters that stand for the vowel sound. Then invite a volunteer to fill in the missing letters. Continue with other spelling words.

Teacher to Teacher

Say a simple sentence, such as, "I ironed the **shirt**." Ask children to stretch the sentence by adding **r**-controlled words. For example:

I ironed the **purple** shirt.
I ironed the **purple** shirt **yesterday**.
I ironed the **purple** shirt **yesterday afternoon**.

S. Santa Teresa
Philadelphia, PA

118

Integrating the Language Arts

Objectives
• To use oral and written language to extend the theme concept
• To recognize consonant digraphs and **r**-controlled vowels in context

Background Information

The Statue of Liberty was built in France by sculptor Frédéric-Auguste Bartholdi. It was taken apart and shipped to the United States in 1885, where it was put together again. The Statue of Liberty and its base reach a combined height of more than 300 feet. The statue weighs 225 tons. One index finger is 8 feet long, and a fingernail is 13 inches by 10 inches. The Statue of Liberty is one of the largest sculptures in the world.

★ Teaching the Lesson

Materials: pictures of the Statue of Liberty; map of the United States

• Have children look at the pictures and share what they know about the Statue of Liberty.

• Read aloud the paragraph on page 119. Then help children find New York City on the map; it is the location of the Statue of Liberty.

• Ask children to search the text for words with consonant digraphs and **r**-controlled vowels.

Oral Language Development
Ask the concluding question on page 119. To get the discussion started, ask children why their ancestors (or their families) came to America. Write responses on the board.

ESL Activities
Refer to page 89L.

Let's read and talk about the Statue of Liberty.

Meet Miss Liberty. That's what some people call this statue. She stands on an island in New York harbor and greets people who come to the United States. Miss Liberty is over 100 years old. She was a gift to us from the people of France. She's 152 feet high on a base that's 150 feet high. She holds the torch of freedom above her head.

Why do you think Miss Liberty holds the torch of freedom above her head?

LESSON 58: Compound Words, **y** as a Vowel, Consonant Digraphs, and **r**-controlled Vowels in Context

Reading and Writing Connection

Materials: books about the Statue of Liberty

Give children access to books about the Statue of Liberty, and encourage them to learn more about Miss Liberty and how she was built.

Invite children to think about what they would say to the man who sculpted the Statue of Liberty. Then have them write thank-you notes to him.

Social Studies Connection

Materials: world map, pushpins

Tell children that around the turn of the 19th century, many immigrants entered the United States by ship through New York Harbor. Explain that Miss Liberty was, for many, the first glimpse of America.

Ask children to find out whether any of their ancestors came to America through Ellis Island. As they share this information, help children mark a world map with pushpins to show where their families came from.

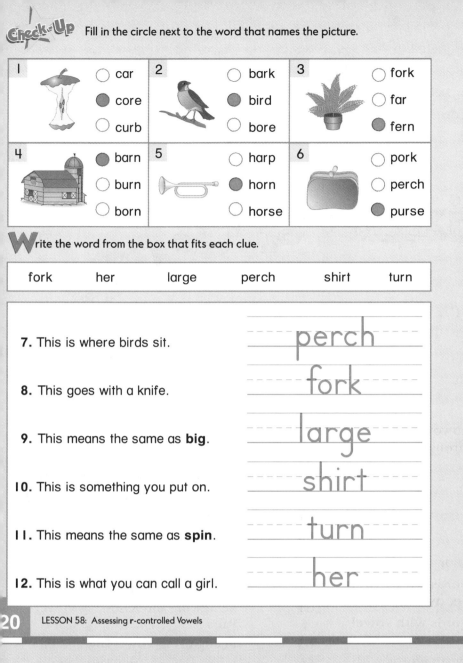

Check-Up Fill in the circle next to the word that names the picture.

1. ○ car ● core ○ curb
2. ○ bark ● bird ○ bore
3. ○ fork ○ far ● fern
4. ● barn ○ burn ○ born
5. ○ harp ● horn ○ horse
6. ○ pork ○ perch ● purse

Write the word from the box that fits each clue.

fork	her	large	perch	shirt	turn

7. This is where birds sit. perch

8. This goes with a knife. fork

9. This means the same as **big**. large

10. This is something you put on. shirt

11. This means the same as **spin**. turn

12. This is what you can call a girl. her

20 LESSON 58: Assessing r-controlled Vowels

Reteaching *Activities*

Like Miss Liberty
Materials: index cards, pocket chart, Phonics Picture Cards listed below

Write these words on index cards, and put them in a pocket chart: **barn, car, star, corn, horn, horse, fern, letter, zipper, bird, shirt, purse,** and **turtle.** Then place picture cards for the same words facedown on a table. Have children take turns choosing a picture card and finding the word card that names it.

Play Your Cards
Write **r**-controlled vowel words on separate index cards. Have children work in groups. Appoint a dealer in each group to give four or five cards to each player. Then direct each dealer to lay down a card and say, for example, "**yard, ar.**" Explain that the other players may either lay down a card with the same **r**-controlled vowel or pass if they do not have a match. Have a different player start each round. The first player to lay down all his or her cards wins.

Assessing the Unit

Check-Up Say **ar**-, **or**-, **er**-, **ir**-, and **ur**-words, and have volunteers write them on the board. Correct any spelling errors. Remind children that **er, ir,** and **ur** all stand for the same sound. Then review how to indicate an answer choice by filling in a circle.

Read aloud the directions and have children identify the pictures at the top of page 120. You may wish to have children complete this section before going over the directions for and assigning the exercise at the bottom of the page.

Observational Assessment Review the observational notes you have recorded throughout this unit. Use these notes to help assess overall performance and progress.

Student Skills Assessment After children have completed the assessment on page 120, use the results and your observations to record your evaluation of each child's skills on pages 207–208 of the Student Edition.

Writing Conference Meet with each child to discuss the work in his or her portfolio. Encourage children to talk about their writing as you review the samples together. Take notes on children's comments and your own insights regarding progress. Use these notes to help you evaluate how well the child is applying phonics skills to writing.

Encourage children to revise one or more of their portfolio writings. Suggest that they use **ar**-, **or**-, **er**-, **ir**-, and **ur**-words in their revisions.

Group together for the *Reteaching Activities* children who need further practice with **r**-controlled vowels.

After reteaching, you might turn to page 89C of the Teacher's Edition for alternative assessment methods.

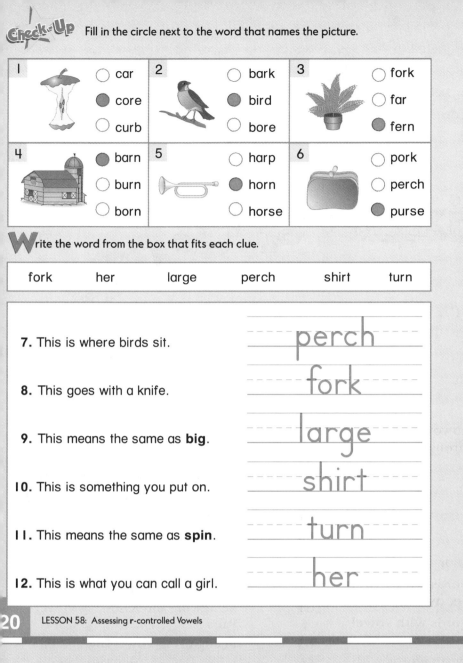

A Rainbow of Colors

Theme:
Green, blue, yellow, brown—
colors all around!

Overview

Unit 6 introduces children to vowel pairs, digraphs, and diphthongs through the theme of colors.

Objectives

- To enjoy a poem about color
- To recognize and write words with vowel pairs **ai, ay, ea, ee, oa, oe, ow, ui, ue, ie**
- To recognize and write words with vowel digraphs **ea, oo, au, aw**
- To recognize, spell, and write words with diphthongs **ou, ow, oi, oy, ew**

Thematic Teaching

Have children tell the colorful things or places they most enjoy. Provide additional reading material about colors.

Display the Poetry Poster "What Is Brown," and refer to it throughout the unit.

Individual Lessons

Lesson	Skill Focus
59	Introduction to Vowel Pairs, Vowel Digraphs, and Diphthongs
60	Recognizing Vowel Pairs **ai** and **ay**
61	Recognizing Vowel Pairs **ea** and **ee**
62	Reviewing Vowel Pairs **ai, ay, ea,** and **ee**
63	Recognizing Vowel Pairs **oa, oe, ow, ui, ue,** and **ie**
64	Reviewing and Assessing Vowel Pairs
65	Recognizing Vowel Digraph **ea**
66	Recognizing Vowel Digraph **oo**
67	Recognizing Vowel Digraphs **au** and **aw**
68	Reviewing and Assessing Vowel Digraphs **ea, oo, au,** and **aw**
69	Recognizing and Writing Diphthongs **ou** and **ow**
70	Writing and Reviewing Diphthongs
71	Connecting Spelling and Writing
72	Integrating the Language Arts

Take-Home Book: *Colors All Around*

Mary O'Neill

When Mary O'Neill was a little girl, she wrote and directed plays that were performed for her younger brothers and sisters. She harnessed that talent and spent the first part of her adult life writing ads. Eventually O'Neill became the head of her own advertising agency. When she was sixty-two years old, O'Neill joined the Peace Corps; while serving in West Africa and Latin America, she taught journalism and writing to the native peoples.

Curriculum Integration

Spelling   A *Spelling Connection* appears in every lesson.

Writing   Children write poems, descriptions, metaphors, song lyrics, newspaper articles, and reports on pages 124, 134, 136, 146, and 147.

Science   Activities related to science are found on pages 126, 134, 142, and 144.

Art   Opportunities for creativity through art appear on pages 124, 136, and 144.

Optional Learning Activities

Multisensory Activities   Every lesson offers a variety of learning styles—visual, auditory, tactile, or kinesthetic.

Multicultural Connection   Children celebrate cultural diversity in activities on pages 128, 134, and 142.

Thematic Activities   *Extending the Skill Across the Curriculum* in each lesson provides a cross-disciplinary application of thematic activities.

Assessment Strategies

Multiple strategies such as *Observational Assessments,* portfolios, written middle- and-end-of-the-unit assessments, and the *Skills Checklist* at the back of the Student Edition will help you assess children's mastery of phonics skills throughout Unit 6

Resources

Work by Mary O'Neill
Hailstones and Halibut Bones. New York: Doubleday, 1990.

Theme-Related Sources
Color Songs, Crayon Stories. Ashforton Music Group, 1991.

Florian, Douglas. *A Painter.* New York: Greenwillow, 1993.

Hailstones and Halibut Bones. Robert Waterman, 1993.

Assessment

In Unit 6 children focus on recognizing and writing vowel pairs, vowel digraphs, and diphthongs. The following are suggestions for evaluating these skills through informal/ formal, observational, objective, portfolio, and performance assessments. You may also wish to refer to *Using Technology* for alternative assessment activities.

Informal/Formal Assessment

The tests on pages 121D, 121E, and 121F assess children's mastery of the skills of recognizing and writing vowel pairs, vowel digraphs, and diphthongs. These tools may be used informally at the beginning of the unit to identify a starting point for individual or class instruction or formally at the end of the unit to assess children's progress.

Observational Assessment

Specific opportunities for observation are highlighted in the lesson plans and throughout the unit. *Multisensory Activities, Theme Activities,* and *Spelling Connection* offer additional chances for observation.

Objective Assessment

Use the assessment pages throughout the unit. Determine the area(s) in which children would benefit from more instruction; then refer to *Reteaching Activities* found throughout the unit in the Teacher's Edition. Finally, reassess children's progress.

Portfolio Assessment

Ask children to use color names to describe the area around them. For example, children might say, "The walls in my classroom are gray." Then invite children to write a story describing how they would like the world to be colored. For example, "The walls in my classroom are bright yellow." Have them illustrate their story. Display the stories and illustrations on a bulletin board titled "Color My World."

Performance Assessment

Review the vowel digraphs and vowel diphthongs. Have children brainstorm words with the digraphs and diphthongs. List the words on the board. Tell children to write two funny rhyming sentences that include color names and words with digraphs and diphthongs. Provide this model:

A small **blue jay**
Saw some **brown hay**
And a **green hoe**
By the farmer's **toe**!

Have children present their rhymes.

Using Technology

Have children complete the activities on pages 121K–121L of the Teacher's Edition.

Answer Key

Page 121D

1. mail 2. clue 3. green 4. suit 5. toast 6. tray 7. stream
8. pie 9. snow 10. grow 11. weeds 12. hoe 13. juicy

Page 121E

1. pool 2. feather 3. yarn 4. tooth 5. launch 6. spread
7. hood 8. shawl 9. boots 10. sweater 11. goose 12. fawn
13. moose 14. hawk 15. sauce 16. sausage 17. bread 18. cookie

Page 121F

1. house, south, brown 2. toys, enjoy, foil 3. chew, threw
4. sound, loud, frown 5. join, joy, boil 6. plow
7. dew 8. moist 9. hound

_____

- -

_____

Permission to duplicate this page is granted to users of *Sadlier Phonics*.

Write a word to answer each riddle.

1	2	3
I can be letters or postcards. I rhyme with **sail**.	I am a hint to help you get an answer. I rhyme with **glue**.	I am flat. I am made with bread. I rhyme with **coast**.

4	5	6
You can carry your lunch on me. I rhyme with **clay**.	I am a small river. I rhyme with **dream**.	I am white and cold. I rhyme with **blow**.

Circle the word that makes sense in each sentence.

7. I like to _____ tomatoes in my garden.   sweep   grow

8. Each day I pull out the _____.   paint   weeds

9. Soon my tomatoes will be red and _____.   easy   juicy

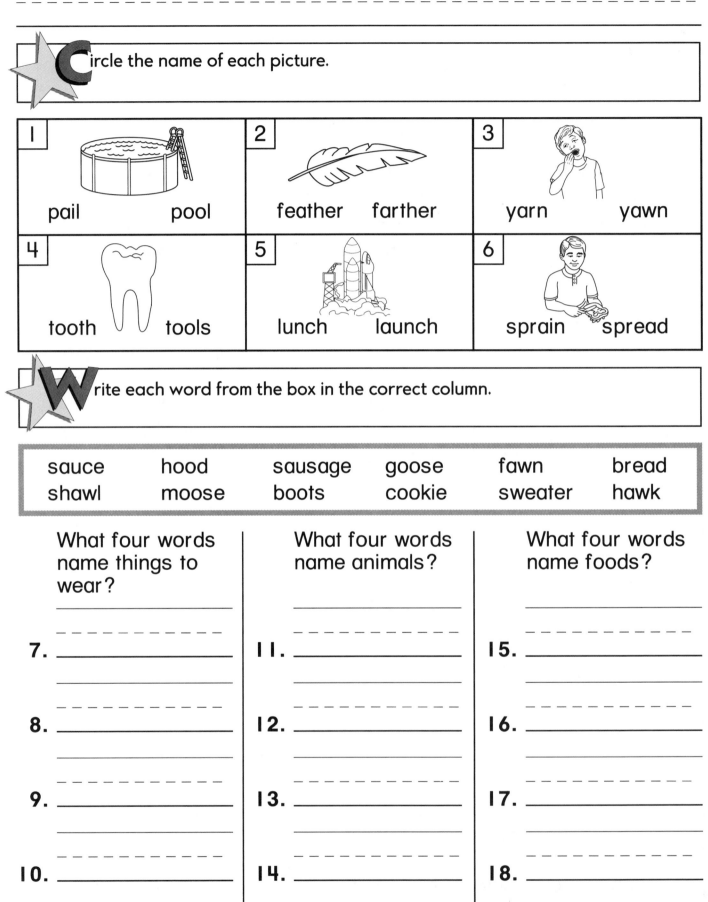

Circle the name of each picture.

1. pail pool	2. feather farther	3. yarn yawn
4. tooth tools	5. lunch launch	6. sprain spread

Write each word from the box in the correct column.

sauce	hood	sausage	goose	fawn	bread
shawl	moose	boots	cookie	sweater	hawk

What four words name things to wear?	What four words name animals?	What four words name foods?
7. _____	11. _____	15. _____
8. _____	12. _____	16. _____
9. _____	13. _____	17. _____
10. _____	14. _____	18. _____

    Blackline Master 24: Assessing Vowel Digraphs **ea, oo, au, aw**

Circle the words in each row that have the same vowel sound as the name of the picture in the box.

1		house	south	knew	brown
2		toys	crowd	enjoy	foil
3		crown	chew	threw	owl
4		sound	loud	frown	flew
5		ground	join	joy	boil

Underline the word that answers each question.

6	Which word means to dig up the ground?	7	Which word is small drops of water on the grass?
	couch play		oil tower
	broil plow		dew blouse
8	Which word means wet or damp?	9	Which word is a kind of dog?
	threw moist		pouch crew
	spoil frown		hound point

Game Time

▲▽▲▽▲▽▲▽▲▽▲▽ Pot of Gold Ahead! ▲▽▲▽▲▽▲▽▲▽

Blackline Master 26 p.121H

Objective: To read words with vowel digraphs

Players: pairs

Materials: construction paper, glue, scissors, number cubes

❁ Duplicate Blackline Master 26 and give a copy to each pair. Have children glue the page onto construction paper, color the rainbow, and cut out the words and leprechaun markers at the bottom. Tell partners to choose markers and color them different colors.

❁ Direct players to place the words facedown in a pile and to take turns rolling a number cube, moving their markers, and following the directions where they land. Explain that "FREE SPACE" means to stay put until the next turn; otherwise players who correctly read the chosen words may advance the number of spaces indicated.

❁ The first player to reach the pot of gold wins.

❁ You might make cards with words from other units and have the class play again.

▲▽▲▽▲▽▲▽▲▽▲▽ Flower Power ▽▲▽▲▽▲▽▲▽▲▽

Blackline Master 27 p.121I

Objective: To sort words with diphthongs according to their vowel sound

Players: individuals

Materials: crayons, scissors, glue, construction paper

❁ Duplicate Blackline Master 27 and give a copy to each child. Have children lightly color the flower parts any colors they choose and cut out each part. Then have them glue each illustrated flower center onto a separate sheet of construction paper.

❁ Direct children to name each picture and then glue around it the petals that have words with the same vowel sound as the picture name.

❁ Children may enjoy making their own petals and centers with other words and pictures.

▲▽▲▽▲▽▲▽▲▽▲▽ Over the Rainbow ▲▽▲▽▲▽▲▽▲▽

Objective: To read words with vowel pairs

Players: whole class

Materials: mural paper, crayons, scissors, index cards, beanbag (optional)

❁ Draw a rainbow on mural paper and have children color it. Then cut it out and lay it on the floor.

❁ On index cards write words with vowel pairs, such as: **snail, chain, hay, tray, green, queen, peach, bean, soap, goal, hoe, toe, row, low, fruit, juice, glue, clue, pie,** and **tie.**

❁ Ask children, one at a time, to read a word. If they read the word correctly, have them jump over the rainbow or toss a beanbag over the rainbow to the child who will read next.

❁ To vary the game, you might read the words and ask children to spell them. You might also use words containing vowel digraphs or diphthongs.

Pot of Gold Ahead!

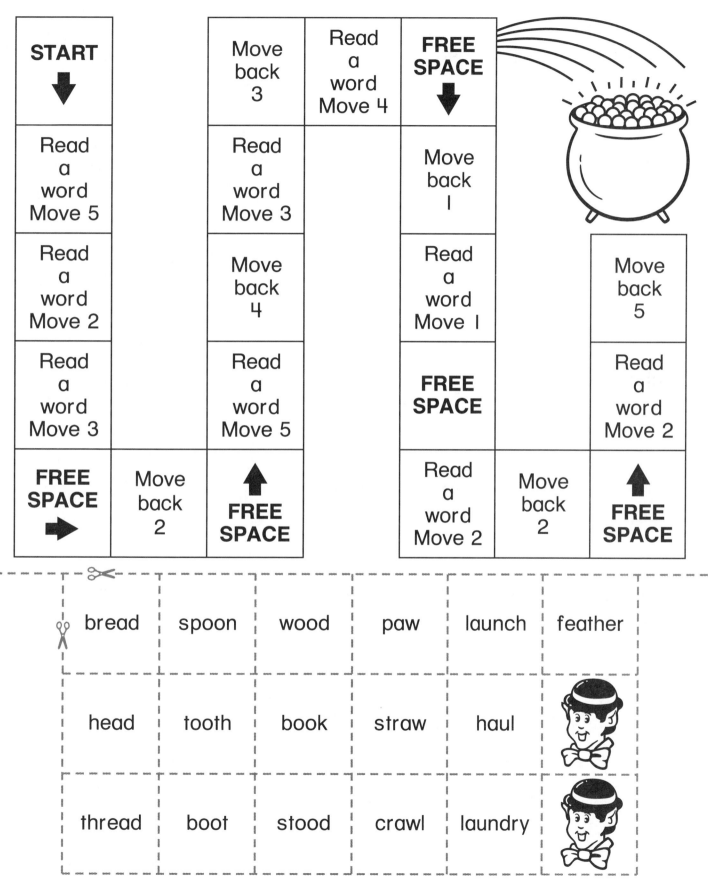

		Move back 3	Read a word Move 4	**FREE SPACE** ↓	
START ↓		Read a word Move 3		Move back 1	
Read a word Move 5		Move back 4		Read a word Move 1	Move back 5
Read a word Move 2		Read a word Move 5		**FREE SPACE**	Read a word Move 2
Read a word Move 3					
FREE SPACE ➡	Move back 2	**FREE SPACE** ↑		Read a word Move 2	Move back 2	**FREE SPACE** ↑

bread	spoon	wood	paw	launch	feather
head	tooth	book	straw	haul	
thread	boot	stood	crawl	laundry	

Flower Power

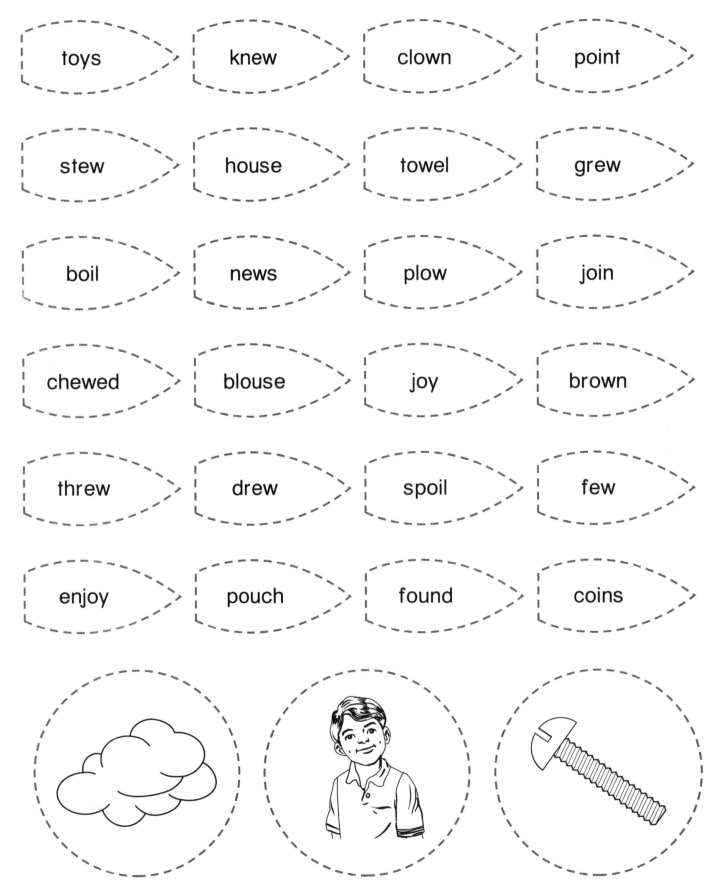

toys knew clown point

stew house towel grew

boil news plow join

chewed blouse joy brown

threw drew spoil few

enjoy pouch found coins

ESL Activities

Shades of Brown
Page 121

Bring in a variety of brown objects, preferably those with distinctive textures, scents, or shapes; for example: cinnamon sticks, tree bark walnuts, brown straw, soil, and so on. Pass the objects around and present pertinent vocabulary to help children describe each object's characteristics.

Favorite Browns
Page 121

Teach children the song "My Favorite Things." Then have them sing about their favorite brown things. Have students work in groups to write and illustrate their new song.

Terrific Trains
Page 124

Bring in pictures of various types of trains, such as commuter, subway, and freight. Discuss the different trains, and invite children to tell about trains on which they have ridden. Provide small boxes, pieces of wood, pipe cleaners, glue, and other materials, and have children make trains.

Train Sights *Page 124*

Bring to class several large, colorful pictures of country and city scenes. Seat children in rows, and tell them to imagine they are riding a train across the country.

Teach the class the sentence starter: "From the train I can see…." Then hold up the pictures one at a time, and call on children to name and/or describe what they see. After each child has had a turn, encourage the class to imagine and describe other scenes that might be viewed from a train.

What Does It Mean?
Page 134

Have children work in pairs, preferably more advanced speakers with beginners. Direct each pair to list words from the story that have the sound of **ea**. Tell partners to write each word's contextual meaning and a new sentence containing the word. Invite pairs to share their work.

A Place to Visit
Page 134

Have children work in groups to write a short story about a make-believe land they would like to visit. In preparation, list potential vocabulary on the board. Include words with the vowel digraph **ea**, and encourage children to use those and other **ea** words in their stories.

Seasonal Fun
Page 138

Have children work in groups. Assign each group a season, and direct each group member to

write a paragraph about a favorite activity, a special event, or a special visit made during that season. Encourage the class to use words that contain vowel digraphs **au** and **aw**. Use the following prompts to guide children:
- Tell what you did first, next, last.
- Describe the scene and the weather.
- Tell who was with you.

Visit to an Aunt
Page 138

On an experience chart, write the sentences from page 138 in story format. Direct children to perform each action as you recite the story together. Then have children write additional sentences to extend the story.

Flowering Big Book
Page 147

Have children work in groups to write and illustrate pages for a big book about flowers and plants. Provide illustrated reference books about plant life. Also provide craft items such as crepe paper, drawing materials, pipe cleaners, and styrofoam so that children can make three-dimensional flowers to go with their big book.

TECH TALK

Silly Diphthongs

Objectives
- To review the vowel diphthongs **ou**, **ow**, **oi**, **oy**, and **ew**
- To use Kid Works™ 2* to write silly sentences that contain words with diphthongs

Preparation
Show pictures of mountains and ask children to describe what they see. Write the word **mountains** on the board. Ask a volunteer to circle the diphthong **ou**. Then read *Mountains* by Norman Barrett (Watts). Ask children who have gone hiking or skiing to describe the scenery. Add words to the Theme Words chart, and have children identify the vowel diphthongs.

One Step at a Time

1 Have children work independently or in small groups.

2 Tell children to use the Story Writer feature of Kid Works™ 2 to write a sentence for each diphthong. Direct children to choose pictures from the picture boxes to write and then save a rebus silly sentence.

3 Have children select "Story Illustrator" and draw a picture for the silly sentence they wrote. Have them save the picture.

4 Have children go back to Story Writer and click on the Picture Box to pull up the picture that matches their silly sentence. Guide them to place the picture at the beginning of the sentence and to print the sentence and picture.

5 Direct children who want to hear their silly sentences to choose "Story Player" and to listen.

Class Sharing

Have children take turns sharing their silly sentences. Assemble children's sentences in a class booklet. Place the booklet in the Reading Corner for children to peruse at their leisure.

The clown's frown flew away.

Are You Blue?

Objectives
- To review vowel pairs, diphthongs, and digraphs
- To use E-mail to learn about colors

Preparation
Be sure to allow for on-line time. The journal *Classroom Connect* is a good resource to help you open communications with other classes. Tell children that they are going to compare colors in their classroom with colors in other classrooms. Then brainstorm with children what items they would like to compare; for example, hair color, eye color, color of chalkboards, color of desks, and so on. List these items on chart paper, and display the list.

One Step at a Time

1. Have children work in small groups. Provide each group with an E-mail address for another second-grade class. Tell children to write on paper a message to the other class about what they are studying—phonics concepts and colors. Tell them also to include a list of things to compare, such as those previously discussed and listed on chart paper.

2. Direct children to enter their messages and to compile the comparison information in chart form on the computer. Tell them to underline or italicize the digraphs, diphthongs, and vowel pairs.

3. Guide children to communicate their method of recording and highlighting information to the other class. Then have each group E-mail its information and a request for a response to its assigned class.

Class Sharing

Have all the groups assemble their information. Tell children to prepare a report for the rest of the class. Explain that they should be as innovative as possible. Provide a variety of media opportunities. Allow time for children to rehearse and present their reports. You might want to videotape the performance.

Singing in Colors

Play *Color Songs, Crayon Stories* (Ashforton Music Group). Invite children to sing with the recording. Ask them to name the colors and topics that are mentioned. List these on the board, and ask volunteers to identify digraphs, diphthongs, or vowel pairs.

Have children work in small groups. Tell each group to choose one of the songs and to practice singing it. Allow time for each group to sing their song. You might want to record the performances.

All referenced software is listed under Computer Resources on page T46.

Literature Introduction to Vowel Pairs, Vowel Digraphs, and Diphthongs

Objectives
- To enjoy a poem about colors
- To identify words with vowel pairs, vowel digraphs, and diphthongs

Starting with Literature

- Ask children to name their favorite color and tell what comes to mind when they think of that color. Then have children turn to page 121. Ask what color the poet has written about.

- Read the poem aloud. Then reread it, and invite children to join in. Ask them to point out the rhyming words. Help children note how the poet uses brown in descriptions that are not usually linked with color, such as "the color of work" and the "smell of the Sunday roast."

Developing Critical Thinking

Ask a volunteer to read the questions at the bottom of the page. Encourage children to share their own thoughts about color.

Introducing the Skill

Explain that two letters together sometimes stand for one vowel sound, such as **ow** in **brown, oa** in **road,** and **oo** in **good.** Have children find these words in the poem.

Practicing the Skill

Read the poem line by line, and have children point out words that have two vowels together or a vowel plus **w.** (At this point, accept all words, even though some may be exceptions to rules in the following lessons.)

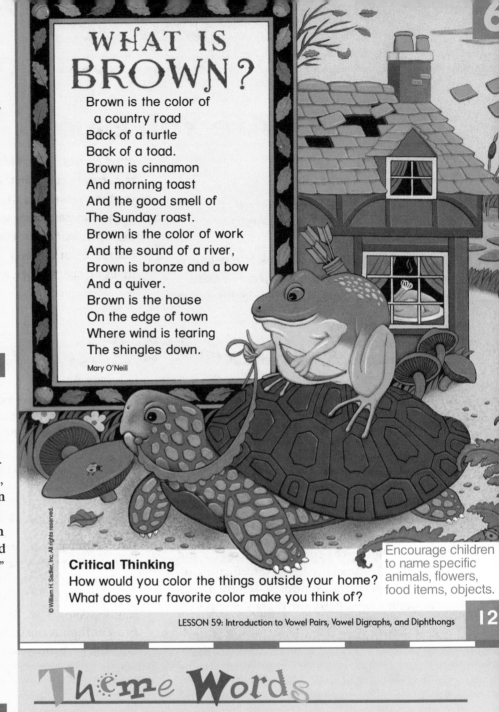

WHAT IS BROWN?

Brown is the color of
a country road
Back of a turtle
Back of a toad.
Brown is cinnamon
And morning toast
And the good smell of
The Sunday roast.
Brown is the color of work
And the sound of a river,
Brown is bronze and a bow
And a quiver.
Brown is the house
On the edge of town
Where wind is tearing
The shingles down.

Mary O'Neill

Critical Thinking
How would you color the things outside your home? What does your favorite color make you think of?

Encourage children to name specific animals, flowers, food items, objects.

LESSON 59: Introduction to Vowel Pairs, Vowel Digraphs, and Diphthongs   **12**

Theme Words

Color Craze Invite children to close their eyes and imagine a world without color. Have them share their feelings, and use responses to start a list of theme words on chart paper. Ask children to use their favorite colors in descriptive phrases such as "tall green grass," and "beautiful blue sky." Add their phrases to the list.

Throughout the unit, use and add to the list of theme words. At the end of the unit, draw a "rainbow" of misspelled theme words on the board. Invite volunteers to reach the pot of gold at the end of the rainbow by correctly spelling the words. Give a gold star to each child who spells a word correctly.

Dear Family,

As your child progresses through this unit about colors, she or he will review vowel pairs and learn about vowel digraphs and diphthongs. Read the definitions and examples together.

vowel pair: two vowels that come together to make one long vowel sound (**green**, **gray**)

vowel digraph: two vowels that come together to make a long sound, a short sound, or a special sound (**bread**, **hook**, **pause**, **lawn**)

diphthong: two letters blended together to make one vowel sound (**brown**, **house**, **coin**, **toy**)

● Read the poem "What Is Brown?" on the reverse side.

● Look for words that have vowel pairs, vowel digraphs, or diphthongs. (**brown**, **road**, **toad**, **toast**, **good**, **Sunday**, **roast**, **sound**, **bow**, **house**, **town**, **down**)

● Talk about other colors that you see every day.

PROJECT

Ask your child to draw a rainbow on a large sheet of paper. When your child learns a word that has a vowel pair, vowel digraph, or diphthong, suggest that he or she write it under the rainbow. Your child can practice reading the words and using them in sentences.

brown gray
new hook
cloud boy

Apreciada Familia:

En esta unidad, sobre los colores, su niño aprenderá vocales apareadas, vocales digrafas y los diptongos. Lea las definiciones y los ejemplos con su niño.

vocales apareadas: dos vocales que al unirse producen un sonido largo (**green**, **gray**).

vocales digrafas: dos vocales que al unirse producen un sonido largo, corto o especial (**bread**, **hook**, **pause**, **lawn**).

diptongos: dos letras que al unirse producen un sonido (**brown**, **house**, **coin**, **toy**).

● Lea la poesía, "What Is Brown?" en la página 121.

● Busquen palabras que tengan pares de vocales, vocales digrafas y diptongos (**brown**, **road**, **toad**, **toast**, **good**, **Sunday**, **roast**, **sound**, **bow**, **house**, **town**, **down**).

● Hablen de los colores que ven todos los días.

PROYECTO

Pida al niño dibujar un arco iris en un papel grande. Cuando el niño aprenda palabras con vocales apareadas, digrafas o diptongos puede escribirlas debajo del arco iris. Luego puede practicar leyendo y usando las palabras en oraciones.

LESSON 59: Introduction to Vowel Pairs, Vowel Digraphs, and Diphthongs—Phonics Alive at Home

---

Phonics Alive at Home

● The *Phonics Alive at Home* page is intended to involve families in their children's reading and writing development through activities that apply phonics skills.

● In Unit 6, the *Phonics Alive at Home* page includes activities related to the unit theme, "A Rainbow of Colors." The page also pertains to the phonics focus on vowel pairs, vowel digraphs, and diphthongs.

● Have children remove page 122 from their books. Suggest that they discuss the page and complete the suggested project at home with family members.

● Encourage children to bring their rainbows to school to share with the class.

● As you work through the unit, provide ample opportunities for children to share personal experiences related to colors, books with colorful illustrations, or stories they have written about color-related topics.

● Ask children to bring in an item from home, such as a toy, book, picture, or article of clothing that is their favorite color.

ESL Activities

ESL activities are referenced throughout this unit. These activities benefit the ESL child in your classroom by providing additional language experiences. Choose the activities that best meet the diverse needs of your class.

For ESL activities related to "What Is Brown?" refer to page 121J.

Take-Home Book

The Take-Home Book for Unit 6, *Colors All Around,* is found on student pages 219–220. It may be enjoyed by children and family members alike. Use the fold-up book to reinforce the phonics skills on vowel pairs, vowel digraphs, and diphthongs taught in this unit. You may choose to use the book at the end of the unit, or send it home at an appropriate time.

Recognizing Vowel Pairs ai and ay

Objectives
- To recognize and write words with vowel pairs **ai** and **ay**
- To write words with vowel pairs **ai** and **ay** in a story

Warming Up

Reviewing Digraphs sh and ch
- Have children write the words below on strips of paper, cut the strips apart, and put the words in order in sentences:
  —shrubs at Shelly shop. sells the
  —chops into cheesecake. for Chad chunks cherries the
- Ask children to read each sentence aloud and name the consonant digraph they hear most often.

★ Teaching the Lesson

Materials: Phonics Picture Card **jay**

- Write this poem on chart paper:
  The sun is out, no **rain today**.
  What a **day** to go out and **play**!
  In the garden is a **snail**.
  Ruff sees it and wags his **tail**.
  I see birds—black and **gray**,
  The one I like is the big blue **jay**.

- Display the picture card for **jay**. Have children identify the vowel sound in the picture name. (long **a**)
- Together read the poem several times; call attention to the long **a** words. Have volunteers circle the letters that stand for the long **a** sound.
- Have children read aloud the Helpful Hint on page 123. Elicit from students that **ai** and **ay** are vowel pairs and that they stand for the long **a** sound.

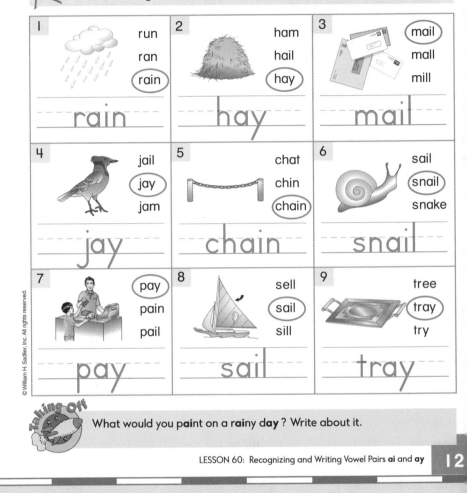

Remember! If there are two vowels in a one-syllable word, the first vowel is usually long and the second vowel is silent. These two vowels together are a **vowel pair**.

The vowel pairs **ai** and **ay** stand for the long **a** sound in **rain** and **hay**. Circle the long **a** word that names each picture. Write the word.

1. run / ran / (rain) — rain
2. ham / hail / (hay) — hay
3. (mail) / mall / mill — mail
4. jail / (jay) / jam — jay
5. chat / chin / (chain) — chain
6. sail / (snail) / snake — snail
7. (pay) / pain / pail — pay
8. sell / (sail) / sill — sail
9. tree / (tray) / try — tray

What would you **paint** on a **rainy day**? Write about it.

LESSON 60: Recognizing and Writing Vowel Pairs **ai** and **ay**   12

Multisensory *Activities*

Visual ■ Tactile

Chains of Color
Materials: scissors, tape, colored construction paper

On the board write long **a** words with **ai** and **ay**. Have children write four or five of the words on strips of colored paper. Then have them work in small groups to make word chains by taping the strips in interlocking rings. Have children hang the chains around the room and read the words.

Auditory ■ Visual

Say the Names
Materials: Phonics Picture Cards **jay, rain, snail, hay, spray, pail, train**

Display the poem from *Teaching the Lesson.* Hold up picture cards **jay, rain,** and **snail.** Ask children to name the pictures and find the names in the poem. Then display the other picture cards. Have children name and spell each word aloud while classmates check their spelling.

Use a word from the box to complete each sentence. Then read the story.

| day | Gail | hay | sail | trail |

The Silver Train

A train ride is fun on a sunny

day. Look out and you'll see a farm

with bales of golden _hay_. There's a

lake and a boat with a white _sail_. And

there's my friend _Gail_! She's riding a

black horse along a _trail_.

What else might you see on a train ride? Write about it.

Accept any reasonable response.

24   LESSON 60: Writing Vowel Pairs **ai** and **ay**

Spelling Connection

Read the words and sentences aloud. Invite volunteers to spell each word orally or write it on the board.

snail	I found a **snail** in the garden.
chain	Lock your bike with the **chain**.
hay	We saw bales of **hay** in the field.
day	Which **day** of the week do you like best?
paint	Pablo uses watercolors to **paint**.

Teacher to Teacher

Have one player in a group of four deal index cards with **ai** and **ay** words on them. Direct each child to fan his or her cards so that the player on the left can draw one. That player then reads the word and uses it in a sentence. If successful, the card is discarded and play continues; if not, that player keeps the card. Whoever runs out of cards first is the winner.

Margaret Ann Murphy
West Chester, PA

Practicing the Skill

● Read aloud the directions on page 123, and identify the pictures together. Then have children complete the page.

● Make sure children understand the directions on page 124. Fill in the first word together. Then point out where children will write their own sentences at the bottom, and have them complete the page.

● Have children do _Taking Off_ on page 123 alone or in pairs.

Extending the Skill Across the Curriculum

(Art/Poetry)

Theme Activity

Materials: paints, brushes, paper

● Ask children to tell how the different parts of the day might remind them of particular colors. Then share the theme book cited below.

● Have children paint a picture of any time of day.

● Write the poem below on the board. Have children copy it, attach it to their pictures, and underline the words with long **a** vowel pairs.

> **Today**, tonight, along the **way**
> I see the colors of the **day**.
> Sky of blue or **gray** or black,
> Like **trails** of **paint** across and back.

● List color names on the board. Ask children to write their own poems to describe their pictures.

Theme Book

Bragg, Ruth Gembicki. _Colors of the Day_. Boston: Picture Book Studio, 1992. Colorful events of one day.

Portfolio

Have children save their poems in their portfolios.

ESL Activities

Refer to page 121J.

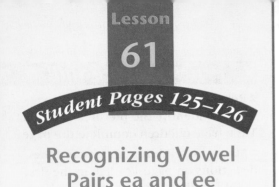
Recognizing Vowel Pairs ea and ee

Objectives
● To recognize and write words with vowel pairs **ea** and **ee**
● To categorize **ea** and **ee** words

Warming Up

Reviewing Digraphs th and wh
● Write **thirty** and **wheat** on the board. Have children say the words. Ask a child to circle the digraphs.

● Tell children to name an associated word that begins with **th** or **wh** for each group of words. Then say: cat, face, hair (**whiskers**); pins, needle, thimble (**thread**); rain, storm, lightning (**thunder**); ocean, large, mammal (**whale**); rose, stem, sharp (**thorn**).

★ Teaching the Lesson

● Write this poem on chart paper:

Can you see me hiding in the **tree**?
Green like the **leaf** that's under me.
I can't be **seen** looking too **real**,
Or I may be a bird's next **meal**.

● Read the poem aloud. Ask which animal "me" is. Then invite children to join in a second reading.

● Have children identify the **ea** and **ee** words. Help them generalize that **ea** and **ee** can often stand for the long **e** sound.

● Together read the Helpful Hint on page 123. Then have volunteers circle examples of **ea** and **ee** words in the poem.

Observational Assessment
*Ask individual children to read the poem again. Note whether they read the **ea** and **ee** words correctly.*

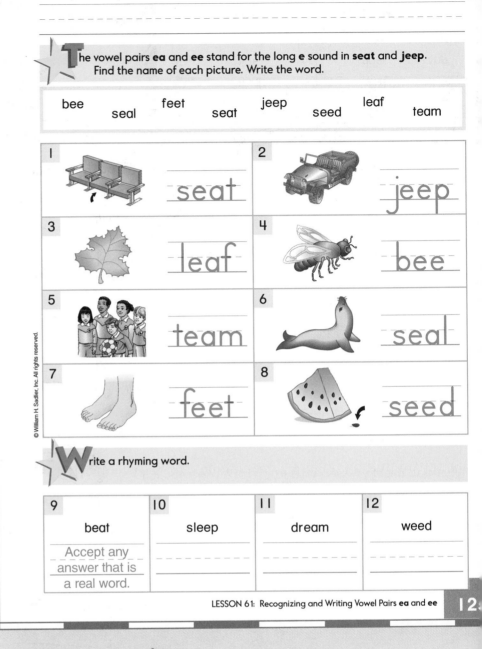

The vowel pairs **ea** and **ee** stand for the long **e** sound in **seat** and **jeep**. Find the name of each picture. Write the word.

| bee | seal | feet | seat | jeep | seed | leaf | team |

1. seat
2. jeep
3. leaf
4. bee
5. team
6. seal
7. feet
8. seed

Write a rhyming word.

9 beat	10 sleep	11 dream	12 weed
Accept any answer that is a real word.			

LESSON 61: Recognizing and Writing Vowel Pairs **ea** and **ee**

12

Multisensory *Activities*

Visual ■ Tactile

Green Are the Leaves
Materials: green paper, scissors, tape, Phonics Picture Cards **bee, green, jeans, jeep, team, tree, sheep, wheat, leaf, peas, queen, wreath, seal, teeth, knee, screen**

Draw a tree on the board. Place the picture cards in a pocket chart. On the chalk ledge, display sixteen paper "leaves" with the picture names on them. Ask children to choose a card, say its name, and tape the corresponding leaf to the tree.

Auditory ■ Kinesthetic

The Knees Have It
Ask children to stand. Say each of these words: **tree, hide, clean, jeep, net, leaf, best, bean, sheep, wheat, shell, green, feet, nine,** and **peach**. Have children tap their knees when they hear a long **e** sound.

Ask volunteers to spell each long **e** word, tapping their knees as they say each letter. Then have the class spell the word together. Write the words on the board as children spell them.

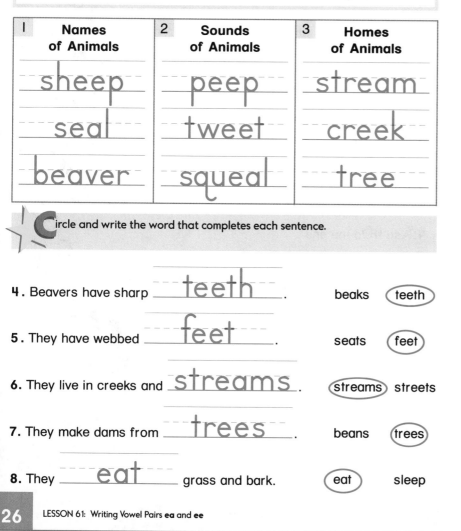

Write each word under the correct heading.

peep	stream	sheep	creek	tweet
seal	beaver	tree	squeal	

1 Names of Animals	2 Sounds of Animals	3 Homes of Animals
sheep	peep	stream
seal	tweet	creek
beaver	squeal	tree

Circle and write the word that completes each sentence.

4. Beavers have sharp ___teeth___.   beaks   (teeth)

5. They have webbed ___feet___.   seats   (feet)

6. They live in creeks and ___streams___.   (streams)   streets

7. They make dams from ___trees___.   beans   (trees)

8. They ___eat___ grass and bark.   (eat)   sleep

26

LESSON 61: Writing Vowel Pairs **ea** and **ee**

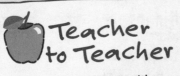

Practicing the Skill

● Invite volunteers to read the directions on page 125 aloud and identify the pictures.

● Read through the word box on page 126. Show children how to write selections in the correct column. Then read aloud the directions for the second exercise, and have children complete both pages.

Extending the Skill Across the Curriculum

(Language Arts/Science)

Theme Activity

Materials: drawing paper, crayons

● Have children reread the poem used in *Teaching the Lesson.* Encourage them to tell what they know about animals that are difficult to see.

● Share the theme books cited below. Then discuss how animals use color to disguise and protect themselves.

● Ask children to name an animal that uses color to camouflage itself. Have them draw a scene that includes the hidden animal. Have children imagine they are the animal in their pictures. Then have them write a few sentences telling how and where they hide themselves. Provide sentence starters such as:

It is hard to **see** me because…
I do not look **real** because…
I can hide on a **leaf** because…
I can hide on (in) a **tree** because…

● Assemble pictures and sentences in a class book titled "Hide and Seek." Place the book in the class library.

Theme Books

Coldrey, Jennifer, ed. *Hide and Seek.* New York: G.P. Putnam's Sons, 1986. How animals hide.

Sowler, Sandie. *Amazing Animal Disguises.* New York: Alfred A. Knopf, 1992. Animal camouflage.

126

Reviewing Vowel Pairs
ai, ay, ea, ee

Objectives
- To review vowel pairs **ai, ay, ea, ee**
- To write words with vowel pairs **ai, ay, ea, ee** in a poem

Warming Up

Reviewing Digraphs kn and wr
- Have children write **kn** and **wr** on two sheets of scrap paper. Leaving a blank space for the digraph, write these words on the board: **knee, wren, wreath, knock, wrong, know, write, knight, wreck, knob, kneel,** and **wrist**.
- Say each complete word, and have children hold up the **kn** or **wr** paper for the digraph they hear. Then have a volunteer write **kn** or **wr** in the blank space on the board.

★ Teaching the Lesson

- Ask: "What eats fish and is gray or brown?" Tell children they can solve the riddle by working through each of the steps below. Then read each step aloud.

1. Write **gain**.
2. Change the **g** to **r**. (**rain**)
3. Change the **n** to **l**. (**rail**)
4. Change the **ai** to **ea**. (**real**)
5. Change the **r** to **s**. (**seal**)

- Have children try another riddle. Ask: "What can you fill with sand at the beach?"

1. Write **meat**.
2. Change the **t** to **l**. (**meal**)
3. Change the **m** to **s**. (**seal**)
4. Change the **ea** to **ai**. (**sail**)
5. Change the **s** to **p**. (**pail**)

Follow the directions to make new words and find the answer to each riddle.

What are hard and white and sometimes fall out?
START with: **gray**

1. Change the **gr** to **tr**. — tray
2. Change the **ay** to **ee**. — tree
3. Change the **tr** to **t**. — tee
4. Add **th** to the end. — teeth

What is gold or silver, short or long, weak or strong?
START with: **real**

5. Change the **r** to **m**. — meal
6. Change the **ea** to **ai**. — mail
7. Change the **l** to **n**. — main
8. Change the **m** to **ch**. — chain

LESSON 62: Reviewing Vowel pairs **ai, ay, ea, ee**

12

Multisensory *Activities*

Tactile ■ Visual

Green Paint or Clay
Materials: green finger paint or green clay, paper

Invite children to use finger paint and paper to write words with **ai, ay, ea,** and **ee**. Alternatively, distribute clay, and have children form words from clay "ropes." Have children read each other's words. If clay is used, invite children to trace over the words with their fingers.

Visual ■ Tactile

Take a Train or a Jeep
Materials: construction paper, scissors, crayons

Cut a **train** engine from construction paper. Have children outline and cut out rectangular train cars with wheels. On each car, have children write an **ai** or **ay** word. Mount the train on the wall, and have children read the words. Repeat the activity with a **jeep** and trailers with **ea** and **ee** words.

Complete each line of the poem by writing a word from the box.
Read the poem, and underline all the **ai** words and **ay** words.
Circle all the **ea** words and **ee** words.

bee	keep	play	peak	tails	trail

GREEN GRASS

(Green) is the grass under the snail.

Get down close to (see) its ___trail___.

Black is the (jeep) making a (squeak).

Will it ever (reach) the (peak) ?

White is the (seed) I planted so (deep).

Here is a pumpkin you can (keep).

Blue is the jay in the old oak (tree).

Out of a hive comes a buzzing (bee).

Silver is the train on (steel) rails.

Dogs run by and wag their ___tails___.

Yellow is the sun that shines today.

Let's go out. It's time to ___play___.

28 LESSON 62: Reviewing Vowel Pairs **ai, ay, ea, ee**

Spelling Connection

Read aloud the words and sentences below. Invite volunteers to spell each word orally or write it on the board.

pail   Fill the **pail** with water.
today It is Pete's birthday **today**.
keep   You may **keep** the book.
gray   The sky turned **gray** before it rained.
meals We eat our **meals** in the kitchen.

Multicultural Connection

Tell the class that in ancient China, calligraphers (writers) and painters made their own colored ink. Explain that they made some ink from pearl powder and ground jade, a semi-precious stone. For colors, they used plants—indigo for blue—or minerals—cinnabar for red and malachite for green. Have children imagine they have to make their own ink. Ask what they might use from nature to produce a given color.

Practicing the Skill

● Ask a volunteer to read aloud the directions on page 127. Explain that the riddles here are just like those children solved earlier.

● Read aloud the instructions and the words in the box on page 128. Point out that each answer rhymes with the last word in the line before.

● Have children complete both pages.

Extending the Skill Across the Curriculum

(Language Arts)

Theme Activity

● Extend the rhyme on page 128 by writing the lines below on the board; omit the words in parentheses. Beside the lines, list the missing words: **sleet, weed, spray, rain, meal,** and **play**.

Green is the grass, gold is the grain,
Gray is the sky, down comes the
    (**rain**).

Black is the jeep, out on the street,
Soon it will be icy, and covered with
    (**sleet**).

White are the seeds that I planted
    today.
Bring out the hose and give them a
    (**spray**).

Blue is the jay with a squawk and a
    squeal,
Looking around for his next hearty
    (**meal**).

Brown are the leaves along the way.
We jump on a heap, and start to
    (**play**).

Red is the flower that comes from a
    seed.
Just yesterday, it looked like a
    (**weed**).

● Have children choose a word from the list to complete each rhyme.

128

Lesson 63

Student Pages 129–130

Recognizing Vowel Pairs oa, oe, ow, ui, ue, ie

Objective
● To recognize and write words with vowel pairs **oa, oe, ow, ui, ue, ie**

Warming Up

Reviewing Final Digraphs

Assign one of the consonant digraphs **ch, sh, th,** and **ck** to each child. Then say these words: **sack, bench, dash, both, catch, fresh, fifth, clock, each, north, snack, truck, lunch, dish,** and **lock.** Tell children to stand when they hear their consonant digraph and then say its letters.

★ Teaching the Lesson

Materials: Phonics Picture Cards **fruit, pie, blue**

● Read aloud "What Is Brown?" on the Poetry Poster. Ask a child to identify words with the long **o** sound.

● On the board write **road, toad, toast, roast,** and **bow.** Ask a child to circle the two letters that stand for the long **o** sound in each word. Explain that although **w** is not a vowel, when it is combined with **o,** the letters can stand for the long **o** sound. Then write **toe** on the board. Point out that **oe** also stands for long **o.**

● Write these sentences on the board: "I like fruit pie. Blueberry is my favorite." Then display the picture cards. Ask children to match each picture with its name on the board. Point out the **ui** and **ue** spellings for long **u,** and the **ie** spelling for long **i.**

129

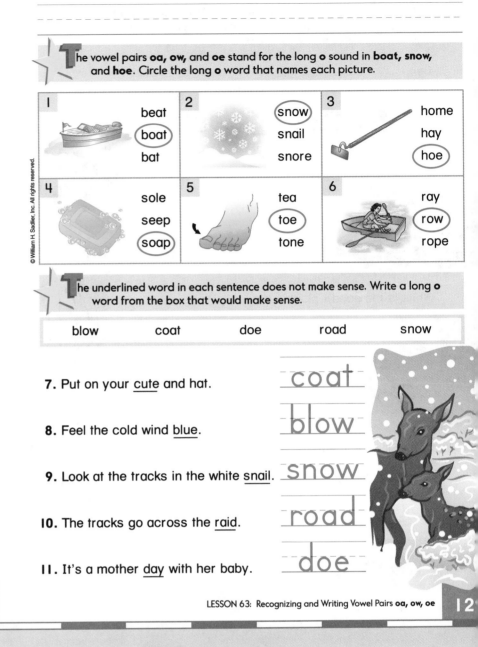

The vowel pairs **oa, ow,** and **oe** stand for the long **o** sound in **boat, snow,** and **hoe.** Circle the long **o** word that names each picture.

1. beat / (boat) / bat
2. (snow) / snail / snore
3. home / hay / (hoe)
4. sole / seep / (soap)
5. tea / (toe) / tone
6. ray / (row) / rope

The underlined word in each sentence does not make sense. Write a long **o** word from the box that would make sense.

| blow | coat | doe | road | snow |

7. Put on your <u>cute</u> and hat. — coat

8. Feel the cold wind <u>blue</u>. — blow

9. Look at the tracks in the white <u>snail</u>. — snow

10. The tracks go across the <u>raid</u>. — road

11. It's a mother <u>day</u> with her baby. — doe

LESSON 63: Recognizing and Writing Vowel Pairs **oa, ow, oe**

12

Multisensory *Activities*

Visual ■ Tactile

Build the Snowmen

Materials: construction paper, scissors, markers, tape

Cut out three snowman faces and hats. Mount them on the bulletin board, and label each **oa, oe,** or **ow.** On each of fifteen white circles, write **coach, float, foam, road, roast, throat, toast, blow, grown, know, show, snow, hoe, toe,** or **doe.** Have children build the snowmen by reading a word and taping it to the correct snowman.

Auditory ■ Tactile

Fruit Pies

Materials: construction paper, scissors

Cut two circles into eight wedges each. On one set of wedges write **cried, die, fried, lie, pie, tie, tied,** and **tried.** On the other write **blue, clue, glue, Sue, due, fruit, juice,** and **suit.** Mix up the wedges. Have children choose wedges and piece together the two long vowel "pies."

The vowel pairs **ui** and **ue** stand for the long **u** sound in **fruit** and **glue**. The vowel pair **ie** stands for the long **i** sound in **tie**. Circle the word that names each picture.

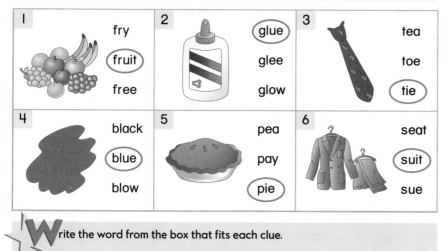

1	fry ~~fruit~~ free	2	(glue) glee glow	3	tea toe (tie)
4	black (blue) blow	5	pea pay (pie)	6	seat (suit) sue

Write the word from the box that fits each clue.

fruit	glue	tie	pie	juice

7. This can come from an orange.   juice

8. This can grow on a tree.   fruit

9. This can make things stick.   glue

10. This is something you bake.   pie

11. This is something you wear.   tie

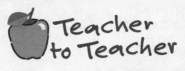

Spelling Connection

Read aloud the words and sentences below. Invite volunteers to spell each word orally or write it on the board.

road	The **road** was bumpy.
toe	Sue stubbed her **toe** on a chair.
row	Joan sits in the third **row**.
clue	Give me a **clue** to the riddle.
juice	Oranges make good **juice**.
pie	Miguel likes blueberry **pie**.

Teacher to Teacher

Mount pictures of these items on separate cards: **pail, haystack, beak, beet, boat, bow, pie, fruit, glue,** and **toe**. Have each child pick a card, identify the vowel pair, and, on the board, list as many words as possible with the same vowel pair.

Second Grade Teacher
Lincoln, NE

Practicing the Skill

• Read the directions on page 129 together, and have children identify the pictures. Do the first item in the second exercise.

• Have children identify the pictures on page 130. Ask a volunteer to read the directions for both exercises. Then have children complete both pages.

Extending the Skill Across the Curriculum

(Language Arts/Health)

Theme Activity
Materials: magazines, scissors, glue, large construction paper

• Share the theme books cited below. Then go over the food pyramid in *What We Eat*, and draw a blank food pyramid on chart paper. Remind children of what each layer represents.

• Explain that the pyramid reminds us to eat less of the foods at the top, and more of those at the bottom.

• Have children name favorite foods. Write them in the correct layers of the pyramid. Emphasize words with vowel pairs, such as **fruit, meat, beans, cheese, grains,** and so on.

• Talk about the colors of foods. List foods and their colors on the board, and point out vowel pairs; for example, bananas and lemons (**yellow**), **peas** and **beans** (**green**), **blueberries** (**blue**), and **roast beef** (**brown**).

• Have children work in small groups to make a collage of foods of the same color.

Theme Books

Lynn, Sara and James, Diane. *What We Eat*. New York: Thomson Learning, 1992. The food pyramid, recipes, and projects.

McMillan, Bruce. *Growing Colors*. Lothrop, New York: Morrow 1994. Vibrantly colored fruits and vegetables.

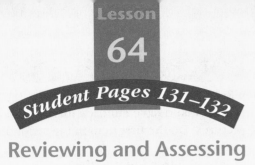

Reviewing and Assessing Vowel Pairs

Objectives
- To review vowel pairs **oa, oe, ow, ui, ue, ie**
- To write words with vowel pairs **oa, oe, ow, ui, ue, ie**
- To use words with **oa, oe, ow, ui, ue, ie** in sentences

Warming Up

Reviewing ar-Words

Draw two large stars on the board. Write **star** in the center of one and **spark** in the center of the other. Have children work in pairs to copy the stars. Then have them write at each point a word that rhymes with the word in the center.

★ *Teaching the Lesson*

Materials: Phonics Picture Cards **toad, snow, toe, tie, blue, suit**

- Write this puzzle on the board:

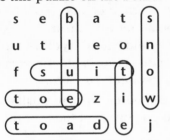

- Read aloud the story below. Have volunteers choose the correct picture card for each blank and then say the word. Ask others to find and circle the words in the puzzle.

   Outside, the road was covered with white (snow). Before I went out, I fed my pet (toad). I was in a hurry and stubbed my (toe). I put on my snow (suit). Mom said to (tie) my new (blue) scarf around my neck.

Write the name of each picture. Then find and circle the words in the puzzle. Look across and down.

1	toad	2	hoe
3	bowl	4	fruit
5	blue	6	tie
7	toe	8	pie

```
h  o  e  a  b  c
d  f  r  u  i  t
b  o  w  l  f  o
l  g  t  i  e  a
u  p  i  e  h  d
e  i  t  o  e  j
```

LESSON 64: Reviewing Vowel Pairs **oa, ow, oe, ui, ue, ie**

13

Multisensory *Activities*

Visual ■ Tactile

Fruit Bowl

Materials: plastic bowl, construction paper, scissors

Have children draw fruit shapes on construction paper and then cut them out. Ask children to write one word with a vowel pair on each shape and place it in the bowl. You may want to assign vowel pairs to partners and make word lists available to them. Have children practice reading the words in the "fruit bowl."

Auditory ■ Visual

Seek and Find

Materials: large-grid paper

Give each child a sheet of grid paper on which to make a word search puzzle similar to the one in *Teaching the Lesson*, but with different vowel pair words. Let children use their books, or provide a chalkboard list of words with **ai, ay, ea, ee, oa, oe, ow, ue, ui,** and **ie** for reference. Have children exchange puzzles and find the hidden words.

1. tie
2. blue
3. hoe
4. snail
5. leaf
6. pay

Circle and write the word that completes each sentence.

7. Look at the __fruit__ in this bowl.   (fruit)   freeze

8. The lemons are __yellow__.   yelling   (yellow)

9. The limes are a pretty shade of __green__.   (green)   grain

10. The plums are __blue__.   (blue)   blow

11. Do you know the color of the __peach__?   poach   (peach)

32   LESSON 64: Assessing Vowel Pairs

Reteaching *Activities*

Can You Match It?

Materials: Phonics Picture Cards
green, boat, snow, toe, tie, blue, fruit; index cards

Display the picture cards. Write the picture names on index cards. Have children name the vowel pairs and say the vowel sounds as they match the words to the pictures.

Who Knows?

Materials: index cards, hole punch, yarn

On separate index cards, write **oa, oe, ow, ue, ui,** and **ie.** Punch a hole in each card, and loop yarn through it. Ask children to wear the cards around their necks and sit in a circle. Say a word with a vowel pair. Write it on the board, but leave a blank for the vowel pair. Have children name the missing vowel pair and the person who is wearing it. Then have a child complete the word.

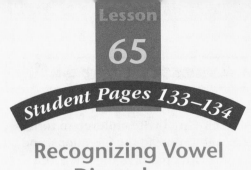

Recognizing Vowel Digraph ea

Objectives

● To distinguish between the short **e** and long **e** sounds of **ea**

● To read and write **ea** words in context

Warming Up

Reviewing or-Words

Write these words on the board: **corn, horse, north, more, orange, shore, store, short, tore, porch, morning,** and **short**. Ask children to use any of the **or**-words in phrases to complete these sentence starters:

> As I walked around the **corner**…
> The **storm**…
> At the **fort**…

★ *Teaching the Lesson*

● Write this poem on the board and underline the boldfaced words:

> Brown is the color
>   of pumpernickel **bread**.
> Brown is the color
>   of my new **bedspread**.
> Brown is the color
>   of yummy **gingerbread**.
> Brown is the color
>   of the hair on my **head**.

● Have children read the poem together and then identify the sound they hear in the underlined words. (short **e**) Have volunteers circle the letters that stand for short **e**.

● Read aloud the Helpful Hint on page 133. Explain that vowel digraph **ea** can also stand for the long **e** sound in words such as **beak, leaf,** and **clean** as well as for the long **a** sound in words such as **break, great,** and **steak**.

A **vowel digraph** is two vowels together that stand for one sound. The vowel sound can be long or short, or the vowel digraph can have a sound of its own.

The vowel digraph **ea** can stand for the short **e** sound in **bread**. Circle and write the word that names each picture. Color the pictures in which **ea** has the short **e** sound.

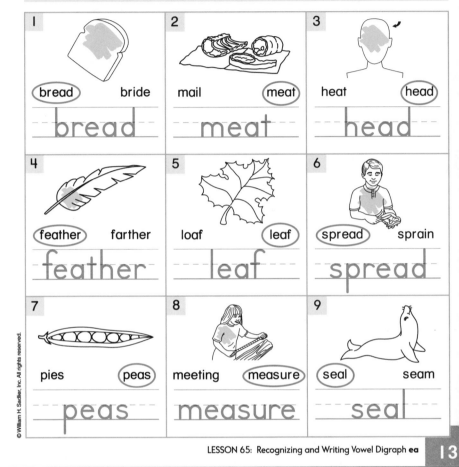

LESSON 65: Recognizing and Writing Vowel Digraph **ea** 13

Multisensory *Activities*

Visual ▪ Tactile

Words of a Feather

Materials: construction paper, scissors, feather patterns, tape, glue

Have children trace and cut out ten feathers each. Ask them to write a word with vowel digraph **ea** on each feather. Measure a strip of paper around each child's head. Fasten the ends to make a headband. Have children glue their feathers to the headbands and then read one another's feather words.

Visual ▪ Auditory

Treasure Chest

Materials: two small boxes, blank flash cards

Write vowel digraph **ea** words from pages 133 and 134 on blank flash cards. Present the boxes as "treasure chests," and challenge children to put **ea** words with a short **e** sound in one chest and **ea** words with a long **e** sound in the other. Then have children take turns drawing a treasure from each chest and reading it aloud.

Read the story. Underline the words in which **ea** has the long **e** sound. Write the words in which **ea** has the short **e** sound on the lines below.

Welcome to Rainbow Land

Jean grabbed a leather coat. Joan grabbed a sweater. They went out after breakfast. Something was wrong! The sky was pink instead of blue. The leaves on the trees were silver.

"I'm not ready for this," Jean said. "I'm going back to bed."

"Wait," said Joan. "There's a trail of yellow beans. Let's see where they lead."

Jean and Joan followed the trail to a peach meadow. Just ahead they saw a green gingerbread house.

leather	sweater
breakfast	instead
ready	meadow
ahead	gingerbread

What happened next? Write about it. Try to use some of these words: **feather, heavy, spread, thread, weather**.

LESSON 65: Recognizing and Writing Vowel Digraph **ea**

34

Spelling Connection

Read aloud the words and sentences below. Invite volunteers to spell each word orally or write it on the board.

bread   Rashan likes rye **bread**.
head   The bird's **head** was red.
feather   Kiesha found a **feather** from a bluebird.
spread   Martin **spread** peanut butter on his toast.
heavy   The donkey carried a **heavy** load.

Multicultural Connection

Tell children that some Indian tribes in the Amazon Basin wear headdresses made of parrot and egret feathers. Explain that these tribes also use dyes made from plants to decorate their faces and bodies for ceremonies, hunts, and war; they believe these decorations bring them good luck.

Invite children to tell how these face and body decorations are similar to our society's use of cosmetics and clothing.

Practicing the Skill

Reread the Helpful Hint on page 133, go over the directions, and have children complete the page. Then read the story on page 134 together. Have children identify the words with vowel digraph **ea** and write those with the short **e** sound. Conclude with *Taking Off*.

Extending the Skill Across the Curriculum

(Science/Poetry)

Theme Activity

● Write this poem on the board:

I see a bird **ahead** of me,
Pretty **feathers** I can see.
Let me watch you **spread** your wings,
And fly through **meadows** as you sing.

Read the poem with children. Ask them to point out words with vowel digraph **ea** and tell whether they have the sound of long or short **e**.

● Read aloud the theme book cited below. Then make a concept map about birds. Emphasize kinds of birds, feather colors, and habitats.

● Have each child draw a picture of a bird and write one or two facts about it.

Observational Assessment
*As children read aloud the poem, determine whether they use context clues to pronounce each **ea** digraph.*

Theme Book

Flora. *Feathers Like a Rainbow: An Amazon Indian Tale*. New York: Harper Collins, 1989. How Amazonian birds got their color.

Portfolio

Have children add their bird facts and pictures to their portfolios.

ESL Activities

Refer to page 121J.

Recognizing Vowel Digraph oo

Objectives
● To recognize the two sounds of vowel digraph **oo**
● To recognize and write words with vowel digraph **oo**

Warming Up

Reviewing r-Controlled Vowels
Materials: Phonics Picture Cards **star, corn, fern, bird, purse**

Display the picture cards, and say each name. Ask what vowel sounds children hear in each picture name. Have children write the words on the board. Remind children that **er, ir,** and **ur** can all stand for the same sound.

★ *Teaching the Lesson*

Materials: Phonics Picture Cards **spoon, book**

● Write the following rhymes on the board, and read them together:

The sun was out at **noon,**
But at night I saw the **moon.**

I gave my Dad a recipe **book;**
He's the one who likes to **cook.**

● Point out the two sounds of digraph **oo**. Hold up the picture cards, and write their names on the board. Underline **oo** in each.

● On the board write **shook, spool, boot, stood, tool,** and **good**. Have children circle words that have the same **oo** sound as **spoon**. Have them underline those that have the same sound as **book**.

The vowel digraph **oo** can stand for the vowel sound in **moon** or the vowel sound in **hook**. Write the name of each picture.

1. moon
2. hook
3. wood
4. spoon
5. broom
6. book
7. pool
8. boot
9. hood
10. tooth
11. cook
12. roof

LESSON 66: Recognizing and Writing Vowel Digraph **oo**   13

Multisensory *Activities*

Visual ■ Auditory

Football on the Loose
Materials: flash cards

Write **oo** words from pages 135 and 136 on flash cards. Draw a football field on the board. Mark each ten-yard line and the end zones. Then have children in two teams take turns reading the flash card words. For each word read correctly, a team gains ten yards. Mark each team's progress on the field. Award six points for each "touchdown."

Tactile ■ Auditory

Cool Cookies
Materials: construction paper, scissors, crayons, empty oatmeal cylinder

Ask children to draw "cookies" on construction paper and then cut them out. Have children write an **oo** word on each cookie. Make a "cookie jar" from an oatmeal cylinder, and place the cookies in it. Have children take turns picking a cookie from the jar and reading the **oo** word.

Write an **oo** word to answer each question.

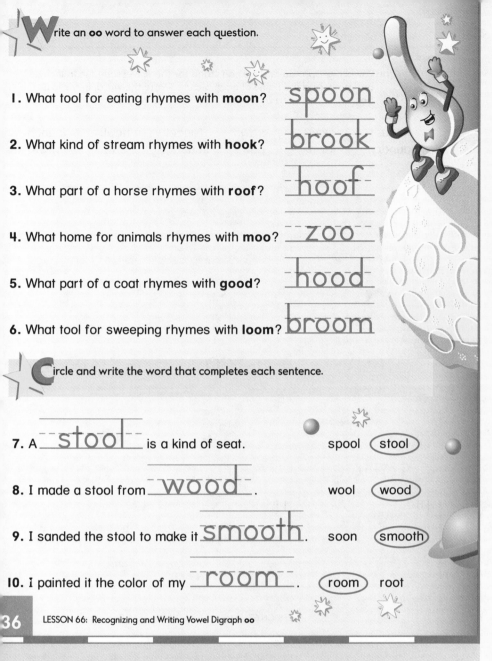

1. What tool for eating rhymes with **moon**? spoon

2. What kind of stream rhymes with **hook**? brook

3. What part of a horse rhymes with **roof**? hoof

4. What home for animals rhymes with **moo**? zoo

5. What part of a coat rhymes with **good**? hood

6. What tool for sweeping rhymes with **loom**? broom

Circle and write the word that completes each sentence.

7. A stool is a kind of seat. spool (stool)

8. I made a stool from wood. wool (wood)

9. I sanded the stool to make it smooth. soon (smooth)

10. I painted it the color of my room. (room) root

36 LESSON 66: Recognizing and Writing Vowel Digraph **oo**

Spelling Connection

Read aloud the words and sentences below. Invite volunteers to spell each word orally or write it on the board.

book Tim left the **book** at school.
moon The full **moon** was shining brightly.
tooth Nina has a loose **tooth**.
wood The table is made of **wood**.
spoon Ling's baby sister eats with a little **spoon**.

Practicing the Skill

• Read the directions on page 135 together, and identify the pictures.

• Read the directions on page 136, and do the first item together. For the second activity, suggest that children try both word choices in each sentence to decide which one makes sense.

• Have children complete both pages.

Extending the Skill Across the Curriculum

(Language Arts/Art)

Theme Activity

Materials: large box of crayons, drawing paper

• Have children name colors, and list the names on the board. Suggest that children look for names in a large box of crayons. Invite them to try combining two colors to make a third; for example: red and yellow (orange), yellow and blue (green, chartreuse), red and blue (purple, violet, magenta).

• Share the theme book cited below. Then have children make a color book with **oo** captions. Elicit ideas such as "I wear my red **hood** in **cool** weather," or "I eat **good food** with a silver **spoon**." To get the class started, write on the board: **boot, wood, broom, pool, tooth, brook, food, smooth, good, cookie, cool, school,** and **bloom**.

• Have children illustrate one sentence per page. Bind the pages together into individual books for children to share with the class.

Theme Book

Greeley, Valerie. *White Is the Moon.* New York: Macmillan, 1990. The whole spectrum of color.

Portfolio

Have children place the color books in their portfolios.

Recognizing Vowel Digraphs au and aw

Objectives
- To recognize and write words with vowel digraphs **au, aw**
- To write **au, aw** words in context

Warming Up

Reviewing Initial Blends
- Write the following words on the board; omit the blends: **snake, slippers, skates, smoke, spider, squirrel, stripes, snow, brick, crow, dress, grapes, pretty, truck, frog, cream, blanket, cloud, flag, flowers, gloves, plum, plant,** and **sled**. List the blends separately. Then write these color names on the board: **red, orange, yellow, green, blue, purple, brown, black, gray,** and **white**.
- Have children supply the blend for each word and name a color associated with the word. Invite children to use each word and color name in an oral sentence.

★ *Teaching the Lesson*

- Write this rhyme on chart paper:
  One day in **August**, just at **dawn**,
  I looked outside and **saw** a **fawn**.
  My footsteps **caused** the **fawn** to jump,
  And run away across the **lawn**.
- Have children close their eyes and visualize the scene as you read the rhyme aloud. Then reread it together.
- Invite volunteers to find the words that contain the vowel digraphs **au** and **aw**. Have them circle the digraphs and read the words aloud. Help children to recognize that **au** and **aw** can make the same sound.

The vowel digraphs **au** and **aw** can stand for the vowel sound in **launch** and **paw**. Find the name of each picture. Write the word. In the last box, write the word that is not used and draw a picture to go with it.

August	claw	crawl	faucet	hawk	launch
laundry	lawn	paw	sausage	saw	straw

1 launch	2 paw	3 sausage
4 crawl	5 straw	6 hawk
7 faucet	8 laundry	9 saw
10 August	11 claw	12 Children should draw a picture for **lawn**. lawn

LESSON 67: Recognizing and Writing Vowel Digraphs **au** and **aw**   13

Multisensory *Activities*

Visual ■ Auditory

Paw Prints

Materials: construction paper, encyclopedia or animal book, scissors, tape

Show pictures of animal paw prints from an encyclopedia or other book. Have children draw paw prints on construction paper and then cut them out. Have children write an **au** or **aw** word on each print. Tape the prints to the wall to make a "trail." Encourage children to read the words on the trail.

Visual ■ Tactile

Straw Words

Materials: construction paper, drinking straws, glue, scissors

Have each child write a few **au** and **aw** words in large block letters on construction paper. Direct children to cut drinking straws into pieces and glue the pieces on the outlines of the letters. Encourage them to exchange papers and practice reading the words as they trace the straw letters with their fingers.

Circle the words that have the same vowel sound as **launch** and **paw**.

(sauce)   clue   (haul)   play
(fault)   (yawn)   head   (cause)
(pause)   thread   (shawl)   breath
(jaw)   (fawn)   spread   (draw)

Fill in the circle next to the word that completes the sentence. Write the word in the sentence.

1. Last **autumn** I stayed with Aunt Paula.
   - ○ auto
   - ● autumn

2. We woke up at **dawn**.
   - ○ drawn
   - ● dawn

3. We looked out and saw a brown **hawk**.
   - ● hawk
   - ○ law

4. It had a hooked beak and sharp **claws**.
   - ○ thaws
   - ● claws

5. We also saw a spotted **fawn**.
   - ● fawn
   - ○ yawn

6. It ran across Aunt Paula's **lawn**.
   - ● lawn
   - ○ jaw

7. It **paused** to look back at us.
   - ○ caused
   - ● paused

Taking Off

Write about something you like to do in the autumn.

38   LESSON 67: Recognizing and Writing Vowel Digraphs **au** and **aw**

Spelling Connection

Read aloud the words and sentences below. Invite volunteers to spell each word orally or write it on the board.

haul The truck will **haul** the trash away.

August The weather is hot in **August**.

paw There were **paw** prints in the snow.

crawl Paul saw a rabbit **crawl** under the fence.

draw Carlo likes to **draw** animals.

Computer Connection

Invite children to enter the green door—the Wooden Blocks Room—of Beginning Reading™ (Sierra) to review consonant blends and consonant digraphs. When Bananas, the talking chimpanzee, pronounces a sound, have children use the mouse to click on the block with two letters that stand for that sound. You might use this activity after Lesson 69 to review consonant blends, digraphs, and diphthongs.

Practicing the Skill

- Read aloud the directions on page 137, and together identify the pictures. Have children complete the page.
- Review both sets of directions on page 138. Then have children complete the page.
- Encourage partners to brainstorm ideas for *Taking Off* before they write.

Extending the Skill Across the Curriculum

(Language Arts/Music)

Theme Activity

- Write this poem on the board, using a second color for the **au** and **aw** words:

  Turkey's in the **straw**,
   white on gold,
  Turkey's in the **straw**,
   white on gold,
  Turkey's in the **straw**,
   white on gold,
  On an **autumn** morning.

  Recite the poem with the class.

- You might substitute the verses below. Write each on the board.

  Hawk's in the tree,
   brown and white...
  Chicken's on the **lawn**,
   likes green grass...
  Paula's making **sauce**
   tomato red...
  Mama wears a **shawl**,
   blue and green...

- Encourage children to make up their own lyrics with other **au** and **aw** words.

Observational Assessment

*After children sing, point to **au** and **aw** words to determine whether each child can read the words.*

ESL Activities

Refer to page 121J.

Reviewing and Assessing Vowel Digraphs
ea, oo, au, aw

Objectives
● To review vowel digraphs **ea**, **oo**, **au**, **aw**

● To write words with digraphs **ea**, **oo**, **au**, **aw**

Warming Up

Reviewing Final Blends
On the board draw a ladder with ten rungs. Write one of these final blends on each rung: **st, lt, mp, nk, ld, ft, nt, nd, sk,** and **ng**. Have children copy the ladder and then "climb" it by writing an appropriate word on each rung.

★ *Teaching the Lesson*

Materials: Phonics Picture Cards **thread, August, paw, book, spoon**

● On the board draw blank lines for the letters in this puzzle, but fill in the **T** in *thread*:

T H R E A D
A U G U S T
P A W
B O O K
S P O O N

● Display the picture cards. Have children name each picture and print the letters on the lines. Then ask them to solve this riddle: "What birds can be gray, brown, or white, and enjoy mice for lunch?" Explain that the answer can be found in the puzzle.

● On the board write **broom, sneak, fault, thaw, stood, yawn, pause, head,** and **cook**. Have children say the words and circle the vowel digraphs.

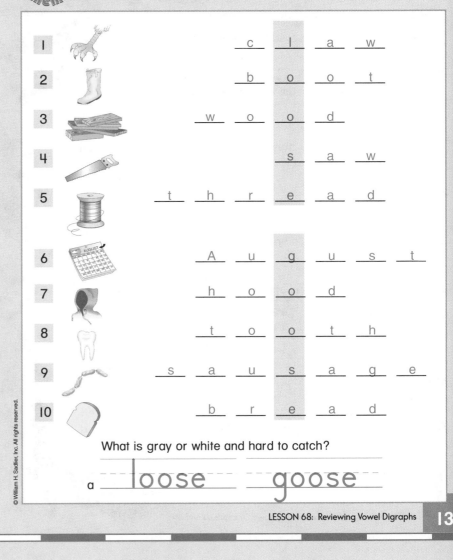

Write the name of each picture in the puzzle. Then read the shaded letters down to find the answer to the question.

1. c l a w
2. b o o t
3. w o o d
4. s a w
5. t h r e a d
6. A u g u s t
7. h o o d
8. t o o t h
9. s a u s a g e
10. b r e a d

What is gray or white and hard to catch?

a loose goose

LESSON 68: Reviewing Vowel Digraphs **13**

Multisensory *Activities*

Visual ■ Tactile

Gingerbread Cookie Words
Materials: "gingerbread" boy and girl patterns, construction paper, scissors, tape

Assign vowel digraphs to small groups of children. Ask the groups to trace the patterns several times, cut out the paper "cookies," and write on each a word with their digraph. Have each group tape its cookies together, hang them around the room, and read the words.

Visual ■ Kinesthetic

Look for the Loop
Materials: two lengths of yarn, bean-bag, flash cards

Make two large concentric yarn loops on the floor. On flash cards write words with vowel digraphs **ea, oo, au,** and **aw**. Alternating between two teams, have a child read a word. If it is read correctly, he or she may toss the beanbag into the loops. Give ten points for the center loop and five for the outer loop.

Check-Up Color the box that contains the vowel digraph in each picture name. Write the word.

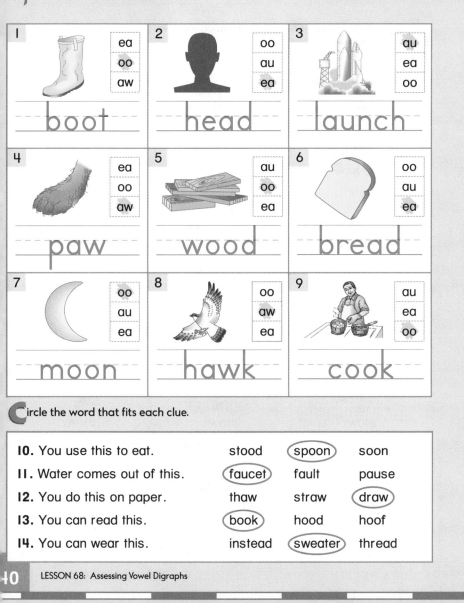

1. ea / **oo** / aw — boot
2. oo / au / **ea** — head
3. **au** / ea / oo — launch
4. ea / oo / **aw** — paw
5. au / **oo** / ea — wood
6. oo / au / **ea** — bread
7. **oo** / au / ea — moon
8. oo / **aw** / ea — hawk
9. au / ea / **oo** — cook

Circle the word that fits each clue.

10. You use this to eat.	stood	(spoon)	soon
11. Water comes out of this.	(faucet)	fault	pause
12. You do this on paper.	thaw	straw	(draw)
13. You can read this.	(book)	hood	hoof
14. You can wear this.	instead	(sweater)	thread

LESSON 68: Assessing Vowel Digraphs

40

Check-Up Have children turn to page 139. Ask volunteers to read the directions and identify the pictures. Then read the directions on page 140 together, and have children identify the pictures. On the board, show children how to color the box for the correct vowel digraph and then write the picture name. For the exercise at the bottom of the page, tell children to read all answer choices before they choose the correct one. Then have children complete both pages.

Observational Assessment Review any observational notes you have recorded on how well children recognize and pronounce vowel digraphs **ea, oo, au,** and **aw**.

Student Skills Assessment Use the checklist on Student Edition pages 207–208 to record your observations of each child.

Writing Conference Meet with each child to discuss the work in his or her portfolio. Encourage children to talk about and critique their writing as you review the samples together. Make notes on their progress.

Encourage children to review their previous writing to find vowel digraphs they may have used. Encourage them also to revise and add to their portfolio work, and to remove work they no longer enjoy.

Group together students who need further instruction on vowel digraphs for the *Reteaching Activities.*

Reteaching *Activities*

August Ahead
Materials: August calendar page, counters, number cube

Write an **ea, oo, au,** or **aw** word on each day of a large August calendar page. Give each child a counter. Have players, in turn, roll a number cube and move that number of spaces. If the player reads the word on that date correctly, he or she places his or her counter there. If not, the player returns to the original space and waits for another turn.

Moon Launch
Materials: tape; Phonics Picture Cards **thread, August, moon, book, paw;** flash cards

Display the picture cards on the chalk ledge. Above each, write its digraph. On flash cards write **ea, oo, au,** and **aw** words. Draw a moon on the board. Have a child choose a flash card, read the word, and tell which picture name has the same digraph. Then have children "launch" their words to the moon by taping them around the moon.

Recognizing and Writing Diphthongs ow and ou

Objectives
- To distinguish between the two sounds of **ow**
- To identify the sound of diphthongs **ow, ou**
- To read and write words with **ow, ou** in context

Warming Up

Reviewing Soft and Hard c and g
On the board write **can, dice, gum, giant, city, gem, cow, gull, stage, cent, cuff,** and **game**. Invite children to work in pairs to sort the words. Discuss the categories children use.

★ Teaching the Lesson

- Write "How now brown cow?" on the board. Read the question with children. Call attention to the **ow** sound in each word.
- Substitute **slow crow** for **brown cow,** and read the new question. Call attention to the long **o** sound in **slow** and **crow.**
- Substitute **loud cloud** for **brown cow,** and read the new question. Call attention to the **ou** sound in **loud** and **cloud.**
- Lead children to recognize that:
  the letters **ow** can stand for two vowel sounds—long **o** as in **slow,** or **ow** as in **brown;**
  the letters **ow** blend together to make the sound in **brown;**
  the letters **ou** blend together to make the sound in **cloud;**
  the **ou** sound in **cloud** is the same sound as **ow** in **brown.**

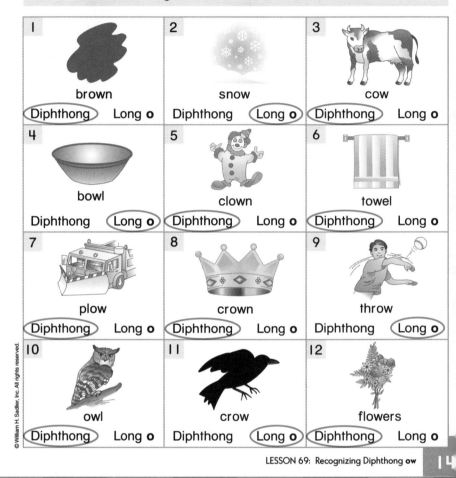

A **diphthong** is two letters blended together that stand for one vowel sound.

The diphthong **ow** can stand for the vowel sound in **brown.** Say the name of each picture. Circle **Diphthong** if the word has the vowel sound in **brown.** Circle **Long o** if the word has the vowel sound in **snow.**

1. brown — (Diphthong) Long **o**
2. snow — Diphthong (Long **o**)
3. cow — (Diphthong) Long **o**
4. bowl — Diphthong (Long **o**)
5. clown — (Diphthong) Long **o**
6. towel — (Diphthong) Long **o**
7. plow — (Diphthong) Long **o**
8. crown — (Diphthong) Long **o**
9. throw — Diphthong (Long **o**)
10. owl — (Diphthong) Long **o**
11. crow — Diphthong (Long **o**)
12. flowers — (Diphthong) Long **o**

LESSON 69: Recognizing Diphthong **ow**

14

Multisensory *Activities*

Auditory ▪ Kinesthetic

Brown or Yellow?

Materials: paper plates, brown and yellow crayons

Have children color or label one side of a paper plate brown and the other side yellow. Say each **ow** word on page 141. Direct children to show the brown side when they hear the **ow** sound, as in **brown,** and the yellow side when they hear the long **o** sound, as in **yellow.**

Visual ▪ Kinesthetic

Flower Power

Materials: construction paper, scissors, crayons, glue

On the board, list words with diphthongs **ow** and **ou,** such as **brown, down, crown, how, owl, flower, cloud, about, pouch, cloud, found,** and **sound.** Have children make two daisy-like flowers, and label one flower center **ow** and the other **ou.** Invite children to write **ow** words and **ou** words on the proper petals.

141

The diphthong **ou** in **cloud** stands for the same vowel sound as the diphthong **ow** in **brown**. Circle the word that names each picture.

1		2		3	
	(cloud) claw clown		crane (crown) crowd		how horse (house)

4		5		6	
	porch (pouch) peach		(blouse) blues blaze		cash catch (couch)

Use a word from the box to complete each sentence.

brown	clouds	down	mountains	owl	sound

7. Let's go hiking in the _mountains_ .

8. Look up to see the _clouds_ in the sky.

9. Look _down_ to see the valleys below.

10. Sh! Don't make a _sound_ .

11. Maybe we'll hear a _brown_ bear growling.

12. Maybe we'll hear a gray _owl_ hooting.

42 LESSON 69: Recognizing and Writing Diphthongs **ow** and **ou**

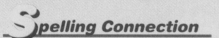

Spelling Connection

Read the words and sentences below. Ask volunteers to spell each word orally or write it on the board.

out The opposite of in is **out**.
house The **house** had a red roof.
flower Daffodils are my favorite **flower**.
cloud A gray **cloud** floated across the sky.
down It took less time to hike **down** the mountain.

Multicultural Connection

Tell children that in the Himalayan mountain country of Tibet, priests or monks called *lamas* have a great respect for nature. Explain that each year the lamas hold a festival called *Mani Rimdu* and that for the festival, the lamas dye sand from a river to make beautiful circular pictures called *mandalas* (MUHN duh-luhs) to represent the circle of life. When the festival is over, the sand is returned to the river. Ask children why returning the sand might be important.

Practicing the Skill

● Review the Helpful Hint and the directions on page 141. Do the first two items together.

● Have volunteers read the directions and identify the pictures on page 142. Together, do the first item in each exercise. Then have children complete both pages.

Extending the Skill Across the Curriculum

(Language Arts/Science)
Theme Activity
Materials: index cards, tape

● Use a K-W-L chart. Ask what children already know about mountains, and list responses under "What I Know." Ask what they want to know, and list responses under "What I Want to Know."

● Share the theme book cited below. Then ask children for any new knowledge, and record it under "What I Learned."

● Write the paragraph below on the board. Leave blank spaces for the words in parentheses:

There are (**mountain**) ranges (**around**) the world. In North America, the tallest mountains are in Alaska. The Andes are in (**South**) America. The world's highest mountains, the Himalayas, are (**found**) in Asia. (**Down**) in the valleys, many (**flowers**) can (**sprout**). Some mountains are white with snow. Others appear gray, green, (**brown**), or even purple.

● Display the words **mountain, around, South, found, down, flowers, sprout,** and **brown** on index cards. Invite children to tape the missing word into the blank space as they each read a sentence.

Theme Book
Barrett, Norman. *Mountains.* New York: Franklin Watts, 1989. Colorful photos.

Lesson 70

Writing and Reviewing Diphthongs

Objectives
- To recognize the sounds of diphthongs **oi, oy, ew**
- To read and write words with **oi, oy, ew** in context
- To review diphthongs **ow, ou, oi, oy, ew**

Warming Up

Reviewing y as a Vowel
Write **jelly, story, cry, sly, city, try,** and **heavy** on the board. Invite children to sort the words by the sound of **y**. Have children explain why they used certain categories.

★ Teaching the Lesson

- On the board write "Mr. **Choi enjoys oyster stew**." Call on a volunteer to read the sentence aloud. Underline the words **Choi, enjoys,** and **oyster**. Ask children to say these words and listen for the vowel sound they share. Lead children to conclude that the letters **o** and **i** and the letters **o** and **y** blend together to make the same vowel sound.
- Ask children what vowel sound they hear in the word **stew**. (oo) Call on a volunteer to underline the letters (**ew**) that blend together to make the sound.
- Have children generate a list of words for each diphthong. (For **oi**, you might work with the phonogram **oil**.)

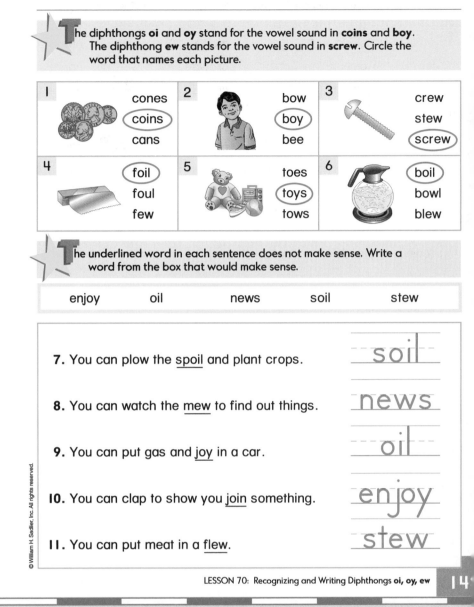

The diphthongs **oi** and **oy** stand for the vowel sound in **coins** and **boy**. The diphthong **ew** stands for the vowel sound in **screw**. Circle the word that names each picture.

| 1 | cones / **coins** / cans | 2 | bow / **boy** / bee | 3 | crew / stew / **screw** |
| 4 | **foil** / foul / few | 5 | toes / **toys** / tows | 6 | **boil** / bowl / blew |

The underlined word in each sentence does not make sense. Write a word from the box that would make sense.

| enjoy | oil | news | soil | stew |

7. You can plow the <u>spoil</u> and plant crops. — soil

8. You can watch the <u>mew</u> to find out things. — news

9. You can put gas and <u>joy</u> in a car. — oil

10. You can clap to show you <u>join</u> something. — enjoy

11. You can put meat in a <u>flew</u>. — stew

LESSON 70: Recognizing and Writing Diphthongs **oi, oy, ew**

14

Multisensory *Activities*

Auditory ■ Kinesthetic

Be Joyful! Make Noise!
Materials: party horns or other noise-makers (optional)

Distribute noisemakers. Invite children to listen as you say these words, pausing after each: **coins, cones, moist, mist, choice, oil, point, choose, boy, boo, toys, blue, boil, tools, broil, soil, sail, Roy, say, soy, nose, eek, paint,** and **noise.** Tell children to make noise when they hear a word with the sound of **oi** or **oy.**

Visual ■ Tactile

Newspaper Crew
Materials: newspapers, scissors, glue, construction paper

Distribute the materials. Invite children to cut out **ew** words from newspapers or cut letters from construction paper to spell **ew** words. Have children make collages of the words to share with classmates. You might also have children make collages of words with diphthongs **ow, ou, oi,** and **oy.**

Write the name of each picture. Then find and circle the words in the puzzle. Look across and down.

1. boy
2. brown
3. cloud
4. cow
5. foil
6. house
7. screw
8. toys

```
b  r  o  w  n  d
o  a  t  o  y  s
y  f  o  i  l  c
c  l  o  u  d  r
c  o  w  b  c  e
h  o  u  s  e  w
```

44   LESSON 70: Reviewing Diphthongs

Spelling Connection

Read aloud the words and sentences below. Invite volunteers to spell each word orally or write it on the board.

boys — Girls and **boys** flew colorful kites.

coins — Asi collects **coins** from other countries.

soil — Troy hoed the **soil** in the garden.

knew — Andy **knew** the answer to the problem.

blew — The wind **blew** the leaves.

Computer Connection

Have children use Sound It Out Land™ 3 (Conexus) to explore with Vowel Owl the phonetic sounds of vowel digraphs and diphthongs. Children can learn important sounds by listening to Vowel Owl sing to the night sky. Direct them to choose words that demonstrate the sounds on Vowel Owl's vowel digraph and diphthong cards. Challenge children to say the words and vowel sounds as they match them.

Practicing the Skill

• Have children turn to page 143. Review the directions and the sounds of the diphthongs. Ask volunteers to identify the pictures. Do the first item in each exercise together.

• Call on volunteers to read the directions and identify the pictures on page 144. Have children write the answer to the first item and circle that word in the puzzle.

• Ask children to complete both pages.

Extending the Skill Across the Curriculum

(Art/Science)

Theme Activity

Materials: uniformly sized paper circles, paints (including yellow and brown), tape

• Invite children to explore how colors can fool the eye. Ask a volunteer to paint one circle yellow. Have another volunteer paint a circle dark brown.

• Tape the painted circles next to each other on the bulletin board. Tell children to stand at the opposite end of the room and say which circle looks larger. Then invite partners to paint two circles with different colors, one light and the other dark. Have them repeat the experiment. Track results on a chart.

• Elicit from children that light colors make objects appear larger. Explain that light colors reflect light, while dark colors absorb it.

• Have children find and circle words in the chart that contain diphthongs.

• Children can find more "eye teasers" and color experiments in *Science Tricks and Magic* by Gaby Waters (EDC Publishing).

144

Connecting Spelling and Writing

Objectives
● To say, spell, and write words with vowel digraphs and diphthongs
● To write a descriptive paragraph using spelling words

Warming Up

Reviewing Compound Words
Have children come up with compound word clues for classmates to solve. Provide this example:

tip + toe =? (**tiptoe**)

★ Teaching the Lesson

● On the board write "**Thread** comes in lots of colors." Read the sentence with children. Ask which word has the short **e** sound. Invite a volunteer to underline the letters that stand for that sound. (**ea**)

● Write the vowel digraphs **ea, oo, au,** and **aw** in a row across the board. In another row, write the diphthongs **ow, ou, oi, oy,** and **ew**. Say the vowel sound that each set of letters makes.

● Together, say each spelling word on page 145, spell it, and say it again. Invite volunteers to write each word on the board under the vowels in its name.

● Challenge children to use each word in a sentence.

Practicing the Skill

Have children read the directions and the spelling words on page 145. Ask volunteers to read the vowel digraphs and diphthongs. Then have children complete the page.

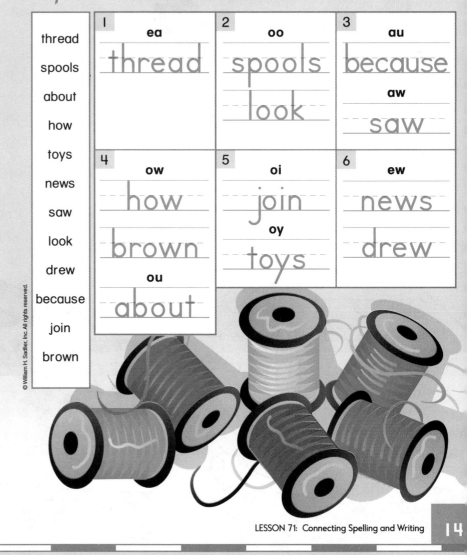

Spell and Write Say and spell each word in the box. Then write each word under the vowels in its name.

thread
spools
about
how
toys
news
saw
look
drew
because
join
brown

1 ea	2 oo	3 au
thread	spools	because
	look	aw
		saw

4 ow	5 oi	6 ew
how	join	news
brown	oy	drew
ou	toys	
about		

LESSON 71: Connecting Spelling and Writing

145

Multisensory *Activities*

Auditory ■ Kinesthetic

Spelling for Points
Materials: number cube, index cards

Write the spelling words on index cards. Randomly place the cards face-down on a table. Have children work in pairs and take turns spelling for points. Player 1 rolls a number cube. Player 2 chooses a card and reads the word. If Player 1 spells the word correctly, she or he earns the number of points showing on the cube.

Kinesthetic ■ Visual

Spelling Quilt
Materials: two-inch colored paper squares, glue, crayons, construction paper

Give each child twelve squares. Have children glue the squares on a sheet of paper in a quilt pattern. Ask children to write a spelling word on each square, using a different color crayon for each vowel digraph or diphthong. Have children use a crayon to make "stitch marks" around the squares.

Spell and Write

Think of something you can make from spools. Write a paragraph to describe it. Use one or more of your spelling words.

thread	spools	about	how	toys	news
saw	look	drew	because	join	brown

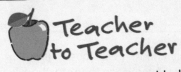

I can make

LESSON 71: Connecting Spelling and Writing

Spelling Connection

Have children form a circle to play "bounce and spell." Say a spelling word, and bounce a ball to a child. The child should say the first letter of the word and then bounce the ball to a classmate, who says the second letter, and so on. If a child says the wrong letter, the next player should correct it before adding a letter. Have a recorder write each letter on the board as the word is spelled.

Teacher to Teacher

Make three spiderwebs from black yarn, and mount them on the bulletin board. Cut three spiders from paper, and label them "Vowel Pair," "Vowel Digraph," and "Vowel Diphthong." Attach each to a web. Have children write words on paper bug shapes. Invite them to tape the bugs to the correct spiderweb.

Sharon Obrimski
Savannah, GA

The Writing Process

Tell children that they will write a paragraph to describe something made from spools. Explain that to describe an item means to tell what it looks like and what it does. Have children read the directions on page 146.

Brainstorm Invite children to share their ideas about items that can be made from spools. Talk about the objects shown on the page. Then have children generate a list of objects they might make.

Write Have children write drafts on paper. Encourage children to use words that tell about color, shape, and size.

Revise Suggest that children check their writing and make sure they have used descriptive words. Have them go back and underline spelling words they have used.

Publish Have children write their descriptions on page 146. Ask them to exchange papers and draw what has been described.

Extending the Skill

Provide spools and materials such as twine, feathers, glue, beads, and paint that children can use to make spool "thingamajigs" (like those items they wrote about on page 146).

Choose a child's "thingamajig," and work with the class to write on the board a paragraph on how to make it. Write a topic sentence and use words such as *first* and *next* to give clear directions. Ask a child to copy the paragraph onto chart paper for display along with the thingamajigs.

Portfolio

Children may wish to add their descriptions to their portfolios.

Integrating the Language Arts

Objectives
- To use oral and written language to extend the theme concept
- To demonstrate recognition of vowel pairs, vowel digraphs and diphthongs in context

Background Information

One quality of flowers that attracts animals is color. Animals that are active in the day, such as bees, birds, and butterflies, seem to like blue, purple, pink, red, and yellow flowers. These colors are bright in the daylight sun but cannot be seen at night. Animals that are active at night, such as bats and moths, are attracted to white or very pale-colored flowers, which stand out in the darkness.

★ *Teaching the Lesson*

- Focus children's attention on the photos on page 147. Ask how flowers are similar and different. Invite children to tell about their favorite flowers.
- Ask a volunteer to read the text aloud. Draw attention to the flower names, and discuss why they are appropriate. Encourage thoughtful responses to the questions.
- Challenge children to point out vowel digraphs and diphthongs on this page.

Oral Language Development
Encourage children to talk about the flowers they like the most. Ask why people grow colorful flowers.

ESL Activities
Refer to page 121J.

Look and Learn!   Let's read and talk about colorful flowers.

bluebells

strawflowers

striped maple

Flowers can be many colors. Bluebells are blue, and so is ground ivy. Daisies and snowdrops are white. Some trees have green flowers and leaves. Strawflowers may be red, pink, yellow, violet, or white.

If you enjoy flowers, see if you can plant a garden. Watch it bloom into a rainbow. Watch for birds and butterflies that stop by.

If you had a garden, what would you plant in it? Why?

daisy

snowdrops

LESSON 72: Vowel Pairs, Vowel Digraphs, and Diphthongs in Context

14

Reading and Writing Connection

Supply children with books about flowers. Encourage them to choose a particular flower and read about it. Then ask children to write about the flowers they chose by answering these questions:

> What is the name of the flower?
> What colors can it be?
> How tall can it grow?
> In what parts of the world can it grow?

Social Studies Connection

Explain that tulips are colorful spring flowers that grow from bulbs and that originated in the Mediterranean area and central Asia. Tell children that tulips from Turkey were brought to Holland; then Dutch and German settlers brought them to North America. Today, tulip festivals are held in many North American cities, including Michigan City, IN, and Ottawa, Canada.

Help students trace the "migration" of the tulip on a map or globe.

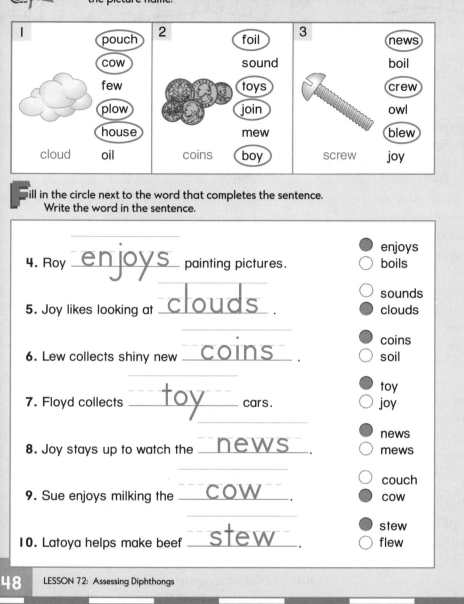

Check-Up Circle the words in each list that have the same vowel sound as the picture name.

1
- pouch ⟨circled⟩
- cow ⟨circled⟩
- few
- plow ⟨circled⟩
- house ⟨circled⟩

cloud

2
- foil ⟨circled⟩
- sound
- toys ⟨circled⟩
- join ⟨circled⟩
- mew

coins

oil

3
- news ⟨circled⟩
- boil
- crew ⟨circled⟩
- owl
- blew ⟨circled⟩

screw

boy ⟨circled⟩

joy

Fill in the circle next to the word that completes the sentence. Write the word in the sentence.

4. Roy **enjoys** painting pictures.
   - ● enjoys
   - ○ boils

5. Joy likes looking at **clouds** .
   - ○ sounds
   - ● clouds

6. Lew collects shiny new **coins** .
   - ● coins
   - ○ soil

7. Floyd collects **toy** cars.
   - ● toy
   - ○ joy

8. Joy stays up to watch the **news** .
   - ● news
   - ○ mews

9. Sue enjoys milking the **cow** .
   - ○ couch
   - ● cow

10. Latoya helps make beef **stew** .
   - ● stew
   - ○ flew

48 LESSON 72: Assessing Diphthongs

Reteaching *Activities*

Diphthong Stew
Materials: colored construction paper, scissors, container

Ask children to cut three or four vegetable shapes from the paper. List **oi**, **oy**, and **ew** words for them to copy on their shapes. Tell children they will make diphthong stew by reading a word, identifying the diphthong, and then adding the shape to the "stew pot."

Clouds Over the Mountain
Materials: construction paper, index cards

Cut and label a cloud shape from white paper and a mountain shape from brown paper. Mount them on the board. Write **ou** and **ow** words on index cards. Have children read each card and place it under the shape or color that has the same spelling.

Assessing the Skills

Check-Up Review the spelling of each diphthong. Have children name words that contain each one. Then ask children to identify the pictures at the top of page 148. Have a volunteer read the directions. Point out that more than one word in each list should be circled. For the second exercise, tell children to try both words in the sentences before choosing the one that makes sense.

Observational Assessment Review the observational notes you have recorded throughout this unit. Use the notes to help you assess overall performance and progress.

Student Skills Assessment Use the assessment on page 148 and your observations to record your evaluation of each child's skills on Student Edition page 207.

Writing Conference Meet with each child to review the samples of work in her or his portfolio. Encourage children to talk about their writing as you review the samples together. Make notes about each child's progress to add to their portfolios. You might also encourage children to add new work to their portfolios or to edit an earlier writing sample.

Group together for the *Reteaching Activities* children who need further instruction on diphthongs. You might then use the alternative assessment methods on page 121C.

Take-Home Book Remind children to complete the Take-Home Book for Unit 6 at home.

PLANNING RESOURCE

NUMBERS COUNT

Theme:
*On the street or in a book—
numbers everywhere I look.*

Overview

Unit 7 introduces children to contractions, plurals, inflectional endings, and words ending in **le** by using numbers.

Objectives

- To enjoy a poem about numbers
- To recognize, write, and spell words with plural and inflectional endings, contractions, and words ending in **le**

Thematic Teaching

Discuss with children how they use numbers in their daily lives. Consider children's experiences and prior knowledge when selecting activities from the lessons. Provide additional reading material about numbers.

Display the Poetry Poster "Numbers, Numbers," and refer to it throughout this unit.

Individual Lessons

Lessons	Skill Focus
73	Introduction to Contractions and Word Endings
74–75	Recognizing and Writing Contractions
76	Connecting Spelling and Writing
77	Reviewing and Assessing Contractions
78	Recognizing and Writing Plural Endings **s** and **es**/Changing **y** to **i**
79	Reviewing and Assessing Plural Endings
80	Recognizing and Writing Inflectional Endings **s** and **es**/Changing **y** to **i**
81	Writing Words with Inflectional Endings **ing** and **ed**
82	Dropping Silent **e** Before Adding Inflectional Endings **ing** and **ed**
83	Doubling Final Consonants Before Adding Inflectional Endings **ing** and **ed**
84	Recognizing and Writing Words Ending in **le**
85	Changing **y** to **i**/Reviewing Inflectional Endings
86	Connecting Spelling and Writing
87	Integrating the Language Arts

Take-Home Book: *Shopping with Milo*

Lee Blair

"Numbers, Numbers" was written by Leland Blair Jacobs, who used the pseudonym Lee Blair. Blair was a teacher as well as a writer, and began his teaching career in a one-room schoolhouse in Michigan. Although Blair taught all grade levels—from elementary school through college—when he wrote, he especially wanted to create works that would make reading fun for young children.

Curriculum Integration

Writing Children write descriptions, narratives, poetry, diaries, and reports on pages 154, 156, 166, 174, 176, and 177.

Math Activities involving math are found on pages 152, 154, 160, 164, 166, 168, 170, 172, and 177.

Social Studies An opportunity for children to relate to social studies appears on page 174.

Optional Learning Activities

Multisensory Activities Every lesson includes activities that offer a variety of learning styles—visual, auditory, tactile, or kinesthetic.

Multicultural Connection Children celebrate cultural diversity in activities on pages 160, 170, and 174.

Thematic Activities The *Extending the Skill Across the Curriculum* aspect of each lesson applies the unit theme to various disciplines.

Assessment Strategies

Multiple strategies such as *Observational Assessments*, portfolios, written middle- and end-of-the-unit assessments, and the *Skills Checklist* at the back of the Student Edition will help you assess children's mastery of phonics skills throughout Unit 7.

Resources

Work by Leland B. Jacobs
Just Around the Corner: Poems About the Seasons. New York: Henry Holt, 1993

Theme-Related Resources
In Search of the Missing Numbers. Davidson & Associates, Inc., 1988.

Moore, Inga. *Six-Dinner Sid.* Old Tappan, NJ: Simon & Schuster, 1991.

Assessment

In Unit 7 children focus on recognizing contractions and word endings. The following are suggestions for evaluating these skills through informal/formal, observational, objective, portfolio, and performance assessments. You may also wish to refer to *Using Technology* for alternative assessment activities.

Informal/Formal Assessment

The tests on pages 149D, 149E, and 149F assess whether children have mastered recognizing and writing contractions and word endings. These tools may be used informally at the beginning of the unit to identify a starting point for individual or class instruction or formally at the end of the unit to assess children's progress.

Observational Assessment

Specific opportunities for observation are highlighted in the lesson plans. In addition, there are many opportunities throughout the unit to observe children recognizing and writing contractions, plural endings, inflectional endings **ing** and **ed**, and words ending in **le**. Opportunities for observation might include *Multisensory Activities, Spelling Connection,* and *Computer Connection.*

Objective Assessment

Use the assessment pages throughout the unit. After completing each assessment page, determine the area(s) in which children would benefit from more instruction; then refer to *Reteaching Activities* found throughout the unit in the Teacher's Edition. After reteaching the skill, reassess children's progress.

Portfolio Assessment

Have children write a "One" story. Tell them to choose a topic about anything they have studied in phonics this year. Tell children to write the story in the first person singular. Model this "One" story for the children:

> I went to visit a museum. I looked at one thing. It was an Egyptian mummy. It was covered in gold.

Ask children to exchange stories with a partner. Direct each partner to rewrite the story as a "More Than One" story. Then model this "More Than One" story starter:

> We went to visit two museums. We looked at two things. They were two Egyptian mummies....

Performance Assessment

Provide children with old magazines. Direct children to cut out stories and glue them on sheets of construction paper.

Tell children to circle the contractions and the plurals in the stories. Then tell them to write the two words that make up each contraction and to make the plural words singular.

Using Technology

To evaluate children's progress, have them complete the *Tech Talk* activities on pages 149K–149L of the Teacher's Edition.

Answer Key

Page 149D

1. c	2. i	3. l	4. k	5. f	6. g
7. j	8. d	9. a	10. b	11. h	12. e
13. I'm	14. isn't	15. doesn't	16. can't	17. We'll	18. it's

Page 149E

1. eagle	2. purple	3. pebble	4. turtle	5. apple
6. circle	7. gobble	8. marble	9. pickle	10. puzzles
11. table	12. castle	13. little		

Page 149F

1. knocks 2. wishes 3. hides 4. watches 5. plays 6. riding
7. sweeping 8. planning 9. sharing 10. skipping 11. dropping
12. liking 13. aiming 14. jogging 15. tracing 16. learn 17. get
18. grin 19. shine 20. march 21. frame 22. run 23. pick 24. slice

Find the two words that have the same meaning as each contraction. Then write the letter of the contraction next to the two words.

a. they're   b. haven't   c. she's   d. let's
e. didn't   f. you'll   g. aren't   h. you've
i. they've   j. he's   k. shouldn't   l. that's

1. she is _____

2. they have _____

3. that is _____

4. should not _____

5. you will _____

6. are not _____

7. he has _____

8. let us _____

9. they are _____

10. have not _____

11. you have _____

12. did not _____

Write the contraction for the two underlined words in each sentence.

13. <u>I am</u> helping Dad build a deck. _____

14. That <u>is not</u> an easy job. _____

15. He <u>does not</u> want to make a mistake. _____

16. <u>We will</u> finish the deck on Monday. _____

Write a word from the box to answer each riddle.

| marble | pebble | purple | eagle | gobble | turtle |

1 I am a large bird.

_____

- - - - - - - - - -

_____

2 I am a color.

_____

- - - - - - - - - -

_____

3 I am a little stone.

_____

- - - - - - - - - -

_____

4 I am an animal with a hard shell.

_____

- - - - - - - - - -

_____

5 I am the sound a turkey makes.

_____

- - - - - - - - - -

_____

6 I am a small glass ball.

_____

- - - - - - - - - -

_____

Fill in the circle next to the word that makes sense in each sentence.

7. Doing jigsaw _____ is a hobby of mine.

○ handles
○ puzzles

8. My first puzzle was a picture of a _____ .

○ middle
○ castle

9. It had 1000 _____ pieces.

○ little
○ bottle

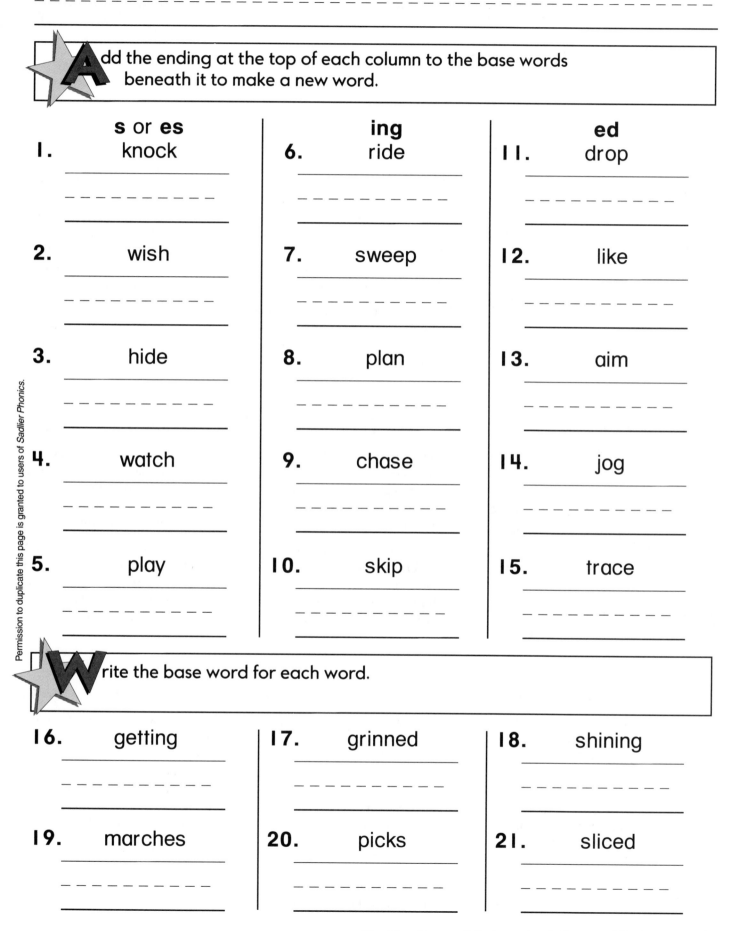

Add the ending at the top of each column to the base words beneath it to make a new word.

s or **es**

1. knock

2. wish

3. hide

4. watch

5. play

ing

6. ride

7. sweep

8. plan

9. chase

10. skip

ed

11. drop

12. like

13. aim

14. jog

15. trace

Write the base word for each word.

16. getting

19. marches

17. grinned

20. picks

18. shining

21. sliced

Game Time

▲▽▲▽▲▽▲▽▲ Contraction Concentration ▲▽▲▽▲▽▲▽

Blackline Master 31 p.149H

Objective: To identify the two words a contraction stands for

Players: pairs

Materials: construction paper, glue, scissors

❂ Duplicate Blackline Master 31 and give a copy to each pair. Have partners glue their copy onto construction paper and cut out the cards. Then direct children to mix up the cards and place them facedown in six rows of four.

❂ Invite children to play a memory game by matching contractions with words that have the same meaning.

❂ Have one partner in each pair turn over two cards. Explain that if the cards match, the player may pick them up and take another turn; if the cards do not match, they should be turned facedown and the other player given a turn.

❂ Tell partners to add up the points on their cards once all cards have been matched. The player with the most points wins the game.

▲▽▲▽▲▽▲▽ Count on Correct Endings ▲▽▲▽▲▽▲▽

Blackline Master 32 p.149I

Objective: To build words by adding inflectional endings s, es, ed, and ing

Players: pairs or small groups

Materials: construction paper, scissors, glue

❂ Duplicate Blackline Master 32 and give a copy to each child. Have children glue their copies onto construction paper and cut out the cards.

❂ Invite partners to take turns adding inflectional endings **s**, **es**, **ed**, or **ing** to the given base words. Tell children to use the single-letter cards to double the final conso-

nant, if necessary, before adding an ending card. Suggest that if an **e** needs to be dropped from the base word, they simply cover the **e** with the ending card.

❂ Encourage children to check one another's words for accuracy and to use the newly built words to make up sentences related to the unit theme "Numbers Count!"

▲▽▲▽▲▽▲▽▲ Contraction Bull's-Eye! ▲▽▲▽▲▽▲▽▲

Objective: To identify the two words a contraction stands for

Players: two teams

Materials: chalk or masking tape, word cards, beanbag

❂ Use chalk or masking tape to outline three concentric circles on the floor. Mark the center bull's-eye circle twenty points, the middle circle ten, and the outside circle five. On the chalk ledge, display word cards for contractions and for the words that stand for those contractions.

❂ Give one child a beanbag. Direct that child to choose a contraction,

find the two words it stands for, and then use the contraction in a sentence. If the player uses the word correctly, invite her or him to toss the beanbag at the target to find how many points his or her team receives.

❂ Alternate between the teams, and record points to see who wins.

Contraction Concentration

5	10	5	10
didn't	wasn't	aren't	won't

5	20	5	10
we'll	you'll	she's	they're

5	10	5	20
I've	it's	let's	he's

| you will | was not | I have | did not |

| they are | let us | we will | are not |

| he has | will not | it is | she is |

Count on Correct Endings

plan	splash	s
hope	stop	es
wag	pass	ed
smile	hum	ing
reach	chase	n
count	show	p
mix	dance	t
jog	flip	g
help	skate	x
wave	drip	m

ESL Activities

Number Rhythms
Page 149

Guide children in tapping out the rhythm of the poem as they recite it. Then have the class illustrate on posterboard items the poem describes as having numbers. Help children attach rulers or cardboard rollers to their posters as handles. Recite the poem together again, and direct children to hold up their number signs when the part illustrated is mentioned.

Number Skits
Page 149

Have children work in groups. Assign each group a stanza of the poem to perform as a skit. Provide skit outlines for beginning ESL students. Encourage children to devise props and present their skits to the class.

One or More
Page 159

On separate index cards, write the base words on page 159. Hold up a card, and ask a volunteer to read the word and use it in a sentence. Call on another child to say and spell the plural form and then to say the plural form of the original sentence. Continue through all the cards.

Creative Journals
Page 168

Invite children to keep a class journal of special activities in which they participate throughout the week. Encourage them to use some of the past tense words learned in the unit.

Imaginative Models
Page 170

Present various pictures of competitions, such as the Olympic Games, the Indy 500, organized athletics, and chess matches. Initiate a discussion of contests and competitions, and ask children to tell about memorable competitions in which they have participated or that they have witnessed. Provide materials for children to draw or make models of either a favorite real competition or a fantasy one. Then have them write brief past-tense descriptions explaining the real or imaginary competition.

Endings in Action
Page 174

Distribute posterboard and markers. Invite children to choose a verb to illustrate in its **ing** and **ed** forms. Direct them to divide their posterboard in half and make two pictures that distinctly show the action in progress and the completed action. Have each child include beneath each picture a caption that contains the featured word.

Decorative Clocks
Page 177

Present pictures of instruments used throughout the world to measure time. Include ancient timepieces, such as sundials, hourglasses, and rock formations. Explain how each instrument works. Then provide craft materials for children to construct decorative clock faces with movable hands.

Collage of Clocks
Page 177

Ask children to locate pictures of clocks in magazines, catalogs, or advertising flyers and to bring the pictures to class. Have each child glue her or his clock onto construction paper and write beneath it a caption that begins: "It is _____ o'clock. It is time to…." Tell children to use the time shown on their clock or make up a time if none is visible. Together, make a giant clock collage.

TECH TALK

Picturing Double

Objectives
- To review plural endings **es, ies,** and **s**
- To use drawing features on a program such as Kid Works™ 2* to review plurals

Preparation
Read aloud *So Many Cats* by Beatrice Scenk de Regniers (Houghton Mifflin). Have children identify the plural words as they occur in the story. Write these words on the board. Ask volunteers to explain how each of the words was made plural and to name each singular form.

One Step at a Time

1 Direct children on Kid Works™ 2 to access the Icon Maker to make and select noun icons. Tell them to choose appropriate icons from the blue box or use the drawing tools to make their own.

2 Have children make three different icons for words whose plurals have an **es** ending, three for **ies**, and three for **s**. Tell them to enter the singular and plural forms of each word in the text box beneath each picture.

3 Tell children to save each labeled icon in the My Words box and then click on "New" under "File" to clear the easel.

4 Encourage children to say each singular and plural icon name and then press Enter to hear the computer say the same.

5 Direct children to click on the Print button in the My Words box to print their work.

Class Sharing

Ask volunteers to share their icon pages. Have them read aloud the singular and plural forms of each picture name and tell how the plural was formed.

baby
babies

bus
buses

drum
drums

Missing Numbers

Objectives
- To identify words ending in **ed**, contractions, and plural endings
- To use a writing program such as Storybook Weaver® Deluxe* to write and illustrate a story about a day without numbers

Preparation
Read a story about the history of numbers. You might display pictures of early number systems and an abacus. Explain to children that numbers have been a part of life for many years.

Ask children to name all the different places they see numbers. Write responses on the board. Then say, "I got up at seven A.M. I ran to catch the Number 3 bus to school." Ask the class to name the numbers you said. Then ask a volunteer to tell the class what he or she did before coming to school and to specify the time of each activity. Have children raise their hands every time they hear a number. Keep a tally on the board. Then ask children to imagine a day without numbers. Ask them how they could tell the same story without using numbers.

One Step at a Time

1. Have children work individually or in small groups. Direct children using Storybook Weaver® Deluxe to select "Start a New Story" from the opening screen.

2. Tell children to select "Title" and then enter a title for their story (e.g., "A Day Without Numbers"). Then have them select "Author" to enter their name and "Border" to include a decorative border on their title page.

3. Tell children to use any of the ideas talked about in class or their own ideas to write a story about a day without numbers.

4. Have children select "Picture and Text" to enter sentences and "Scenery," "Objects," and "Color" to illustrate each page. Tell them to use the Musical Note icon to add sound.

5. Direct children to print their stories.

Class Sharing

Encourage children to share their stories. Ask the class to determine which story was the funniest, the most clever, and so on.

Number Songs

Provide copies of the words to songs or rhymes about numbers, such as "One, Two, Buckle My Shoe," or "One Little, Two Little Indians." If possible, play recordings of the songs or rhymes. Write the words on the board. Have children identify each plural word and then explain how it was made plural. Have the class work in groups to practice singing or chanting one of the songs or rhymes and to write additional verses. Allow time for class presentations.

All referenced software is listed under Computer Resources on page T46.

Literature Introduction to Contractions and Word Endings

Objectives
- To enjoy a poem about numbers
- To identify plurals, inflectional endings, and contractions

Starting with Literature

- Ask children to find all the numbers pictured on page 149. Then read aloud "Numbers, Numbers." Have children join in as you read it again.
- Ask children to list the places in the poem where numbers are found. Then have them list the names of other places where they see numbers. Have children share their lists.

Developing Critical Thinking
Read aloud the questions at the bottom of page 149. Invite children to imagine and tell about what might happen during a day without numbers.

Introducing the Skill

Tell children that, in this unit, they will learn about *plurals*, words that mean more than one; the word endings **es, ing, ed,** and **le**; and about *contractions*, ways to express two words as one word.

Practicing the Skill

Ask children to skim the poem on page 149 for words that end in **s** or **es**. Explain that each of these words indicates that there are more than one of each item. Then ask children to say the singular of each word.

ESL Activities
Refer to page 151J

NUMBERS, NUMBERS

Numbers in the grocery store
   About the things we eat,
Numbers on the doorways,
   And in the city street.

Numbers on the calendar,
   On signs that flash or glow,
Numbers on the telephone,
   Or tickets for the show.

Numbers on the buses,
   On money that I spend,
Numbers on the stamps I put
   On letters that I send.

Numbers on the highways, yes,
   And numbers in a book!
It seems I'm seeing numbers
   Almost everywhere I look!

Lee Blair

Critical Thinking
Why are numbers important in your life?
What kinds of problems would people have
if there were no numbers?

LESSON 73: Introduction to Contractions and Word Endings

14

Theme Words

Numbers Count Ask volunteers to tell their age, height, phone number, home address, and zip code. Then ask what their responses have in common. (All responses contain numbers.) Reread the poem "Numbers, Numbers" on page 149. Ask children to tell of other places they have seen numbers. List their responses on chart paper. Throughout the unit, add phrases from children's responses to the list, and use them in activities.

At the end of the unit, use the list to assess children's ability to recognize contractions, plurals, inflectional endings, and words ending in **le**.

Dear Family,

As your child progresses through this unit about numbers, he or she will learn about the following kinds of words and word endings.

> **contraction:** two words written as one with one or more letters left out (**isn't = is not; I'll = I will**)
>
> **plural:** word that means more than one (**book_s, peach_es**)
>
> **word endings s, ed, ing:** endings that can be added to a word to make new words (**need_s, help_ed, skipp_ed, jump_ing, bak_ing**)

- Read the poem "Numbers, Numbers" on the reverse side.
- Look for plurals (**number_s, thing_s, doorway_s, sign_s, ticket_s, buse_s, letter_s, highway_s**), contractions (**I'm**), and words that end in **ing** (**see_ing**).
- Talk about places where you see numbers.

PROJECT

Make a word bank by putting a slit in the top of a shoebox. Whenever your child learns a new contraction, plural word, or word that ends in **s**, **ed**, or **ing**, have him or her write the word on a card and "deposit" it in the bank. Your child can "withdraw" words and use them in sentences.

Apreciada Familia:

En esta unidad, sobre los números, su niño aprenderá los siguientes tipos de palabras y terminaciones.

> **contracción:** una palabra formada por la abreviación de dos palabras (**isn't = is not; I'll = I will**).
>
> **plural:** palabras que indican más de uno (**book_s, peach_es**).
>
> **palabras que terminan en s, ed, ing:** letras que se añaden al final de una palabra (**need_s, help_ed, skipp_ed, jump_ing, bak_ing**).

- Lea la poesía, "Numbers, Numbers" en la página 149.
- Busquen los plurales (**number_s, thing_s, doorway_s, sign_s, ticket_s, buse_s, stamp_s, letter_s, highway_s**); una contracción (**I'm**); y la palabra que termina en **ing** (**see_ing**).
- Hablen de los lugares donde ven números.

PROYECTO

Hagan un banco de palabras haciendo una abertura en la parte de arriba de una caja de zapatos. Cada vez que el niño aprenda una contracción, un plural, o una palabra que termine in **s**, **ed**, o **ing**, pídale escribir la palabra en una tarjeta y "depositarla" en el banco. El niño puede "retirar" palabras para escribir oraciones.

LESSON 73: Introduction to Contractions and Word Endings—
Phonics Alive at Home

Phonics Alive at Home

- *Phonics Alive at Home* is intended to involve families in their children's reading and writing development through activities that apply phonics skills.
- The *Phonics Alive at Home* page 150 includes a project related to the unit theme "Numbers Count!" It also has activities that pertain to the phonics focus on contractions, plurals, inflectional endings, and words ending in **le**.
- Have children tear out and take home page 150. Invite them to discuss the page and complete the project with family members. Encourage children to bring their completed projects to school to share with classmates.
- Provide ample opportunities for children to talk about their experiences with numbers in activities such as shopping, playing games, measuring, using money, and reading books, newspapers, and magazines.
- Encourage children to bring to class items that have numbers on or in them. Have each child explain what the numbers are and tell why the numbers are important.

ESL Activities

Opportunities for ESL activities are provided and referenced throughout this unit. These activities benefit the ESL children in your classroom by providing additional language experiences. Choose the activities that best meet the diverse needs of your class.

For ESL activities related to "Numbers Count!" refer to page 151J.

Take-Home Book

Include family members in class-related activities by sending children home with a book of their own. The fold-up book *Shopping with Milo*, which can be found in the Student Edition on pages 221–222, is for shared reading enjoyment and encourages children to apply their newly learned phonics skills related to contractions and word endings. Use the Take-Home Book as the final activity in the unit, or send it home at another appropriate time.

Recognizing and Writing Contractions

Objective
● To recognize and write contractions made with **not** and **will**

Warming Up

Reviewing Vowel Digraphs
● On chart paper write the following:

Three toothless tigers took ten threads.
Five foolish fawns fished for feathers.
Seven smooth snakes sold sweaters.

Have volunteers read the sentences aloud and circle the vowel digraphs.

● Ask children which of the numbers from one to ten are not used in the sentences. Then have children write sentences about these numbers.

★ Teaching the Lesson

● On the board write these sentences:

I **do not** want to ride Bus 28.
I **don't** want to ride Bus 28.
I **will** ride Bus 34 instead.
I**'ll** ride Bus 34 instead.

Have volunteers read the sentences aloud. Explain that **don't** and **I'll** are short ways of writing **do not** and **I will**. Point out the apostrophe, and explain that it takes the place of the missing letter(s).

● On the board write **aren't, can't, isn't, hasn't, couldn't, she'll, we'll, they'll,** and **you'll**. Have a volunteer read each contraction. Help children write the two words from which it is made and identify the letters that have been left out. Explain that **won't** is an exception to the rule and that it means **will not**.

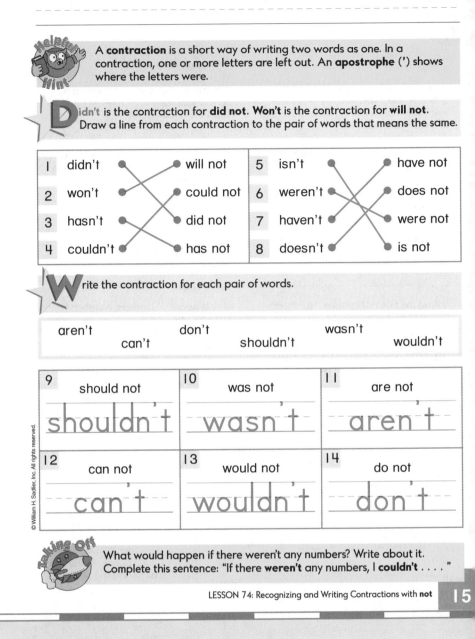

A **contraction** is a short way of writing two words as one. In a contraction, one or more letters are left out. An **apostrophe** (') shows where the letters were.

Didn't is the contraction for **did not**. **Won't** is the contraction for **will not**. Draw a line from each contraction to the pair of words that means the same.

1	didn't	will not
2	won't	could not
3	hasn't	did not
4	couldn't	has not

5	isn't	have not
6	weren't	does not
7	haven't	were not
8	doesn't	is not

Write the contraction for each pair of words.

aren't   don't   wasn't
can't   shouldn't   wouldn't

9 should not	10 was not	11 are not
shouldn't	wasn't	aren't
12 can not	**13** would not	**14** do not
can't	wouldn't	don't

What would happen if there weren't any numbers? Write about it. Complete this sentence: "If there **weren't** any numbers, I **couldn't** . . . . "

LESSON 74: Recognizing and Writing Contractions with **not** 15

Multisensory *Activities*

Auditory ■ Visual

Connecting Contractions
Materials: index cards

On index cards write **didn't, she'll, I'll, he'll, wasn't,** and **doesn't,** and **he will, was not, I will, she will, does not,** and **did not.** Give contraction cards to one group and phrase cards to another group. Ask a child to read aloud the contraction on his or her card. Have the child with the matching phrase card stand and say the phrase.

Visual ■ Kinesthetic

What's Your Bus Number?
On the board write:
1. I don't want to miss my bus.
2. I'll be first in line.
3. They'll take Bus 56 to school.
4. He hasn't ridden a bus before.
5. He'll ride Bus 8 downtown.

Have children number a sheet of paper from 1 to 5 and write each contraction as two words. Ask volunteers to replace the contractions on the board with the appropriate words.

She'll is the contraction for **she will**. Draw a line from each contraction to the pair of words that means the same.

1	she'll ●	● we will	4	they'll ●	● I will
2	you'll ●	● she will	5	he'll ●	● he will
3	we'll ●	● you will	6	I'll ●	● they will

Write the contraction for the underlined words in each sentence. Then use the bus schedule to write two sentences of your own. Include a contraction in each sentence.

Place	Bus Number		Place	Bus Number
Zoo	57		Pine Lake	15
Downtown	25		Museum	32
Library	12		Skate Way	6
Central Park	30		South Mall	27

7. <u>I will</u> take Bus 12 to the library.

8. <u>She will</u> go downtown on Bus 25.

9. <u>He will</u> take Bus 15 to the lake.

10. Hurry or <u>you will</u> miss the bus!

11. _Children's sentences should be based on the bus schedule and_

12. _include contractions with **will**._

I'll
She'll
He'll
you'll

52 LESSON 74: Recognizing and Writing Contractions with **will**

Practicing the Skill

● Read aloud the Helpful Hint at the top of page 151. Review both sets of directions, and do the first item in each exercise together. Then have children complete the page.

● Have children work in pairs to do the *Taking Off* activity. Encourage them to use words from the *Theme Words* list. Then invite pairs to share their sentences.

● Read aloud the directions to the first exercise at the top of page 152. Do the first item together, and then have children complete the exercise. Review the directions for the second exercise. Again, do the first item together, and have children complete the page.

Extending the Skill Across the Curriculum

(Language Arts/Math)
Theme Activity
● Share the theme books cited below. Have children skim the books to find contractions. List them on chart paper.

● Write this subtraction story on the board: "Art has 24 crayons. He'll keep 15 and give the rest to Lars. How many crayons will Art give to Lars?" Write "24 - 15 = ?" below the story. Ask a volunteer for the answer. Then have children write it in a sentence with a contraction. (e.g., **He'll** give Lars 9 crayons.) Continue with other subtraction stories.

Theme Books

Delton, Judy. *My Mom Made Me Go to School.* New York: Delacorte Press, 1991. A boy does not want to go to kindergarten.

O'Donnell, Elizabeth Lee. *Maggie Doesn't Want to Move.* New York: Macmillan, 1987. A child is sad about moving.

Lesson 75

Student Pages 153–154

Recognizing and Writing Contractions

Objective
● To recognize and write contractions made with **am, is, are, have, has, us**

Warming Up

Reviewing Diphthongs
Materials: Phonics Picture Cards **house, screw, coins**

● Write this story on the board:

The **boy** wearing Number 8 ran **around** the track. He **grew** tired as his feet **pounded** the **ground**, but he **drew** energy from the **sound** of the **crowd**. He smiled with **joy** as he **threw** himself across the finish line.

● Invite children to read the story aloud. Display the picture cards. Have children say each picture name and find words in the story with the same vowel sounds.

★ Teaching the Lesson

● Write these sentences on chart paper:

Let us run in some races.
Let's run in some races.
I am going to run the 50-yard dash.
I'm going to run the 50-yard dash.

Have students read each sentence aloud. Explain that **let's** and **I'm** are contractions of **let us** and **I am**. Ask volunteers to identify the letters replaced by the apostrophes.

● On the board write **he is, she is, we are, you are, that is, what is, it is, they are, he has, she has,** and **I have**. Help children to name and write the contraction for each phrase.

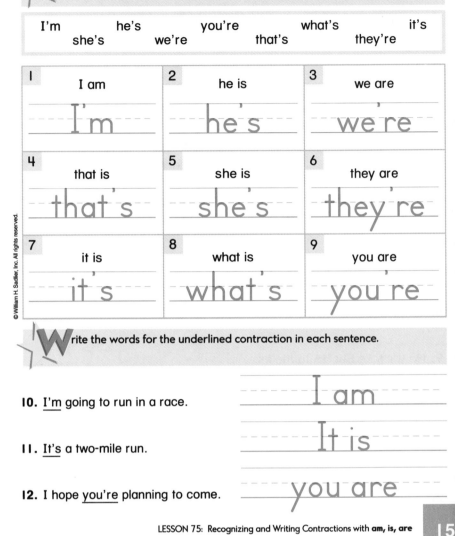

'm is the contraction for **I am**. **He's** is the contraction for **he is**. **We're** is the contraction for **we are**. Write the contraction for each pair of words.

I'm he's you're what's it's
she's we're that's they're

1. I am — I'm	2. he is — he's	3. we are — we're
4. that is — that's	5. she is — she's	6. they are — they're
7. it is — it's	8. what is — what's	9. you are — you're

Write the words for the underlined contraction in each sentence.

10. <u>I'm</u> going to run in a race. — I am

11. <u>It's</u> a two-mile run. — It is

12. I hope <u>you're</u> planning to come. — you are

LESSON 75: Recognizing and Writing Contractions with **am, is, are**   153

Multisensory Activities

Visual ■ Kinesthetic

Contraction Equations
On the board write:

I	is
she	am
he	are
we	have
you	has
they	

Below the columns write **I + am = I'm.** Have children write eleven contraction equations, each of which matches a word from the first column with one from the second. Tell them to use all eleven words.

Visual ■ Auditory

What's the Answer?
On the board write:

When you add me to 8, the sum is 17. <u>I am</u> what number? (9)

<u>We have</u> found 4 dimes. <u>You have</u> found 2 quarters. Which is worth more? (2 quarters)

Have children read the problems aloud, replacing the underlined words with contractions. Have them solve each problem and then write and solve new problems using contractions.

153

She's is the contraction for **she is**. She's is also the contraction for **she has**. **You've** is the contraction for **you have**. **Let's** is the contraction for **let us**. Write the contraction for each pair of words.

I've   he's   she's   they've   let's   you've   we've   it's

1 she has	2 you have	3 let us
she's	you've	let's

4 we have	5 he has	6 I have
we've	he's	I've

7 they have	8 it has	
they've	it's	

Write the words for the underlined contraction in each sentence.

9. I've a new game we can play.

     I have

10. Watch Juan. He's played this game before.

     He has

11. Anita plays well. She's scored thirty points.

     She has

12. It's been fun playing this game with you.

     It has

54   LESSON 75: Recognizing and Writing Contractions with **have, has, us**

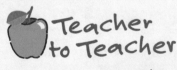

Spelling Connection

Read aloud each word and sentence below. Ask a volunteer to spell the word orally. Have another volunteer write the word on the board.

they're	**They're** going shopping at two o'clock.
I'm	**I'm** going with them.
she's	**She's** buying ten pencils.
he's	**He's** found a book for seventy-five cents.
you've	**You've** only got twenty-five cents left.

Teacher to Teacher

Distribute bumper sticker-size strips of paper and bright-colored markers. Have children choose a theme and write slogans that include contractions. For example: "I'm cool. I'll stay in school." "Let's think green. Plant a tree." "Don't bike without a helmet."

S. Helen Teresa
Trenton, NJ

Practicing the Skill

- Review the contractions at the top of page 153 with students. Read aloud the directions for each exercise. Have children complete the page.
- Follow the same procedure for page 154. Then have children complete the page.

Extending the Skill Across the Curriculum

(Language Arts/Math)

Theme Activity

- Ask children how numbers are used in racing. Add their suggestions to the *Theme Words* list. Then share the theme books cited below.
- Have children work in pairs to scan the books and list the contractions they find. Then have pairs list the words each contraction stands for.
- Have pairs look for numbers in the illustrations and stories. Ask them to share their findings and their lists.
- Have children plan a class race. Have them determine how winners will be chosen and how to record each racer's performance. Then stage the race. Ask children to write a story about the race. Encourage them to use contractions.

Theme Books

Isenberg, Barbara, and Susan Wolf. *The Adventures of Albert, the Running Bear*. Boston: Houghton Mifflin, 1982. Albert Bear escapes and runs in a marathon.

Kessler, Leonard. *The Big Mile Race*. New York: Greenwillow, 1983. Seven animals run in a race.

Observational Assessment

Note which children use the apostrophe correctly in the contractions in their stories.

Portfolio

Have children add their stories to their portfolios.

Connecting Spelling and Writing

Objectives
- To say, spell, sort, and write contractions
- To write dialogue using spelling words

Warming Up

Reviewing Initial Blends
Direct children's attention to the "Numbers, Numbers" Poetry Poster. Invite them to point to and say words that begin with initial consonant blends. (**grocery, store, street, flash, glow, spend, stamps**)

★ Teaching the Lesson

Materials: index cards

- Ask children this riddle: "What time is it when the clock strikes 13?" On the board write this response: "**It's** time to get a new clock." Invite a volunteer to read the response and underline the contraction with **is**.
- Have children write the words **not, is, have, will,** and **us** on index cards.
- Have children say, spell, and say each spelling word again and then hold up the card for the word that is part of the contraction.
- Invite children to use each contraction in a sentence.

Practicing the Skill

Together review the directions on page 155. Ask volunteers to read the spelling words. Then have children complete the page.

Spell and Write — Say and spell each word in the box. Then write each word under the correct heading.

didn't
you'll
I've
we've
that's
can't
let's
it's
I'll
what's
shouldn't
they've

1 Contractions with not
didn't
can't
shouldn't

2 Contractions with is
that's
it's
what's

3 Contractions with have
I've
we've
they've

4 Contractions with will
you'll
I'll

5 Contraction with us
let's

LESSON 76: Connecting Spelling and Writing

15

Multisensory *Activities*

Auditory ■ Kinesthetic

Spelling Relay
Have children line up in four teams. Say the word pair for a spelling contraction, such as **you will**. Have the first child on Team 1 go to the board, write the first letter of the contraction, tag the next team member to write the next letter, and so on. The apostrophe counts as a letter. If a child writes an incorrect letter, the next child must use his or her turn to correct it. Repeat with a new word pair for each team.

Kinesthetic ■ Visual

Choosing Pairs
Materials: index cards

Give each pair of children two sets of twelve index cards. As one child writes the spelling words on a set of cards, the other writes each corresponding word pair. Then have partners mix the cards and spread them facedown. Have each partner turn up two cards at a time. If the cards match, the player keeps them. If not, the cards are returned facedown.

Spell and Write Imagine that your classroom clock could talk. Write what it would say. Use one or more of your spelling words.

didn't	you'll	I've	we've	that's	can't
let's	it's	I'll	what's	shouldn't	they've

7:30 A.M.

56 LESSON 76: Connecting Spelling and Writing

Spelling Connection

Ask a volunteer to point to a spelling word on page 156 so that only the two of you can see it. Invite the other children to guess the spelling word by asking yes/no questions about the words in the contraction; for example, "Is it a contraction with **not**?" When the answer is yes, have the questioner guess the word by saying and spelling it. The child who correctly says and spells the word chooses the next word.

The Writing Process

Tell children that they will be writing what a classroom clock would say if it could talk. Together read the directions on page 156.

Brainstorm Invite children to imagine they are classroom clocks, ticking all day—before, during, and after school. Ask what they might see and hear, how they might feel, and what they, as clocks, might say.

Write Have children write on paper what the clock would say. Remind children to write in the first person.

Revise Have children make sure that they have pretended to be the clock and have used the word *I*. Tell them to check to be sure they used one or more spelling words.

Publish Invite children to bring their clocks to "life" by dramatizing what they have written.

Have children reread their sentences and underline the spelling words they have used.

📁 **Portfolio**
Have children add their clock dialogues to their portfolios.

Extending the Skill

Ask children what a clock might see or experience over the course of a day. Then assign to pairs of children different hours or times of the day. Have the pairs write a few sentences telling what might happen at their assigned time. Use children's sentences to make a chart titled "A Day in the Life of a Clock." Have children illustrate the chart.

Reviewing and Assessing Contractions

Objectives
- To review contractions made with **not, will, am, is, are, have, has, us** and their corresponding word pairs
- To write contractions in sentences

Warming Up

Reviewing Vowel Digraph oo

Materials: Phonics Picture Cards **book** and **moon**

- Display the picture cards. Ask children to name them and identify the two sounds of vowel digraph **oo**.
- On the board write this story:

  Brooke loved to count. She counted things in the **rooms** of her house. She counted 10 pairs of **boots** in a **bedroom**, 18 **spoons** in the kitchen, 12 pieces of **wood** next to the fireplace, 8 **hooks** in the **bathroom**, and 23 **tools** in the garage.

Have a volunteer read the story aloud. Ask children to name the words with the same sounds as **book** and **moon**.

★ Teaching the Lesson

- Write these sentences on the board:
1. I **don't** have a calendar.
2. **Isn't** your birthday in two days?
3. **You'll** be eight years old.
4. **Let's** have a party.

Have volunteers read the sentences aloud and underline the contractions.

- Have children number sheets of paper from 1 to 4. Ask them to write the word pairs for each contraction.

Use the number code to write contractions. Write the letter for each number. Put an apostrophe in the blank space. Then write the words for each contraction.

1 = a	2 = d	3 = e	4 = h	5 = i
6 = l	7 = n	8 = o	9 = r	10 = s
11 = t	12 = u	13 = v	14 = w	15 = y

1. i s n ' t — is not
   5 10 7   11

2. w e ' v e — we have
   14 3 13 3

3. y o u ' r e — you are
   15 8 12 9 3

4. s h e ' l l — she will
   10 4 3 6 6

5. d i d n ' t — did not
   2 5 2 7   11

6. t h e y ' r e — they are
   11 4 3 15 9 3

7. a r e n ' t — are not
   1 9 3 7   11

8. l e t ' s — let us
   6 3 11 10

LESSON 77: Reviewing Contractions   15

Multisensory *Activities*

Visual ■ Auditory

Cooking with Contractions
Write this story on chart paper:

Today we are going to bake 24 muffins. I will find a bowl. Then you will pour in the mix. Do not forget to add 2 eggs and 1 cup of water. Let us set the timer for 20 minutes. I am hungry. I cannot wait to taste the muffins.

Read the story aloud. Then have volunteers write contractions above the words they stand for. Read the rewritten story together.

Visual ■ Tactile

Chain of Contractions
Materials: construction-paper strips, markers, tape

On the board write:

I	is
she	am
we	are
you	have
they	will

Have children use one word from each column to write a contraction on each strip and tape them together in a chain. Display the chain.

157

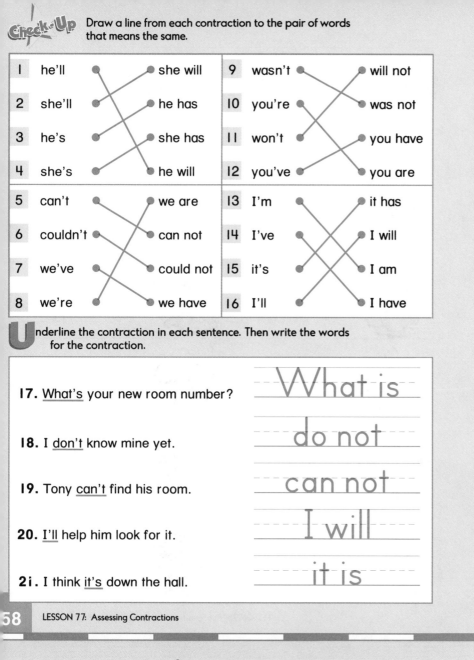

Check-Up Draw a line from each contraction to the pair of words that means the same.

1	he'll	she will	9	wasn't	will not
2	she'll	he has	10	you're	was not
3	he's	she has	11	won't	you have
4	she's	he will	12	you've	you are
5	can't	we are	13	I'm	it has
6	couldn't	can not	14	I've	I will
7	we've	could not	15	it's	I am
8	we're	we have	16	I'll	I have

Underline the contraction in each sentence. Then write the words for the contraction.

17. <u>What's</u> your new room number?   What is

18. I <u>don't</u> know mine yet.   do not

19. Tony <u>can't</u> find his room.   can not

20. <u>I'll</u> help him look for it.   I will

2i. I think <u>it's</u> down the hall.   it is

58   LESSON 77: Assessing Contractions

Assessing the Skills

Check-Up Have volunteers read aloud the directions for the exercises on pages 157–158. Be sure children know what they are to do for each exercise. Do the first item in each exercise with the class. Then have children complete both pages.

Observational Assessment Note how well individual children match contractions with word pairs and use the apostrophe correctly.

Student Skills Assessment Use the checklist on Student Edition pages 330–331 to record your observations of each child.

Writing Conference Meet with each child to discuss a sample of work from her or his portfolio. Encourage the child to talk about any difficulties she or he has had with writing contractions. Make notes about each child's progress, and add them to the child's portfolio for review during your next conference.

Group together students who need further help with contractions for the *Reteaching Activities*.

Reteaching *Activities*

Adding Apostrophes
On the board write:

didnt	shell	Im
well	hes	cant
hasnt	weve	thats
youve	theyll	isnt
wasnt	Ill	dont
shes	theyre	its
theyve	lets	were

Invite children to insert an apostrophe in the correct place in each contraction and then say the two words that have the same meaning. Ask which letter(s) the apostrophe stands for.

From Two to One
On the board write: **we are, let us, they have, we will, she has, they are, was not, I will, you have, do not, she will, I am, that is, were not, can not, he is, did not, we have, they will, is not, what is, should not, it is,** and **he will.** Have children read each phrase aloud. Ask them to write a sentence using a contraction for any word pair. Invite volunteers to read their sentences and spell the contractions.

Recognizing and Writing Plural Endings s and es/Changing y to i

Objectives
● To form plurals by adding **s** or **es** to base words
● To change **y** to **i** before adding **es** to form plurals

Warming Up

Reviewing Vowel Pairs
Invite children to use rhyming words with vowel pairs in sentences. For example, "The st**ai**n in the dr**ai**n is pl**ai**n to see."

★ *Teaching the Lesson*

Materials: Phonics Picture Cards **bus, glass, bench, brush, fox**

● Read aloud the Poetry Poster "Numbers, Numbers." On the board list the plurals **numbers, things, doorways, signs, tickets, buses, stamps, letters,** and **highways**. Remind children that plurals name more than one. Circle the **s** or **es** ending, and read each word together. Then ask children how to make words plural.

● Display the picture cards. Ask volunteers to write each picture name on the board and then add **es** to form its plural. Call attention to the Helpful Hint at the top of page 159. Underline the letter(s) just before the **es** in each plural.

● Display the picture card for **bunny**. Ask children to say its name and its plural. Write **bunny** and **bunnies** on the board. Ask how the plural is formed. Then read the Helpful Hint on page 160.

ESL Activities
Refer to page 151J.

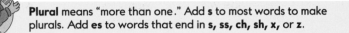

Plural means "more than one." Add **s** to most words to make plurals. Add **es** to words that end in **s, ss, ch, sh, x,** or **z**.

Goats is the plural of **goat**. **Peaches** is the plural of **peach**. Each picture shows more than one. Add **s** or **es** to the word to write the picture name.

1 goat **goats**	2 peach **peaches**
3 dish **dishes**	4 shell **shells**
5 fox **foxes**	6 cone **cones**
7 fork **forks**	8 dress **dresses**
9 dime **dimes**	10 bus **buses**

LESSON 78: Recognizing and Writing Plural Endings **s** and **es**   15

Multisensory *Activities*

Auditory ■ Kinesthetic

Bag It or Box It
Materials: paper bag, box, Phonics Picture Cards **book, brush, cherry, box, bed, chair, glass, watch, lamp, hat, shirt, bench, strawberry**

On the board write **bag** and **box**. Then write the plurals. Label the bag **s** and the box **es**. Place them at the front of the room. Display the picture cards. Have children name each and say its plural. Then have children place the cards in the appropriate container.

Auditory ■ Kinesthetic

Presto, Change-o!
Materials: index cards

On index cards write clues for the plural words on pages 159–160 (e.g., **more than one goat**). On the board write the singular form of each clue word (e.g., **goat**). Invite each child to choose a card, find the matching word on the board, and write **s, es,** or **ies** to form its plural.

Helpful Hint

When a word ends in **y** after a consonant, change the **y** to **i** before adding **es**.

penny + es = pennies   baby + es= babies

Change the **y** to **i** and write the plural of each word.

1 penny	2 baby	3 party
pennies	babies	parties
4 story	5 puppy	6 fly
stories	puppies	flies

Add **es** to each word at the left and write the new word in the sentence.

puppy   **7.** My dog Fleas had five ___puppies___.

baby   **8.** Now they're as helpless as newborn ___babies___.

pony   **9.** Soon they'll be the size of small ___ponies___.

buddy   **10.** The puppies and I are best ___buddies___.

penny   **11.** Their fur is the color of shiny ___pennies___ !

60   LESSON 78: Changing y to i Before Adding Plural Ending **es**

Multicultural Connection

Have children work in small groups to find and identify plurals in one of the books from Jim Haskins's *Count Your Way* series of multicultural counting books (Carolrhoda) or in Muriel Feelings's *Moja Means One: A Swahili Counting Book* (Puffin). Have each group share its results with the class.

Teacher to Teacher

Have the class line up in two teams. Give each team a singular word. Have the first child say its first letter. Then have the other team members spell its plural by taking turns to add a letter. Alternate between teams until every child has had a turn. Teams earn two points for each plural spelled correctly.

Christine Matuszewski
Ramsey, NJ

Practicing the Skill

- Together review the Helpful Hint and the directions on page 159. Identify the picture names. You may also wish to have children name each plural. Do the first two items with the class. Then have children complete the page.

- Review the Helpful Hint on page 160. Then call on volunteers to read the directions and model the first item in each set of exercises. Direct children to complete the page.

Extending the Skill Across the Curriculum

(Language Arts/Math)

Theme Activity

- Go to the library with children, and assemble a collection of counting books. Invite children to explore the books. Talk about the diverse subjects of the books, the order of the numbers (ascending or descending), the range of the numbers, the way the objects are counted (by ones, twos, fives, tens, and so on), and the stories or rhymes in the books.

- Have children work in small groups to design and write their own counting books.

- Invite each group to present its book to the rest of the class. Tell children to point out any plurals they may have used.

- Encourage children to share their books with children in kindergarten and first grade.

Reviewing and Assessing Plural Endings

Objective
● To review and assess plural endings **s** and **es**

Warming Up

Reviewing Initial Consonants

Direct children's attention to the "Numbers, Numbers" Poetry Poster. Invite children to find a word in the poem that has the same initial consonant sound as each of these words: **ten, seven, dime, cent, nine, less, more, half, count, billion.**

★ Teaching the Lesson

● On the board write "number facts" such as these:

There are 24 <u>hour</u> in a day.
There are 12 <u>inch</u> in a foot.
There are 5 <u>penny</u> in a nickel.
There are 2 or more <u>pony</u> in a team.
An octopus has 8 <u>arm</u>.
A triangle has 3 <u>side</u>.
There are more than 190 <u>country</u> in the world.

Call on volunteers to add **s** or **es** to make the underlined words plural.

● Invite children to write "number facts" of their own using the singular forms of words. Have volunteers put their sentences on the board. Call on other volunteers to read the sentences and to say and spell the correct plurals.

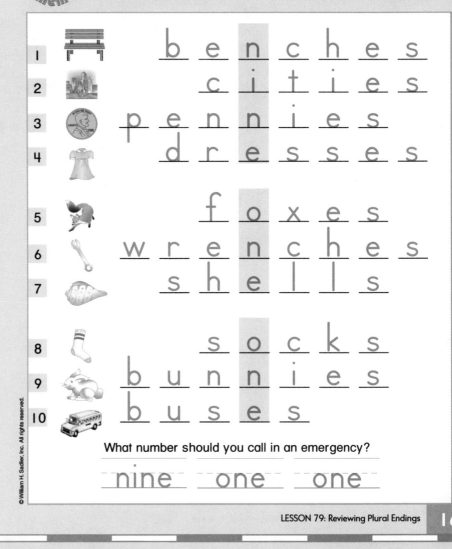

Write the plural of each picture name in the puzzle. Remember to add **s** or **es** and to make spelling changes. Then read the shaded letters down to find the answer to the question.

1. b e n c h e s
2. c i t i e s
3. p e n n i e s
4. d r e s s e s
5. f o x e s
6. w r e n c h e s
7. s h e l l s
8. s o c k s
9. b u n n i e s
10. b u s e s

What number should you call in an emergency?

nine one one

LESSON 79: Reviewing Plural Endings

16

Multisensory *Activities*

Visual ■ Tactile

Plural Facts

Materials: index cards, markers

Distribute an index card to each child. Have children write a singular noun on one side of the card and its plural on the other. Provide these examples:

bench + es = benches
pony + es = ponies
sock + s = socks

Ask volunteers to put their singular nouns on the board. Have others form the correct plurals.

Auditory ■ Kinesthetic

Rhyming Plurals

Write the following list on the board or on chart paper:

 5 **bell**
10 **shell**
15 **box**
20 **fox**
25 **cherry**
30 **berry**

Ask children to add **s** or **es** to rhyming words. Then ask what the number pattern is. (+5) Invite children to continue the pattern.

Check-Up Add **s** or **es** to write the plural of each word. Remember to make spelling changes.

1	pony	2	trunk	3	dress
	ponies		trunks		dresses

4	box	5	sack	6	fly
	boxes		sacks		flies

7	bunny	8	peach	9	straw
	bunnies		peaches		straws

Add **s** or **es** so that the word in **bold** print makes sense in each sentence.

10. There are 10 **penny** in a dime.

11. **Mayfly** live only about 2 hours.

12. **Fox** live only 7 years.

13. Newborn **baby** have 300 bones.

14. There are more than 12,000 kinds of **ant**.

pennies

Mayflies

Foxes

babies

ants

62   LESSON 79: Assessing Plural Endings

Reteaching *Activities*

Nod "Yes" for es

Point out that the plural ending **es** usually makes a one-syllable word sound longer. Give the example **bench, benches**. Then slowly say a series of plural nouns such as **peaches, plums, foxes, dogs, brushes, combs, clocks, watches, wishes, dreams, cars, buses, dresses,** and **pants**. Ask children to nod their heads "yes" whenever they hear a plural that ends in **es**.

One/More Than One

Materials: oaktag or paper, markers, magazines, glue

Have children write and illustrate pairs of singular and plural words from pages 159–162. Children may draw pictures or cut them from magazines. Invite children to use each word in a sentence. Then have them sort their pictures into three groups: add **s**, add **es**, and change **y** to **i** before adding **es**.

Recognizing and Writing Inflectional Endings s and es/Changing y to i

Objectives
● To form new words by adding **s** or **es** to base words
● To change **y** to **i** before adding **es** to form new words

Warming Up

Reviewing Consonant Digraphs
Ask children to share tongue twisters with consonant digraphs. Start with this example: "How much wood would a woodchuck chuck if a woodchuck could chuck wood?"

★ Teaching the Lesson

● On the board write "I run past second base." Ask a volunteer to read the sentence to the class. Change the word **I** to **Jim**. Ask what is wrong with the new sentence. Have another volunteer add an **s** to **run** so that the sentence makes sense.

● On the board write **run, runs; rush, rushes;** and **hurry, hurries**. Ask how the second word in each pair differs from the first. Invite a volunteer to underline the ending **s** or **es** in each pair. Explain that **run, rush,** and **hurry** are all base words. Point out that **s** or **es** can be added to a base word to form a new word. Elicit how the spelling changes when **es** is added to **hurry**.

● List these words on the board: **jump, throw, catch, push, try, carry**. Have children use each word in a sentence. Together add the ending **s** or **es** to each base word. Then have children use each new word in a sentence.

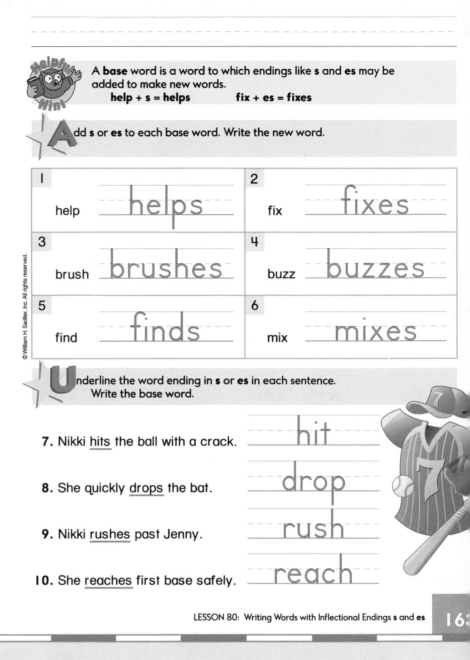

A **base** word is a word to which endings like **s** and **es** may be added to make new words.
help + s = helps   fix + es = fixes

A dd **s** or **es** to each base word. Write the new word.

1 help	helps	2 fix	fixes
3 brush	brushes	4 buzz	buzzes
5 find	finds	6 mix	mixes

U nderline the word ending in **s** or **es** in each sentence. Write the base word.

7. Nikki <u>hits</u> the ball with a crack. __hit__

8. She quickly <u>drops</u> the bat. __drop__

9. Nikki <u>rushes</u> past Jenny. __rush__

10. She <u>reaches</u> first base safely. __reach__

LESSON 80: Writing Words with Inflectional Endings **s** and **es**   163

Multisensory *Activities*

Visual ■ Kinesthetic

Act It Out

With the class, compile a list of verbs (action words) that end in consonants on the board; for example **hop, walk, cry,** and **stretch**. Call on a volunteer to choose a word and act it out for classmates. Have the child who guesses the word go to the board and add either **s** or **es** to the word before choosing another word to act out.

Visual ■ Kinesthetic

The Count Counts

Materials: index cards

On the board write the headings "I" and "He/She." On index cards write action words such as **count, counts, add, adds, subtract, subtracts, match, matches, pass, passes, multiply, multiplies,** and **carry, carries**. Shuffle the cards and place them facedown in a pile. Have each child take a card, read the word, write the word under the correct heading, and use it in a sentence.

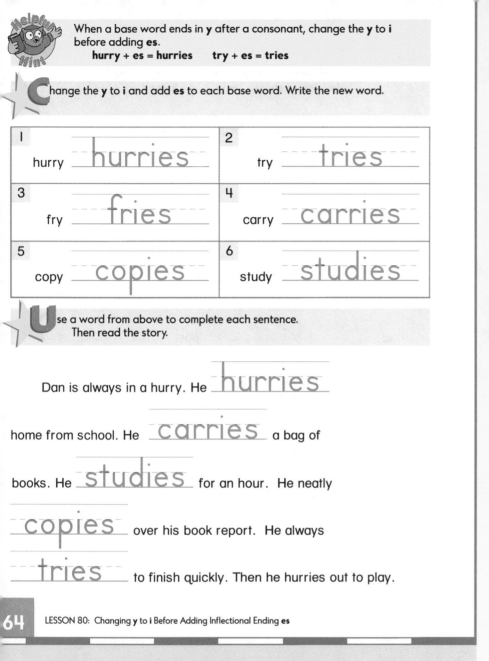

When a base word ends in **y** after a consonant, change the **y** to **i** before adding **es**.

hurry + es = hurries   try + es = tries

Change the **y** to **i** and add **es** to each base word. Write the new word.

1 hurry	hurries	2 try	tries
3 fry	fries	4 carry	carries
5 copy	copies	6 study	studies

Use a word from above to complete each sentence. Then read the story.

Dan is always in a hurry. He **hurries** home from school. He **carries** a bag of books. He **studies** for an hour. He neatly **copies** over his book report. He always **tries** to finish quickly. Then he hurries out to play.

64 LESSON 80: Changing **y** to **i** Before Adding Inflectional Ending **es**

Spelling Connection

Read aloud each word and sentence below. Invite a volunteer to spell the word orally. Have another volunteer write the word on the board.

pitches The pitcher **pitches** the ball to the batter.

catches The catcher **catches** the ball with his glove.

hits The batter **hits** the ball with her bat.

cheers The crowd **cheers** when she hits a home run.

tries Each team **tries** hard to win the game.

Practicing the Skill

● Review the Helpful Hint at the top of page 163. Point out that **help** and **fix** are action words. Call on volunteers to read each set of directions. Then do the first item in each exercise with the class. Have children complete the page.

● Repeat the procedure for the first exercise on page 164. Then read aloud the second set of directions. Have children complete the paragraph. Call on volunteers to read the sentences.

Extending the Skill Across the Curriculum

(Math/Language Arts)

Theme Activity

● Talk with children about numbers in a baseball game. Ask children to give the number of bases (4), innings (9), teams (2), each team's players on the field (9), strikes (3), balls (4), and outs (3). Ask children what numbers their favorite players wear.

● On the board draw a baseball diamond with home plate and three bases. Then invite children to imagine they are sportscasters at a game. Together make up names for the players, and write them on the baseball diamond. On chart paper or on the board, write a step-by-step account of a play as children dictate it, starting with the pitcher throwing the ball. Use phrases such as "strike one," "ball three," and "hits a double (or two-bagger)."

● Read the account with the class. Invite volunteers to go back and underline the action words that end in **s** or **es**.

Writing Words with Inflectional Endings ing and ed

Objective
● To write words with the inflectional endings **ing** and **ed**

Warming Up

Reviewing Diphthongs
Materials: Phonics Picture Cards **brown, boy, screw**

● Write this poem on the board:

> Over in the meadow, in the **soil**
>   near the tree,
> Lived a **brown** mother **mouse** and
>   her little mice three.
> "**Chew**!" said the mother.
> "We **chew**," said the three.
> So they **chewed** leaves with **joy**,
> In the **soil** near the tree.

Then read the poem together.

● Display the picture cards. Have children name each picture and find words in the poem with the same vowel sounds.

★ Teaching the Lesson

● On the board write: "I will be **surfing** on Sunday. Six of us **surfed** on Saturday." Read the sentences aloud. Explain that **surfing** and **surfed** are formed by adding the endings **ing** and **ed** to the base word **surf**.

● Invite children to underline the words ending in **ing** and **ed** and then circle the base words.

Observational Assessment
Note whether children correctly identify base words and endings.

The endings **ing** and **ed** can be added to a base word.
help + ing = helping   help + ed = helped

Add **ing** to each base word. Write the new word.

I help	helping	2 fix	fixing
3 jump	jumping	4 grow	growing
5 find	finding	6 pass	passing

Underline the word ending in **ing** in each sentence. Write the base word.

7. June is <u>helping</u> Azeem do math.

8. They are <u>adding</u> numbers.

9. June and Azeem are <u>trying</u> to solve a problem.

10. They like <u>working</u> together.

help

add

try

work

Multisensory *Activities*

Visual ■ Tactile

Glue Words
Materials: drawing paper, white glue, pencils

On the board write **crawl, rest, walk, fold, scoop, wink, jump, turn, yawn, kick, surf,** and **knock.** Have each child write one of the words on paper, add **ed** or **ing**, and trace over the new word with glue. When the glue dries, have children exchange papers, trace the glue words with their fingers, and identify the base words and endings.

Auditory ■ Visual

Adding the Base Word
Have children fold sheets of paper into three columns and label the columns "base word," "+ ed," and "+ ing." Read aloud these base words, one at a time: **add, show, rest, ask, look, play, surf, pick, lick, cool, sail, stay, help, plow,** and **cook.** Ask students to write each base word in the first column and add endings to make new words in the other two columns.

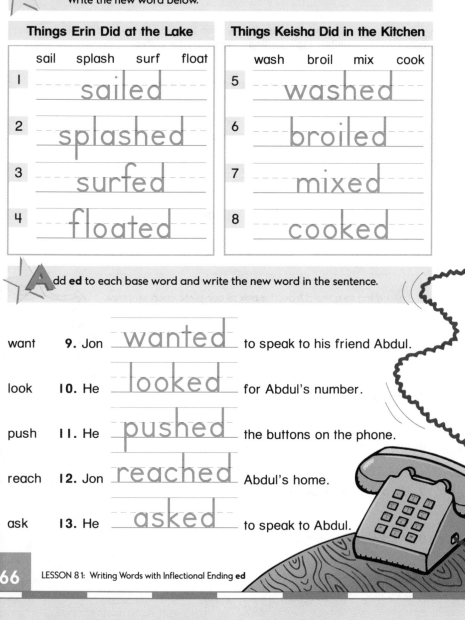

Tell what Erin and Keisha did in the past. Add **ed** to each base word. Write the new word below.

Things Erin Did at the Lake

sail   splash   surf   float

1	sailed
2	splashed
3	surfed
4	floated

Things Keisha Did in the Kitchen

wash   broil   mix   cook

5	washed
6	broiled
7	mixed
8	cooked

Add **ed** to each base word and write the new word in the sentence.

want   9. Jon _wanted_ to speak to his friend Abdul.

look   10. He _looked_ for Abdul's number.

push   11. He _pushed_ the buttons on the phone.

reach   12. Jon _reached_ Abdul's home.

ask   13. He _asked_ to speak to Abdul.

66   LESSON 81: Writing Words with Inflectional Ending **ed**

Spelling Connection

Read aloud each word and sentence below. Call on a volunteer to spell the word orally. Ask another child to write the word on the board.

helping Imani is **helping** Lee with his homework.
washed   I **washed** the dishes after dinner.
called   Noah **called** his mother at work.
adding   She's **adding** numbers with a calculator.
looked   I **looked** all over for my missing sock.

Computer Connection

Have children practice spelling words with Midnight Correction from Spell It 3™ (Davidson & Associates, Inc.). Select word lists that correlate to the words in this unit. Then have children use the Editor to compile a list of **ed** and **ing** words. Make sure children include all the words from this unit, and tell them to write the spelling rule. Print the list, make copies, and distribute it to the class. Have children circle the base words and underline the endings.

Practicing the Skill

• Together read the Helpful Hint, the examples, and both sets of directions on page 165. Do the first item in each exercise with the class. Have children complete the page.

• Explain that words ending in **ed** tell about the past. Then read aloud both sets of directions on page 166. Have children complete the page.

Extending the Skill Across the Curriculum

(Language Arts/Math)

Theme Activity

Materials: paper plates, construction and drawing paper, fasteners, crayons

• Have each child make a clock face by writing 1 through 12 around the edge of a paper plate and attaching two paper hands to the center of the plate. Have children use their clocks to practice telling time.

• Share the theme books cited below. Have children skim the books for words that end with **ing** and **ed**. List them on the board.

• Give each child several sheets of drawing paper. Ask children to write stories about what they did yesterday and what they plan to do tomorrow. Tell them to underline all the **ed** and **ing** endings. Ask volunteers to share their stories.

Theme Books

Fuchshuber, Annegert. *The Cuckoo-Clock Cuckoo.* Minneapolis: Carolrhoda, 1988. A curious cuckoo leaves his clock.

Maestro, Betsy and Giulio Maestro. *Around the Clock with Harriet.* New York: Crown, 1984. Harriet's activities each hour of the day.

Portfolio

Have students add their stories about time to their portfolios.

Student Pages 167–168

Dropping Final e Before Adding Inflectional Endings ing and ed

Objective
- To add inflectional endings **ing** and **ed** to words that end with final **e**

Warming Up

Reviewing Vowel Digraphs
- Write the following on the board:

  telephone b(oo)k
  (Au)gust calendar
  m(ea)suring sp(oo)n
  w(ea)ther map
  sch(oo)l clock

- Have volunteers fill in the blanks with the **ea, oo,** or **au** to complete the words. Ask others to pronounce the words and identify the vowel sounds.
- Ask students what the phrases have in common. (They all have something to do with numbers.)

★ Teaching the Lesson

- Write these sentences on chart paper:
  I like to <u>rake</u> leaves.
  José is <u>raking</u> leaves with me.
  We <u>raked</u> two big piles of leaves.

Have a volunteer read each sentence aloud. Elicit that the base word **rake** ends in **e**. Guide children to see that final **e** is dropped before **ing** or **ed** is added.

- Write these words in a column on the board: **save, like, close, shine, wipe, hike,** and **trade**. Have children make new words by adding **ing** and **ed**. Then have children work with partners to share and compare the new words.

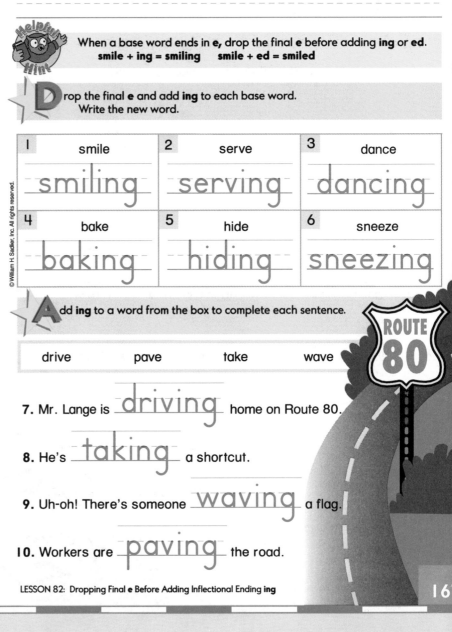

When a base word ends in **e**, drop the final **e** before adding **ing** or **ed**.
smile + ing = smiling   smile + ed = smiled

Drop the final **e** and add **ing** to each base word. Write the new word.

1 smile	2 serve	3 dance
smiling	serving	dancing
4 bake	5 hide	6 sneeze
baking	hiding	sneezing

Add **ing** to a word from the box to complete each sentence.

drive	pave	take	wave

7. Mr. Lange is __driving__ home on Route 80.

8. He's __taking__ a shortcut.

9. Uh-oh! There's someone __waving__ a flag.

10. Workers are __paving__ the road.

LESSON 82: Dropping Final **e** Before Adding Inflectional Ending **ing**

16

Multisensory Activities

Visual ■ Kinesthetic

Waving for Final e
On the board write **wave**. Elicit that it ends with a final **e**. Write these base words on the board: **jump, dance, surf, sail, smile, bake, stay, look, sneeze, skate, rest, care, turn, start, slice, yawn, pave,** and **clean**. Point to one word at a time. Tell students to wave their hands if the word ends in a final **e**. Have volunteers write and read new words by adding **ing** and **ed** to each base word.

Visual ■ Auditory

Matching Rhyming Words
On index cards write: **baking, raking, licking, kicking, telling, selling, hiking, liking, waved, saved, fooled, cooled, sliced, priced, walked,** and **talked**. Spread the cards facedown. Have a child turn over two cards. If the words rhyme, have the child name the base words, tell if they end in silent **e**, and keep the cards. If the words do not rhyme, have the child return the cards.

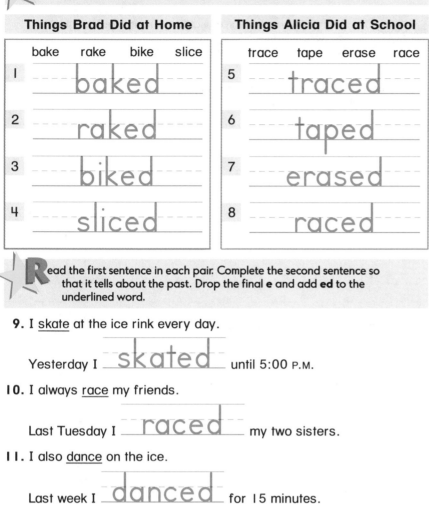

★ **T**ell what Brad and Alicia did in the past. Drop the final **e** and add **ed** to each base word. Write the new word below.

Things Brad Did at Home

bake   rake   bike   slice

1. baked
2. raked
3. biked
4. sliced

Things Alicia Did at School

trace   tape   erase   race

5. traced
6. taped
7. erased
8. raced

★ **R**ead the first sentence in each pair. Complete the second sentence so that it tells about the past. Drop the final **e** and add **ed** to the underlined word.

9. I skate at the ice rink every day.

Yesterday I ___skated___ until 5:00 P.M.

10. I always race my friends.

Last Tuesday I ___raced___ my two sisters.

11. I also dance on the ice.

Last week I ___danced___ for 15 minutes.

Taking Off

Tell how you usually spend time with your friends.
Tell what you did last week.

68 LESSON 82: Dropping Final **e** Before Adding Inflectional Ending **ed**

Spelling Connection

Read aloud each word and sentence below. Ask a volunteer to spell the word orally. Have another volunteer write the word on the board.

baked   I **baked** two pies.
sliced   Bob **sliced** the apples for the pies.
smiled   My mother **smiled** when she saw the pies.
serving   We're **serving** the pies for dessert.
saving   I'm **saving** a piece of pie for my friend Anna.

Computer Connection

Have children write a story about a missing number using a program such as Kid Works 2™ (Davidson & Associates, Inc.). Tell children to decide which number from one to ten is missing. Help them imagine problems they would encounter if, for example, the number 5 was missing. Elicit that children would not be able to get from 4 to 6 when counting, there would be no five o'clock, and so on. Direct children to write, illustrate, and print their story. Display the stories on a bulletin board titled "Where's the Number?"

Practicing the Skill

● Together review the Helpful Hint, the examples, and the directions for each set of exercises on page 167. Do the first item in each exercise with the class. Then have children complete the page.

● Follow the same procedure for page 168. Invite children to complete the exercises. Then have children do the *Taking Off* activity.

Extending the Skill Across the Curriculum

(Language Arts/Math)

Theme Activity

Materials: index cards

● Write these base words on index cards: **bake, chase, dance, grade, sneeze, wave, name, hike, price, race, rake, save, serve, prune, skate, slice, trace, smile, tame, frame, like, wipe, bike, pave, trade, shine,** and **search.** Give one card to each child.

● Review skip counting by 5. Tell children they will write a story by skip counting by 5 and by making sentences that each have a base word with an **ed** or **ing** ending.

● Begin by saying and then writing on the board a sentence such as "I waved to 5 friends." Have a child repeat it and say a new sentence that has **ed** or **ing** added to his or her base word and the next number in the sequence. (e.g., "Now I'm baking 10 cookies.") Write the new sentence on the board. Continue with all the base words.

● Invite each child to the board to circle the word ending in **ing** or **ed** in his or her sentence. Then have the child read the sentence to the class.

Observational Assessment

Note how well students pay attention to what has gone before in the story and how well they connect the story line.

ESL Activities

Refer to page 151J.

Lesson 83

Student Pages 169–170

Doubling Final Consonants Before Adding Inflectional Endings ing and ed

Objective
- To write new words by doubling the final consonant before adding inflectional endings **ing** and **ed**

Warming Up

Reviewing Short Vowels
Materials: Phonics Picture Cards

Write **a, i, o, u,** and **e** across the board. Give each child one of these picture cards: **ant, bat, ham, hand, tag, van, cap, bib, hill, lid, pin, six, box, doll, log, ox, pot, top, bug, cub, cup, rug, sun, bus, duck, bed, egg, jet, pen,** and **ten.** Ask each child to name the picture, identify the short vowel sound, and place the card on the chalk ledge under the appropriate vowel.

★ Teaching the Lesson

- On chart paper write the following:

  I **clap** at the end of a concert.
  I am **clapping** my hands.
  Once I **clapped** 30 times!

Have volunteers read the sentences aloud. Elicit that the base word **clap** is a short vowel word that ends in a consonant. Help children see that the final consonant **p** is doubled before adding **ing** or **ed** to form a new word.

- In a column on the board, write **hop, stop, hum, drip, mop, nap,** and **slip.** Have volunteers make new words by adding **ing** and **ed.** Have each child say and spell the new word and explain the rule for its spelling.

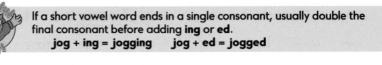

If a short vowel word ends in a single consonant, usually double the final consonant before adding **ing** or **ed**.
jog + ing = jogging   jog + ed = jogged

Double the final consonant and add **ing** to each base word. Write the new word.

1. jog	2. skip	3. wag
jogging	skipping	wagging
4. knit	5. cut	6. grab
knitting	cutting	grabbing

Underline the word ending in **ing** in each sentence. Write the base word.

7. Jim is <u>swimming</u> laps in the pool.   swim

8. He swims back and forth without <u>stopping</u>.   stop

9. Jim is <u>getting</u> lots of exercise.   get

10. He is <u>planning</u> to swim six laps tomorrow.   plan

Multisensory *Activities*

Visual ■ Auditory

Word Values

Assign a dollar value to each letter of the alphabet: A = $1, B = $2, and so on to Z = $26. On the board write: **flip, chop, knit, shop, snap, grin, nod,** and **dip.** Have children make two new words from each base word by adding **ing** and **ed.** Then have children use calculators to find the value of each new word by adding the values of its letters.

Auditory ■ Kinesthetic

Listen! Act! Write!

Read aloud each sentence below. Ask children to listen for the action words. After each sentence is read, have a volunteer write the action word on the board and then perform the action.

Joel **snapped** his fingers.
Miya is **grinning**.
Ming **jogged** in place.
Tony **nodded** his head.
Doug **rubbed** his hands together.

Tell about the past. Add **ed** to a word from the box to complete each sentence. Then read the story.

clap	hum	tap	plan	pat

Last summer our town had a frog-jumping contest.

I <u>planned</u> to win with my frog Tiny. I knew just

what to do. At the start, I <u>tapped</u> Tiny on the

head for good luck. I also <u>hummed</u> a good-luck

song. Then I <u>patted</u> Tiny on the back to get

him started.

On his first jump, Tiny leaped eleven feet! I

<u>clapped</u> and jumped up and down.

What happened on Tiny's second and third jumps? Finish the story.

Children should use complete sentences, written in the past tense,

to tell the story outcome.

70

LESSON 83: Doubling Final Consonant Before Adding Inflectional Ending **ed**

Spelling Connection

Read aloud each word and sentence below. Ask a volunteer to spell the word orally. Have another volunteer write the word on the board.

jogging   I'm **jogging** two miles today.

hopped   The bird **hopped** across the lawn.

swimming   Josh is **swimming** laps in the pool.

rubbed   The cat **rubbed** against my leg.

shopping   I'm **shopping** for a new shirt.

Multicultural Connection

Together read the Chinese folktale *Two of Everything*, by Lily Toy Hong (A Whitman). In this story a man finds a magical brass pot and discovers that everything that falls into the pot doubles. Then read *A Grain of Rice*, by Helena Clare Pittman (Bantam). In this story a farmer saves a princess. For his reward, he asks for one grain of rice to be doubled every day for 100 days.

Have students use calculators to explore the doubling patterns.

Practicing the Skill

● Together read the Helpful Hint, the examples, and the directions for both exercises on page 169. Have children complete the page.

● Read aloud the directions at the top of page 170. Complete the first sentence with the class. Then have children complete the page.

Extending the Skill Across the Curriculum

(Language Arts/Math)

Theme Activity

● On chart paper write this poem:

Two little bunnies
<u>Hopping</u> by a tree.
Four little bunnies
<u>Napping</u> by me.
Six little bunnies
<u>Stopping</u> by the door.
Eight little bunnies
<u>Scrubbing</u> the floor.

● Read the poem aloud. Have volunteers identify the base word of each underlined word. Then invite volunteers to recite the poem by replacing **ing** with **ed**.

● Ask children to predict the next number in the poem. (10) Then, on the board, write number patterns such as those below. Have children complete the patterns.

1, 2, 3, <u>(4)</u>, 5, <u>(6)</u>, 7
10, 20, 30, <u>(40)</u>
5, 10, 15, <u>(20)</u>
3, <u>(6)</u>, 9, 12

● Have children work in pairs to make up more number patterns. Ask them to exchange papers with other pairs and complete the patterns.

Observational Assessment

*Note whether children remember to change the **ing** ending to **ed** when they recite the poem.*

ESL Activities

Refer to page 151J.

Recognizing and Writing Words Ending in le

Objective
● To recognize and write words ending in **le**

Warming Up

Reviewing Diphthongs
Materials: Phonics Picture Cards **cloud, screw, toys**

● On the board write the following:

A **clown counted coins** for the **crowd**.

A **cow chewed** a **few flowers**.

A **boy plowed outside** for three **hours**.

An **owl flew around** the **house**.

● Have children read the sentences aloud. Display the picture cards. Ask volunteers to name the picture and circle the words that have the same vowel sound.

★ Teaching the Lesson

Materials: Phonics Picture Cards **turtle, juggle**

● Display the picture cards. Have children name the pictures. Ask volunteers to write the names on the board. Elicit that both **turtle** and **juggle** end in **le**. Together read the words in the box on page 171 to practice the sound of this ending.

● On the board write this sentence:

The **little turtle** found one **purple pebble** in the **middle** of a **puddle**.

Have a volunteer read the sentence to the class. Invite other volunteers to underline the words ending in **le**. Have the class say these words.

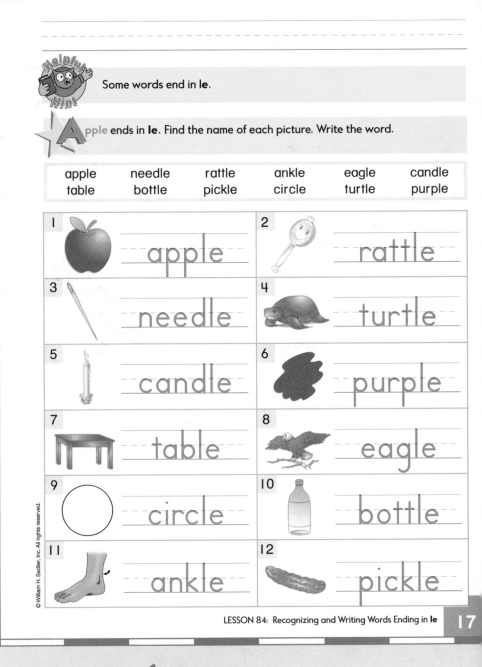

Some words end in **le**.

Apple ends in **le**. Find the name of each picture. Write the word.

apple	needle	rattle	ankle	eagle	candle
table	bottle	pickle	circle	turtle	purple

1. apple
2. rattle
3. needle
4. turtle
5. candle
6. purple
7. table
8. eagle
9. circle
10. bottle
11. ankle
12. pickle

LESSON 84: Recognizing and Writing Words Ending in **le**   **171**

Multisensory *Activities*

Visual ■ Auditory

Riddles That Puzzle

Write these words on the board: **eagle, triangle,** and **table**. Have volunteers say the words and circle the **le** endings. Then ask the riddles below. Invite children to choose one of the words from the list to answer each riddle.

I have three sides. What am I? **(triangle)**

I have four legs. What am I? **(table)**

I have two wings. What am I? **(eagle)**

Visual ■ Auditory

Are You Able to Unscramble?

Write the following on the board:

The **beetle** ate an (palpe). **(apple)**

I put a (dancel) in the **middle** of the table. **(candle)**

Handle the glass (lotbet) with care. **(bottle)**

The (telitl) girl loved her **uncle**. **(little)**

Have children unscramble the words in parentheses. Then have them say the words and read the sentences.

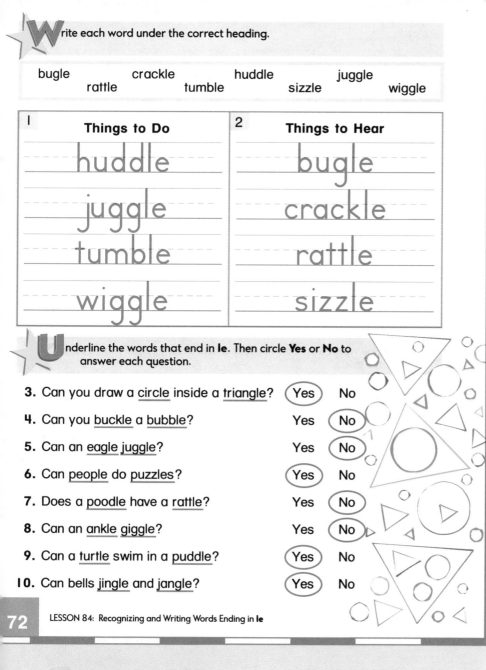

Write each word under the correct heading.

bugle   crackle   huddle   juggle
    rattle   tumble   sizzle   wiggle

1 Things to Do	2 Things to Hear
huddle	bugle
juggle	crackle
tumble	rattle
wiggle	sizzle

Underline the words that end in **le**. Then circle **Yes** or **No** to answer each question.

3. Can you draw a circle inside a triangle?   (Yes) No

4. Can you buckle a bubble?   Yes (No)

5. Can an eagle juggle?   Yes (No)

6. Can people do puzzles?   (Yes) No

7. Does a poodle have a rattle?   Yes (No)

8. Can an ankle giggle?   Yes (No)

9. Can a turtle swim in a puddle?   (Yes) No

10. Can bells jingle and jangle?   (Yes) No

72   LESSON 84: Recognizing and Writing Words Ending in **le**

Spelling Connection

Read aloud each word and sentence below. Call on a volunteer to spell the word orally. Ask another volunteer to write it on the board.

turtle	The **turtle** had a hard shell.
apple	I ate an **apple** for a snack.
candle	I put one **candle** in each cupcake.
little	The **little** kitten slept on the pillow.
table	Please set the **table**.

Practicing the Skill

● Together read the Helpful Hint and the directions on page 171. Identify the pictures together. Then have children complete the page.

● Read aloud the directions for both exercises on page 172. Do the first items together. Then have children complete the page.

Extending the Skill Across the Curriculum

(Math/Art)

Theme Activity

Materials: construction paper, paper plates, scissors, glue, hole punch, yarn

● Ask children what they know about jungles. Then share the theme book cited below. Reread selected pages. Ask children to raise their hands when they hear a word that ends in **le**.

● On the board draw and label a **circle**, a **triangle**, and a **rectangle**.

● Have children make elephant masks. Have them cut two construction-paper triangles for ears and a long rectangle for a trunk. Have them glue the shapes on paper plates and then cut two circles for eyes. Punch holes in the sides of the plates through which to thread yarn.

● On the board write these sentences:

Two elephants **whistle** in the **jungle**.
Three elephants **huddle** in the **jungle**.
Four elephants **giggle** in the **jungle**.
Five elephants form a **circle**.
Six elephants **wiggle** and **waggle**.

Ask volunteers to circle the words that end with **le**.

● Help children put on their masks. Have the "elephants" act out the sentences.

Theme Book

Mahy, Margaret. *17 Kings and 42 Elephants*. New York: Dial, 1987. A royal procession through a jungle.

Lesson 85

Changing y to i/ Reviewing Inflectional Endings

Objectives
- To change **y** to **i** before adding **ed** to base words
- To review inflectional endings **s**, **es**, **ing**, **ed**

Warming Up

Reviewing Soft and Hard c
Have children skim the "Numbers, Numbers" Poetry Poster to find a word that begins with soft **c** (**city**) and a word that begins with hard **c**. (**calendar**)

★ Teaching the Lesson

Materials: index cards

- Complete this sentence with children and write it on the board: "Yesterday we studied _____." Ask what ending was added to the word **study** to tell about the past. (**ed**) Have a child write the base word **study** on the board. Elicit that **y** was changed to **i** before adding **ed**.
- On index cards write **study, studied, copy, copied, try,** and **tried**. Have children sort the cards into base words and words that tell about the past. Ask how the base words and the words with inflectional endings are alike. Lead children to see that when a base word ends in a consonant and **y**, the **y** is changed to **i** before **ed** is added.
- On the board write the headings **s or es, ing, ed**. Have children add the endings to the base words **walk, march, jog, hike,** and **hurry**. Ask volunteers to explain spelling changes.

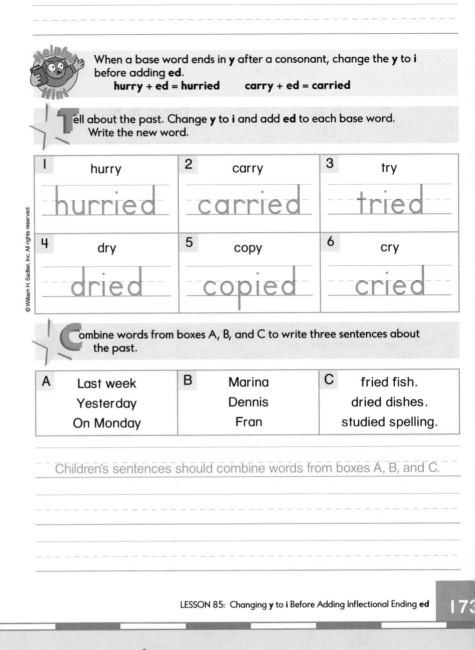

When a base word ends in **y** after a consonant, change the **y** to **i** before adding **ed**.
hurry + ed = hurried   carry + ed = carried

Tell about the past. Change **y** to **i** and add **ed** to each base word. Write the new word.

1 hurry	2 carry	3 try
hurried	carried	tried
4 dry	5 copy	6 cry
dried	copied	cried

Combine words from boxes A, B, and C to write three sentences about the past.

A	B	C
Last week	Marina	fried fish.
Yesterday	Dennis	dried dishes.
On Monday	Fran	studied spelling.

Children's sentences should combine words from boxes A, B, and C.

Multisensory *Activities*

Visual ■ Auditory

Add an Ending
Materials: index cards

On the board write the headings **s or es, ing, ed**. On index cards write base words from pages 163–174. Place the cards facedown in a pile. Invite children to choose a card and come to the board to write the base word with each ending. Have other children use each new word in an oral sentence.

Auditory ■ Kinesthetic

Yesterday's News
Materials: yesterday's newspaper

Together read the lead paragraph from several articles about interesting events that occurred yesterday. Then ask children to tell what happened yesterday. Write the sentences they dictate on the board. Invite volunteers to underline words that end in **ed** or **ing**. Have other children write the base words.

Complete each column by adding the ending at the top to the base word.

	s or es	ing	ed
1 paint	paints	painting	painted
2 rush	rushes	rushing	rushed
3 chase	chases	chasing	chased
4 try	tries	trying	tried

Write the base word.

5 sleeps	6 winning	7 flipped
sleep	win	flip
8 making	9 pitches	10 saved
make	pitch	save
11 quitting	12 dries	13 studied
quit	dry	study

LESSON 85: Reviewing Inflectional Endings

Spelling Connection

Read aloud each word and sentence below. Have a volunteer spell the word orally. Ask another volunteer to write it on the board.

sleeps	The baby **sleeps** in a crib.
chases	The dog **chases** the cat around the house.
fixes	The plumber **fixes** the sink.
making	What are you **making** with the clay?
stopped	I **stopped** at the library to find a book.

Multicultural Connection

Background Information Calendars based on the phases of the moon have been used for thousands of years. Some cultures and religions today use a lunar calendar to determine special dates. Many Native Americans celebrate each new moon of the year.

Activity Read aloud the poems in *Thirteen Moons on Turtle's Back: A Native American Year of Moons*, by Joseph Bruchac and Jonathan London (Putnam). Invite children to use an almanac or calendar to find the date of the next new moon.

Practicing the Skill

● Together read the Helpful Hint and the two sets of directions on page 173. Have children complete the page.

● Ask volunteers to read both sets of directions on page 174. Do the first item in each exercise together. Have children complete the page.

Extending the Skill Across the Curriculum

(Language Arts/Social Studies)

Theme Activity

● Share the theme books cited below. Tell children to raise their hands when they hear a word ending in **s, es, ing,** or **ed.** Have them identify each base word.

● Point out that the boy and the mouse began their diaries in January and ended them in December. Then have children work in small groups to research these questions about calendars:

How did July get its name?
What holiday is the third Monday in January?
How did December get its name?
What holiday is the last Monday in May?

● Have children keep a diary for a week. Tell them to circle any words ending in **s, es, ing,** and **ed.** Ask volunteers to share their diaries if they wish to do so.

Theme Books

McPhail, David. *Farm Boy's Year.* New York: Atheneum, 1992. A boy's life on a farm in the 1800s.

Oakley, Graham. *The Diary of a Church Mouse.* New York: Atheneum, 1987. A mouse keeps a diary.

Portfolio

Have students add their diaries to their portfolios.

ESL Activities

Refer to page 151J.

Lesson 86

Student Pages 175–176

Connecting Spelling and Writing

Objectives
- To say, spell, sort, and write words with inflectional endings
- To write a rhyme using spelling words

Warming Up

Reviewing Plural Endings s and es

Materials: Phonics Picture Cards

Display picture cards with objects such as **balloon, bunny, bus, cake, chair, cherry, duck, glass, shirt, strawberry, truck,** and **watch**. On the board write the headings **s** and **es**. Ask children to name each picture. Invite volunteers to the board to write its plural under the correct heading.

★ Teaching the Lesson

- On the board write the sentence "I like **jumping** rope." Read the sentence together. Ask which word ends in **ing**. Together say, spell, and say the word again. Ask whether any changes were made to the base word before the ending **ing** was added. (no)
- Repeat the procedure for the other spelling words. Have children explain spelling changes.
- Invite children to use each spelling word in a sentence.

Practicing the Skill

Together review the directions, spelling words, and categories for sorting the words on page 175. Ask a volunteer to explain where to write the first word on the list. Then have children complete the page.

Spell and Write — Say and spell each word in the box. Then write each word under the correct heading.

brushes, carried, hurried, jogging, jumping, raked, running, smiling, stopped, tries, washed, wiped

1. **No Base Changes** — brushes, jumping, washed
2. **Change y to i** — carried, hurried, tries
3. **Drop Final e** — raked, smiling, wiped
4. **Double Final Consonant** — jogging, running, stopped

LESSON 86: Connecting Spelling and Writing — 175

Multisensory *Activities*

Auditory ■ Visual

Guessing Game

Give a series of clues for each spelling word. Invite children to guess the possibilities at each stage and use the process of elimination to write the word. For example:

> It has no base changes.
> (**brushes, jumping, washed**)
> It has 7 letters. (**brushes, jumping**)
> It ends in es. (**brushes**)

Visual ■ Kinesthetic

Filling Shapes

On the board draw connected boxes to show the shape of each spelling word. For example, here is the shape of the word **brushes**:

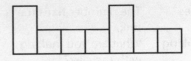

Say a spelling word. Ask a child to come to the board, find the word shape, and fill it in.

175

Spell and Write Read the playground rhyme. Then add one or two verses. Use one or more of your spelling words.

brushes	carried	hurried	jogging	jumping	raked
running	smiling	stopped	tries	washed	wiped

I went outside to count the stars.
I made a mistake and counted cars.
I went inside to bake a pie.
I made a mistake and baked a fly.

Spelling Connection

Draw a tic-tac-toe grid on the board. Have children form teams. Assign each team one of the categories for sorting the spelling words on page 175. Have players on each team take turns writing spelling words from the appropriate category in the squares. The first team to write three in a row gets first choice of category for the next game.

The Writing Process

Tell children that they will write verses for a playground rhyme. Together read the directions on page 176. Ask volunteers to read the words in the box.

Brainstorm Ask children about their favorite playground rhymes. Then read the rhyme on page 176. On the board write the rhyme pattern:

I went _____ to _____.
I made a mistake and _____.

Brainstorm a list of places to go and things to do. Invite children to suggest silly rhymes.

Write Have children write their verses on paper. Encourage them to have fun making up their rhymes.

Revise Have children read their verses to themselves to make sure they have followed the rhyme scheme. Have them make sure they have used spelling words. Then have children write their rhymes on the page.

Publish Invite children to share their verses with the class. Then have children go back and underline spelling words they have used.

Portfolio

Have children add their rhymes to their Portfolios.

Extending the Skill

Children may enjoy putting together a book of playground rhymes. Assign each child one page. Invite children to write their favorite rhymes or their own versions of those rhymes and to illustrate them. Collect the rhymes, add a cover, bind the book, and display it in the classroom or school library.

Integrating the Language Arts

Objectives
● To use oral and written language to extend the theme concept
● To demonstrate ability to recognize contractions, plurals, inflectional endings, and words ending in **le** in context

Background Information

One of the earliest known clocks was the Egyptian water clock, a bowl with a small hole in the bottom. As water dripped out of the bowl, the water level was measured to tell how much time had passed. Sundials were used to tell time in Egypt, Greece, and Rome. These objects measure time by the shadow cast by the sun.

★ Teaching the Lesson

● Read page 177 aloud and identify the clocks. (pocket watch, classroom clock, clock radio, digital wristwatch) Point out which are analog or digital. Discuss unusual clocks children have seen.
● Have children identify plurals, contractions, inflectional endings, and words ending in **le** on page 177.

Oral Language Development
Invite children to imagine what it would be like not to have clocks or watches. Ask what problems might arise. Have children suggest ways to know the time without a clock.

ESL Activity
Refer to page 151J.

Let's read and talk about clocks.

What time is it? Let's look at a clock to find out. Analog clocks have faces with numbers 1 to 12 and hands that point to the minutes and the hour. Digital clocks don't have hands. The hour and the minutes are separated by a : . The number before the : tells the hour. The number after the : tells the minutes past the hour.

What would happen if people didn't have clocks or watches?

Reading and Writing Connection

Supply groups of children with encyclopedias and books about clocks. Have them explore questions about interesting kinds of clocks. For example: How does the clock work? What does it look like? Where and when was it used? Have each group appoint a recorder to write down facts and an illustrator to draw pictures. Then invite each group to present its report to the class.

Mathematics Connection

Display a time zone map of the United States for children to study. Help them to locate the city where they live. Tell them that the time decreases by one hour for every time zone to the left and increases by one hour in each zone to their right. Encourage students to use the map to find the present time in other cities around the country.

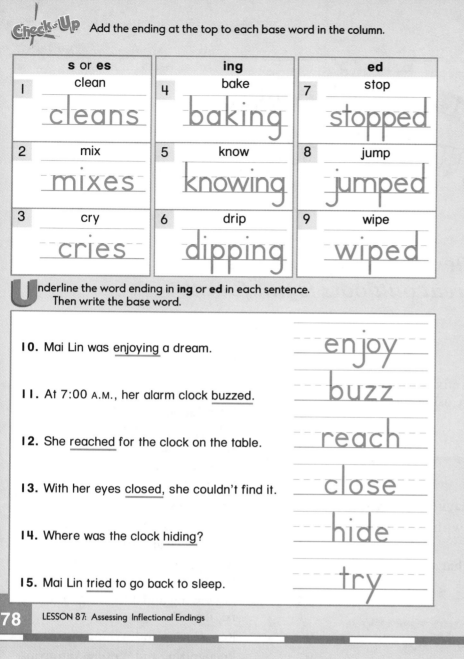

s or es	ing	ed
1 clean **cleans**	4 bake **baking**	7 stop **stopped**
2 mix **mixes**	5 know **knowing**	8 jump **jumped**
3 cry **cries**	6 drip **dipping**	9 wipe **wiped**

Underline the word ending in **ing** or **ed** in each sentence.
Then write the base word.

10. Mai Lin was <u>enjoying</u> a dream. **enjoy**

11. At 7:00 A.M., her alarm clock <u>buzzed</u>. **buzz**

12. She <u>reached</u> for the clock on the table. **reach**

13. With her eyes <u>closed</u>, she couldn't find it. **close**

14. Where was the clock <u>hiding</u>? **hide**

15. Mai Lin <u>tried</u> to go back to sleep. **try**

78 LESSON 87: Assessing Inflectional Endings

Reteaching *Activities*

How Does It End?
On the board write **s or es**, **ed**, and **ing** and **looked**, **passes**, and **shaping**. Help children identify each base word. Then review how each word is formed from its base word. Show flash cards of the base words used in this unit. Ask children how each word is spelled when each of the endings on the board is added to the word.

Make a Great Ending
Write the following words on flash cards: **count, reach, bake, wag, jump, fix, trace, win, help, fish, race,** and **chop**. Display the words in a pocket chart. Invite children to select a base word from the pocket chart, say it, choose an ending, and then say and write the new word. Have children return the base-word cards to the pocket chart so that they can be used again. Finally, have children match the cards with all words that have that base word.

Assessing the Unit

Unit Test Review when and how the spellings of words change when inflectional endings **s**, **es**, **ing**, or **ed** are added. Together read the directions for both exercises on page 178. Do the first, fifth, and ninth items with the class. Then have children complete the page.

Observational Assessment Review the notes you recorded throughout this unit. Use them to help assess children's overall performance and progress.

Student Skills Assessment Use the assessment on page 178 and your observations to record your evaluation of each child's skills on pages 330–331 of the Student Edition.

Writing Conference Meet with each child to discuss a portfolio writing sample that he or she did during this unit. Encourage the child to talk about the work as you review it together. Take notes, and use these and previous notes to help evaluate the child's writing and application of phonics skills. Encourage the child to write more or to edit a piece of writing. Have the child add these pieces to his or her portfolio.

Group together students who need further instruction for the *Reteaching Activities*.

At this time you might refer to the alternative assessment methods on page 149C.

Take-Home Book Remind children to complete the *Take-Home Book* for Unit 7 at home.

PLANNING RESOURCE

OUTDOOR FUN

Theme:
*Summer, Winter, Spring or Fall—
the great outdoors is fun for all.*

Overview

Unit 8 introduces suffixes, prefixes, synonyms, antonyms, and homonyms by using the theme of outdoor fun.

Objectives

- To enjoy a poem about playing on a swing
- To read and write words with suffixes and prefixes
- To read and write words that are synonyms, antonyms, and homonyms

Thematic Teaching

Ask children what outdoor activities they most enjoy. Provide additional reading material on related topics.

Display the Poetry Poster "Swinging," and refer to it throughout the unit.

Individual Lessons

Lesson	Skill Focus
88	Introduction to Suffixes, Prefixes, Synonyms, Antonyms, Homonyms
89	Suffixes **ful, less, ness**
90	Writing and Reviewing Suffixes **ly, ful, less, ness**
91	Suffixes **er** and **est**
92	Reviewing and Assessing Suffixes
93	Prefixes **re** and **un**
94	Writing and Reviewing Prefixes **re, un, dis**
95	Reviewing and Assessing Prefixes **re, un, dis**
96	Recognizing and Writing Synonyms
97	Recognizing and Writing Antonyms
98	Recognizing and Writing Homonyms
99	Reviewing Synonyms, Antonyms, and Homonyms
100	Connecting Spelling and Writing
101	Integrating the Language Arts

Take-Home Book: *A Wonderful Day*

Curriculum Integration

Writing   Children write captions, letters, story endings, comparisons, reports, details, and descriptions on pages 182, 184, 192, and 200.

Science   Activities related to science appear on pages 182, 184, 196, and 200.

Social Studies   An opportunity for children to relate to social studies is found on page 198.

Math   An application of phonics skills to math appears on page 186.

Art   Children express their creativity through the activity on page 192.

Optional Learning Activities

Multisensory Activities   Each lesson contains activities that appeal to all learning styles—visual, auditory, tactile, or kinesthetic.

Multicultural Connection   Children celebrate cultural diversity in the activities on pages 182, 190, and 198.

Thematic Activities   The *Extending the Skill Across the Curriculum* aspect of every lesson applies the unit theme to various disciplines.

Assessment Strategies

Multiple strategies such as *Observational Assessments,* portfolios, written middle- and end-of-the-unit assessments, and the *Skills Checklist* at the back of the Student Edition will help you assess children's mastery of phonics skills taught throughout Unit 8.

Resources

Theme-Related Resources

Ancona, George. *My Camera.* New York: Crown, 1992.

Head First and Belly Down. Nancy Schimmel and Candy Forest, 1992.

Hort, Lenny. *How Many Stars in the Sky?* New York: Morrow, 1991.

Medearis, Angela Shelf. *Dancing with the Indians.* New York: Holiday House, 1991.

Mott, Evelyn Clarke. *Balloon Ride.* Walker & Co., 1991.

Sheldon, Dyan. *Under the Moon.* New York: Dial, 1994.

Three Days on a River in a Red Canoe. GPN/WNED-TV, 1983.

Assessment

In Unit 8 children focus on recognizing and writing suffixes, prefixes, synonyms, antonyms, and homonyms. The following are suggestions for evaluating these skills through informal/formal, observational, objective, portfolio, and performance assessments. You may also wish to refer to *Using Technology* for alternative assessment activities.

Informal/Formal Assessment

The tests on pages 179D, 179E, and 179F assess whether children have mastered recognizing and writing suffixes, prefixes, synonyms, antonyms, and homonyms.

These tools may be used informally at the beginning of the unit or formally at the end of the unit to assess children's progress.

Observational Assessment

Specific opportunities for observation are highlighted in the lesson plans. In addition, there are many opportunities throughout the unit to observe children identifying and writing suffixes, prefixes, synonyms, antonyms, and homonyms. Other opportunities for observation might include *Multisensory Activities*.

Objective Assessment

Use the assessment pages throughout the unit. After completing each assessment page, determine the area(s) in which children would benefit from more instruction; then refer to *Reteaching Activities* found throughout the unit in the Teacher's Edition. After reteaching the skill, reassess children's progress.

Portfolio Assessment

Show pictures of historical places in the United States. Ask what historical places children have visited. Help children locate each historical place on a wall map of the United States.

Have children work in small groups to choose one historical place. Tell them to research information about it. Have each group write five exciting facts about its chosen place.

Performance Assessment

Set up five stations around the classroom. Have one station each for suffixes, prefixes, synonyms, antonyms, and homonyms. Try to have several activities at each station. Tell children to chose one activity at each station. Activities might include a cloze paragraph where children fill in the missing word; a tape recording of words where children identify synonyms, antonyms, or homonyms; or a tape recording where children supply synonyms, antonyms or homonyms.

Provide answer keys for children after they have completed the work at all of the stations.

Using Technology

To evaluate children's progress, have them complete the *Tech Talk* activities on pages 179K–179L of the Teacher's Edition.

Answer Key

Page 179D
1. help 2. star 3. kind 4. big 5. nice 6. sun 7. seed 8. pony
9. good 10. loud 11. use 12. hot 13. swiftly 14. hopeful
15. families 16. windier 17. soreness 18. slower 19. breathless
20. longest

Page 179E
1. unfair 2. repaint 3. uncover 4. reheat 5. unlock 6. untrue
7. dishonest 8. reread 9. disagree 10. refill 11. distrust 12. retell 13. unable 14. rejoin 15. uneasy 16. disliked 17. unafraid

Page 179F
1. boat/ship 2. sack/bag 3. friend/pal 4. shout/yell
5. fast/quick 6. nearly/almost 7. below/under
8. night/evening 9. full 10. dry 11. sad 12. last 13. sink
14. bottom 15. left 16. big 17. right/write 18. meet/meat
19. knight/night 20. some/sum 21. one/won 22. knew/new

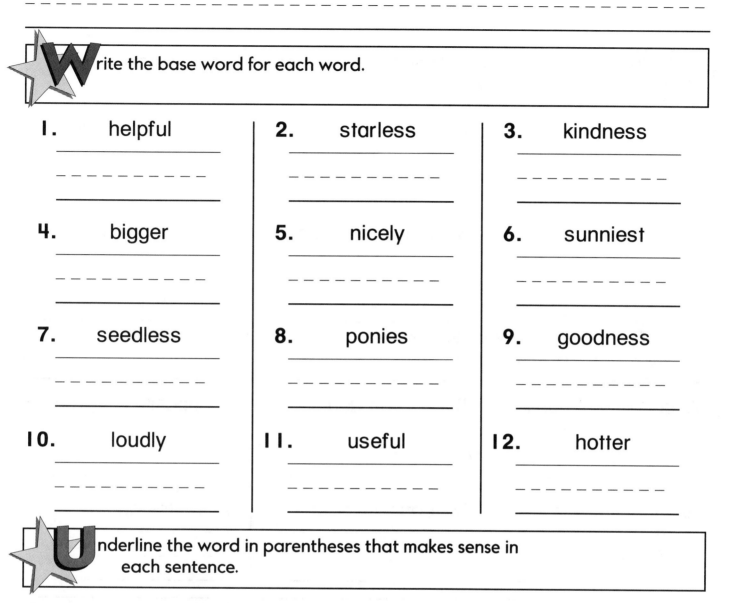

Write the base word for each word.

1. helpful

2. starless

3. kindness

4. bigger

5. nicely

6. sunniest

7. seedless

8. ponies

9. goodness

10. loudly

11. useful

12. hotter

Underline the word in parentheses that makes sense in each sentence.

13. Mike and Gloria ran (nearly, swiftly) in the race.

14. They were (colorful, hopeful) that one of them would win.

15. Many (families, stories) ran together.

16. The first half of the race was (easiest, easier) than the second half.

17. During the last mile, Mike felt a (soreness, loudness) in his legs.

18. He ran a little (slowest, slower) than Gloria.

19. They were both (wireless, breathless) at the finish line.

20. This was the (longest, longer) race they had ever run.

U se the prefixes **re** or **un** to make new words that mean the same as the words given.

1. not fair

_____

2. paint again

_____

3. opposite of cover

_____

4. heat again

_____

5. opposite of lock

_____

6. not true

_____

U se the prefixes **re** or **dis** to make new words that mean the same as the words given.

7. opposite of honest

_____

8. read again

_____

9. opposite of agree

_____

10. fill again

_____

11. opposite of trust

_____

12. tell again

_____

F ill in the circle next to the word that makes sense in each sentence.

13. Last year I was _____ to go to the city pool.

○ unseen
○ unable

14. At first I felt _____ about swimming.

○ unfair
○ uneasy

15. Then I discovered that I no longer _____ the water.

○ disliked
○ displeased

Blackline Master 34: Assessing Prefixes

Draw a line from a word in the first column to a word in the second column that has **the same** or **nearly the same** meaning.

1	boat ●	● pal	5	fast ●	● almost
2	sack ●	● ship	6	nearly ●	● under
3	friend ●	● yell	7	below ●	● evening
4	shout ●	● bag	8	night ●	● quick

In each column, fill in the circle in front of the word that means the opposite of the word at the top.

9. empty	10. wet	11. happy	12. first
○ big	○ damp	○ sad	○ front
○ full	○ water	○ smile	○ last
○ open	○ dry	○ good	○ out

13. float	14. top	15. right	16. little
○ full	○ over	○ turn	○ big
○ boat	○ bottom	○ under	○ over
○ sink	○ close	○ left	○ new

Circle the two words in each row that sound the same but have different meanings.

17. right   white   ride   write

18. met   meet   meat   mat

19. note   knight   knot   night

20. some   sum   same   seem

Game Time

▲▽▲▽▲▽▲▽▲▽▲▽▲ Mile High Hike ▲▽▲▽▲▽▲▽▲▽▲▽

Blackline Master 36 p.179H

Objective: To read words with suffixes and prefixes and identify base words

Players: pairs

Materials: scissors, crayons

- Duplicate Blackline Master 36 and give a copy to each pair. Have each partner cut out a hiking-boot marker and color it.

- Direct both partners to start at the bottom of the mountain and take turns climbing up one side and down the other. Explain that to move, players should jump over one another's boots so that each player lands on every other word.

- Tell players to read each word on which they land, identify its suffix or prefix, and use the word in a sentence.

- To vary the game, have players say words that have the same suffix or prefix as those on which they land.

▲▽▲▽▲▽▲▽▲▽▲▽▲▽ Outdoor Fun ▽▲▽▲▽▲▽▲▽▲▽▲▽▲

Blackline Master 37 p.179I

Objective: To identify pairs of words as synonyms, antonyms, or homonyms

Players: individuals

Materials: drawing paper, scissors, glue

- Duplicate Blackline Master 37 and give a copy to each child.

- Have children cut out the three larger boxes at the top of the blackline master and glue each to the top of a separate sheet of paper. Then have them draw a big boat, tree, or road on each sheet to match the heading.

- Have children cut out the boxes with the pairs of words. Tell them to decide whether each pair is a synonym, antonym, or homonym and glue the words onto the correct pages.

- Encourage children to add to their drawings new pairs of words they read or hear in conversation.

▲▽▲▽▲▽▲▽▲▽ Surf the Biggest Wave ▲▽▲▽▲▽▲▽▲▽

Objective: To write words with suffixes and prefixes

Players: whole class

Materials: mural paper, surfboard patterns, crayons, scissors, construction paper

- Draw a big wave on mural paper, and post it on a bulletin board. Distribute surfboard patterns, and have each child trace and cut out a surfboard. Tell children to color their boards but to leave space in the center to write a word.

- Make two columns on the board. In column 1 write base words such as **join, glad, true, honest, hope, care, slow, quick, cold, hot, early, bumpy, bunny,** and **city.** In column 2 write corresponding suffixes and prefixes, such as **ful, re, ly, es, dis, un, est, less, er,** and **ness.**

- Call on a student to match a base word with a suffix or prefix. If he or she can write the new word correctly on the board, invite the child to copy the word onto his or her surfboard and tack it to the wave.

Mile High Hike

tallest

unable | dislike

fearless | loudly

sunnier | kindness

retell | stories

neatly | bumpiest

unclear | cheerful

hotter | seedless

repaint | pennies

START | **STOP**

Outdoor Fun with Words

Synonym Boat	Antonym Tree	Homonym Road

fast quick	first last	shout yell	plain plane
big little	sail sale	smile frown	leave go
road rode	boat ship	blew blue	front back
dry wet	right write	house home	sink float
rush hurry	strong weak	meat meet	big large
over under	one won	pail bucket	no know

ESL Activities

Poets Are We *Page 179*

Direct children to be seated in a circle. Write the poem on chart paper, and display it in the middle of the circle. Together, recite the poem, tap out its rhythm, and review the rhyme pattern. Then recite lines or phrases and call on children to supply the words that come next. Finally, invite children to compose new lines that match the poem's rhythm and rhyme scheme.

Big Adventures
Page 183

Have children work in groups. Give each group a list of words that end with the suffixes studied. Include some words not mentioned in the text. Direct the groups to use most or all of their words to write stories about a child's adventure. (Keep this purpose in mind when you prepare the lists.) Have the groups share their stories.

Vacation Tips
Page 187

Initiate a discussion of possible vacation spots. Encourage children to tell about special attractions and popular places in their homelands. Have children work in groups to prepare pages for a class brochure. First, have the groups discuss and compare their favorite vacation places. Tell them to use words that end in **er** and **est** to describe the different sites and what a vacationer might enjoy doing at each place. Then have each group select two or three vacation sites and write a page describing each. Remind them to include words with suffixes, particularly **er** and **est**. Allow time for class presentations. Then help children edit their work; have them write and illustrate final versions and underline the suffixes. Combine all the pages into a class "vacation brochure."

Race for Meaning
Page 194

Have children work in groups. Use prefix words from the text to make a set of word cards for each group. Direct group members to work together to write the meaning of each of their words. The first group to write correct meanings for all their words wins. Have each group read its list of meanings aloud. Call on volunteers to use each prefix word in a sentence.

Double Day *Page 197*

Have children work in pairs. Assign each pair two contrasting scenarios related to the unit theme "Outdoor Fun." You might use: rainy day spent inside/sunny day outside; outdoor fun with friends/alone; winter/summer day outside; nighttime/daytime outdoor fun; working/playing outdoors. Direct partners to use synonyms and antonyms to write five pairs of sentences that compare what they might see or do in the two scenarios. Have each partner represent one scenario to present the pair's sentences to the class; for example:

- It is **dark** and rainy **outdoors**. It is **bright** and warm **outside**.
- I **like playing** baseball with my friends. I **enjoy working** outside with my family.

Help the class identify the synonyms and antonyms.

The World's Parks
Page 205

Invite children to tell about national parks, aside from the Grand Canyon, they may know of or have visited. Present pictures and information about well-known parks or refuges throughout the world. Provide reference materials and have children work in groups to research famous parks in the United States or abroad. Have each group write and illustrate a brief report on a park of its choice for class presentation.

TECH TALK

Synonym It!

Objectives
- To help children use synonyms
- To use a writing and painting program such as Kid Works™ 2* to write a synonym story

Preparation
Play the audio cassette *Head First and Belly Down* by Nancy Schimmel and Candy Forest. Stop the tape at certain words and ask children to name another word that they might use instead of the word indicated. List the word and the synonyms named on the board.

One Step at a Time

1. Write the following paragraph on the board.

   Joseph likes to bring his lunch when he hikes in the forest. He is very careful to put the wrapper in his backpack and never to throw trash in the forest. He stays on the trail and does not pick the forest plants. He leaves the forest as clean as it was when he got there.

2. Have a volunteer read the paragraph. Then erase certain words and ask children to name other words with nearly the same meaning that would be suitable (e.g., **hikes/walks, forest/woods**). Then brainstorm with the class other outdoor activities they enjoy.

3. Tell children on Kid Works™ 2 to use the Story Writer feature to write stories about an outdoor activity. Encourage them to

   include words that have synonyms and to underline or italicize those words. Also suggest that children use the Cat icon from the side menu to have the computer replace words in the story with symbols.

4. Direct children to select "Story Illustrator" to access the tools, colors, and stamps. Invite them to illustrate their "Synonym It" stories. Have them store their illustrations in "Picture Box" at the bottom of the screen in the Story Writer feature. Then have children select "Story Writer" to retrieve their illustrations and place them at the beginning of their texts.

5. Have children use the Story Player feature to print their illustrated stories.

Class Sharing

Have children exchange their stories with a partner. Tell partners to replace the underlined or italicized words with synonyms. Display the stories in the Reading Corner.

Change That Word!

Objectives

- To review antonyms, synonyms, homonyms, suffixes, and prefixes
- To use a writing program, such as The Amazing Writing Machine™* to write a story about the environment
- To use E-mail to exchange information about different environments with other children

Preparation

Read aloud *Balloon Ride* by Evelyn C. Mott (Walker). Show children the photographs as you read. Ask volunteers to describe what the young girl saw as she traveled in the balloon. Have students tell how objects look different when looked down on from the balloon.

One Step at a Time

1. Have children work in small groups.

2. Ask children to describe the environment in which they live. List their responses on the board.

3. Direct children to use The Amazing Writing Machine™ to write a description of their environment.

4. Tell children to edit their stories. Have them use synonyms, homonyms, and antonyms to improve their stories.

5. Have children use a drawing and painting program to illustrate their stories.

6. Direct children to print their stories and E-mail them to other second-grade classes.

Class Sharing

Have children design a bulletin board on which to display their stories along with stories children from other classes may have E-mailed back. Ask children to mark on a wall map the locations of the other classes. Then have children use the information they received to describe those places.

Travelin' Around the Countryside

Show the video *Three Days on a River in a Red Canoe* (GPN/Wned-TV). Have children describe the river and the environment around the river. Write children's responses on the board. Identify certain words for which children will be able to name homonyms, antonyms, and synonyms.

Have children work in small groups. Tell them to write a story titled "Three Days at (your school)." Ask children to brainstorm and then list what they want to include in their video. Then help them write a script. Allot time for children to videotape their stories.

All referenced software is listed under Computer Resources on page T46.

Student Pages 179–180

Literature Introduction to Suffixes, Prefixes, Synonyms, Antonyms, Homonyms

Objectives
● To enjoy a poem about a swing
● To identify suffixes, prefixes, synonyms, antonyms, homonyms

Starting with Literature
● Discuss the illustration on page 179. Ask the class what the girl can see from her swing.
● Recite the poem. Explain that the poet has included notes on how to read the stanzas. Read the poem with the class.

Developing Critical Thinking
Ask a volunteer to read the questions at the bottom of page 179. Encourage children to answer imaginatively.

Introducing the Skill
● Tell children they will learn about suffixes and prefixes—word parts that come at the end or beginning of a base word to change its meaning and make a new word. On the board, add **ly** to **slow** to exemplify *suffix*.
● Tell children they will also learn about words that have the same or opposite meanings. Use **quicker** from the poem and **faster** to exemplify *synonym*.

Practicing the Skill
Ask children to identify in the poem's second verse the words made of a base word and a special ending. Ask them to find in the first verse a word that is the opposite of **high**.

ESL Activities
Refer to page 179J.

179

Swinging

Slowly, slowly, swinging low,
Let me see how far I go!
Slowly, slowly, keeping low,
I see where the wild flowers grow!

(Getting quicker):
   Quicker, quicker,
   Swinging higher,
   I can see
   A shining spire!
   Quicker, quicker,
   Swinging higher,
   I can see
   The sunset's fire!

   Faster, faster,
   Through the air,
   I see almost
   Everywhere.
   Woods and hills,
   And sheep that stare—
   And things I never
   Knew were there!

(Getting slower):
   Slower, slower, now I go,
   Swinging, dreaming, getting low;
   Slowly, slowly, down I go—
   Till I touch the grass below.

Irene Thompson

Critical Thinking
What do you think is the best part about going high on a swing?
If you could put a swing anywhere, where would you put it? Why?

LESSON 88: Introduction to Suffixes, Prefixes, Synonyms, Antonyms, and Homonyms

17

Theme Words

Outdoor Fun Ask children to name any outdoor activities they enjoy; use their responses to begin a chart of theme words. Have children also name words associated with each activity, and add these to the chart as well. Return to the theme word chart and add to it throughout the unit to reflect a growth in words and phrases used by children.

Have each child select one outdoor activity they would like to do and think of words to describe that activity. Encourage them to use the language skills learned in this lesson and include words with suffixes or prefixes, as well as words that are synonyms, antonyms, and homonyms. Have children use these words and those listed on the word chart to compose a paragraph about the activity.

Dear Family,

As your child progresses through this unit about outdoor fun, she or he will learn about the following kinds of word parts and words.

suffix: word part added to the end of a word to change its meaning or make a new word (**careful**)

prefix: word part added to the beginning of a word to change its meaning or make a new word (**reload**)

synonyms: words that have the same meaning (**fast/quick**)

antonyms: words that have the opposite meaning (**up/down**)

homonyms: words that sound the same but have different spellings and meanings (**blue/blew**)

● Read the poem "Swinging" on the reverse side.

● Look for words with the suffixes **ly** and **er** (**slowly**, **quicker**, **higher**, **faster**, **slower**). Also look for synonyms (**quicker/faster**) and antonyms (**quicker/slower**, **faster/slower**).

● Talk about ways you and your family have outdoor fun.

PROJECT

Help your child draw a kite and cut it out. Attach a tail. Encourage your child to write new words on small pieces of paper and tape them to the tail.

Apreciada Familia:

En esta unidad, sobre el recreo, su niño aprenderá otros tipos de palabras y partes de palabras.

sufijos: letras que se añaden al final de una palabra y que cambian su significado o hace una nueva (**careful**).

prefijos: letras que se añaden al principio de una palabra y que cambian su significado o hacen una nueva (**reload**).

sinónimos: palabras que tienen el mismo significado (**fast/quick**).

antónimos: palabras que significan lo opuesto (**up/down**).

homónimos: palabras que tienen el mismo sonido pero diferente significado y se escriben diferentes (**blue/blew**).

● Lea, "Swinging" en la página 179.

● Busquen palabras que tengan los sufijos **ly, er** (**slowly**, **quicker**, **higher**, **faster**, **slower**). Busquen los sinónimos (**quicker/faster**) y los antónimos (**quicker/slower**, **faster/slower**).

● Hablen de lo que hace su familia para divertiese fuera de la casa.

PROYECTO

Ayude a su niño a dibujar y recortar una cometa. Atele una cola. Anime al niño a escribir palabras en pedacitos de papel y pegarlas en la cola de la cometa.

LESSON 88: Introduction to Suffixes, Prefixes, Synonyms, Antonyms, and Homonyms—Phonics Alive at Home

ESL Activities

Throughout this unit, ESL activities are referenced. These activities benefit the ESL child in your classroom by providing additional language experiences. Choose the activities that best meet the diverse needs of your class.

For ESL activities related to "Swinging," refer to page 179J.

Take-Home Book

In Unit 8, children will appreciate and share with family members the Take-Home Book *A Wonderful Day*, found on student pages 223–224. This fold-up book enhances students' knowledge of the suffixes, prefixes, synonyms, antonyms, and homonyms taught in the unit. Send this component home with children at any appropriate time during the unit.

Phonics Alive at Home

● The *Phonics Alive at Home* page is intended to involve families in the development of their children's reading and writing through activities that apply specific phonics skills.

● In Unit 7, the *Phonics Alive at Home* page includes discussion and a project related to both the unit theme of "Outdoor Fun" and the phonics focus on suffixes, prefixes, synonyms, antonyms, and homonyms.

● Have children tear page 180 out of their books. Read the headings, and discuss the contents of the page with the class. Point out the bilingual layout and explain its purpose.

● Direct children to complete the project at home with family members. Encourage them to bring their completed kites to school to share with the class.

● Provide ample opportunities for children to share stories they have written, books they have read, or experiences they have had that relate to the unit theme.

● Ask children to start collecting pictures from newspapers or magazines that show people having fun outdoors. Use the pictures to make a bulletin-board collage that may be added to and referred to throughout the unit.

Suffixes ful, less, ness

Objectives
● To write words ending in **ful, less,** and **ness** in context
● To match **less** and **ness** words and meanings

Warming Up

Reviewing Inflectional Endings
On the board write **play, dig, chase, jog, rake, jump, hide, run, sail, skip, skate,** and **swim.** Have volunteers write the **ing** form of each word and use it in a sentence.

★ Teaching the Lesson

● Write this rhyme on chart paper, and have a child recite it:

> Last year I found a **homeless** pup;
> I taught her tricks, like jumping up.
> My **playful** pup and I have fun;
> She has a **quickness** when we run.

● Ask children to identify the base words in **homeless, playful,** and **quickness.** Tell them each ending is called a *suffix,* a word part added to the end of a word to change its meaning. Explain that **less** means "without," so **homeless** means "without a home"; **ful** frequently means "full of," so **play-ful** means "full of play"; **ness** means a "condition," so **quickness** means "condition of being quick." (Certain **ful** words such as **useful** and **harmful** may need further clarification.)

● On the board write **cheerful, seed-less, kindness, colorful, tasteless,** and **thickness.** Have children give the base word, the suffix, and the meaning of each word.

 A **suffix** is a word part added to the **end** of a base word to change its meaning or make a new word.

fear + ful = fearful	fear + less = fearless
soft + ness = softness	soft + ly = softly

The suffix **ful** means "full of." **Fearful** means "full of fear." Add the suffix **ful** to each base word. Write the new word below.

Words that Describe People or Things		Words that Describe Feelings	
help grace play use		cheer fear hope thank	
1	helpful	5	cheerful
2	graceful	6	fearful
3	playful	7	hopeful
4	useful	8	thankful

Write about the puppy. Use a word that ends in the suffix **ful.**

Accept any reasonable response. Children

might describe the puppy as "playful."

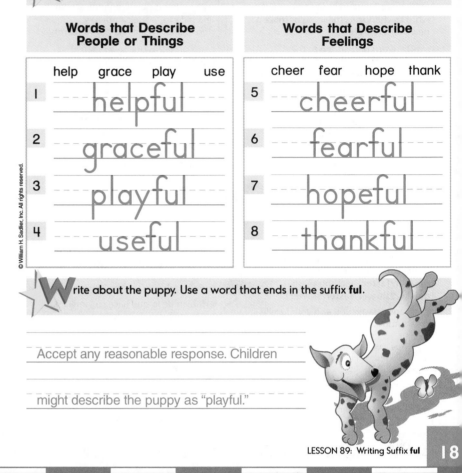

LESSON 89: Writing Suffix **ful** | 8

Multisensory *Activities*

Auditory ▪ Visual

Be Careful, Not Careless!
Materials: large index cards

On index cards write suffixes **ful** and **less,** and the words **cheer, color, fear, harm, help, hope, pain, thank,** and **use.** Place the suffix cards on the chalk ledge; distribute the word cards to children. Have each child with a card place it beside one of the suffixes, read the new word, and tell its meaning. Redistribute the word cards and have children repeat the process with the other suffix. Be sure all children participate.

Visual ▪ Auditory

Quickness Counts
On the board write: **loudness, soft-ness, darkness, quickness, sickness, flatness,** and **roundness.** Say the following phrases, and have children choose a word from the list to match each.

a rabbit's fur (**softness**)
a starless night (**darkness**)
a ball (**roundness**)
top of a desk (**flatness**)
not feeling well (**sickness**)
very noisy (**loudness**)
deer running (**quickness**)

The suffix **less** means "without." **Fearless** means "without fear." The suffix **ness** means "a state of being." **Softness** means "being soft." Find and write the word that goes with each definition.

cloudless	darkness	fearless	loudness	softness	useless

1 without fear	2 being soft	3 being loud
fearless	softness	loudness

4 without use	5 without clouds	6 being dark
useless	cloudless	darkness

Use a word from above to complete each sentence.

7. Cleo is a brave and _fearless_ hunter.

8. Don't be fooled by the _softness_ of her fur.

9. Don't be fooled by the _loudness_ of her purr.

10. It's _useless_ to try to keep her indoors.

11. She goes out and hunts on sunny, _cloudless_ days.

12. She goes out and hunts in the _darkness_ of the night.

Spelling Connection

Read aloud each word and sentence below. Have one volunteer spell a word orally and another write it on the board.

playful	The puppy is **playful**.
helpful	Tad is **helpful** with chores.
seedless	Gina likes **seedless** grapes.
careless	Do not be **careless** with your math answers.
kindness	Our neighbors always show us **kindness**.

Multicultural Connection

Background Information Because of the great amount of snow that falls in Norway's mountains, skiing has been the country's most popular sport for over 2,000 years. When people from Norway emigrated to other countries, they brought skiing with them. Today the sport is popular around the world.

Activity Ask children how skiing might help them get around in a lot of snow. Discuss whether skiing is an easy sport to learn in your area.

Practicing the Skill

● Call attention to the Helpful Hint for adding suffixes on page 181. Then read aloud all the directions. Tell children they may use a **ful** word from the first section to write about the picture.

● Review the definitions and instructions on page 182. Stress the overlap between the two sections. Then have children complete both pages.

Extending the Skill Across the Curriculum

(Language Arts/Science)

Theme Activity

Materials: globe, flashlight

● Shine a flashlight on a globe to model while you explain that the northern hemisphere has less daylight during the winter than during the summer because of the position of the sun and Earth.

● Invite students to explain the relationship between the four seasons and the varying length of days from season to season. Ask them to tell at what time of year they most enjoy the outdoors and why they enjoy it.

● Tell children that from September to March in northern Norway, people do not tend to spend much time outdoors because it is dark almost all day. Have the class locate Norway and your state on the globe. Encourage children to read books like the one cited below about Norway's "dark days." Then have them use the words **darkness, blackness,** and **brightness** to write descriptions of Norwegian days.

Theme Book

Emberley, Michael. *Welcome Back, Sun*. New York: Little, Brown, 1993. A Norwegian family awaits the sun.

Portfolio

Have children add their descriptions to their portfolios.

Writing and Reviewing Suffixes ly, ful, less, ness

Objectives
- To write words ending in **ly** in context
- To review suffixes **ful, less, ness, ly**

Warming Up

Reviewing Vowel Pairs

Ask children to say and write words that contain one of these vowel pairs: **ai, ay, ea, ee, oa, oe, ow, ui, ue,** and **ie**.

★ Teaching the Lesson

- Read to the class "Swinging" on page 179. Then direct children to read silently the first stanza of the poem to find the word that ends in **ly**. Point out that the suffix **ly** often means "in a certain way." Ask a volunteer to tell what **slowly** means.

- On the board write base words to which **ly** can be added, for example, **quick, bright, soft,** and **loud**. Have volunteers add the suffix **ly** to each base word, tell the meaning of the new word, and use it in a sentence.

- On the board write: **fearful, fearless,** and **softness**. Have volunteers underline the suffix in each word, tell its meaning, and then use the word in a sentence.

Observational Assessment
Observe how readily children define each suffix.

ESL Activities
Refer to page 179J.

The suffix **ly** means "in a certain way." **Softly** means "in a soft way." Add the suffix **ly** to a base word from the box and write a new word to answer the question.

bright	soft	loud	glad

1. How does snow fall? — softly

2. How does the sun shine? — brightly

3. How does thunder boom? — loudly

4. How do you greet a friend? — gladly

brave	sweet	slow	quick

5. How does a snail crawl? — slowly

6. How does a hero act? — bravely

7. How does a deer run? — quickly

8. How does a bird sing? — sweetly

Taking Off — Write a question of your own that can be answered with a word that ends in **ly**. Exchange questions with a classmate.

LESSON 90: Writing Suffix **ly**   18

Multisensory *Activities*

Visual ■ Kinesthetic

How Do You March?

Materials: index cards

On index cards write **quickly, softly, slowly, loudly, quietly, swiftly,** and **nicely**. Have children stand in a line facing you. Hold up a card and invite a volunteer to read it. Then direct all children to march in place in a way that demonstrates the word. Use all the cards; have children identify each base word and suffix.

Visual ■ Auditory

Shining Brightly

Materials: dark blue mural paper, yellow crayon

Make a mural of the night sky. Include about twenty stars, and label each with a word ending in **ful, less, ness,** or **ly** (see pages 181–184). Point to one star. Ask a volunteer to read and define its label and then draw a line connecting it to another star. Continue the process for each connected star.

Find and write the word that goes with each definition.

| bravely | cheerful | fearless | hopeful | loudness |
| slowly | kindness | sadly | useless | |

1 without fear	2 being loud	3 in a slow way
fearless	loudness	slowly

4 full of cheer	5 in a sad way	6 without use
cheerful	sadly	useless

7 being kind	8 full of hope	9 in a brave way
kindness	hopeful	bravely

Add the suffix **ful, less, ness,** or **ly** so the word in **bold** print makes sense in each sentence. Write the new word.

10. Julie waited for a **cloud** night.   cloudless

11. She **quick** set up her telescope.   quickly

12. She saw the stars shining **bright**.   brightly

13. They twinkled in the **dark**.   darkness

84   LESSON 90: Reviewing Suffixes **ful, less, ness, ly**

Spelling Connection

Read aloud each word and sentence below. Have one volunteer spell a word orally and another write it on the board.

brightly   The stars were shining **brightly**.
darkness   The sky was filled with **darkness**.
colorful   The northern lights are **colorful**.
clearly   The signs were **clearly** marked.
cordless   **Cordless** phones must be recharged.

Computer Connection

Have children complete the Bullfrog Log Game from Spell It 3® (Davidson & Associates). Direct children to use the Junior Word List of words that end in the suffix **ly**. Then have them make a new list of words with the Editor. Tell children to include words that have the suffixes **ness, ful, less,** and **ly**. Then have them complete the Bayou Word Preview to practice the words.

Practicing the Skill

Read aloud the instruction box on page 183; have children complete the exercise. For page 184, have children read the directions and do one item in each exercise; then have them complete the page. Direct children to conclude with *Taking Off* on page 183.

Extending the Skill Across the Curriculum

(Language Arts/Science)

Theme Activity

● Make a KWL chart about stars. In the K column, write what children say they know about stars. In the W column, write what they want to know.

● Encourage children to read theme books, such as the one cited below, for information on stars. After research time, ask children what they learned. Record responses in the chart's L column.

● On chart paper, write this story; leave blanks for the suffixes:

One **cloudless** night I climbed a hill to watch the stars. I was **breathless** at the top. The night was filled with **darkness** except for the **brightly** sparkling stars. When I saw the **colorful** northern lights, I was **hopeful** that I would see a shooting star. With my telescope I saw more **clearly**. I was very excited to see....

● Have volunteers fill in the suffixes. Then invite children to use words ending in **ness, ly,** and **ful** to finish the story on paper. Provide theme books and the KWL chart for reference. Encourage sharing.

Theme Books

Kinsey-Warnock, Natalie. *On a Starry Night*. New York: Orchard Books, 1994. The night sky on a farm.

Portfolio

Have children add their story endings to their portfolios.

Suffixes er and est

Objectives
- To change the spelling of base words before adding **er** or **est**
- To write words ending in **er** and **est** in context

Warming Up

Reviewing Words Ending in le
Have children work in pairs. Invite them to write and exchange questions that include words ending in **le**(s). For example: Can a **turtle whistle**? Can **people** eat **apples**?

★ Teaching the Lesson

- Say, "(Child's name) runs fast, but a cat runs faster," and write **fast** and **faster** on the board. Ask what suffix was added to **fast** to compare the way a child and cat run. Circle **er**. Explain that **er** means "more" and is used when comparing two things.

- Say, "A cheetah is the fastest runner of all animals." Add the word **fastest** to the list on the board. Ask children to name the suffix added to **fast** to compare the cheetah's speed with that of other animals. Circle **est**. Explain that **est** means "most" and that it is used when comparing more than two things.

- Invite volunteers to read aloud the Helpful Hints on pages 185 and 186. Provide examples to clarify the double consonant and **y**-to-**i** spelling changes pointed out in the second hint. Then use classroom objects such as erasers, boxes, and books to illustrate **small, smaller, smallest; big, bigger, biggest;** and **heavy, heavier, heaviest.**

Helpful Hint

The suffix **er** is added to a base word to compare two things. The suffix **est** is added to compare more than two things.
small   small**er**   small**est**

★ **C**ompare the things. Add **er** or **est** to the base word and write the new word.

1	2	3
small	smaller	smallest

★ **A**dd **er** and **est** to each base word. Write the new word.

	er	**est**
4. fast	faster	fastest
5. cold	colder	coldest
6. soft	softer	softest
7. kind	kinder	kindest

Taking Off

Write three sentences to describe a race between a turtle, a snail, and an inchworm. Use the words **slow, slower,** and **slowest**.

LESSON 91: Writing Suffixes **er** and **est**   18

Multisensory *Activities*

Visual ■ Auditory

High, Higher, Highest
Recite again "Swinging" on page 179. Then direct children to read the poem silently to find the words that end in **er**. Write the words on the board as children name them, and ask volunteers to use each word in a sentence that compares two things. Then change each suffix to **est**, and have other volunteers use the new words in sentences that compare more than two things.

Visual ■ Kinesthetic

Picture This
On the board write **dark, high, long, thin, big, hot, windy, happy,** and **sunny**. Assign a base word to each child. Direct children to fold a sheet of paper into thirds and to write and illustrate their base word in one third. Then have them write and illustrate their base word with **er** and **est** in the other two thirds. Invite them to share their pictures and explain the changes made to the base words.

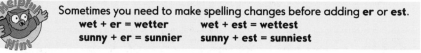

Sometimes you need to make spelling changes before adding **er** or **est**.

| wet + er = wetter | wet + est = wettest |
| sunny + er = sunnier | sunny + est = sunniest |

Double the final consonant and add **er** and **est** to each word. Write the new words.

	er	est
1. wet	wetter	wettest
2. thin	thinner	thinnest
3. big	bigger	biggest
4. hot	hotter	hottest

Change the **y** to **i** and add **er** and **est** to each word. Write the new words.

	er	est
5. sunny	sunnier	sunniest
6. bumpy	bumpier	bumpiest
7. happy	happier	happiest
8. lucky	luckier	luckiest

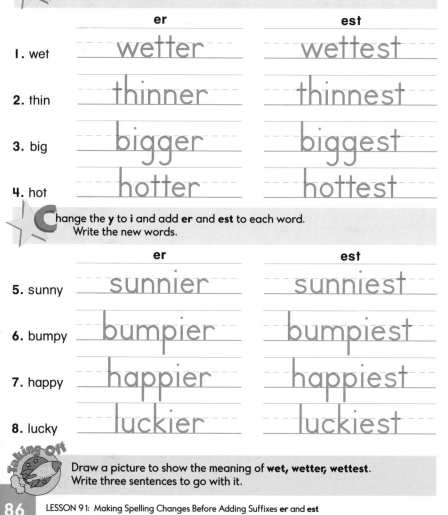

Taking Off
Draw a picture to show the meaning of **wet, wetter, wettest**. Write three sentences to go with it.

86 LESSON 91: Making Spelling Changes Before Adding Suffixes **er** and **est**

Spelling Connection

Read aloud each word and sentence below. Have one volunteer spell a word orally and another write it on the board.

fastest	Kim is the **fastest** swimmer on the team.
bigger	A bus is **bigger** than a car.
windier	Monday was **windier** than Tuesday.
hottest	August is often the **hottest** month.
darker	Starless nights are **darker** than nights lit by stars.

Practicing the Skill

Review the Helpful Hint on page 185. With the class, read both sets of directions and do the first two items in the first exercise before having children complete the page. Repeat the procedure for page 186. Then encourage children to try *Taking Off* on each page.

Extending the Skill Across the Curriculum

(Math/Language Arts)

Theme Activity

Materials: rulers, tape measures, yardsticks, written direction sheets

• Invite the class to go on a scavenger hunt in the classroom. Have each child work with a partner. Give each pair a ruler, tape measure, and yardstick. Give oral and written directions such as the following.

Find something that is:
  a. about 2 inches long
  b. more than 2 inches long
  c. less than 2 inches long
  d. about 4 feet tall
  e. less than 4 feet tall

• Invite each pair to list on the board the objects they found. Discuss the results as a class. Have children use words ending in **er** and **est** to compare the objects found.

• Invite children to look at the illustrations in the theme book cited below to make more comparisons.

📖 **Theme Book**

Diagram Group. *Comparisons*. New York: St Martin's Press, 1980. Illustrated source book for exploring measurement.

Observational Assessment
*During discussion note which children use **er** and **est** correctly.*

Reviewing and Assessing Suffixes

Objective
• To review and assess suffixes **er, est, ful, less, ness, ly, er, est**

Warming Up

Reviewing Consonant Digraphs
On the board list consonant digraphs **th, sh, wh, ch, ck, kn,** and **wr,** and the words **thick, ship, chat, then, shown, white,** and **know.** Challenge children to replace the digraph(s) in each word with one or more from the list to write a new word.

★ Teaching the Lesson

• Together, read the Poetry Poster "Swinging." Call on volunteers to point out words in the poem that contain **er.** Write these words on the board, and ask volunteers to use each in a sentence that compares two things. For example, "I am quick, but you are **quicker.**"

• Erase the suffix **er** from each word. Then invite volunteers to add **est** to the base words and to use the new words in sentences.

• On the board write **slowly, helpful, fearless,** and **quickness.** Ask volunteers to underline the suffix in each word and then use the suffix to define the word; for example, **slowly** means "in a slow way."

• Review the Helpful Hints on pages 181, 185, and 186. Call attention to the "suffix facts" such as, **fear + ful = fearful.** Invite children to write additional "suffix facts" to illustrate further each hint.

ESL Activities
Refer to page 179J.

Read the first sentence in each pair. Complete the second sentence by adding **er** or **est** to the word in **bold** print. Remember to make spelling changes if you need to.

1 Rabbits, zebras, and lions all run **fast.**

The lion is the ___fastest___ of the three animals.

2 Milly swings up **high** into the sky.

Mat swings up ___higher___ .

3 Jack is **tall.**

Jill is even ___taller___ .

4 90°F is **hot.**

95°F is ___hotter___ .

5 All the pencils are **thick.**

The first pencil is the ___thickest___ .

6 Sometimes Zach is a **messy** eater.

His baby sister is ___messier___ .

LESSON 92: Reviewing Suffixes **er** and **est**   18

Multisensory *Activities*

Visual ■ Kinesthetic

Comparing Apples and Oranges
On the board write incomplete sentences like these:

Apples are juicy, but oranges are _____.

Tortoises are slow, but snails are _____.

Tom is tall, Ricardo is taller, and Feng is _____.

Have children complete each sentence by adding the suffix **er** or **est** to the underlined word. Then challenge them to make up their own comparison sentences.

Visual ■ Auditory

Go to First Base
Materials: index cards

Draw a baseball diamond on the board. On index cards, write words with suffixes from pages 181–188. Ask children, one at a time, to choose a card and read the word. Tell children they can go to first base by naming the base word, to second by defining the word, to third by using the word in a sentence, and to home plate by naming another word with the same suffix.

1 full of fear	2 in a slow way	3 without use
fearful	slowly	useless

4 being dark	5 without a cloud	6 full of cheer
darkness	cloudless	cheerful

7 in a brave way	8 without fear	9 being loud
bravely	fearless	loudness

10 full of hope	11 in a quick way	12 being soft
hopeful	quickly	softness

Underline the word in parentheses that makes sense in each sentence.

13. It was the (**hottest**, **hotter**) day of the year.

14. I (**gladly**, **sadly**) agreed to go for a ride with Uncle Al.

15. We went up (**highest**, **high**) in the sky in a hot air balloon.

16. We flew over the (**taller**, **tallest**) of all the trees.

17. We flew (**faster**, **fast**) than the wind.

18. My brother thinks I'm a (**cloudless**, **fearless**) person.

19. I think I'm the (**luckiest**, **luckier**) person in the world.

20. I will always remember my uncle's (**kindness**, **softness**).

Reteaching *Activities*

Match Words
Materials: index cards

On the board write words with suffixes from pages 181–188. Write each base word on an index card, and display the cards in random order in a pocket chart. Invite children to take turns choosing a card and matching the base word with a word on the board. Have children use the suffix to define the word.

Sort Words
Materials: index cards

On the board write the headings "No Base Change," "Double the Final Consonant," and "Change y to i." Write base words from pages 185–187 on index cards. Invite children to choose a word, add the suffix **er** or **est**, and write the new word beneath the appropriate heading. Then challenge children to sort the words beneath the headings "Compares Two Things" and "Compares More Than Two Things."

Assessing the Skills

Check-Up Read the directions for the review on page 187 together. Ask children to explain when they must change the spelling of a base word before adding **er** or **est**. Model the first item for the class before asking children to complete the page.

The assessment on page 188 is a tool that will help you evaluate children's progress toward mastering suffixes. Before assigning the page, ask children to name a suffix used to compare two things and a suffix used to compare more than two things. Then read the directions together, model the first item in each set, and have children complete the page.

Observational Assessment Use your observational notes to decide whether reteaching is necessary.

Student Skills Assessment Record your evaluation of each child's mastery of his or her phonics skills on the checklist on pages 207–208 of the Student Edition.

Writing Conference Arrange conferences with individual children to review writing recently added to their portfolios. Encourage children to talk about how their writing is improving. Take notes on how well each child has been applying phonics skills to progress in writing. Pay particular attention to whether children seem able to incorporate suffix word-forms fluidly into their writing or whether the new words disrupt their progress.

Group together children who need further instruction on suffixes. Then conduct the *Reteaching Activities*.

Prefixes re and un

Objective
● To write words beginning with the prefixes **re** and **un** in context

Warming Up

Reviewing Contractions
Write these contractions on the board: **didn't, they'll, that's, we're, you've, let's, I'll, couldn't, you'll, don't, they're, I've,** and **shouldn't**. Have the class work in two teams. Ask a volunteer from Team 1 to say the first word of each contraction and a volunteer from Team 2 to say the second word. Switch roles halfway through.

★ Teaching the Lesson

● Invite one child to spell the word **spell** and another to respell the word. Write **respell** on the board and circle the prefix **re**. Tell children that the word part **re** added to the beginning of a word is a *prefix* that means "again," so **respell** means "spell again."

● Use ribbon to tie a bow; then ask a child to untie it. Write **untie** on the board and circle the prefix **un**. Do the same with **unhappy**. Tell children that **un** is a *prefix* that can mean "opposite of" or "not." Ask volunteers to tell the meanings of the words on the board and to name each prefix and base word.

● Write on the board **refill, remake, rebrush, unfair, unlock, unseen,** and **uncover**. Have children circle the prefix, underline the base word, and explain the meaning of each word.

A **prefix** is a word part added to the **beginning** of a base word to change its meaning or make a new word.
re + tie = retie   un + happy = unhappy   dis + honest = dishonest

The prefix **re** means "again." **Retie** means "tie again." Use the prefix **re** to write a word for each definition.

1 tie again	2 tell again	3 join again
retie	retell	rejoin
4 place again	5 fill again	6 pack again
replace	refill	repack
7 load again	8 use again	9 check again
reload	reuse	recheck

Add the prefix **re** to each base word and write the new word in the sentence.

pack   10. Josh had to ___repack___ his backpack.

fill   11. Deb had to ___refill___ the canteens.

tie   12. We'll leave as soon as I ___retie___ my shoe.

LESSON 93: Writing Prefix **re**   189

Multisensory *Activities*

Visual ■ Kinesthetic

Able or Unable?
On the board write the following list without the parentheticals:

    fold, unfold (paper)
    cover, uncover (hat)
    button, unbutton (coat)
    open, reopen (door)
    read, reread (book)
    tie, untie, retie (shoelace)
    write, rewrite (pencil)

Read the words with the class. Then ask volunteers to use classroom objects to demonstrate each group of words.

Visual ■ Auditory

Spell or Respell
On the board write: **build, lock, pack, true, tell, heat, happy, paint, seen,** and **write**. Direct children to add the prefix **un** or **re** to a word to answer clues you give. Give these clues: heat again; opposite of pack; not true; write again; opposite of lock; build again; not seen; tell again; paint again; not happy.

The prefix **un** means "not" or "to do the opposite of." **Unhappy** means "not happy." **Unpack** is the opposite of **pack**. Add the prefix **un** to the word in **bold** print to complete each sentence.

1. Someone who is not **happy** is _unhappy_.

2. The opposite of **pack** is _unpack_.

3. If something is not **safe**, it's _unsafe_.

4. The opposite of **button** is _unbutton_.

5. If you are not **able** to swim, you are _unable_ to swim.

6. The opposite of **roll** is _unroll_.

Add the prefix **un** to each base word and write the new word in the sentence.

safe   7. Without a helmet, skating is _unsafe_.

able   8. I've looked, but I'm _unable_ to find my helmet.

pack   9. I guess I'll _unpack_ my skating gear.

roll   10. I'll _unroll_ my sleeping bag and camp out instead.

90

LESSON 93: Writing Prefix **un**

Reviewing Prefixes
re, un, dis

Objectives
● To write words with the prefix **dis** in context
● To review prefixes **re, un, dis**

Warming Up

Reviewing Inflectional Endings

Read aloud the poem "Swinging." Direct children to raise their hands whenever they hear a word with the inflectional ending **ing**. Ask volunteers to write each **ing** word on the board, circle the inflectional ending, and underline the base word.

★ *Teaching the Lesson*

● Write these sentences on the board:
  Lee **likes** camping.
  Terry **dislikes** camping.
  Telling the truth is being **honest**.
  Telling a lie is being **dishonest**.

● Discuss how the meanings of **likes** and **honest** change when the prefix **dis** is added. Elicit from children that **dis** means "not" and that the new word is the *opposite* of the base word.

● On the board, write the base words listed below. Invite volunteers to add the prefix **dis** to each and then read the new word.

  loyal   trust
  agree   pleased
  appear   obey

● On the board write:
  Biking without a helmet is _____.
  Tina must _____ her camera with film.

Call on volunteers to fill in the blanks with words that begin with the prefix **re, un,** or **dis**.

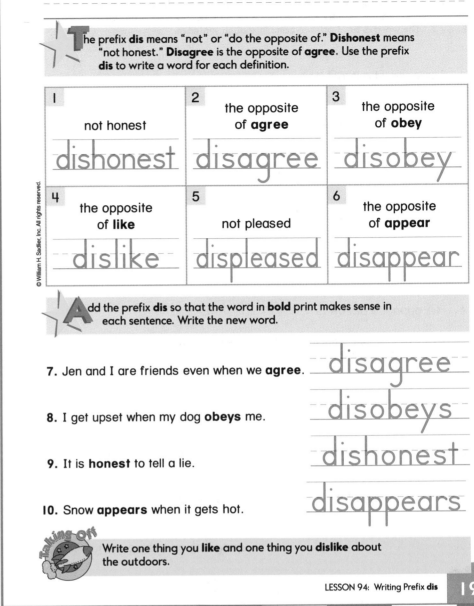

The prefix **dis** means "not" or "do the opposite of." **Dishonest** means "not honest." **Disagree** is the opposite of **agree**. Use the prefix **dis** to write a word for each definition.

1 not honest	2 the opposite of **agree**	3 the opposite of **obey**
dishonest	disagree	disobey
4 the opposite of **like**	5 not pleased	6 the opposite of **appear**
dislike	displeased	disappear

Add the prefix **dis** so that the word in **bold** print makes sense in each sentence. Write the new word.

7. Jen and I are friends even when we **agree**.   disagree

8. I get upset when my dog **obeys** me.   disobeys

9. It is **honest** to tell a lie.   dishonest

10. Snow **appears** when it gets hot.   disappears

Taking Off Write one thing you **like** and one thing you **dislike** about the outdoors.

LESSON 94: Writing Prefix **dis**   191

Multisensory *Activities*

Visual ■ Kinesthetic

Discover the Meaning

Materials: index cards, pocket chart, posterboard, red paper

Write these words on index cards and put them in a pocket chart: **dislike, dishonest, displease, disloyal, disobey, disappear, distrust, disorder, dismount, disapprove,** and **disconnect**. Write each word's meaning on red paper, and display the papers around the room. Invite children to match the definitions to the correct words.

Visual ■ Auditory

Instant Replay

Materials: construction paper

Assign to each child some of the words with prefixes from pages 179–184. Distribute strips of construction paper, and tell children to write one word on each strip. Direct them to fold back the prefix part of the strip to show only the base word. Have each child work with a partner to practice reading the words with and without the prefixes by turning the flap back and forth.

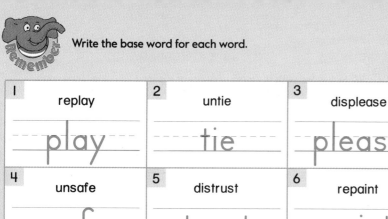

Write the base word for each word.

1 replay play	**2** untie tie	**3** displease please
4 unsafe safe	**5** distrust trust	**6** repaint paint
7 disagree agree	**8** rejoin join	**9** unafraid afraid

Fill in the circle next to the prefix that completes the word and makes sense in the sentence.

10. Let's take pictures before the sun ___appears.	● dis	○ un
11. Here's a good spot to ___pack our bags.	● un	○ dis
12. We'll ___load the camera so we don't run out of film.	○ dis	● re
13. Hold still or the pictures will be ___clear.	○ re	● un
14. That's a good shot of a boy ___locking his bike.	● un	○ dis
15. It's time to ___pack our bags and head home.	○ dis	● re

𝒮pelling Connection

Read aloud each word and sentence below. Have one volunteer spell a word orally and another write it on the board.

disorder   The bookshelf is in **disorder**.

dislikes   Tom **dislikes** loud music.

disconnect   Do not **disconnect** the phone.

rewind   **Rewind** the tape before returning it.

untie   Try to **untie** the ribbon without cutting it.

Practicing the Skill

● Review the meaning of the prefix **dis** at the top of page 191. Go over all directions, and have children complete the page. Use *Taking Off* to conclude this lesson's practice work.

● Tell children to write the base words of the words given in the first exercise on page 192. Then instruct them to mark the ovals of the prefixes they choose in the second exercise.

Extending the Skill Across the Curriculum

(Language Arts/Art)

Theme Activity

Materials: white and colored paper

● Write this paragraph, with blanks for the prefixes, on chart paper:

> Are your photos in **disorder**? Have they been **unseen** for years? Are they blurry and **unclear**? Have you **discovered** anything interesting? Ask your family whether you may choose some outdoor photos to **review** at school.

● Have children fill each blank with **un, re,** or **dis.** Then share the photography theme book cited below.

● Ask children to bring in two or three photos of interesting outdoor activities to frame. Show the class how to glue each picture onto a piece of white paper slightly bigger than the photo. Then have them glue that paper onto a colored sheet slightly larger than the white one.

● Have children include funny captions. Then make a photo display titled "Discover Outdoor Fun."

Theme Book

King, Dave. *My First Photography Book.* New York: Dorling Kindersly, 1994. Vivid photos for beginners.

Portfolio

After dismantling the display, have children add their photos and captions to their portfolios.

Reviewing and Assessing Prefixes re, un, dis

Objective
● To review and assess prefixes **re, un, dis**

Warming Up

Reviewing Plural

Ask a volunteer to tell the meaning of the word *plural*. On the board list these words: **book, clown, fox, owl, peach, cape, fish, buzz, swing,** and **sandwich.** Call on children to write each plural and to use it in a sentence.

★ *Teaching the Lesson*

● Say, "I like to lie in a hammock and **reread** my favorite book." Repeat the sentence. Ask which word begins with a prefix.

● Review the Helpful Hint on page 189. Ask children to name words that begin with the prefixes **re, un,** and **dis.** Write the words on the board and have volunteers use each word's prefix to define the word. For example, **reuse** means "use again." Then invite children to use each word in a sentence.

ESL Activities
Refer to page 179J.

Write a word with the prefix **re, un,** or **dis** for each clue. Then read the shaded letters down to find the answer to the question.

1	join again	r e j o i n
2	opposite of **tie**	u n t i e
3	opposite of **trust**	d i s t r u s t
4	draw again	r e d r a w
5	opposite of **load**	u n l o a d
6	opposite of **obey**	d i s o b e y
7	not true	u n t r u e
8	fill again	r e f i l l
9	use again	r e u s e
10	not able	u n a b l e

What can you do in the summer sun?

Have a lot of outdoor fun !

LESSON 95: Reviewing Prefixes 193

Multisensory *Activities*

Auditory ■ Visual

Bingo

Materials: nine-by-nine bingo grids, strips of paper

Generate a long, chalkboard list of nine-letter words that begin with prefixes **re, un,** and **dis.** Give each child a grid and strips of paper as "chips." Direct children to write any nine of the words horizontally in the spaces. Then randomly define the listed words. Have children cover words you define that appear on their grids. Three words covered wins.

Visual ■ Kinesthetic

Concentration

Materials: index cards

Have children work in pairs. Give each pair twelve cards. Ask children to write on half of the cards words that begin with **re, un,** and **dis**—two words per prefix. On the remaining cards, have them write a definition for each word. Tell partners to place each set facedown in a pile and to alternate turning over cards to match words with definitions.

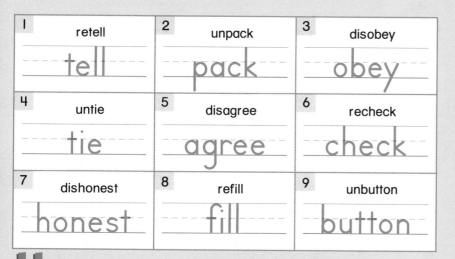

1 retell _tell_	2 unpack _pack_	3 disobey _obey_
4 untie _tie_	5 disagree _agree_	6 recheck _check_
7 dishonest _honest_	8 refill _fill_	9 unbutton _button_

Underline the word in parentheses that makes sense in each sentence.

10. Mom says that my treehouse is (**unable**, **unsafe**).

11. That (**disagrees**, **displeases**) Mom.

12. It makes me (**unhappy**, **unroll**), too.

13. We have to (**reuse**, **replace**) wood that has rotted.

14. We have to (**repaint**, **replay**) the whole thing.

15. We have to (**reload**, **retie**) the rope ladder.

16. I (**dislike**, **disappear**) scratchy sandpaper.

17. I'm (**untied**, **unable**) to reach the roof.

18. It's (**unclear**, **unafraid**) how we'll ever finish.

19. I wish I could (**disappear**, **distrust**) now!

20. I'd better stop complaining and (**refill**, **rejoin**) Mom at work.

LESSON 95: Assessing Prefixes

Reteaching *Activities*

What Do You Do?

On the board list words with prefixes from pages 189–194. Tell children you are going to ask questions that begin "What do you do…?" Direct them to choose from the word list to answer. Use conditional clauses such as:

if your shoelace is untied?
   (**Retie** it.)
before taking off your
   jacket? (**Unbutton** it.)

Know/Don't Know

Materials: index cards

On index cards, write words with prefixes from pages 189–194. On the back of the cards, write the definitions of the words. Have children work in groups. Give a set of cards to each group to study and quiz one another. You might have children sort the cards into "know" and "don't know" piles and work until each child's "don't know" pile disappears.

Assessing the Skills

Check-Up Have children read the directions on page 193. Call on a volunteer to explain how to complete the puzzle. Remind children that the page is a review. Then have them complete the page.

The assessment on page 194 is a tool that will help you evaluate children's progress mastering prefixes. Before assigning the page, ask a volunteer to restate the meaning of the prefixes **re, un,** and **dis**. (again; not; to do the opposite of) Read the directions together, and model the first item in each section. Then have children complete the page.

Observational Assessment Use your observational notes to decide whether reteaching is necessary.

Student Skills Assessment Turn to the checklist on pages 207–208 of the Student Edition, and record your evaluation of each child's skills' mastery.

Writing Conference Arrange conferences with individual children to review the writing they have recently added to their portfolios. Encourage children to talk about their photo captions and to point out particular phonics skills that are demonstrated in the captions. Ask children whether looking back on their work helps them see writing improvement that they might not have otherwise noticed. Take notes on each child's progress; use these notes to determine whether children are applying phonics skills successfully.

Group together children who need further instruction on prefixes. Then conduct the *Reteaching Activities*.

ESL Activities
Refer to page 179J.

Student Pages 195–196

Recognizing and Writing Synonyms

Objectives
- To recognize and write synonyms
- To rewrite a story using synonyms

Warming Up

Reviewing Vowel Digraphs

On the board write **oo, ea, ea, au,** and **aw**. Tell children you are going to ask riddles that can be answered with two words containing the same digraph. Use the following:

You toast it for this meal.
   (**bread/breakfast**)
It is tomato gravy you can put on these links. (**sauce/sausage**)
It is a chef who can make these sweet treats. (**cook/cookies**)
This young deer has these instead of feet. (**fawn/paws**)

★ *Teaching the Lesson*

- Write the following story on the board; underline the selected words:

I <u>enjoy</u> visiting my aunt. Her <u>home</u> is near the <u>sea</u>. We walk along the beach and watch the <u>big</u> <u>boats</u>. When the air is <u>breezy</u>, we wear our <u>jackets</u>. I take a <u>bucket</u> for collecting <u>beautiful</u> shells, which I use to make <u>presents</u>.

- Next to the story write: **pretty, windy, like, ocean, pail, house, gifts, ships, large,** and **coats**. Have a volunteer read the story aloud. Tell children that each underlined word can be matched with a word in the list that has about the same meaning. Explain that words that mean the same or nearly the same are called *synonyms*. Have volunteers write each story word next to its synonym in the list.

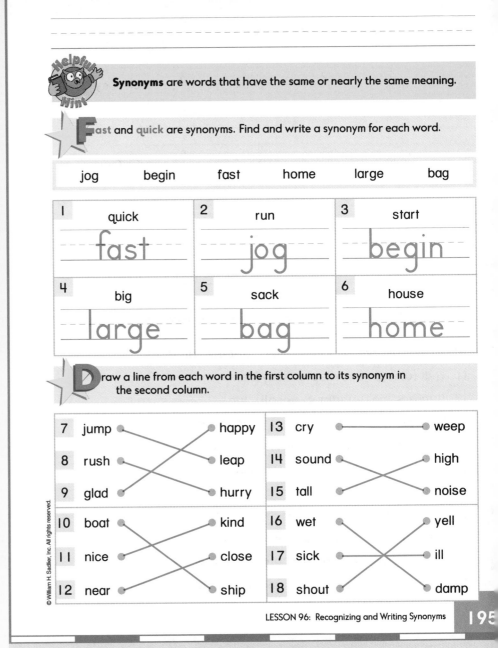

Synonyms are words that have the same or nearly the same meaning.

Fast and **quick** are synonyms. Find and write a synonym for each word.

| jog | begin | fast | home | large | bag |

1 quick	2 run	3 start
fast	**jog**	**begin**
4 big	5 sack	6 house
large	**bag**	**home**

Draw a line from each word in the first column to its synonym in the second column.

7	jump	—	leap
8	rush	—	hurry
9	glad	—	happy
10	boat	—	close
11	nice	—	kind
12	near	—	ship

13	cry	—	weep
14	sound	—	noise
15	tall	—	high
16	wet	—	ill
17	sick	—	yell
18	shout	—	damp

LESSON 96: Recognizing and Writing Synonyms **195**

Multisensory *Activities*

Auditory ■ Visual

Synonym Match

Materials: index cards

On separate index cards write **quick, sack, nap, friend, glad, weep, wet, yell, woods, below, almost,** and **enjoys.** Give one card to each child. Tell children to hold up their word when they hear you say its synonym. Say these words, one at time: **fast, bag, sleep, pal, happy, cry, damp, shout, forest, under, nearly,** and **likes.**

Visual ■ Auditory

Twins on Leaves

Materials: paper, leaf patterns, scissors

Assign a different pair of synonyms to each child. Have each child trace and cut out two leaves, write each word on a leaf, and then staple the leaves together fan-style at the stem or base so that both words can be read. Display the leaves on a bulletin board for children to read.

Circle the word in each list that means the same or nearly the same as the word in **bold** print.

1 **home**	2 **below**	3 **leave**	4 **pail**
door	over	stay	(bucket)
(house)	in	here	spoon
car	(under)	(go)	water
work	out	slow	sink

Write the word from the box that is a synonym for the word in **bold** print.

hike	likes	little	pal	tapped	trail

5. My **friend** Goldie likes to walk in the woods.　　pal

6. She **enjoys** collecting leaves.　　likes

7. One day Goldie went for a **walk**.　　hike

8. She decided to explore a new **path**.　　trail

9. She followed the path to a **small** house.　　little

10. Goldie **knocked** on the door.　　tapped

Taking Off

Was anyone home? Finish the story. In your sentences, you might use synonyms for the words **big** and **small**.

96 LESSON 96: Recognizing and Writing Synonyms

Spelling Connection

Read aloud each word and sentence below. Have one volunteer spell a word orally and another write it on the board.

gift Mom gave me a **gift** for my birthday.

forest Many insects live in the **forest.**

bucket Naomi filled the **bucket** with shells.

hurry Ted had to **hurry** to school.

nearly We collected **nearly** 100 bottles to recycle.

Practicing the Skill

● Have children review the meaning of *synonym*, given in the Helpful Hint on page 195. Then select volunteers to read the directions for each exercise. Do one item in each exercise together before having children complete the page. Follow the same procedure for page 196.

● Once children have completed both pages, invite them to do the *Taking Off* activity on page 196. Allow time for children to share their story endings with the class.

Extending the Skill Across the Curriculum

(Language Arts/Science)

Theme Activity

● Present the words **insects** and **bugs** as often-used synonyms. Point out that people all over are familiar with insects, or bugs. Invite children to share memorable experiences they have had with insects or bugs. List on the board bugs children have seen. Have children read theme books such as those cited below and report back to the class on insects of their choice.

● List these words on the board, and ask children to name synonyms for each of them: **big** (large, huge); **sacks** (bags); **thin** (skinny); **dirt** (soil); **earth** (ground); **small** (little, tiny); **long** (lengthy); **harm** (hurt); **gently** (carefully); **bold** (brave); **leap** (jump); **scampering** (running); **swaying** (swinging); and **plucks** (picks).

Theme Books

Souza, D.M. *Insects in the Garden*. Minneapolis, MN: Carolrhoda Books, 1991. Grasshoppers and mantises are highlighted.

Ryder, Joanne. *My Father's Hands*. New York: Morrow, 1994. A father helps his daughter discover the insect world.

Lesson 97

Student Pages 197–198

Recognizing and Writing Antonyms

Objectives
- To recognize and write antonyms
- To rewrite a story using antonyms

Warming Up

Reviewing Diphthongs
Read aloud each sentence below, and have children identify the three words with the same diphthong.

Wrap the **broiled** meat in **foil** to keep in the **moisture**.

It took **about** an **hour** to climb the **mountain**.

Troy ate **soybeans** and **oysters**.

The **crew chewed** gum and **blew** bubbles.

The **clown** with a **flower** took a **bow**.

★ Teaching the Lesson

- Write this rhyme on chart paper:

  Fast or slow, high or low,
  Sink or float, come or go.
  Short or long, weak or strong,
  Walk or run, right or wrong.

- Read the rhyme together. Ask children what they notice about the meanings of many of the words. Tell children that words with opposite or nearly opposite meanings are called *antonyms*. Have children identify each set of antonyms in the rhyme.

- Ask children to name an antonym for each of these words: **hot, inside, happy, wet, easy,** and **front**.

- Refer children to the poem "Swinging" on page 179, and have them find sets of antonyms in the poem.

ESL Activities
Refer to page 179J.

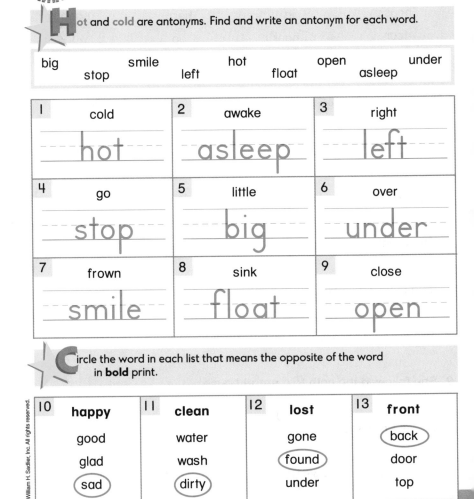

Antonyms are words that have the opposite or nearly the opposite meaning.

ot and **cold** are antonyms. Find and write an antonym for each word.

| big | smile | hot | open | under |
| stop | left | float | asleep | |

1 cold hot	2 awake asleep	3 right left
4 go stop	5 little big	6 over under
7 frown smile	8 sink float	9 close open

ircle the word in each list that means the opposite of the word in **bold** print.

10 **happy**	11 **clean**	12 **lost**	13 **front**
good	water	gone	(back)
glad	wash	(found)	door
(sad)	(dirty)	under	top

LESSON 97: Recognizing and Writing Antonyms

197

Multisensory *Activities*

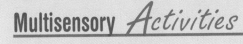

Visual ■ Kinesthetic

Win or Lose
Materials: index cards, pocket chart, shoe boxes

Have the class work in two teams. On the board write a list of words that have distinct opposites. On index cards write each word's antonym; display the cards in a pocket chart. Position two shoe boxes as "goals" for each team. Have players pull out cards with words that mean the opposite of the listed words and place them in their goal.

Visual ■ Tactile

In or Out of the Pool
Materials: index cards, boxes

Have children write ten pairs of antonyms, each word on a separate index card. Tell them to work with a partner and randomly place all their cards facedown in a shirt box "swimming pool." Then direct partners to alternate turning over two cards. If the cards are antonyms, the player takes the cards; otherwise, the cards stay in the pool.

197

Read about Cam. Then write a story about her friend Mac. Tell how he is the opposite of Cam. Replace each word in bold print with an antonym.

Cam is a **tall girl**. **She** sits in the **last** row of **her** class. **She** has **long** hair and freckles. **She always** wears glasses. When **she** writes, **she** uses **her right** hand.

Cam likes **winter** sports. **She** enjoys skating. Even on the **coldest** days, you'll find Cam outdoors.

Mac is a short boy. He sits in the first row of his class. He has short hair and freckles. He never wears glasses. When he writes, he uses his left hand.

Mac likes summer sports. He enjoys skating. Even on the hottest days, you'll find Mac outdoors.

98   LESSON 97: Recognizing and Writing Antonyms

Spelling Connection

Read aloud each word and sentence below. Have one volunteer spell a word orally and another write it on the board.

empty   The ice rink is **empty** in the summer.

under   Your shoe is **under** the table.

found   Someone **found** my lost dog.

strong   Exercise helps build **strong** muscles.

asleep   Tina fell **asleep** at 8:00.

Multicultural Connection

Background Information Although many people think the game of soccer originated in England, there is evidence that games in which players kicked balls and did not use their hands were played in ancient China and Japan. In the United States, soccer was introduced by immigrants and has since become increasingly popular.

Activity Discuss with children why soccer is called "football" in England. Ask them how English football differs from American football.

Practicing the Skill

● Review the meaning of antonyms on page 197. Have volunteers read the directions and lead the class through the first item in each exercise. Then have children complete the page.

● Read aloud the directions on page 198. Tell children to use extra paper if necessary to write their stories.

Extending the Skill Across the Curriculum

(Language Arts/Social Studies)

Theme Activity

● Talk with children about sports that are typically associated with winter and cold weather or summer and warm weather. Mention some sports that are highlighted at the summer and winter Olympic Games.

● List on the board typical summer and winter activities. Summer might include baseball, softball, swimming, soccer, and bicycling; winter might include football, skiing, ice skating, sledding, and hockey.

● Write the following stories about summer and winter sports on chart paper. Have children name antonyms for the underlined words. Write responses above the corresponding words.

Maria's favorite <u>summer</u> activity is swimming. She can't wait for the pool to <u>open</u> each June. <u>First</u>, she learned to <u>float</u> on her back. Now, she swims in the <u>shallow</u> end. Maria likes to watch her friend Julie dive off the <u>high</u> board. Maybe next year Maria will swim <u>faster</u>.

Omar likes to ice skate in the <u>winter</u>. The weather is <u>cold</u>, so he dresses warmly. Omar takes lessons to become a <u>good</u> skater. He already knows how to skate <u>fast</u> and how to <u>stop</u> <u>quickly</u>. Jumps are the <u>hardest</u>. Omar practices so that he will become a <u>strong</u> skater.

Lesson 98

Recognizing and Writing Homonyms

Objectives
- To recognize and write homonyms
- To write homonyms in sentences

Warming Up

Reviewing r-Controlled Vowels
Write the words below on the board; leave a blank for each missing vowel and **r** that appear together. Ask children to imagine they are walking outdoors and to name things they might see. Tell them to use words with the **r**-controlled vowels.

b__n	p__k	ac__n
b__d	t__tle	flow__
riv__	h__se	y__d
p__ch	d__t	c__b
f__m	th__n	spid__

★ *Teaching the Lesson*

- Write this chant on chart paper:

    A sailor went to sea, sea, sea,
    To see what he could see, see, see,
    And all that he could see, see, see,
    Was the bottom of the deep blue
        sea, sea, sea.

- Have children read the chant aloud. Ask them to identify words that sound the same. Point out the different spellings, and tell children that words that sound the same but are spelled and defined differently are called *homonyms*.
- Write these sentences on the board:

    A **bee** might **be** near the hive.
    The wind **blew** my **blue** hat away.
    Dad bought a **sail** on **sale**.
    I **ate** **eight** peanuts on our hike.

Ask volunteers to circle the homonyms and explain why they are homonyms.

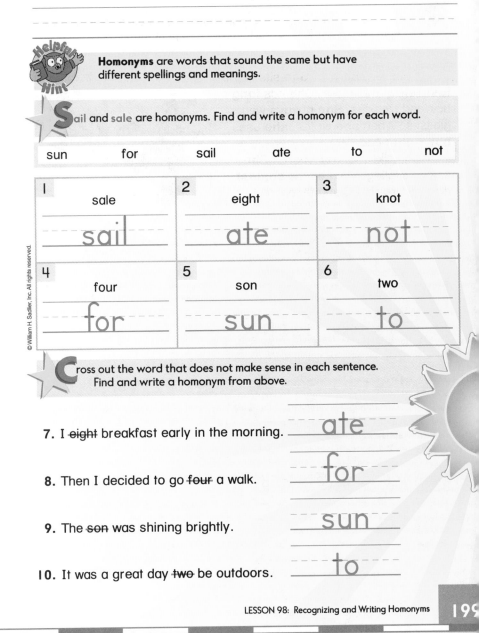

Homonyms are words that sound the same but have different spellings and meanings.

Sail and *sale* are homonyms. Find and write a homonym for each word.

sun	for	sail	ate	to	not

1 sale	2 eight	3 knot
sail	ate	not
4 four	**5** son	**6** two
for	sun	to

Cross out the word that does not make sense in each sentence. Find and write a homonym from above.

7. I ~~eight~~ breakfast early in the morning. _____ ate

8. Then I decided to go ~~four~~ a walk. _____ for

9. The ~~son~~ was shining brightly. _____ sun

10. It was a great day ~~two~~ be outdoors. _____ to

LESSON 98: Recognizing and Writing Homonyms 199

Multisensory *Activities*

Visual ■ Kinesthetic

I Have an Eye for Words

Materials: colored construction paper "blocks"

Write pairs of homonyms on colored paper "blocks," one word per block. Around the room, display one block from each pair; distribute the other blocks to children. Have each child, one at a time, walk around the room to search for the homonym block for his or her word. Then have children use the words in sentences.

Visual ■ Auditory

Write the Right Word

Write the sentences below on the board. Have children replace the incorrect word with its homonym.

Nights wore shining armor.
Did you **male** the letter?
I bit into a juicy **pair**.
She wore a wedding **wring**.
The dog wagged its **tale**.
Summer begins in a **weak**.
Can you **here** the music?
The house is made of **would**.
A **heard** of cows ate grass.
Sue **red** two books last week.

Circle two words in each box that sound the same but have different spellings and meanings.

1	(tale)	tall	2	ride	(right)	3	reed	(road)
	(tail)	tell		(write)	white		ride	(rode)
4	knot	note	5	(dear)	deep	6	weed	(weak)
	(night)	(knight)		(deer)	deal		(week)	wood

Circle and write the word that completes each sentence.

7. Lashanda and I ___made___ little toy boats.   (made) maid

8. Mine was red and hers was ___blue___.   blew (blue)

9. We put paper ___sails___ on the top.   sales (sails)

10. We put our boats in the ___creek___.   (creek) creak

11. We decided to race ___our___ boats.   hour (our)

12. The wind ___blew___ the sails.   (blew) blue

13. Lashanda and ___I___ clapped.   eye (I)

14. Lashanda ___won___ the race.   one (won)

200

LESSON 98: Recognizing and Writing Homonyms

Spelling Connection

Read aloud each word and sentence below. Have one volunteer spell each word orally and another write it on the board.

deer   Ravi saw two **deer** on the path.
would   I **would** like to see a moose.
night   Sometimes animals come out at **night**.
meet   I would not like to **meet** a bear in the woods.
heard   We **heard** the hoot of an owl.

Practicing the Skill

● Have children review the meaning of *homonym* in the Helpful Hint on page 199. Go over all directions. Remind children to cross out words used incorrectly in the second exercise. Then have them complete the page.

● Read aloud the directions for both exercises on page 200. Then have children complete the page.

Extending the Skill Across the Curriculum

(Language Arts/Science)

Theme Activity

● Ask children to describe outdoor places where they enjoy walking. Then share with the class nature poems from the theme book cited below. Have children point out any homonyms they hear.

● Write the following story on chart paper; underline each homonym.

I like to walk in the early morning <u>son</u>. Sometimes the sky is <u>blew</u> and cloudless. The <u>flours</u> look <u>sew</u> pretty with drops of <u>do</u> on them. <u>Eye</u> sometimes walk along the <u>creak</u>. Last <u>weak</u> I saw a <u>dear</u>. On other days I stroll to the <u>see</u>. I like to <u>bee</u> <u>their</u> to watch white <u>sales</u> on the water. If I close my eyes, I can <u>here</u> the waves.

Read aloud the story. Challenge children to replace each underlined word with a homonym that makes sense and to list on paper the homonym pairs.

Theme Book

Paladino, Catherine. *Land, Sea, & Sky: Poems to Celebrate the Earth*. New York: Little, Brown, 1993. Nature poems and photos.

Portfolio

Suggest that children put their homonym lists in their portfolios.

Reviewing Synonyms, Antonyms, and Homonyms

Objectives
- To write synonyms, antonyms, and homonyms in a crossword puzzle
- To match synonyms and antonyms
- To write homonyms in context

Warming Up

Reviewing Compound Words
On the board write the sentences below. Have children use two words in each to make a compound word.

We put the new **sail** on the **boat**.
The **bee** flew back to its **hive**.
Keesha put the **mail** in the **box**.
The **light** from the **moon** is bright.
Sue put a **cloth** on the **table**.

★ Teaching the Lesson

- Have children look at the poem "Swinging" on page 179. Ask them to find the word **quicker** in the poem; then ask them to find a *synonym* for **quicker** and an *antonym* for **quicker**.
- Write these words on the board: **sea, eye, threw, new,** and **stair**. Ask children to search the poem for *homonyms* for the words on the board. Discuss the different spellings and meanings of each homonym pair.
- Write these sets of words on the board, and have children identify them as synonyms, antonyms, or homonyms: **asleep/awake, wish/hope, forest/woods, nose/knows, simple/easy, wide/narrow, float/sink, fix/repair, flower/flour, lost/found, plane/plain,** and **thin/thick**.

ESL Activities
Refer to page 179J.

201

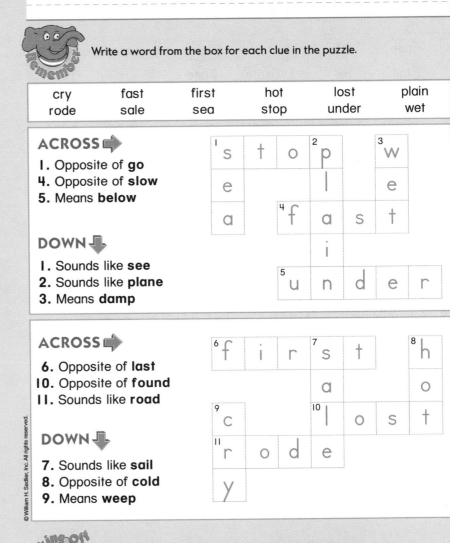

Write a word from the box for each clue in the puzzle.

cry	fast	first	hot	lost	plain
rode	sale	sea	stop	under	wet

ACROSS ➡
1. Opposite of **go**
4. Opposite of **slow**
5. Means **below**

DOWN ⬇
1. Sounds like **see**
2. Sounds like **plane**
3. Means **damp**

Puzzle 1 answers:
1. s t o p
2. p (l a n e) → l, 3. w e t
e
a / 4. f a s t
i
5. u n d e r

ACROSS ➡
6. Opposite of **last**
10. Opposite of **found**
11. Sounds like **road**

DOWN ⬇
7. Sounds like **sail**
8. Opposite of **cold**
9. Means **weep**

Puzzle 2 answers:
6. f i r s t, 7. (s a)... 8. h
o
9. c / 10. l o s t
11. r o d e
y

Write a sentence using two or more homonyms. For example, "We **rode** down the **road** and saw a **plane** land on the **plain**."

Multisensory *Activities*

Visual ■ Tactile

Pick and Choose
Materials: index cards

Write the headings "Synonyms" and "Antonyms" on the board. On separate index cards, write sea/ocean; stay/remain; low/high; cry/laugh; old/new; home/house; talk/chat; buy/sell; hard/soft; begin/start; breezy/windy; front/back; glad/happy; search/look; few/many; before/after.

Have children arrange the cards under the correct headings.

Auditory ■ Visual

Let's Do What's Due
Materials: drawing paper

Assign to each child a homonym pair (e.g., **flower/flour, pair/pear, knight/night, road/rode, ant/aunt, blew/blue, sale/sail**). Tell children to divide a sheet of drawing paper in half and to illustrate one word on each side. Direct them also to write each word in a sentence below its illustration. Put the pages together into a class book.

Draw a line from a word in the first column to its synonym in the second column.

1	home		nap
2	sleep		ill
3	sick		house

4	bag		begin
5	friend		pal
6	start		sack

Draw a line from a word in the first column to its antonym in the second column.

7	little		front
8	long		big
9	back		short

10	out		open
11	close		in
12	awake		asleep

Cross out the word that does not make sense in each sentence. Find and write the correct word.

I	new	to	made	wood

13. Dad ~~maid~~ a swing for me.   made

14. He used a piece of ~~would~~ for the seat.   wood

15. Dad and ~~eye~~ hung the swing in a tree.   I

16. I like my ~~knew~~ swing.   new

17. Watch me swing ~~two~~ and fro.   to

202   LESSON 99: Reviewing Synonyms, Antonyms, and Homonyms

Spelling Connection

Read aloud each word and sentence below. Have one volunteer spell a word orally and another write it on the board.

below The whale disappeared **below** the surface.

nearly Zoe **nearly** touched the whale.

begin It is time to **begin** the search.

wood The boat was made of **wood**.

empty Our thermos was **empty**.

Practicing the Skill

● Ask a volunteer to read aloud the directions on page 201. Do the first items across and down together; then have children complete the crossword.

● Ask volunteers to read aloud all the directions on page 202. Stress that the first exercise focuses on synonyms; the second, antonyms; the third, homonyms. Then have children complete the page.

● Use *Taking Off* on page 201 to promote creativity in writing. Allow time for class sharing.

Extending the Skill Across the Curriculum

(Language Arts/Science)

Theme Activity

● Ask children to tell about animals they have observed in their neighborhoods or at a zoo.

● Tell children that some people go on whale-watching boat trips. Explain that whales are mammals—they give birth to live young and breathe air with their lungs. Children might enjoy reading about whale watching. Suggest the theme book cited below.

● On the board write:

The humpback whale was <u>large</u>.
We saw whales <u>leap</u> into the air.
Two whales swam on the <u>left</u> side of the boat.
Whales must keep their skin <u>dry</u>.
Whales live in the <u>see</u>.
The whale's <u>tale</u> was black.

Have volunteers write synonyms above the first two underlined words, antonyms above the second two, and homonyms above the last two.

Theme Book

Weller, Frances Ward. *I Wonder If I'll See a Whale*. New York: Philomel, 1991. On a whale boat.

Observational Assessment

Observe whether children can correctly identify synonyms, homonyms, and antonyms.

202

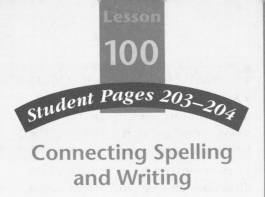

Connecting Spelling and Writing

Objectives
- To say, spell, sort, and write homonyms
- To write a poem using spelling words

Warming Up

Reviewing Contractions
Have children name contractions for word pairs such as: **does not, she will, you have, we are, I am,** and **he is.**

★ Teaching the Lesson

- On the board write the question "Can you see the sea?" Ask a volunteer to read the question and underline the homonyms. Remind children that homonyms sound the same but have different meanings.

- Say a spelling word, and use it in a sentence. For example: "**to**; Let's go **to** the lake." Invite children to say the word, spell it, and then say the word again. Have them do the same for its homonym. Ask a volunteer to use the homonym in a sentence.

- Continue with these sentences:
  Is this boat for **sale**? (**sail**)
  I have a **new** boat. (**knew**)
  My boat has **four** sails. (**for**)
  The wind **blew** the boat. (**blue**)
  I never sail at **night**. (**knight**)

Practicing the Skill

Read with the class the directions and the spelling words on page 203. Then have children complete the page.

Spell and Write Say and spell each word in the box. Then write six pairs of homonyms.

new	
blew	
sale	
too	
for	
to	
knew	
night	
sail	
knight	
blue	
four	

1. new / knew
2. blew / blue
3. sale / sail
4. too / to
5. for / four
6. night / knight

LESSON 100: Connecting Spelling and Writing   203

Multisensory *Activities*

Auditory ■ Kinesthetic

Homonym Riddles

Invite children to write homonym pairs to answer riddles such as these:

What goes on a boat and goes on in a store? (**sail/sale**)

What names a color and tells about the wind? (**blue/blew**)

What names a time of day and someone who wears armor? (**night/knight**)

Kinesthetic ■ Visual

Picture Dictionary

Materials: index cards

Have each child write a spelling word on one side of an index card. Ask them to illustrate the word or write its meaning on the other side. Gather the cards, and hold up each picture or definition one at a time. Direct children to study the clue and then say the word, spell it, and say the word again. Turn the card around so that children can check their spelling.

new	blew	sale	too	for	to
knew	night	sail	knight	blue	four

LESSON 100: Connecting
Spelling and Writing

204

Spelling Connection

Suggest that children write definitions for each pair of homonyms on page 204. Then direct them to use the definitions as clues to link each pair of words in a simple crossword puzzle. Provide this sample.

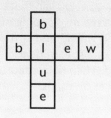

Across: What the wind did
Down: The color of the sky

Computer Connection

Have children use Reading & Phonics Challenge!™ (Brighter Child™ Interactive) for Grade 2 to practice skills taught in this unit. Children can use the menu to practice classifying compound words, antonyms, and synonyms, as well as contractions, prefixes, and inflectional endings **ing** and **ed**.

The Writing Process

Tell children that they will write a poem about summer. Point out that a poem can be a "word picture"(picture painted in words) and that it may or may not have words that rhyme. Have a volunteer read aloud the directions on page 204.

Brainstorm Ask children to tell what they think of when they hear the word *summer*. Elicit what they can see, taste, hear, smell, and touch during the summer. Record their responses in five columns, one for each sense, on the board.

Write Have children write their poems on separate sheets of paper. Tell them to try to include spelling words from page 203. If children seem to need help getting started, provide a sample couplet, such as:

> Blue skies,
> Peach pies.

Revise Suggest that children reread their poems to check whether they have painted a word picture. When they are satisfied with their images, have children write final versions of their poems in the space provided on page 204.

Share Have volunteers take turns reading their poems to the class.

Publish Ask children to illustrate their poems for a class book.

Observational Assessment
Observe whether children are adept at painting a picture in words.

Extending the Skill

Invite children to write additional poems about any of the other seasons. Suggest that they make a five-column "sense list" of what that season makes them think of and include items from the list in their new poems. Direct children to illustrate their poems, and incorporate them into the class book.

204

Integrating the Language Arts

Objectives
- To use oral and written language to extend the theme
- To recognize suffixes, prefixes, synonyms, antonyms, and homonyms in context

Background Information

The walls of the Grand Canyon reveal colorful layers of rock that were once part of a mountain range. The running water of the Colorado River carved this large canyon into the earth millions of years ago. Many animals, including mules, deer, mountain lions, bobcats, coyotes, bats, birds, and squirrels, live within the canyon.

★ Teaching the Lesson

- Have children look at the pictures on page 205. Discuss possible captions. Ask children to share what they already know about the Grand Canyon.

- Have a volunteer read aloud the text. Then ask children to skim the text for words that have prefixes and suffixes. Next, have them name synonyms for **boat, trail,** and **walk;** antonyms for **biggest, least, oldest, far, after,** and **down;** and homonyms for **to, do,** and **for**.

Oral Language Development
Ask children what they think it would be like to hike into the canyon. Have them describe an imaginary hike or mule ride into the depths of the canyon.

ESL Activities
Refer to page 179J.

Let's read and talk about Grand Canyon National Park.

20¢

It's the biggest. It's the oldest. It's the most unusual. It's Grand Canyon National Park, and it's filled with things to do. You can take a tour bus. You can take a boat. If you're twelve years old, you can ride a mule. Anyone can choose a trail and go for a hike. But don't go too far. Remember that after you walk down, you have to climb back up!

Think about hiking down into the Grand Canyon. What would be fun? What would be difficult?

LESSON 101: Suffixes, Prefixes, Synonyms, Antonyms, and Homonyms in Context **205**

Reading and Writing Connection

Help children locate the Grand Canyon on a map of the western states. Distribute outline maps of the states touched by the canyon, and have children color the canyon and Colorado River.

Provide research materials about the Grand Canyon. Have children work in groups to write reports on a Grand Canyon topic, such as Native Americans who live in or near the canyon; indigenous animals or plants; fossils; hiking; rafting on the Colorado River; canyon legends.

Social Studies Connection

Tell children that several Native American peoples live on land around the Grand Canyon. Point out that the Navajo and Hopi tribes live just east of the canyon, and the Havasupai people live in a small canyon off the Grand Canyon. Explain that the name *Havasupai* means "people of the blue-green water" and comes from the color of a stream near the tribe's homeland. Then help children locate these places on maps.

Check-Up Circle the word in each list that means the **same** or **nearly the same** as the word in **bold** print.

1 **run**	2 **big**	3 **glad**	4 **shout**
walk	small	sleepy	(yell)
legs	(large)	(happy)	whisper
(jog)	thin	sad	talk

5 **begin**	6 **rush**	7 **noise**	8 **quick**
write	soon	hear	slow
(start)	go	quiet	(fast)
end	(hurry)	(sound)	still

Circle two words in each row that have **opposite** meanings.

9.	(stop)	look	car	(go)
10.	door	(front)	(back)	open
11.	smooth	(clean)	garden	(dirty)
12.	(in)	(out)	last	next
13.	(left)	new	quiet	(right)
14.	below	(lost)	(found)	weak

Circle two words in each box that **sound the same** but have different spellings and meanings.

15		16		17	
mad	(made)	(knot)	(not)	reed	ride
mud	(maid)	note	knit	(road)	(rode)

18		19		20	
door	(dear)	(blew)	blend	tall	(tail)
(deer)	do	blind	(blue)	tell	(tale)

206   LESSON 101: Assessing Synonyms, Antonyms, and Homonyms

Reteaching *Activities*

Same and Different

List these words on the board: **sack, begin, ship, weep, repair, pal, glad, home, giggle, gift, swift, ocean, tiny, tardy,** and **damp.** Challenge children to name synonyms for each word.

Write another list that includes **before, hot, laugh, dirty, easy, first, float, happy, lost, night, open, over, quiet, left,** and **shallow.** Invite the class to name antonyms for each word.

It Blew Across the Blue Sky

Materials: mural paper, index cards, small shopping bag

On mural paper, draw a hot-air balloon with a small shopping bag "basket." On the balloon write: **blue, by, dear, eight, flour, here, knight, know, meat, new, oar, pain, plane, rap, right, sea, some, sun, threw, two, wait, weak, whole, won,** and **would.** On index cards, write matching homonyms. Have children find the homonyms and "send up" the cards in the basket.

Assessing the Skills

Check Up Have children review the Helpful Hint definitions of *synonym, antonym,* and *homonym* on pages 195, 197, and 199. Then have a volunteer read aloud the directions on page 206. Suggest that students label the appropriate sections **S** (synonym), **A** (antonym), and **H** (homonym). Then have them complete the page.

Observational Assessment Review observational notes you have made throughout this unit. Use them to assess children's progress with suffixes, prefixes, synonyms, antonyms, and homonyms and to decide whether reteaching is necessary.

Student Skills Assessment Use the results of the assessment on page 206 to fill in the checklist on pages 207–208 of the Student Edition.

Writing Conference Meet with each child individually to discuss his or her portfolio writing from this unit. Encourage children to discuss particular strengths and improvements, and to identify difficult areas for future focus. Make notes about each child's progress to determine whether the child is applying phonics skills successfully. Challenge children to consider whether they could make their work better by substituting synonyms or antonyms for some of the words used.

Group together students who need further instruction on synonyms, antonyms, or homonyms. Then conduct the *Reteaching Activities.*

At this time, you might refer to the alternative assessment methods on page 179C of the Teacher's Edition.

Take-Home Book Remind children to complete at home the *Take-Home Book* for Unit 8.

Name _____   Year 19___ – 19___

STUDENT SKILLS ASSESSMENT CHECKLIST

☑ Assessed   ☒ Retaught   ■ Mastered

Unit 1

Initial, Medial, and Final Consonants
❑ Initial Consonants
❑ Final Consonants
❑ Medial Consonants

Unit 2

Short Vowels
❑ Short Vowel **a**
❑ Short Vowel **i**
❑ Short Vowel **o**
❑ Short Vowel **u**
❑ Short Vowel **e**

Unit 3

Long Vowels
❑ Long Vowel **a**
❑ Long Vowel **i**
❑ Long Vowel **o**
❑ Long Vowel **u**
❑ Long Vowel **e**

Unit 4

Variant Consonant Sounds and Consonant Blends
❑ Soft and Hard **c**
❑ Soft and Hard **g**
❑ Initial **l**-blends
❑ Initial **r**-blends
❑ Initial **s**-blends
❑ Final Consonant Blends

Unit 5

Compound Words, y as a Vowel, Consonant Digraphs, and r-controlled Vowels
❑ Compound Words
❑ Two-Syllable Words
❑ **y** as a Vowel
❑ Initial Consonant Digraphs **th, sh, wh, ch**
❑ Final Consonant Digraphs **ck, th, sh, ch**
❑ Consonant Digraph **kn**
❑ Consonant Digraph **wr**
❑ **ar**-words
❑ **or**-words
❑ **er**-words, **ir**-words, **ur**-words

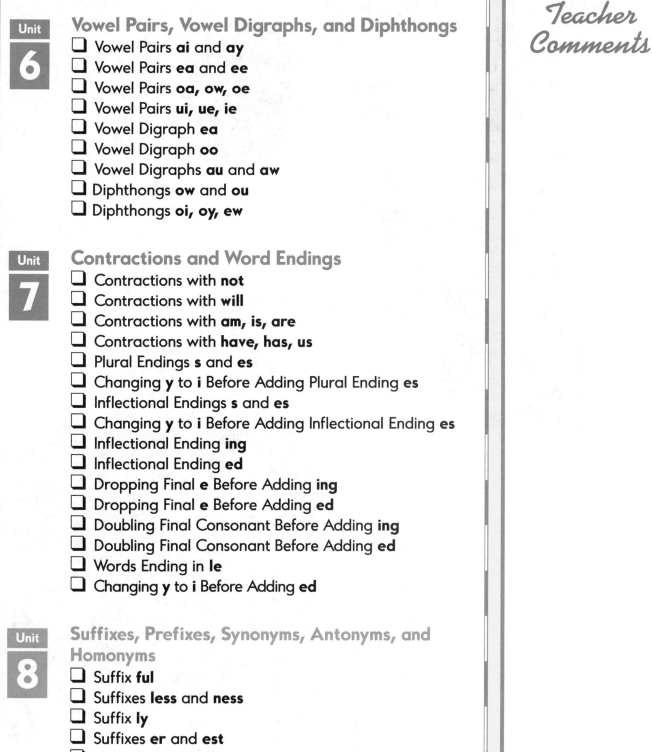

Unit 6 — **Vowel Pairs, Vowel Digraphs, and Diphthongs**
- ❏ Vowel Pairs **ai** and **ay**
- ❏ Vowel Pairs **ea** and **ee**
- ❏ Vowel Pairs **oa, ow, oe**
- ❏ Vowel Pairs **ui, ue, ie**
- ❏ Vowel Digraph **ea**
- ❏ Vowel Digraph **oo**
- ❏ Vowel Digraphs **au** and **aw**
- ❏ Diphthongs **ow** and **ou**
- ❏ Diphthongs **oi, oy, ew**

Unit 7 — **Contractions and Word Endings**
- ❏ Contractions with **not**
- ❏ Contractions with **will**
- ❏ Contractions with **am, is, are**
- ❏ Contractions with **have, has, us**
- ❏ Plural Endings **s** and **es**
- ❏ Changing **y** to **i** Before Adding Plural Ending **es**
- ❏ Inflectional Endings **s** and **es**
- ❏ Changing **y** to **i** Before Adding Inflectional Ending **es**
- ❏ Inflectional Ending **ing**
- ❏ Inflectional Ending **ed**
- ❏ Dropping Final **e** Before Adding **ing**
- ❏ Dropping Final **e** Before Adding **ed**
- ❏ Doubling Final Consonant Before Adding **ing**
- ❏ Doubling Final Consonant Before Adding **ed**
- ❏ Words Ending in **le**
- ❏ Changing **y** to **i** Before Adding **ed**

Unit 8 — **Suffixes, Prefixes, Synonyms, Antonyms, and Homonyms**
- ❏ Suffix **ful**
- ❏ Suffixes **less** and **ness**
- ❏ Suffix **ly**
- ❏ Suffixes **er** and **est**
- ❏ Spelling Changes Before Adding **er** and **est**
- ❏ Prefix **re**
- ❏ Prefix **un**
- ❏ Prefix **dis**
- ❏ Synonyms
- ❏ Antonyms
- ❏ Homonyms

Teacher Comments

Name _____

Friends of Mine

3

Jan is my pen pal. We write letters to each other.

Fold

Fold

Think about your best friend and what you like to do together. Then draw a picture.

Kareem is my buddy. We ride bikes together on Saturdays.

8

9

T27

Directions: Help your child cut and fold the book. Read it together several times. Have your child identify beginning and ending consonants.

UNIT 1: Take-Home Book

Name

Water's Song

Water lapping on the sand.

Fold

Fold

Seas carrying giant ships
Taking people on long trips.

8

Oceans sending pretty shells,

T29

Directions: Help your child cut and fold the book. Read it together several times. Have your child find the rhyming words. Ask what vowel sounds are in the words.

UNIT 2: Take-Home Book

Raindrops falling on city blocks,

Rivers cutting through the land,

Fold

Fold

Waves crashing on ocean rocks

Water pumped from farmers' wells.

1

Tree Leaves and Seeds

Fold

3

Pine trees and blue spruce have needles for leaves. They keep their leaves all year.

Fold

Draw a picture of a leaf or a seed. Write its name.

8

Some seeds are inside fruit. Can you describe the seed of an apple, an orange, a lime, a date, or a peach?

6

Directions: Help your child cut and fold the book. Read it together several times.
Have your child find words with vowels that say their own names.

UNIT 3: Take-Home Book

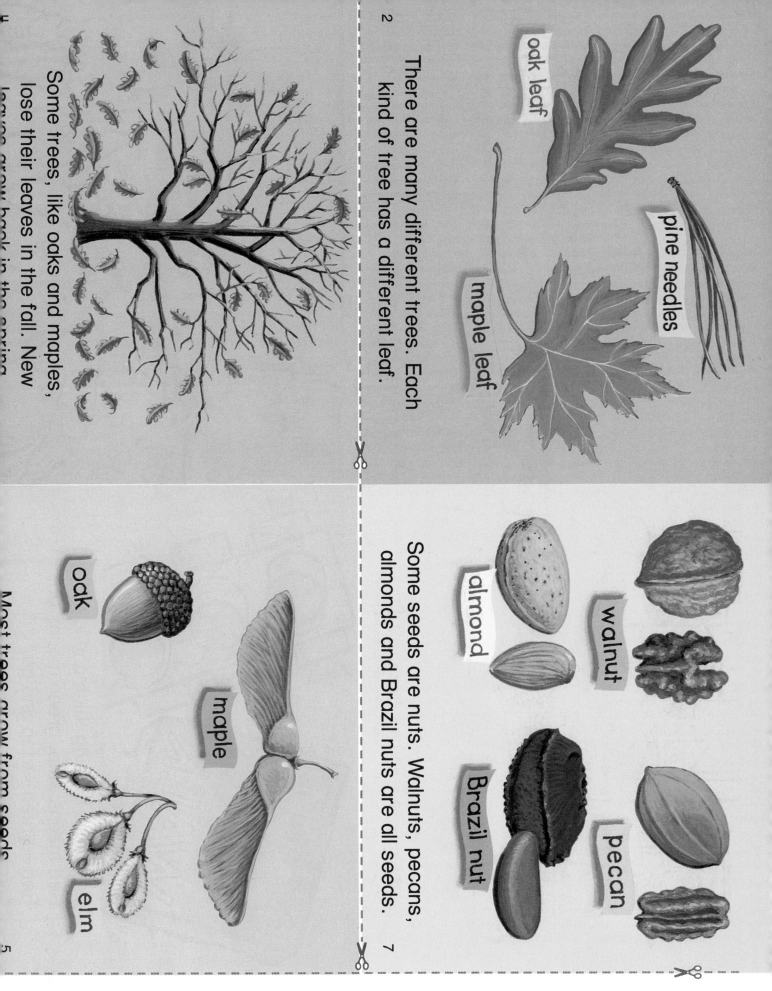

2

There are many different trees. Each kind of tree has a different leaf.

oak leaf

pine needles

maple leaf

4

Some trees, like oaks and maples, lose their leaves in the fall. New leaves grow back in the spring.

5

Most trees grow from seeds.

oak

maple

elm

7

Some seeds are nuts. Walnuts, pecans, almonds and Brazil nuts are all seeds.

almond

walnut

Brazil nut

pecan

Name _____

City Beat

Cars and trucks are slow or fast,
Blocks of people move right past.
Slow—fast—move right past.

Uptown, downtown, children say,
It's the place to live and play.
Uptown—downtown—live and play.

Lights are blinking, high and low,
Red means stop, green means go.
Red—green—stop and go.

DON'T WALK
WALK

8

6

Directions: Help your child cut and fold the book. Read it together several times.
Have your child find words with consonant blends like **tr** and **sp** and words
with soft and hard **c** and **g** like **cent, cat, gym,** and **goat.**

T33

UNIT 4: Take-Home Book

East—west —city's best.
Think the city is the best.
Boys and girls from east and west

Up—down—make it quick!
Elevators go up quick.
Giant buildings made of brick,

Trains—folks—to and fro.
Trains with folks go to and fro.
Under streets, down below,

Sing—dance—to the beat.
Spinning feet step to the beat.
Music, dancing, friends to meet,

Fold

Name _____

Magic Carpet Ride

Fold

1

Inside the trunk under some shirts was a purple carpet. The note on the carpet said, "I will take you anywhere you wish to go."

Fold

3

If you had a magic carpet, where would you go? Draw a picture and write about it.

8

Then the children visited China.
They saw a furry panda eating bamboo.

6

Directions: Help your child cut and fold the book. Read it together several times. Have your child find words with consonant digraphs **th**, **sh**, **wh**, **ch**, **ck**, **wr**, and **kn**. Look for compound words and words with **ar**, **or**, **ir**, and **ur**.

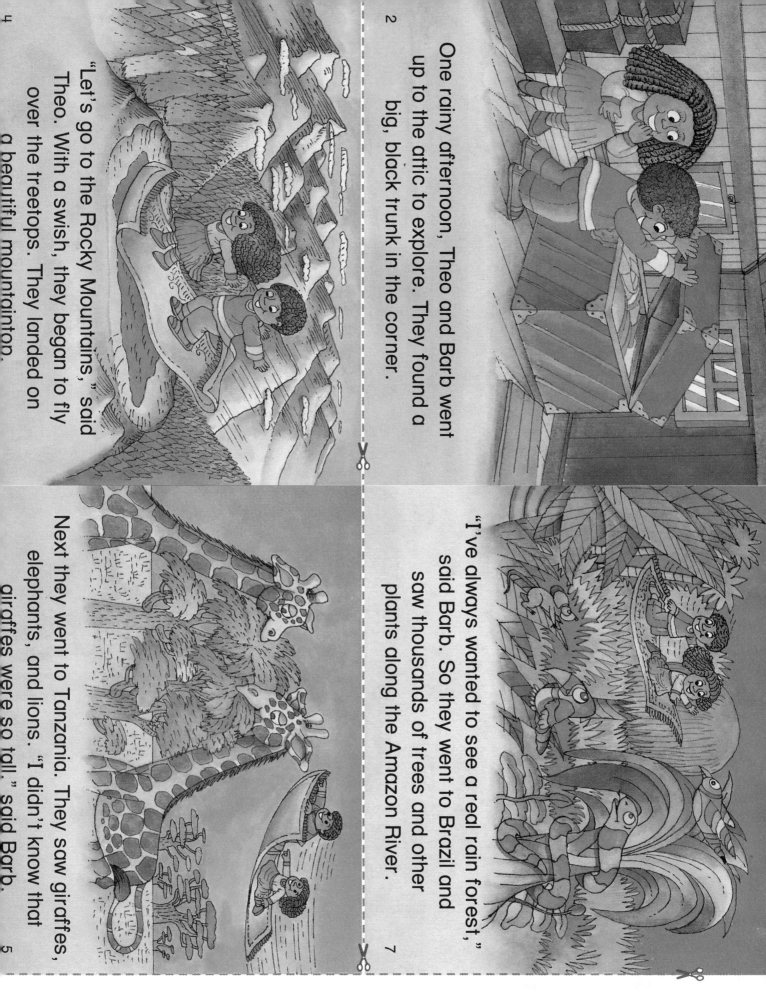

2

One rainy afternoon, Theo and Barb went up to the attic to explore. They found a big, black trunk in the corner.

4

"Let's go to the Rocky Mountains," said Theo. With a swish, they began to fly over the treetops. They landed on a beautiful mountaintop.

7

"I've always wanted to see a real rain forest," said Barb. So they went to Brazil and saw thousands of trees and other plants along the Amazon River.

5

Next they went to Tanzania. They saw giraffes, elephants, and lions. "I didn't know that giraffes were so tall," said Barb.

COLORS ALL AROUND

Name _____

White is snow that covers the street.

Fold

Fold

Blue is the sea where fish swim around,
Moving so smoothly without a sound.

8

Brown is a deer with her spotted fawn.

6

Directions: Help your child cut and fold the book. Read it together several times. Have your child find words with vowel digraphs **ea, oo, aw,** and vowel diphthongs **ow, ou, oi, ew**. Look for words with vowel pairs that make a long sound.

UNIT 6: Take-Home Book

Red is a strawberry, juicy and sweet.

4

Green is a meadow moist with dew.

Fold

Fold

Yellow is the sun that we see at dawn.

7

Orange is the pumpkin whose face I drew.

5

Name _____

Shopping with Milo

GROCERY STORE

FRUIT

PEARS 4/99¢

Peaches $1.00/Pound

Fold

Fold

Milo pays for his groceries. The cashier says, "Here's 29 cents change." Which coins should Milo get?

Thanks for helping Milo!

8

2 dimes, 1 nickel, 4 pennies

There's a sale on juice boxes. "Let's see," Milo says. "I'll get one box for Sara and one for Tara, one for Moe and one for Joe. Oh, and I can't forget me!" Juice boxes come 6 to a pack. Does Milo need more than one pack?

no

yes no

6

Directions: Help your child cut and fold the book. Read it together several times. Have your child find words that are contractions and words that end in **s**, **es**, and **ing**.

UNIT 7: Take-Home Book

Milo thinks, "An apple a day keeps the doctor away. Maybe I'll eat an apple every day next week." How many apples should Milo buy for next week?

1 apple   7 apples   12 apples

Let's help Milo with his shopping. Circle the best answer to each question.

Milo says, "I'll start with fruit." One pound of peaches costs $1.00. Milo gets 3 pounds. How much will he spend on peaches?

$1.00 $3.00 $8.00

$ 3.00

Fold

Fold

APPLES

JUICES

1 OR 2 ?

A WONDERFUL DAY

1

3

Fold

8

That night the colorful lights were
like twinkling stars.

Fold

Then we got into an empty seat at the bottom
of the Ferris wheel. As we rode to the top,
we could see the cars and the road below us.
This was the tallest ride I've ever been on.
It was taller than my apartment building!

6

T41

Directions: Help your child cut and fold the book. Read it together several times. Have your child find words
with suffixes and prefixes. Then ask your child to think of words that mean the same or the opposite of words
you choose. Look for homonyms for these words: **two (to), hour (our), eye (I), road (rode), knight (night)**.

UNIT 8: Take-Home Book

4

Next we rode on an unusual roller coaster. The cars went upside down around a huge loop. I was thankful when that ride ended!

2

Last summer my family went to the biggest amusement park I've ever seen. There were hundreds of families there.

First we went on the merry-go-round. The music played loudly as our horses moved up and down.

Fold

Fold

5

3

Songs and Rhymes

Baa, Baa, Black Sheep

Baa, baa, black sheep,
Have you any wool?
Yes, sir, yes, sir,
Three bags full;
One for my master,
And one for my dame,
And one for the little boy
Who lives in the lane.

Down by the Station

Down by the station,
  early in the morning,
See the little pufferbellies all in a row,
See the engine driver pull
  the little throttle,
Chug, chug! Toot, toot! Off we go!

Little Boy Blue

Little Boy Blue, come blow your horn,
The sheep's in the meadow,
The cow's in the corn.
Where's the little boy that
  looks after the sheep?
Under the haystack, fast asleep!

Merrily We Roll A-Long

Mer-ri-ly we roll a-long,
  roll a-long, roll a-long,
Mer-ri-ly we roll a-long,
  o'er the deep blue sea.

Mary Had a Little Lamb

Mary had a little lamb,
  little lamb, little lamb.
Mary had a little lamb,
  its fleece as white as snow.

It followed her to school one day,
  school one day, school one day.
It followed her to school one day,
  which was against the rule.

It made the children laugh and play,
  laugh and play, laugh and play.
It made the children laugh and play
  to see a lamb at school.

The Mulberry Bush

Here we go round the mulberry bush,
The mulberry bush, the mulberry bush,
Here we go round the mulberry bush,
So early in the morning.

Oh Where, Oh Where Has My Little Dog Gone?

Oh where, oh where has my
  little dog gone?
Oh where, oh where can he be?
With his ears cut short and his
  tail cut long,
Oh where, oh where can he be?

Rub-a-dub-dub

Rub-a-dub-dub,
Three men in a tub;
And who do you think they be?
The butcher, the baker,
The candlestick maker,
And all of them gone to sea.

Row, Row, Row Your Boat

Row, row, row your boat,
Gently down the stream,
Merrily, merrily, merrily, merrily,
Life is but a dream.

This Little Piggy

This little piggy went to market,
This little piggy stayed home;
This little piggy had roast beef,
This little piggy had none.
And this little piggy cried
"Wee, wee, wee,"
All the way home.

Twinkle, Twinkle, Little Star

Twinkle, twinkle, little star,
How I wonder what you are.
Up above the world so high,
Like a diamond in the sky.
Twinkle, twinkle, little star,
How I wonder what you are.

The Wheels on the Bus

The wheels on the bus go
   round and round,
Round and round, round and round.
The wheels on the bus go
   round and round,
All around the town.

The driver on the bus says,
"Move on back.
Move on back. Move on back."
The driver on the bus says,
"Move on back",
All around the town.

The people on the bus go
   up and down,
Up and down, up and down.
The people on the bus go
   up and down,
All around the town.

The babies on the bus go,
   "Wa, wa, wa,
Wa, wa, wa; wa, wa, wa"
The babies on the bus go,
   "Wa, wa, wa",
All around the town.

Working On the Railroad

I've been working on the railroad,
All the live-long day.
I've been working on the railroad,
Just to pass the time away;
Can't you hear the whistle blowing,
Rise up so early in the morn;
Don't you hear the captain shouting,
"Dinah, blow your horn!"

Dinah, won't you blow,
Dinah, won't you blow,
Dinah, won't you blow your horn?
Dinah, won't you blow,
Dinah, won't you blow,
Dinah, won't you blow your horn?

Three Little Kittens

Three little kittens,
They lost their mittens,
And they began to cry:
"Oh, Mother dear, see here, see here,
Our mittens we have lost!"
"What, lost your mittens?
You naughty kittens!
Then you shall have no pie."
"Meow! Meow! Meow! Meow!"

Three little kittens,
They found their mittens,
And they began to cry:
"Oh, Mother dear, see here, see here,
Our mittens we have found!"
"What, found your mittens?
You darling kittens!
Then you shall have some pie."
"Meow! Meow! Meow! Meow!"

Helpful Hints
for children, teachers, and parents

Consonants
The letters **b, c, d, f, g, h, j, k, l, m, n, p, q, r, s, t, v, w, x, y,** and **z** are **consonants**.

Vowels
The letters **a, i, o, u,** and **e** are **vowels**. **Y** at the end of a word can have the sound of long **i** or long **e**: **fly, city**. **W** can be part of a **vowel digraph** or **diphthong**: **p<u>aw</u>, br<u>ow</u>n**.

Short Vowels
If a syllable or word has only one vowel and it comes at the beginning or between two consonants, the vowel is likely to be **short**: **m<u>a</u>p, f<u>i</u>n, r<u>o</u>d, t<u>u</u>g, n<u>e</u>t**.

Long Vowels
If there are two vowels in a one-syllable word, the first vowel is usually **long** and the second vowel is silent: **r<u>ai</u>n, v<u>i</u>ne, r<u>o</u>se, t<u>u</u>be, s<u>ea</u>t**.

Soft c and Soft g
C or **g** followed by **e, i,** or **y** usually has the **soft** sound: **<u>c</u>ity, sta<u>g</u>e**.

Consonant Blend
A **consonant blend** is two or three consonants sounded together in a word so that each letter is heard: **<u>gl</u>obe, <u>tr</u>ain, <u>st</u>amp, <u>v</u>est**.

Compound Word
A **compound word** is made up of two or more smaller words: **starfish**.

Consonant Digraph
A **consonant digraph** is two consonants together that stand for one sound: **<u>ch</u>in, <u>kn</u>ee, <u>wr</u>ist, so<u>ck</u>**.

r-controlled Vowels
An **r** after a vowel gives the vowel a new sound: **b<u>ar</u>n, c<u>or</u>n, f<u>er</u>n, b<u>ir</u>d, t<u>ur</u>tle**.

Vowel Pair
A **vowel pair** is two vowels together that stand for a long sound: **r<u>ai</u>n, s<u>ea</u>t**.

Vowel Digraph
A **vowel digraph** is two vowels together that stand for a long sound, a short sound, or a special sound: **br<u>ea</u>d, m<u>oo</u>n, b<u>oo</u>k, l<u>au</u>nch, p<u>aw</u>**.

Diphthong
A **diphthong** is two letters blended together that stand for one vowel sound: **br<u>ow</u>n, cl<u>ou</u>d, c<u>oi</u>ns, b<u>oy</u>, scr<u>ew</u>**.

Contraction
A **contraction** is a short way of writing two words as one: **didn't = did not, she'll = she will**.

Plural
Plural means "more than one." Add **s** to most words to make plurals: **goat<u>s</u>**.
  Add **es** to words that end in **s, ss, ch, sh, x,** or **z**: **peach<u>es</u>**.
  When a word ends in **y** after a consonant (**penny**), change the **y** to **i** before adding **es**: **penni<u>es</u>**.

Inflectional Endings
The endings **s, es, ing,** and **ed** can be added to a base word: **help<u>s</u>, fix<u>es</u>, fix<u>ing</u>, fix<u>ed</u>**. *See pages 164, 167, 169, and 173 for rules on making spelling changes.*

Suffix
A **suffix** is a word part added to the end of a base word to change its meaning or make a new word: **fear<u>ful</u>, fear<u>less</u>, soft<u>ness</u>, soft<u>ly</u>, fast<u>er</u>, fast<u>est</u>**.

Prefix
A **prefix** is a word part added to the beginning of a base word to change its meaning or make a new word: **<u>re</u>tie, <u>un</u>happy, <u>dis</u>honest**.

Synonyms
Synonyms are words that have the same or nearly the same meaning: **fast/quick**.

Antonyms
Antonyms are words that have the opposite or nearly the opposite meaning: **hot/cold**.

Homonyms
Homonyms are words that sound the same but have different spellings and meanings: **sail/sale**.

The Amazing Writing Machine is a trademark of:
Broderbund Software, Inc.
P.O. Box 6125
Novato, CA 94948-6125
(1-800-521-6263)

Bailey's Book House is a registered trademark of:
Edmark Corporation
P.O. Box 97021
Redmond, WA 98052
(1-800-426-0856)

Beginning Reading is a trademark of:
Sierra On-Line
P.O. Box 85007
Bellevue, WA 98015-8507
(1-800-743-7725)

The Book of Shadowboxes: A Story of the ABC's is available by:
EduQuest an IBM Company
4111 Northside Parkway
Atlanta, GA 30328
(1-800-426-4338)

Flying Colors is a trademark of:
Davidson & Associates, Inc.
P.O. Box 2961
Torrance, CA 90509
(1-800-556-6141)

Kid Phonics is a trademark of:
Davidson & Associates, Inc.
P.O. Box 2961
Torrance, CA 90509
(1-800-556-6141)

Kid Pix Studio is a registered trademark of:
Broderbund Software-Direct
P.O. Box 6125
Novato, CA 94948-6125
(1-800-521-6263)

Kid Works (2) is a trademark of:
Davidson & Associates, Inc.
P.O. Box 2961
Torrance, CA 90509
(1-800-556-6141)

Microsoft® Fine Artist is by:
Microsoft Corporation
1 Microsoft Way
Redmond, WA 98052
(1-800-426-9400)

Phonics is a registered trademark of:
Dinosoft Software
9801 Dupont Avenue South
Bloomington, MN 55431
(612-881-3738)

Reader Rabbit (2 Deluxe) is a registered trademark of:
The Learning Company
6493 Kaiser Drive
Fremont, CA 94555
(1-800-852-2255)

Reading Maze is a registered trademark of:
Great Wave Software
5353 Scotts Valley Drive
Scotts Valley, CA 95066
(1-800-423-1144)

Reading & Phonics Challenge! is a trademark of:
Brighter Child™ Intereactive
150 E. Wilson Bridge Road
Suite 145
Columbus, OH 43085
(310-552-2424)

Read, Write, & Type! is a trademark of:
The Learning Company
6493 Kaiser Drive
Fremont, CA 94555
(1-800-852-2255)

Sound It Out Land (2, 3) is a trademark of:
Conexus
5252 Balboa Avenue, Suite 605
San Diego, CA 92117
(619-268-3380)

Spell Dodger! is a trademark of:
Arcadia Productions
P.O. Box 2961
Torrance, CA 90509
(310-793-0620)

Spell It (3) is a registered trademark of:
Davidson & Associates, Inc.
P.O. Box 2961
Torrance, CA 90509
(1-800-556-6141)

Storybook Weaver (Deluxe) is a registered trademark of:
MECC
6160 Summit Drive North
Minneapolis, MN 55025
(612-569-1500)

For other applicable software, please consult a local software dealer.

CREDITS

Photo

Neal Farris: Cover

Diane J. Ali: 177 *center*.

Animals Animals/ Earth Scenes–
Richard Shiell: 147 *top*;
E. R. Degginger: 147 *bottom center & top left*;
Robert Maier: 147 *left*.

The Art Institute of Chicago/ photograph ©1995, All rights reserved: 89 *left*.

Cate Photography: 24, 104, 127, 209, 210.

Valerie Henschel: 212 *bottom right*.

Ken Karp: 15 *bottom*, 177 *left*.

Kohout Productions/ Root Resources: 147 *top right*.

Richard Nowitz: 89 *right*.

R. Pasley/ Viesti Associates: 87 *right*.

The Picture Cube/ D. & I. MacDonald: 211 *bottom left*;

John Coletti: 219 *top right*;

Emily Stone: 223 *top right*; Stanley Rown: 224 *left*.

H. Armstrong Roberts: 34, 65 *right*, 117, 118 *top*, 147 *bottom right*, 147 *bottom left*, 177 *bottom right*, 220 *bottom left*.

Kevin Schafer: 211 *bottom right*, 212 *bottom left*, 220 *top left*.

Jeremy Stafford-Deitsch/ Ellis Nature Photo: 219 *bottom left*.

The Stock Market/ Lew Long: 15 *top right*; Roy Morsch: 15 *center right*; ChromoSohm: 65 *left*;
Kunio Owaki: 119 *right*;
R. Berenholtz: 119 *left*; Peter Vadnai: 118 *background*;
Thomas Braise: 223 *top left*.

SUPERSTOCK: 220 *bottom right*.

Thayer Syme/ FPG International: 219 *top left*.

Tony Stone Images/ Ian Murphy: 15 *top left*; David Hiser: 15 *center left*;

Don Spiro: 35; Doug Armand:

45 *background*, 223 *background*;
Suzanne & Nick Geary: 45 *right*;
Joe Ortner: 87 *center right*;
Doris DeWitt: 87 *center left*;
Hugh Sitton: 87 *left*;
Mark Burnside: 177 *top right*;
Hideo Kurihara: 205 *top left*;
Bert Sagara: 205 *top right*;
Rainer Grosskopf: 205 *bottom*;
Terry Vine: 211 *top left*;
Peter Timmermans: 212 *top left*;
Jeanne Drake: 219 *bottom right*;
Chip Henderson: 224 *right*.

Mark Turner: 220 *top right*.

Larry Ulrich Photography: 211 *top right*, 212 *top right*.

Prescott Behn: 47B.

Louis Lensky Covey Foundation: 67B.

HarperCollins Publishers: 89B.

Wayne Sproul/International Stock Photo: 89A/89B.

Art

Bart Goldman: Cover, Digital Imaging

Dirk Wunderlich: Cover, Illustration

JoLynn Alcorn: 138
Diane J. Ali: 5A
Shirley Beckes: 19
Ken Bowser: 149A, 149B, 149
Jenny Campbell: 40, 52, 67A, 67B, 67
Chi Chung: 17A, 17B, 17
Peter Church: 121A, 121B, 121
Diane deGroat: 179A, 179B
Karen Dugan: 179
Arthur Friedman: 33, 43, 44, 94, 105, 106, 134, 217, 218
Tom Graham: 20, 37

Adam Gordon: 5A, 5B, 5F, 47G, 65, 67I, 89I, 89J, 121H,121I, 179H, 223, 224
Myron Grossman: 77, 117, 118, 144
Laurie Hamilton : 72, 115, 124
Steve Henry: 75
Joan Holub: 23
Megan Jeffery: 82
Andy Levine: 59, 102, 109, 159, 166, 170, 183
Jason Levinson: 28, 50, 55, 60
Patrick Merrill: 89B, 89
John Nez: 61, 63, 64
Iva O'Conner: 110
Olivia: 129, 145, 146, 155, 156
Chris Reed: 36
Cindy Rosenheim: 27
Roz Schanzer: 10, 22, 26, 73, 85, 86, 187, 198

Theresa Smith: 47A, 47B, 47
Sally Springer: 13, 30, 58, 70
Daryl Stevens: 101, 112, 116, 128, 154, 167, 175, 176, 185
Matt Straub: 215, 216
Steve Sullivan: 6, 18, 48, 68, 90, 122, 150, 180
Don Tate: 96, 100, 131, 136, 163,172, 181, 193, 199
Vicki Wehrman: 213, 214
Jenny Williams: 11, 54
Susan Williams: 114, 203, 204
Toby Williams: 221, 222

Functional art:

Diane Ali, Batelman Illustration, Moffit Cecil, Adam Gordon, Larry Lee, John Quinn, Sintora Regina Vanderhorst